FULL EMPLOYMENT IN
A FREE SOCIETY

FULL EMPLOYMENT
IN A
FREE SOCIETY

A Report by

William H

LORD BEVERIDGE

ııı

Misery generates hate

London
GEORGE ALLEN & UNWIN LTD

FIRST PUBLISHED IN NOVEMBER 1944
SECOND IMPRESSION DECEMBER 1944
THIRD IMPRESSION 1945
FOURTH IMPRESSION WITH A NEW PREFACE 1953
SECOND EDITION 1960
SECOND IMPRESSION 1967

PRINTED IN GREAT BRITAIN
by Photolithography
BY JOHN DICKENS AND CO LTD
NORTHAMPTON

CONTENTS

LIST OF CHARTS

References to paragraphs in the Appendices have the letter A, B, or C prefixed to the number of the paragraph. Numbers without a letter prefixed relate to paragraphs in the main text.

Prologue

FULL EMPLOYMENT SIXTEEN YEARS AFTER

This book was completed and published first in 1944. The whole of what was published then is printed today without change. Full employment in Britain has been accomplished. One of the possible dangers of full employment, foreseen in Part V of this book—inflation diminishing the value of money—has come upon us. I have added, therefore, this Prologue under the name shown above, describing in the light of today full employment and inflation, and examining thereafter the practical problem of whether and how inflation can be brought to an end, while preserving both sides of my original title—Full Employment and A Free Society.

Today's prologue replaces an earlier new preface added in the edition of 1953. While everything else in this volume stands as in 1944, I have with the help of Mr. Oswald George been able to carry on to the present date or near it some of the original statistics, such, for example, as those of Disallowances of Unemployment Benefit given in Table 20. These and other later statistics, though not relevant to the subject of this prologue, may well be of interest to students of full employment. They will be published as soon as convenient in the *Journal* of the Association of Incorporated Statisticians with which both Oswald George and I have many contacts.

I. FULL EMPLOYMENT

Full employment means having more vacancies for workers than there are workers seeking vacancies. It does not mean having no unemployment at all. In a progressive society there will be changes in the demand for labour, qualitatively if not quantitatively, and some men will be unemployed while waiting to pass from one job to the next. In 1944, as a guide to the amount of such temporary idleness as we might expect under full employment, I suggested a figure of 3 per cent of the total labour force, as likely to be idle at any time. Maynard Keynes, when he saw this figure, wrote to me that there was no harm in aiming at 3 per cent, but that he would be surprised if we got so low in practice. I described 3 per cent at the time as "a conservative, rather than unduly hopeful, aim to set for the average unemployment rate of the future under conditions of full employment."[1]

In fact, during the twelve years from 1948 to 1959, the average unemployment rate for Britain, taking all industries together, has been not 3 per cent but half of that, 1·55 in exact terms.

[1] See para. 169 below for this and for basis of the 3 per cent estimate.

The unemployment percentages for each year from 1946 to 1959[1] are as follows :—

1946	..	(2·4)	1953	..	1·6
1947	..	(3·0)	1954	..	1·3
1948	..	1·5	1955	..	1·1
1949	..	1·5	1956	..	1·2
1950	..	1·5	1957	..	1·4
1951	..	1·2	1958	..	2·1
1952	..	2·0	1959	..	2·2

Omitting 1946 and 1947, as years of immediate post-ward disturbance, the year's unemployment rate has never exceeded 2·2 (in 1959) and has been as low as 1·1 (in 1955).

These rates are calculated from statistics published regularly by the Ministry of Labour, in the *Labour Gazette* and elsewhere. Another set of unemployment rates, differing slightly from mine, was published in an article in the *Oxford Economic Papers* of February 1958, with accompanying figures of unfilled vacancies for labour, by J. C. Dow and L. A. Dicks-Mireaux. A chart based on this article, comparing unemployment and unfilled vacancies, from 1946 to 1957 is printed by the Council on Prices, Productivity and Incomes, on page 69 of their first report. The unfilled vacancies greatly exceed the unemployment in the early years, but from 1950 onwards, fluctuate in its neighbourhood, alternatively above and below. Full employment is here.

After World War I, Britain had returned to unemployment, with an average of 14 per cent of its workers idle throughout the inter-war period. After World War II to the present time the unemployment percentage has been 1½ per cent. What has brought this remarkable change, which is probably the largest single cause of British prosperity today?

The change cannot be explained away by describing our time since 1945 as years not of peace but of cold war. The cold war did not begin seriously till 1951, and in any case has made no call for labour remotely comparable to that of hot war.

Employment depends on outlay. Full employment cannot be attained unless outlay, whether public or private, whether for consumption or for investment, is sufficient in total to set up a demand for the whole of the labour that is available for employment. Only the State, by deciding on its own spending and by influencing through taxation and otherwise the spending of its citizens, can ensure enough outlay in total. So in 1944 I named, as the main instrument of a full employment policy, a new type of budget based on manpower, rather than on the assumed limits of taxation[2].

---

[1] The percentages for 1946 and 1947 are bracketed as based on the working of the Unemployment Insurance Acts. The later figures are based on the administration of the National Insurance Act of 1946.

[2] Para. 223. I named as two subsidiary instruments controlled location of industry and organised mobility of labour. Paras. 223-237.

Happily, the idea of a new type of budget had been accepted three years before, in 1941, by Kingsley Wood on the inspiration of Maynard Keynes,[1] who on the ousting of Neville Chamberlain had at last made his way into the Treasury and became its dominant influence.

The budgets of Sir John Simon to 1940 had been old style summaries of Government revenue and expenditure and nothing more. Kingsley Wood in 1941 made a complete change of fashion. He began, not with Government revenue and expenditure, but on a wider survey of "our financial and economic policy in relation to the war" and proceeded "to indicate some of the major problems with which we have to continue to deal," including "the inflationary gap."

The new fashion caught on and lasted. John Anderson, introducing the last war-time budget in April, 1945, started with a White Paper just published, which "seeks to measure the national income, that is to say the total money value of all the goods and services produced by the community and to show how that income has been spent." He announced policies of full employment and of stability of prices and wages.

The Labour Government which came to power in July 1945, in effect made John Anderson's White Paper into an annual. Acutely conscious of the need for economic planning with all facts in mind, they established an Economic Survey recording the past year, and looking forward to the coming years.

The first of the series of Economic Surveys was issued in February 1947 ; in the next year, Stafford Cripps as Chancellor carried the new fashion of budgeting one stage further, by causing the Economic Survey of 1948 and the budget proposals to be discussed together. The Economic Survey continues to this day, as a storehouse of economic history. In it the successive problems of recovery from war are presented in turn : making good the losses of men, equipment and dollars ; devaluation of sterling in 1949 ; impact of re-armament in 1950 ; balance of payment crisis in 1951 ; inflation at intervals throughout. Only the last of these problems can be examined here.

2. INFLATION

In 1944, I called attention to two facts about wage bargaining in Britain : that in the past such bargaining had habitually been conducted sectionally by each craft and trade for itself, and that now a marked and presumably permanent increase in the bargaining strength of labour would result from full employment. In so far as this increase of strength led to labour as a whole gaining a larger share of the total product of industry, I welcomed it. But I went on to a warning : "There is a real danger that

[1] I owe most of what is said here about Keynes to two excellent broadcasts on him made by Professor R. F. Kahn in May 1956. Keynes was even more afraid of full employment leading to inflation than I was. But in the end he accepted full employment as something that we must have in any case.

sectional wage bargaining, pursued without regard to its effect on prices, may lead to a vicious spiral of inflation, with money wages chasing prices and without any gain in real wages for the working class as a whole."[1]

For avoidance of this danger, I made two suggestions. The first was that "the central organisations of labour, such as the Trades Union Congress General Council, should devote their attention to the problem of achieving a unified wage policy which ensures that the demands of individual unions will be judged with reference to the economic situation as a whole." My second suggestion was for greater recourse to arbitration, though I did not think that arbitration could be made compulsory during peace in a free country like Britain.

It is not sufficiently realised today how fully the Labour Government of 1945-50 shared my fears of inflation and how strongly they argued against it.

In January 1947 came a White Paper from the Minister of Labour (George Isaacs) on "Economic Considerations affecting relations between Employers and Workers."[2] This was a long sermon on "the country's very serious economic position" and the overwhelming need for increased production per worker, not merely per hour but per annum. "At present there is too much money chasing after too few goods." Hugh Dalton, in his two budgets that followed in the same year of 1947, said that "we must strengthen still further and without delay our budgetary defences against inflation."

In February 1948, when Stafford Cripps had replaced Hugh Dalton as Chancellor of the Exchequer, came another White Paper on "Personal Incomes, Costs and Prices,"[3] which set out the following doctrine:

> "It is essential that there should be no further general increase in the level of personal incomes without at least a corresponding increase in the volume of production. . . .
>
> "Such an increase . . . can only have an inflationary effect. Unless accompanied by a substantial increase in production, it would drive up prices and charges, adversely affect pensioners, children and other recipients of social service benefits, increase the money cost of our exports and so reduce their saleability, and by black market pressure make it almost impossible to operate the controls necessary in view of the continuing security of supplies and man-power."

There followed a definite conclusion against any rise at the present time in incomes from profits, rent or the like, or in wages or salaries except in exceptional cases, typified by possible need in the national interest to attract labour to a particular under-manned industry. "Each claim for an increase of wages or salaries must be considered on its

[1] See paras. 283-288 below for what I said in 1944 on Determination of Wages.
[2] Cmd. 7018.   [3] Cmd. 7321.

national merits and not on the basis of maintaining a former relativity between different occupations and industries." This conclusion was backed by a warning—that if their views were disregarded, the Government would be ready to use the controls that they still possessed over many prices to prevent higher costs through wages and salaries from leading to higher charges against the consumer.[1]

Stafford Cripps, in the budget of April 1948, rubbed in the moral of the White Paper on Personal Incomes, with all the vigour at his command. In his next budget, of April 1949, he claimed to have brought about "a comfortable and not excessive degree of disinflation, with a better balance between vacancies and workers." He dwelt on his Government's "tremendous achievements" of economic recovery and social security.

Undoubtedly, Government efforts to stimulate output succeeded at times, as in 1949. And retail prices have varied only by a point or two over much of 1958 and 1959. But, as history shows, the efforts of Labour and Conservative Governments alike to stabilise prices since World War II have had little success.

In August 1957, a Council of three persons, including Lord Cohen as Chairman, was established to study and report on Prices, Productivity and Incomes. Before Lord Cohen left for other public duties the Council published three reports relevant to the subject of this prologue.

In the first report, on page five, is a Chart of Retail Prices showing a practically continuous rise from 1946 to 1957, by 4 or 5 per cent each year, by 65 per cent in the eleven years as a whole. Other tables show wages, salaries and profits sharing in the rise ; for the years 1948 to 1956 the total increase for wages and salaries is 81 per cent and that for net company profits is 76 per cent.[2]

Beyond question a persistent cause of rising prices and money cost of living in Britain since World War II has been that which I foresaw in 1944 : the readiness, under full employment, of employers and their associations, on demand by trade unions, to raise money wages in relation to output and to compensate themselves by charging a higher price for the same article. George Isaacs and Stafford Cripps began a battle against poverty-making inflation which is far from being won.

In 1952 the organisation known as Political and Economic Planning published two excellent pamphlets on *Poverty Ten Years After Beveridge* and *Social Security and Unemployment in Lancashire*, whose common theme was destruction of private saving as a way to personal independence in misfortune. The aim of the Beveridge Report of 1942, as had been stated in it more than once, was the practical abolition of public charity— National Assistance under Means Test ; it was to be replaced by security against want given as a right under social insurance, leaving freedom to

---

[1] Para. 10 of Cmd. 7321.

[2] Page 19. Figures given for other forms of gain than wages, salaries and company profits, e.g., by self-employment or by receipt of dividends or rent, show much smaller percentage rises.

every citizen to plan his life and that of his dependants above want. Ten years after, in 1952, more than 2,000,000 needed National Assistance ; social security had been destroyed by endlessly rising prices.

In 1953 the newspapers which reported on 21st May a speech of mine in the House of Lords calling attention to what was happening to social insurance and family life through wage demands and their acceptance by employers leading to higher prices, carried also notice of "three million more in the queue for higher wages."

In January 1956 battle against inflation was announced formally by the Prime Minister in a speech at Bradford. This was followed in February by an admirable broadcast on the same theme by the Chancellor of the Exchequer, Harold Macmillan, and on May 11 by an interview between all the leading Ministers of the Government and the leaders of the Trades Union Congress General Council. The latter admitted the seriousness of Britain's situation and said that they would see the Prime Minister again when they had completed a report on which they were engaged. But the report which came from the T.U.C. at the end of May was mainly a criticism of the Government for provoking higher wage demands, and by mid-June it seemed clear that the T.U.C. were unlikely to advise on wages.[1] A week later some Conservative members in Parliament urged control of prices and wages by law, but the Government rejected this as "not the right solution," without giving an alternative. The *impasse* was complete.

By 1957 average earnings per man had more than doubled as compared with 1946 (rising from 100 to 210), while output per man had risen by little more than a quarter (from 100 to 129).

In 1958 one in four of every man or woman in receipt of a State Security Pension was having to draw National Assistance as well.

In 1959, though prices have changed little, its closing month has witnessed a grant to 800,000 agricultural workers of higher wages and shorter hours, that can hardly fail to raise prices for their product, and demands backed by strike threats for more money and less work by one of the largest trade unions, concerned with transport.

The terms of reference to Lord Cohen's Council recognised that a reasonable stability of prices was desirable ; in opposition to some writers who argue that a continuous if slow rise of prices is good for trade, the Council concluded, after considering society as a whole, that the objective should be to stop inflation, not merely to moderate its course. After naming large classes of society not engaged in trade whether as employers or employees—such as pensioners, holders of fixed interest securities, and owners of land and buildings let at legally controlled rents, they decided that "the arbitrary re-distribution resulting from a steady rise of prices, even if slow, is very unjust." This list of classes subject to injustice by inflation is an interesting echo of the Labour Government's White Paper of 1948 that has been cited above.

[1] *Times*, June 14.

From my early contact with many different conditions of living in our great towns, I have long held the view that maintaining stability in prices is an essential duty of the State, ranking in importance with maintenance of peace abroad and order at home, or abolition of social evils like want, needless disease, squalor and ignorance. I am happy to find myself in full agreement with Lord Cohen's Council.

I believe that, in this, I represent one of the firmest and oldest traditional beliefs of the British people—they want the money in their pockets to keep its value. There is a contrary view sometimes found among professional economists as well as traders. If I understand him rightly, in his latest writings, on "Economic Growth and its Problem of Inflation," appearing in *Economica* of August and November 1959, Nicholas Kaldor who did much admirable work in writing the statistical Appendix C to my 'Full Employment,' inclines to this view. For me, money and prices should be considered from the point of view of ordinary citizens rather than of traders.

Since I wrote this first, I have seen with much interest, in the *Investors' Chronicle*,[1] an article by its editor, demolishing from the business man's point of view, the belief that inflation is beneficial to holders of ordinary shares and other equities. "Ordinary shares," he concludes, "and . . . the economy as a whole—benefit more from increased productivity, than they do from inflation. If only we could get this message across, in place of the defeatist doctrine that inflation is inevitable, how much better off we'd all be."

Lord Cohen's Council, speaking of the time since 1946, said that for Britain "there is no peace-time period of comparable length which shows anything like as big a rise in prices as that of the last eleven years." If one confines one's study to the last 300 years this is true. Prices have always risen in major wars, but they have fallen again when peace returned—after World War I, after the Napoleonic Wars, even after the relatively small Marlborough Wars of 1692-1702.

As has been pointed out by Professor Phelps Brown and Sheila Hopkins, in a fascinating article on "Seven Centuries of the Prices of Consumables compared with Builders' Wage-rates,"[2] features of English price history are the long periods of stable prices disturbed only by bad harvests. Subject to wars, this applies not only to the 300 years now ending but also to most of the first 300 years from 1260 to 1540 for which English prices have been published.[3]

But the intervening years, from 1540 to 1650, yield a different picture—of all but continuous rise of prices, subject again to harvests and to a slight temporary slackening under Elizabeth I. In the later part of this period of just over a century the rise of prices was due to inflow of silver brought by the Spaniards from America and to a considerable extent seized by the

[1] "Inflation and Share Prices," by Harold Wincott, December 25, 1959.
[2] *Economica*, November 1956.
[3] By Thorold Rogers.

English. At the beginning of the period, a rise was brought about by Henry VIII.

Everyone knows that Henry VIII was extravagant in wives, with six of them. Not everyone knows that he was extravagant also in spending—always wanting more money, and that he found money by debasing our currency, that is demanding for the same amount of silver three or four times as many shillings as before. His immediate successors, though they made some attempts to restore a better currency, had little success. Happily for the British tradition, Elizabeth I, soon after she came to the throne in 1558, put this right, called in the bad shillings and gave us good money again, to buy goods, not indeed at the old prices, but at steady prices for a short time, at least, till the American silver began to flow in.

Today we have a number of powerful agencies—trade unions and business associations—in effect debasing our currency, by demanding more shillings for the same or less work or smaller product, an action that in the end does them little good and leaves many others—above all the old—in bitter want. One can only hope that Elizabeth II will find her Government and her people as firm for sound money, as Elizabeth I did. There are, of course, in our wage structure today injustices that call for remedy. But do any of them exceed or equal the injustice being done through destroying by inflation the value of pensions and savings provided for old age?

Inflation has just been the subject of a book written by an old friend of mine, Sir Roy Harrod, and published in 1958, under the title: *Policy Against Inflation*. The book has a standpoint altogether different from mine in this prologue ; it is concerned almost wholly with money and its management, with the gold standard, devaluation, and the like. In a chapter of twenty pages assigned to the topic of wages, out of 250 pages in total, the author recognises that wages may present problems. But in the chapter of conclusions that follows he lays it down firmly that "the recent protracted inflation" (meaning inflation well into 1957 and perhaps beyond) "has been the unavoidable consequence of the devaluation of 1949," rather than a result of wage and price fixings under full employment.

More recently, Roy Harrod has come out with a suggestion that a steady rise of $2\frac{1}{2}$ per cent in real earnings should be held out by employers in general to employees in general.[1] Just how he proposes that such an undertaking should be guaranteed, I have no idea. It requires either that output per employee rises also by $2\frac{1}{2}$ per cent a year, or that British employers and importers, whatever happens to their costs, are able to carry on, without raising the price of anything that wage-earners think important to their way of life.

There are two points only, in regard to inflation, on which I find myself in sympathy today with my old friend.

[1] Letter to *The Times*, January 7, 1960.

One point is his conviction that keeping money stable is an essential duty of the State:

> "The citizen body, including wage-earners themselves, do not wish that the currency should be debased. It is the positive duty of the government to implement the general will in this regard."[1]

He goes on to write of Elizabeth I in the same terms of praise as I do.

The other point is his conviction that if there should be any danger of wage bargaining leading to inflation, the danger ought to be dealt with by direct action of the State to stop such bargaining, rather than by damping down total demand for labour.

But the action that he contemplates, of formal prohibition, for a time at least, of any increase of wages, is far more drastic than anything attempted by any British Government since World War II and all but uniformly rejected by those in charge of wage bargaining. We are bound in Britain to explore more practical remedies for our troubles.

Inflation either now or in the past is by no means confined to Britain or most common there. Some of what I said about past history, I said also in an interview on inflation and social security which I gave in November 1959, to an American journal,[2] following on the same topic the Secretary to the U.S.A. Treasury, Mr. Anderson. I was happy to agree with Mr. Anderson on practically all that he said: that the Government of U.S.A. had a duty to stop inflation and give stable money to its citizens, that only the Government as manager of money could do this, but that the Government could not do this alone, without the co-operation of other agencies in the economic sphere—business institutions and associations of employees and employers which had become important and powerful. All this applies today to the Government of Britain also.

"All power is a trust," wrote Disraeli. But he knew and we know that power may corrupt its owners and be misapplied by them. In the past, power was often used selfishly by inheritors of rank or wealth, used from the right, regardless of the liberties and happiness of ordinary people. Today, under full employment, power won by organisation can be used selfishly from the left and since World War II has been so used at times, to bring unhappiness to common people by destroying the value of their savings and pensions, and making their lives difficult and less free. How can this injustice be prevented for the future? What is the way to stable money in a free society under full employment?

3. THE WAY TO STABLE MONEY

Primary responsibility for the nature and management of money rests with the State. Money is created by the State, not for its purposes only or mainly, but to be used by citizens in managing their affairs and

---

[1] Harrod *op cit.* p. 212.
[2] *United States News and World Report.*

planning the lives of themselves and their dependants from youth to age. Money is an instrument of freedom and happiness. But money can be a good instrument for this on two conditions only : that it is so managed as to lead to full employment, and that it is kept stable in value, at least for the buying of all necessaries of life.

Till recently, neither of these conditions was fulfilled, or even recognised, in the management of money, either in Britain or in other industrial countries like the United States. Till the outbreak of World War II, we had an alternation of booms and depressions in employment, accompanied by alternately rising and falling prices, which we called the trade cycle. Today the responsibility of the State for securing to its citizens both full employment and stable money is recognised not in Britain alone but in many other countries.

But in Britain at least, the powers of the Government are not the same in these two fields of responsibility. Through its control of money, the Government can on its own authority provide for its citizens the priceless gift of full employment ; its duty to provide this is clear. For stable money the Government has no full power today. Its function cannot be put higher than as a duty to ensure in one way or another that the gift of full employment is not misused by some citizens to the damage of others, by inflation destroying the value of money. But the duty of the Government cannot be put lower than this.

The issue before us has many parallels in other fields. Today, for example, the State in Britain is engaged very rightly at great expense in improving facilities for road traffic. If every citizen could be trusted to use those facilities with due regard for others and never to attempt dangerous speeds, the State would have no need to control the use of roads. It is being driven in fact to more and more control.

The State in Britain since World War II has failed till now to keep money stable, because it has tried and failed to obtain free co-operation of the organisations of employees and employers that now settle wages and prices. The rise of prices, following wage demands conceded by employers, has been all but continuous and, to this day, shows no sign of ending.

If the State is to fulfil its accepted duty of preserving the value of money, must it have new powers of control, as a substitute for free co-operation?

Such control might take the form of saying that a rise of certain prices basic to the cost of living needed consent of an impartial authority, could follow a rise of wages only if the wages had been put up by arbitration, and only if the arbitrator recommended that prices rose also. Such control would be a powerful lever for higher output and removal of restrictions on output.

Such control by the State would accord with the responsibilities that the State has undertaken for health, housing, education, traffic, social security (above all of the old), and other forms of welfare. These responsibilities involve vast outlay that would be made larger still by rising prices and would call for higher taxation.

Control of basic prices, leaving choice of employment and determination of wages as now, preserves the essential freedoms of society. It is not open to objection on principle.

But it is far from simple in practice. Defining the articles to which it should apply, enforcing control everywhere, preventing evasion by use of substitutes, would be a heavy task. From experience of price control in two world wars, when it had patriotic acceptance and support, I am by no means anxious to see it return in peace as a possibly contentious measure.

Apart from this, I cannot forget my happy and fruitful dealings with trade unions and their leaders over many years, from their acceptance, in the citizens' interest in 1909, of the breaking in of the State into the field of unemployment insurance hitherto occupied by the trade unions alone, to the help that they gave in 1941-42 to discussion and formulation of social security to put all men and women *equally* above want. Let our Government, whatever its colour, make one more effort to secure freely, from organisations of employees and employers alike, co-operation in keeping our money sound and prices stable.

Should that effort fail, the issue facing us will be clear. If the organisations that now determine wages continue to demand and to give more money for less work, the people of Britain must choose between establishing some State control of prices and suffering endless inflation which will debase our currency, will make saving seem absurd, and will reduce to want and to need for public charity a growing number and proportion of our men and women, in the sunset of their lives.

PREFACE OF 1944

THE work presented here as a Report on Full Employment in a Free Society is a sequel to the Report on Social Insurance and Allied Services which I made to His Majesty's Government in November, 1942. In that Report I named three assumptions of the Plan for Social Security proposed in it, namely a system of children's allowances, a comprehensive health and rehabilitation service, and maintenance of employment. If Social Security is defined as security for the individual, organized by the State, against risks to which the individual will remain exposed even when the condition of the society as a whole is as good as it can be made, both children's allowances and medical treatment are parts of Social Security. Both of these assumptions were dealt with to some extent in my Report, and proposals were made for realizing them. The third assumption, of maintenance of employment and prevention of mass unemployment, was not dealt with there, and no proposals as to how it could be realized were made. Measures to maintain employment are not part of Social Security as defined above; they are measures of general application to make the economic condition of society as a whole healthy. I now complete, so far as I can, the work which I began with my earlier Report.

That earlier Report was prepared by me, at the request of His Majesty's Government, as Chairman of an Inter-Departmental Committee, on which all the other representatives were civil servants. Some seven months after the Committee had been appointed, it was decided by the Government that, in view of the issues of high policy which would arise, the departmental representatives should henceforth be regarded as my advisers and assessors, and that the Report when made should be my Report, signed by my alone, so that the departmental representatives would not be associated in any way with the views and recommendations on questions of policy which it might contain. No one else, therefore, had or has any responsibility for what I said in that Report. At the same time it could not possibly have been made by me, except with the help of the departmental representatives, and without having at my disposal the whole resources of the Government for investigation and consultation. In the Report itself, I expressed my debt to the departmental representatives as strongly as I could, without appearing to associate them in any way with responsibility for the views expressed, which were mine alone. On other occasions I am glad to have been able to express this debt more generously and more fully :

> "There is another remark often made about the Beveridge Report—and that is that the Report is a one-man Report. Now, it is true that the Report is signed by one man only—myself—so that I am the only person that can be hanged for it. No one else can be brought to book for anything whatever that is said in it. No one else is committed to it. But it is not true that the Report was made, or could have been made, by one man sitting and thinking and studying by himself. I had sitting with me a Committee representing all the

Departments concerned with the problems under consideration—all the best experts in the Government service—and very good experts they are. They acted as a Committee in examining witnesses, in discussion and in criticism. They acted as my technical advisers. Without their help in all these ways the Report would have been a very different and much inferior document. I alone am responsible for all that it proposes, just as a Minister alone is responsible for everything that is done in his Department. I was like a temporary Minister for devising this particular piece of post-war reconstruction ; I could not have done the job otherwise."[1]

Only this help and, beyond it, my unrestricted recourse to all the information possessed by the Government made it possible for me, not merely to enunciate general principles, but to suggest the framework of a complete plan which, if accepted, could be used as the basis of legislation.

The present Report is made under different circumstances. Regarding it as a sequel to the earlier Report, I should naturally have been ready to deal with it on the same lines, if that had been the wish of the Government—to make a survey and proposals on my own responsibility but at the request of the Government and with all the help that they could give me. Such a survey could have covered both stages of the problem—demobilization and the permanent structure—in one continuous programme. Since this possibility was not open to me, the present Report is made by myself as a private citizen, and with only such resources as could be made available to a private citizen during the war. This has two consequences. First, the Report is much inferior to what it would have been had I been able to draw, in the same way as for the original Report, upon the resources of the Government. I can only hope that the gap between what I have been able to do as a private citizen and what I did before with the advantages normally reserved for Ministers, will not be too glaring. Second, the present Report is more limited in scope than it might otherwise have been. It does not deal at all with demobilization. It is concerned not with what should happen when total war ends, in order to bring about a smooth transition from war to peace, but with endeavouring to suggest the structure of peace-time industry and economics to which the transition should be made, with a view to preventing any return of mass unemployment. Even for that narrower purpose I should have welcomed any help that the Government had felt able to give me, by way both of expert criticism of my proposals and of information on questions of fact rather than of Government policy. I could have made my own proposals more concrete in many ways—more of a Plan and less of an outline of policy. But the main basis for constructing a better economic system in the next peace than we had in the last peace is to be found, not in the facts of war, but in the study of conditions before the war. On that study, with special reference to unemployment, I was engaged when the war broke out and for most of the first year of war. Part II of this Report and Appendix A are based mainly on this former research ; that Appendix began as a paper to be read at the bi-centenary of the University of Pennsylvania in September 1940.

[1] Speech at the Caxton Hall, 3rd March, 1943, printed in *The Pillars of Security*, pp. 140–1 (George Allen & Unwin, 1943).

Nevertheless, though made by myself in a wholly private capacity, the Report on Policy for Full Employment is no more a one-man affair than was the Plan for Social Security, in the sense that it was made or could have been made by one man sitting and thinking and studying by himself. So far as was possible in the difficult circumstances of the war, I reproduced for myself in this new enquiry the technical assistance which I had obtained from the Government Departments in the first enquiry. I have had continual consultations with economists outside the Government Departments, some of whom have read and criticized nearly all that I have written ; from them I have taken arguments, similes, phrases without number. I have examined memoranda written by many others, and I have discussed the more important of these memoranda with the persons or organizations submitting them. Finally, taking advantage of my association with the Nuffield College and with the admirable series of conferences in connection with the College, organized originally by Mr. G. D. H. Cole, I have submitted most of my proposals in draft to scrutiny by gatherings widely representative of business, of public administration, of labour organisations and of economic science ; the exposition in Part VI of the three conditions of multilateral trade between nations is the fruit of one of these conferences. The new Report remains, like the old one, a document for which no one can be hanged except myself, but it is not one which I could have produced myself, without the cordial and helpful co-operation of many others.

One practical difference—of timing—arises out of the different circumstances in which this Report and my earlier Report were prepared. After I had signed my earlier Report on the 20th November, 1942, by a notable effort of printing the Government were able to publish both the Report and Appendices and its companion volume of Memoranda from Organizations, altogether not far short of 400,000 words, within a fortnight, on 1st December ; they took steps to make an American edition available at similar breakneck speed. The present Report I completed substantially and sent to the printer on 18th May, 1944, but I have no idea when it will see the light. Meanwhile, the Government have published a White Paper on Employment Policy. That cannot be dealt with in any way in the body of my Report, and has not led to any change in the Report, but forms the subject of a postscript.

It is at the request of those who have helped me most, that I do not thank any of my helpers by name, taking freely what they have given freely towards better understanding of our common problems. To one part only of what is written here by another than myself, it has seemed appropriate to attach the name of the author. To my Report on Social Insurance and Allied Services, there was appended a Memorandum by the Government Actuary on the financial aspects of my proposals. So to the present Report is attached in Appendix C a Memorandum by Mr. Nicholas Kaldor on the Quantitative Aspects of the Full Employment Problem in Britain. Mr. Kaldor's figures, naturally, are more speculative than those which could be given by the Government Actuary in 1942 for Social Insurance. They are hardly, I think, more speculative than the actuarial estimates that were made at the introduction of the first limited scheme of unemployment insurance in 1911 or by the Government Actuary at the time of the extension of unemployment insurance in 1920. They are not nearly as visionary as the hopes of those who trust to establishing full employment by leaving things alone. For those who use figures, the Policy for Full Employment can be made most easily intelligible by figures, such as are given by Mr. Kaldor. But the policy does not stand or fall by those figures. It stands on its argument—on the need and on the possibility of intelligent flexible planning with means of adjustment to changing circumstances.

Though naming no other helpers, it would be inappropriate for me not to record, in memory of my long and happy association with the administrators of Labour Exchanges and Unemployment Insurance, the indispensable help given to me by the Ministry of Labour, before this war and in the opening year of the war. The diagnosis of unemployment in Part II and a large part of Appendix A on the International Trade Cycle rest on information, much of it not previously published, which was placed at my disposal from official sources.

I have pleasure in recording the help given to me by the Institute of Statistics at Oxford by statistical computation and by preparing the charts which appear in this Report. The Institute has done much to keep alive independent expert study of economic phenomena during the War. Many of the difficult economic problems briefly noticed in this Report are the subject of special study in a volume on the *Economics of Full Employment* prepared by members of the Institute and published (B. H. Blackwell, Oxford) almost simultaneously with the Report.

I thank my three friends to whose generosity I owe the material means of making my investigation and preparing its results for publication.

The text on my title page I owe to my wife. It comes from the account given by Charlotte Bronte, in the second chapter of *Shirley*, of the hand-loom weavers who one hundred and twenty-five years ago were being driven into unemployment and miserable revolt by the introduction of knitting frames. "Misery generates hate. These sufferers hated the machines which they believed took their bread from them ; they hated the buildings which contained the machines ; they hated the manufacturers who owned the buildings."

This text is my main text. The greatest evil of unemployment is not physical but moral, not the want which it may bring but the hatred and fear which it breeds. So the greatest evil of war is not physical but spiritual, not the ruin of cities and killing of bodies, but the perversion of all that is best in man's spirit, to serve purposes of destruction, hate, cruelty, deceit and revenge.

There is another passage in *Shirley*, describing in Chapter 8 a conversation between a workman and an employer, which illustrates another leading theme of what is written here. "Invention may be all right," says the workman, "but I know it isn't right for poor folks to starve. Them that governs mun find a way to help us. . . . Ye'll say that's hard to do—so much louder mun we shout, then, for so much slacker will t'Parliament men be to set on a tough job." "Worry the Parliament-men as much as you please," replies the employer, "but to worry the mill-owners is absurd." To look to individual employers for maintenance of demand and full employment is absurd. These things are not within the power of employers. They must therefore be undertaken by the State, under the supervision and pressure of democracy, applied through the Parliament men.

The problems dealt with in the present Report are more difficult than those of the earlier Report. My proposals cannot be set out without the use of technical terms and close argument ; economics is a science, not a business of hit and miss. The justification for my proposals cannot be given except by use of statistical data such as occupy Part II and the various Appendices. Those who are content to accept the brief summary of results from these data which appears in Part I can pass from that part direct to Part III and need not proceed to the Appendices. I have endeavoured to free the argument of needless difficulties. I have made the use of indispensable technical language as painless as possible by giving in Appendix D an explanation of terms.

The problems dealt with in the present Report, while technically difficult, are of vital importance to every citizen. I have given in this volume both proposals and the facts and arguments on which they rest. I have endeavoured to make the main results accessible to all, by summarizing them for early publication in a pamphlet with the same title.

But I hope that as many people as possible will desire to understand and to criticize the argument and the data on which it rests. Unemployment cannot be conquered by a democracy until it is understood by them. Full productive employment in a free society is possible but it is not possible without taking pains. It cannot be won by waving a financial wand ; it is a goal that can be reached only by conscious continuous organization of all our productive resources under democratic control. To win full employment and keep it, we must will the end and must understand and will the means.

W. H. BEVERIDGE

June 1944

Part I

INTRODUCTION AND SUMMARY

RELATION OF THE TWO REPORTS

1. THE Report on Social Insurance and Allied Services which I presented to His Majesty's Government in November, 1942, takes freedom from Want as its aim, and sets out a Plan for Social Security to achieve this aim. Want is defined as lack of income to obtain the means of healthy subsistence—adequate food, shelter, clothing and fuel. The Plan for Social Security is designed to secure, by a comprehensive scheme of social insurance, that every individual, on condition of working while he can and contributing from his earnings, shall have an income sufficient for the healthy subsistence of himself and his family, an income to keep him above Want, when for any reason he cannot work and earn. In addition to subsistence income during interruption of earnings, the Report proposes children's allowances to ensure that, however large the family, no child need ever be in Want, and medical treatment of all kinds for all persons when sick, without a charge on treatment, to ensure that no person need be sick because he has not the means to pay the doctor or the hospital.

2. The Report which I now present is a sequel to my earlier Report, in that it is concerned with what was named in that Report as one of the assumptions of Social Security: the assumption that employment is maintained, and mass unemployment prevented. But it is more than a sequel. Maintenance of employment is wanted for its own sake and not simply to make a Plan for Social Security work more easily. The new Report takes as its aim freedom from Idleness and sets out a Policy for Full Employment to achieve that aim. Choice of the term Idleness has two implications. Idleness is a different word from unemployment; freedom from Idleness secured

by full employment does not mean that there must literally be no unemployment at all. Idleness is not the same as Want; it is a positive separate evil from which men do not escape by having an income. These two implications must be examined in turn.

THE MEANING OF FULL EMPLOYMENT

3. What is meant by "full employment," and what is not meant by it? Full employment does not mean literally no unemployment; that is to say, it does not mean that every man and woman in the country who is fit and free for work is employed productively on every day of his or her working life. In every country with a variable climate there will be seasons when particular forms of work are impossible or difficult. In every progressive society there will be changes in the demand for labour, qualitatively if not quantitatively; that is to say, there will be periods during which particular individuals can no longer be advantageously employed in their former occupations and may be unemployed till they find and fit themselves for fresh occupations. Some frictional unemployment[1] there will be in a progressive society however high the demand for labour. Full employment means that unemployment is reduced to short intervals of standing by, with the certainty that very soon one will be wanted in one's old job again or will be wanted in a new job that is within one's powers.

4. Full employment is sometimes defined as "a state of affairs in which the number of unfilled vacancies is not appreciably below the number of unemployed persons, so that unemployment at any time is due to the normal lag between a person losing one job and finding another."[2] Full employment in this Report means more than that in two ways. It means having always more vacant jobs than unemployed men, not slightly fewer jobs. It means that the jobs are at fair wages, of such a kind, and so located that the unemployed men can reasonably be expected to take them; it means, by consequence, that the normal lag between losing one job and finding another will be very short.

5. The proposition that there should always be more vacant jobs than unemployed men means that the labour market should

---

[1] See Explanation of Terms in Appendix D.

[2] This definition is taken from the Nuffield College Statement on *Employment Policy and Organization of Industry after the War*. The Statement adds that full employment in this sense "cannot be completely attained so long as there exist structural maladjustments needing to be put right."

always be a seller's market rather than a buyer's market. For this, on the view of society underlying this Report—that society exists for the individual—there is a decisive reason of principle. The reason is that difficulty in selling labour has consequences of a different order of harmfulness from those associated with difficulty in buying labour. A person who has difficulty in buying the labour that he wants suffers inconvenience or reduction of profits. A person who cannot sell his labour is in effect told that he is of no use. The first difficulty causes annoyance or loss. The other is a personal catastrophe. This difference remains even if an adequate income is provided, by insurance or otherwise, during unemployment; idleness even on an income corrupts; the feeling of not being wanted demoralizes. The difference remains even if most people are unemployed only for relatively short periods. As long as there is any long-term unemployment not obviously due to personal deficiency, anybody who loses his job fears that he may be one of the unlucky ones who will not get another job quickly. The short-term unemployed do not know that they are short-term unemployed till their unemployment is over.

6. The human difference between failing to buy and failing to sell labour is the decisive reason for aiming to make the labour market a seller's rather than a buyer's market. There are other reasons, only slightly less important. One reason is that only if there is work for all is it fair to expect workpeople, individually and collectively in trade unions, to co-operate in making the most of all productive resources, including labour, and to forgo restrictionist practices. Another reason, related to this, is that the character and duration of individual unemployment caused by structural and technical change in industry will depend on the strength of the demand for labour in the new forms required after the change. The greater the pace of the economic machine, the more rapidly will structural unemployment[1] disappear, the less resistance of every kind will there be to progress. Yet another reason is the stimulus to technical advance that is given by shortage of labour. Where men are few, machines are used to save men for what men alone can do. Where labour is cheap it is often wasted in brainless, unassisted toil. The new lands empty of men are the homes of invention and business adventure in peace. Stimulus to labour saving of all kinds is one of the by-products of full employment in war.

7. The full employment that is the aim of this Report means more vacant jobs than unemployed men. It means something else

[1] See Explanation of Terms in Appendix D.

as well. If there were 2 million chronically unemployed men in Britain and $2\frac{1}{4}$ million vacant jobs which they could not or would not fill, there would be more vacant jobs than unemployed men, but to call this state of affairs "full employment" would be mockery. It is not enough to say that there must be more vacant jobs than idle men—more or about as many. It is also necessary to be sure that the number unemployed, or rather the duration of unemployment in the individual case, is not excessive. Full employment, in any real sense, means that unemployment in the individual case need not last for a length of time exceeding that which can be covered by unemployment insurance without risk of demoralization. Those who lose jobs must be able to find new jobs at fair wages within their capacity, without delay. This means that the demand for labour and the supply of labour are related qualitatively as well as quantitatively. The demand must be adjusted to the kind of men available or the men must be capable of adjusting themselves to the demand. In the light of the facts of unemployment set out in Part II, it is clear that the qualitative and local adjustment of demand for labour and supply of labour has to be approached from both ends, that of demand and that of supply. The demands must not only be sufficient in total but must be directed with regard to the quality and the location of the labour that is available. The labour supply must be capable of following the changes of demand that are inseparable from technical advance.

THE PURPOSE OF EMPLOYMENT

8. Idleness is not the same as Want, but a separate evil, which men do not escape by having an income. They must also have the chance of rendering useful service and of feeling that they are doing so. This means that employment is not wanted for the sake of employment, irrespective of what it produces. The material end of all human activity is consumption. Employment is wanted as a means to more consumption or more leisure, as a means to a higher standard of life. Employment which is merely time-wasting, equivalent to digging holes and filling them again, or merely destructive, like war and preparing for war, will not serve that purpose. Nor will it be felt worth while. It must be productive and progressive. The proposals of this Report are designed to preserve all the essential springs of material progress in the community, to leave to special efforts its rewards, to leave scope for change, invention, competition and initiative.

9. In so far as room is left for change and for freedom of movement from job to job, room is left for some unemployment. The aim
of this Report is expressed in numerical terms in paragraph 169 as
a reduction of unemployment to not more than 3 per cent, as compared with the 10 to 22 per cent experienced in Britain between
the wars. But though the Report assumes the continuance of some
unemployment and suggests a figure of 3 per cent, it is the essence
of the proposals made in the Report that this 3 per cent should be
unemployed only because there is industrial friction, and not because
there are no vacant jobs. For men to have value and a sense of
value there must always be useful things waiting to be done, with
money to pay for doing them. Jobs, rather than men, should wait.

PRESERVATION OF ESSENTIAL LIBERTIES

10. The labour market in the past has invariably, or all but
invariably, been a buyer's market rather than a seller's market,
with more unemployed men—generally many more unemployed
men—than unfilled jobs. To reverse this and make the labour market
always a seller's rather than a buyer's market, to remove not only
unemployment but the fear of unemployment, would affect the
working of many existing institutions. It would change and is
meant to change fundamentally the conditions of living and working
in Britain, to make Britain again a land of opportunity for all.
There are some things in Britain which neither full employment
nor the means of achieving it should be allowed to change.

11. The Report, as its title indicates, is not concerned simply
with the problem of full employment. It is concerned with the
necessity, possibility and methods of achieving full employment in
a free society, that is to say, subject to the proviso that all essential
citizen liberties are preserved. The precise effect of the proviso
depends on the list of essential citizen liberties. For the purpose of
this Report they are taken as freedom of worship, speech, writing,
study and teaching; freedom of assembly and of association for
political and other purposes, including the bringing about of a
peaceful change of the governing authority; freedom in choice of
occupation; and freedom in the management of a personal income.
The proviso excludes the totalitarian solution of full employment
in a society completely planned and regimented by an irremovable
dictator. It makes the problem of full employment more complex
in many ways, of which four call for special notice.

12. First, in a free society the governing authority is liable to be

changed at short intervals by peaceful methods of political organization and voting. There must be reasonable continuity of economic policy in spite of such changes of government. The machinery of government, while responsive to general changes of opinion, must be resistant to "lobbies"—that is to say, organized sectional pressures.

13. Second, freedom of association for industrial purposes raises the issue of wage determination. Under conditions of full employment, can a rising spiral of wages and prices be prevented if collective bargaining, with the right to strike, remains absolutely free? Can the right to strike be limited generally in a free society in peace-time?

14. Third, freedom in choice of occupations makes it harder to ensure that all men at all times are occupied productively. It makes it impossible to retain men forcibly in particular work or to direct them to it with the threat of imprisonment if they refuse to go. One assumption underlying this Report is that neither the Essential Work Order nor the powers of industrial direction which have been found necessary in war should be continued when the war is over. In Britain at peace the supply of labour cannot be adjusted by decree to the demand for labour; it can only be guided by economic motives. From another angle, freedom in choice of occupation raises also the issue of industrial discipline. Under conditions of full employment, if men are free to move from one employment to another and do not fear dismissal, may not some of them at least become so irregular and undisciplined in their behaviour, as to lower appreciably the efficiency of industry?

15. Fourth, freedom in the management of a personal income complicates the problem of full employment from another side. If men cannot be forced to buy just what has been produced, this means that the demands for labour and its products cannot be fitted forcibly to the supply. There may be continual changes in the kinds of things on which consumers want to spend their money, that is to say, in the quality of consumers' outlay.[1] There may be changes also in its quantity. For freedom in the management of a personal income includes freedom to decide between spending now and saving[1] so as to have the power of spending later. A totalitarian regime, even if it used money and price and wage differentials to stimulate and guide individual activity, might abolish freedom of saving. It might retain from the national income of each year that portion which it needed for investment,[1] i.e. for the sustenance of

[1] See Explanation of Terms in Appendix D.

persons engaged in making instruments and materials of further production, and might issue to consumers money which, like ration coupons, could not be saved for spending later. In a free society individuals must be allowed to plan their spending over their lives as a whole.

16. Many of the points thus briefly noted will be discussed more fully in Part V, in dealing with the internal implications of a full employment policy. Here it is sufficient to say that none of these freedoms can be exercised irresponsibly. Perpetual instability of economic or social policy would make full employment and any other social reforms futile or impossible. Bargaining for wages must be responsible, looking not to the snatching of short sectional advantages, but to the permanent good of the community. Choice of occupation means freedom in choosing between occupations which are available; it is not possible for an individual to choose to be an Archbishop of Canterbury, if that post is already filled by another. Work means doing what is wanted, not doing just what pleases one. All liberties carry their responsibilities. This does not mean that the liberties themselves must be surrendered. They must be retained.

17. In all the respects named, and possibly in some others, the problem of maintaining full employment is more complicated in a free society than it would be under a totalitarian regime. From one complication of some historic importance the problem, as posed here, is free. The list of essential liberties given above does not include liberty of a private citizen to own means of production and to employ other citizens in operating them at a wage. Whether private ownership of means of production to be operated by others is a good economic device or not, it must be judged as a device. It is not an essential citizen liberty in Britain, because it is not and never has been enjoyed by more than a very small proportion of the British people. It cannot even be suggested that any considerable proportion of the people have any lively hope of gaining such ownership later.

18. On the view taken in this Report, full employment is in fact attainable while leaving the conduct of industry in the main to private enterprise, and the proposals made in the Report are based on this view. But if, contrary to this view, it should be shown by experience or by argument that abolition of private property in the means of production was necessary for full employment, this abolition would have to be undertaken.

DIAGNOSIS OF UNEMPLOYMENT

19. The meaning and purpose of full employment and the limiting conditions under which it is aimed at in this Report have now been stated. The methods to be adopted depend on diagnosis of the evil to be cured. The Report on Social Insurance and Allied Services began with a diagnosis of Want. The present Report takes as its starting-point a diagnosis of unemployment. Part II, on "Unemployment in Peace," sets out, first, the facts of unemployment before the first World War and between the wars, and second, some of the theories of employment and unemployment by which economists have explained these facts. It combines facts and theories in a concluding section on "The New Face of Unemployment" (paragraphs 137–44). The broad results of this diagnosis are as follows:

20. The volume of unemployment at any time in any community depends upon factors of three kinds: on the factors determining the quantity of the effective demand[1] for the products of industry; on the factors determining the direction of the demand; and on the factors determining the manner in which industry responds to the demand. There will be unemployment if effective demand is not sufficient in total to require use of the whole labour force of the community. There will be unemployment if effective demand, though adequate in total, is misdirected, that is to say, is demand for work of a kind which cannot reasonably be performed by the available labour, or in a place to which the available workmen cannot reasonably be expected to move. There will be unemployment if industry is so organized, that in meeting effective demand it carries excessive reserves of labour standing by to meet local and individual variations of demand, or if there are obstacles which prevent labour from following changes in demand.

21. In Britain, throughout the period between the two wars, the demand for labour was seriously deficient in total in relation to the supply. Large parts of the country experienced chronic mass unemployment (paragraphs 75–82). No part of the country had demand for labour exceeding the supply except possibly for particular classes of labour for a few months at the top of each cyclical fluctuation.[1] In 1937, which was the top of a cyclical fluctuation, representing therefore the best that the unplanned market economy could do, there were in Britain $1\frac{3}{4}$ million unemployed, more than 10 per

[1] See Explanation of Terms in Appendix D.

cent of the labour force. There were not in the busiest month of 1937 more than a few thousand unfilled vacancies at the employment exchanges, that is to say there were always many times as many unemployed men as vacant jobs (paragraph 113). In most of the other years between the wars unemployment was much greater than in 1937.

22. The demand for labour was not merely inadequate but misdirected. If the demand as a whole had been so much greater quantitatively as to equal the supply as a whole, but had been directed locally in the same way, that is to say, preserving the same proportions between the different regions of Britain, this demand would have failed to abolish unemployment; there would have been large numbers of unfilled vacancies and of men who could not or would not move to fill them, and could not reasonably be required to do so. No doubt a high demand of this nature would have reduced unemployment by drawing more people away from the depressed areas to the relatively prosperous areas, but it would have done this only at the cost of still greater housing and transport congestion in the prosperous areas, and of still greater breaking up of families, destruction of communities and waste of social capital in the distressed areas. Deficiency of demand and misdirection of demand are two independent evils. A much higher demand than the actual demand, misdirected in the same way, would have left much unemployment untouched. On the other hand, the same total demand directed evenly to all parts of the country, while it would have avoided some of the social evils of concentrated unemployment, would have left the same total of unemployment spread evenly throughout the country. The evil of misdirection lay in the demand being directed to the wrong places rather than in its being directed to the wrong industries. The great changes that did, in fact, occur in the numbers following different industries between the wars show that the labour supply is more fluid as between industries than it is between localities (paragraphs 78–9 and 110–12). It is easier for men and women to change their occupations and it is much easier for boys and girls to choose their first occupations, with reference to the demand in particular industries, than it is for workpeople of any age to move their place of residence. For some people age and family ties make movement almost impracticable. Leaving home in pursuit of new occupations is often a tonic in individual cases, but is a poison if taken in large quantities, involving destruction of communities.

23. The organizational factors in unemployment, which were the

main theme of my first study before the first World War, continued between the wars, bringing about heavy unemployment in particular industries irrespective of the state of demand. The working of these factors and in particular the disorganization of the labour market, is illustrated by the high unemployment rates[1] in particular industries persisting through good times and bad times alike in spite of a rising demand (paragraphs 63–7); by the over-stocking with labour of the building industry, which between 1924 and 1937 simultaneously increased its employment by a half, and doubled its unemployment (paragraph 109): by the chronic 30 per cent of unemployment in dock and harbour service (paragraphs 107–8).

24. Of the various factors in unemployment named above, deficiency of total demand is the most important. It is true that in one sense there is no demand for labour as a whole because every demand is specific: for a person of a particular quality and sex to do particular work in a particular place. In the same sense, there is no supply of labour as a whole; there are only persons of different sexes, ages and mental and physical capacities, in different places, with varying degrees of specialization and adaptability and varying degrees of attachment to the places in which they are. This is true and the existence of friction in the labour market as a factor in unemployment must never be forgotten. But it is also true that the separate demands for labour in each industry and place at any moment add up to a total which in comparison with the total number of separate persons seeking employment at that moment may be relatively high or relatively low. This relation of total demand to total supply is the most important single element in the problem. It affects the position in every industry, without exception, whatever the special circumstances of the industry may be, because depression in one industry reacts upon other industries in two ways. It reduces directly or indirectly the demand for the products of these industries. It increases the number of people seeking employment in them, in relation to the demand. The excessive pressure during depressions to enter other industries which are least affected by it is amply illustrated by the facts set out in paragraphs 71–3.

25. Before the first World War the adequacy of the total demand for labour, except in times of recurrent depression through cyclical fluctuation, was generally taken for granted. The problem of unemployment presented itself as a problem, on the one hand of organizing the labour market so as to shorten the intervals between jobs and to "de-casualize" the casual occupations, and on the other hand

---

[1] See para. 54 and Explanation of Terms in Appendix D.

of mitigating cyclical fluctuation; this was generally supposed to be a monetary phenomenon susceptible of cure by banking policy. After the first World War unemployment in Britain was materially greater than anything experienced before, probably on an average two and a half times as severe as in the thirty years up to 1914 (paragraphs 90-2 and Appendix B, Section 3). The adequacy of total demand could no longer be taken for granted; the new economic theories taught that there was no automatic mechanism for keeping supply of labour and demand for labour painlessly in equilibrium (paragraphs 120-1).

26. The unemployment experienced in the United States between 1930 and the outbreak of the second World War was also materially greater than anything experienced before (paragraph 138 and Table 16). In Britain two factors were at work:

(a) drastic reduction of overseas demand which, through failure of the market economy to develop any compensating home demand, led to chronic structural unemployment during almost the whole period between the two wars;

(b) The cyclical depression which followed 1929 and though less severe in Britain than in the United States was more severe than most previous depressions.

The exceptional unemployment of the United States cannot be attributed to any outside factor such as failure of overseas demand; the depression in the United States was intensified and prolonged by the actions taken by other countries to deal with their difficulties, but to a large extent these were a natural consequence of the depression itself and would be repeated in similar conditions.

27. The Great Depression of 1931-32 was in itself of the same type as previous depressions. Although more severe than anything previously experienced and though its effects in Britain were increased by structural unemployment due to the secular decline of overseas demand, the cyclical movement from 1929 to 1938 is a lineal descendant of the successive fluctuations which have brought insecurity to all advanced industrial countries with an unplanned market economy ever since industry took its modern form (paragraph 100 and Appendix A). So far as the United States is concerned, there is no reason for confidence or even for hope that the economic system which produced this depression, if left to itself, will fail to reproduce similar depressions in future. So far as Britain is concerned, while there was after the first World War a special factor of failure of overseas demand, there is equally no assurance that

other special factors will not recur and if added to cyclical fluctuation will produce intolerable unemployment.

28. Though it is clear that unemployment between the two wars in Britain and in America was worse than it was before the first World War, we are not in a position really to say how bad things were before 1914 because there is no full record. Three facts, however, are certain. First, that in five years out of every six during the last thirty years before the first World War, the demand for labour generated in the British economy was deficient in relation to the supply (paragraph 56). Second, that cyclical fluctuation in Britain in the second quarter of the nineteenth century, though affecting a smaller proportion of the population, was in itself almost as violent as between the two wars (paragraph A 28 in Appendix A). Third, that shifting in the location of industry produced structural unemployment in Britain before the first World War of the same type, though not so serious in scale, as that experienced between the two wars (paragraphs 93–4).

29. While the main evil of unemployment is in its social and human effects upon the persons unemployed and upon the relations between citizens, the purely material loss of material wealth involved in it is serious. If the unused labour resources of Britain between the two wars could have been brought into use it would have been possible without any further change to increase the total output of the community by approximately one-eighth (paragraph 170).

ANALYSIS OF WAR ECONOMY

30. The diagnosis of peace conditions in Part II leaves no doubt as to the central weakness of the unplanned market economy of the past; its failure to generate sufficient steady demand for its products, with local misdirection of demand and disorganization of the labour market as subsidiary weaknesses, all issuing in unemployment. The repeated experience of war is that unemployment disappears. The conditions under which this happens include notorious interference with liberties that are essential for peace—by rationing, by direction of labour, by prohibition of withdrawal of labour in disputes. But the examination of full employment in war that is made in Part III suggests that these interferences arise from the special character of the war objective and its urgency, and are in no way essential to full employment. The examination shows that the supposed distinction between the destructive occupations of those who fight and the productive occupations of the civilian population

is unreal: both classes are required for vital purposes. The experience of war is relevant to peace: that unemployment disappears and that all men have value when the State sets up unlimited demand for a compelling common purpose. By the spectacular achievement of its planned economy war shows also how great is the waste of unemployment. Finally, war experience confirms the possibility of securing full employment by socialization of demand without socialization of production. With that the way is opened for outlining in Part IV a Policy for Full Employment in Peace.

THE NATURE OF A FULL EMPLOYMENT POLICY

31. As unemployment has three distinct sources, action against unemployment must be taken on three lines—of maintaining at all times adequate total outlay;[1] of controlling the location of industry; of securing the organized mobility of labour. The first of these is the main attack: the others are subsidiary—mopping-up operations. Employment depends on outlay, that is to say on the spending of money on the products of industry; when employment falls off, this means that someone is spending less; when employment increases, this means that in total more is being spent. The first condition of full employment is that total outlay should always be high enough to set up a demand for products of industry which cannot be satisfied without using the whole man-power of the country: only so can the number of vacant jobs be always as high as or higher than the number of men looking for jobs. Who is to secure that the first condition is satisfied? The answer is that this must be made a responsibility of the State. No one else has the requisite powers; the condition will not get satisfied automatically. It must be a function of the State in future to ensure adequate total outlay and by consequence to protect its citizens against mass unemployment, as definitely as it is now the function of the State to defend the citizens against attack from abroad and against robbery and violence at home. Acceptance of this new responsibility of the State, to be carried out by whatever Government may be in power, marks the line which we must cross, in order to pass from the old Britain of mass unemployment and jealousy and fear to the new Britain of opportunity and service for all.

32. Assuming that this decision has been taken, the outline of a Policy for Full Employment is set out in Part IV. The essence of the

[1] See Appendix D and paras. 175–9 in Part IV for explanation of the term "outlay."

Policy is the setting up of a long-term programme of planned outlay directed by social priorities and designed to give stability and expansion to the economic system. The main instrument of the Policy is a new type of Budget. The programme is not concerned simply with public outlay—undertaken directly by the State or by local authorities. In a free society the greater part of the total outlay on which employment depends will be the spending of their personal incomes by private citizens. In a society which preserves a large measure of private enterprise in industry, a substantial part of the total outlay will take the form of private business investment. The State, though in a free society it does not seek to control the spending of private citizens, either in amount or in direction, can influence their spending—cannot indeed avoid influencing it by taxation and other forms of fiscal policy. The annual Budget, therefore, is an instrument not only for determining public outlay, but also for influencing private outlay.

33. The long-term programme outlined in Part IV covers outlay of all kinds, under each of five heads. There is communal outlay on non-marketable goods and services, including defence, order, free education, a national health service, roads, drains, and other public works. There is public business investment in industries now under public control or which may be brought under it hereafter, increasing the sector of enterprise in which investment can be expanded steadily. There is private business investment; here through a new organ—described as a National Investment Board—the State, while preserving private enterprise, can, by appropriate measures, co-ordinate and steady the activities of business men. There is private consumption outlay—the largest head of the five; this can be both increased and steadied by State action in re-distributing income, by measures of Social Security, and by progressive taxation. There is a new head—described as joint consumption outlay—under which the State takes the initiative by placing collective orders—for food, fuel and perhaps other necessaries—with a view to re-selling them later to private consumers at a price which may at need be lowered by a subsidy. Under this last head the State can influence both the amount and the nature of private outlay, while still leaving it free.

34. The novelty of the new type of annual Budget will lie in two things: first, that it will be concerned with the income and expenditure of the community as a whole, not only with public finance; second, that it will take the man-power of the country as a datum and plan outlay to that datum rather than by consideration of

financial resources. The Minister introducing the Budget, after estimating how much private citizens may be expected to spend on consumption and on investment together under a condition of full employment, must propose public outlay sufficient, with the estimated private outlay, to bring about that condition, that is to say to employ the whole man-power of the country. This is the cardinal principle. It leaves unsettled the question of how the means are provided to meet this outlay—in particular the division between taxation and borrowing—and the question of the purposes to which outlay is directed—including the division between public and private outlay or between consumption and investment. These and other questions are examined in Part IV, where it is shown that there are several alternative routes to full employment. The best route at any time depends on the circumstances of the time.

35. A long-term programme of planned outlay does not mean an invariable programme. It will be adjusted continuously to changing circumstances by the annual Budget. Its whole character may change gradually, with rising productivity or changing views of social justice. The guiding principle is that of social priorities—of putting first things first. Different societies or the same society at different times may take different views of what comes first, that is to say of what are the most urgent needs. On the view taken in this Report, the most urgent tasks in Britain, once war is over, are, on the one hand, the making of a common attack on the giant social evils of Want, Disease, Ignorance and Squalor, and on the other hand, the re-equipping of British industry, whether in private or public hands, with new and better machinery to ensure a steady increase in the standard of life; industry for this purpose includes agriculture. It is to these tasks that the productive resources of the nation should first be directed, as they become disengaged from total war. These are the common tasks for what is described in this Report as the reconstruction period, perhaps 20 years long, that should follow the transition period, perhaps of two years after total war ends, through which we pass from war to peace; as progress is made with these tasks, new needs will come to the fore and new aspirations will have play. In attacking the four giant evils named above, we shall reduce also the evil of Inequality, at the points where it is most harmful. But when that attack has reached its objectives, it will still be desirable and may appear the best route to full employment to take continuing measures towards a more equitable distribution both of material resources, so that they are spent in place of being saved, and of leisure, so that leisure replaces unemployment.

LOCAL AND QUALITATIVE ADJUSTMENT OF LABOUR DEMAND AND SUPPLY

36. The Policy for Full Employment set out in Part IV, in addition to its main feature of adequate total outlay, includes two subsidiary measures—controlled location of industry and organized mobility of labour. The first of these is required in the main for reasons other than prevention of unemployment: to deal with the Giant Squalor, that is to say with the evils of congestion, over-crowding, ill-health, bad housing, and destruction of urban and rural amenities alike, which are described in the Report of the Royal Commission on the Distribution of the Industrial Population. But need to prevent local misdirection of demand for labour, and the unemployment that may result from it, is an additional reason for this control. It is better, and less of an interference with individual lives, to control business men in the location of their enterprises than to leave them uncontrolled and require workpeople to move their homes for the sake of employment. Control by the State of location of industry is the alternative both to the compulsory direction of labour and to the making of distressed areas. For this new function, a new organ of the State is needed. Planning of Town and Country, Transport, and Housing all hang together and should probably come under the general supervision of a Minister of National Development.

37. The other subsidiary measure is organized mobility of labour, not mobility as such. Naming it does not imply a view that under a full employment policy work-people will constantly need to shift their homes or occupations. On the contrary, most of them will be able to enjoy more stability than ever before. Much fruitless un-guided wandering in search of work will come to an end. The industries which, by practising casual employment, have in the past accumulated and relied on excessive reserves of under-employed labour, will find this impossible under full employment in peace, as they have found it impossible in war. Whether or not the use of the employment exchanges is made compulsory for all classes of vacancies, it should be compulsory in respect of all persons under eighteen, so that the flow of adaptable youth into industries may be wisely directed. Changes in the demand for labour are inseparable from progress, that is to say from the raising of the standard of life. Organized mobility means that if and when change is necessary, men and women shall be willing to change their occupations and their places of work, rather than cling to idleness. It does not mean perpetual motion.

INTERNATIONAL IMPLICATIONS

38. The international implications of a full employment policy form the subject of Part VI of the Report. The vital importance of her overseas trade to Britain requires no emphasis. Britain, in order to maintain any tolerable standard of living, must have certain imports, and after this war, must be able to export more goods in order to pay for those imports, since she has had to sell in the early part of the war many securities representing former investment overseas, which brought imports in payment of interest, and since the earnings of British shipping will for a time at least be seriously reduced. Britain must have imports and exports up to a certain minimum, in order to live; she should endeavour to develop her international trade as far as she can, in order to live better. This does not mean, however, that Britain should delay to adopt a policy of full employment at home, until the attitude of other countries to international trade and the best form which that trade can take are known. On the contrary, the greatest service that Britain can render to other countries, as to herself and to the development of international trade, is forthwith to adopt a policy of full employment at home, making it clear that, for her, overseas trade is a means of raising the standard of life of all countries by fair exchange, and is not a device for exporting unemployment. Once this is clear, Britain should co-operate with other countries in bringing about as much international trade as possible on as free a basis as possible, and should be ready to enter into the widest scheme of international clearing and currency, which has good prospects of permanence.

39. But the prospects for any such scheme depend less on the technical details of the scheme than on the economic policies of the countries taking part. The argument set out in detail in Part VI of the Report leads to the conclusion that any plan for uncontrolled multilateral trading[1] between any group of countries can be permanent and work smoothly, only if each of the countries accept three conditions: first, of pursuing an internal policy of full employment suited to its special circumstances; second, of taking or assenting to all the measures necessary to balance its accounts with the rest of the world, and avoiding want of balance, whether by way of excess or deficiency; third, of displaying reasonable continuity and stability in its foreign economic policy, in respect particularly of the control of trade by tariffs, quotas or other means. The first of these

[1] See paras. 311–13 for explanation of the terms "multilateral trade" and "bilateral trade".

conditions does not mean that failure of a particular country to maintain full employment should lead to its immediate or lasting exclusion from the international trading system. But it does mean that a country which aims at full employment, in making plans for international trade, should take into account not merely the external but also the internal economic policies of other countries and their prospects of stability, and should retain the right to protect itself against the contagion of depression by discrimination in trade and by other measures. It is shown in Part VI that giving this power of protection against the contagion of depression, cannot make the ultimate condition of the depressed country worse.

40. Restoration of the widest possible measure of multilateral trading on the three conditions named above, should be the prime objective of British policy. If, as may well prove possible, a world wide system of multilateral trading is not attainable or is not immediately attainable, the next best course for Britain will be a regional system of multilateral trading, embracing those countries which can accept the conditions named above. The third alternative available to ensure a minimum of imports, without which the British standard of living cannot be maintained, is the making of bilateral agreements with particular suppliers who will also be customers for British exports. In one way or another there is no doubt that the problem of obtaining the necessary minimum of international trade for Britain can be solved. A full employment policy for Britain must be framed in alternatives, and Britain must retain freedom to adopt the second or third best alternative, if the first cannot be secured.

41. The necessity for Britain to have substantial overseas trade means that employment in Britain will be subject to fluctuations of overseas demand. Steps can be taken and all possible steps should be taken in co-operation with other nations to diminish these fluctuations. The new facts as to the international trade cycle set out in Appendix A to the Report and summarized briefly in paragraphs 96–101 suggest that to stabilize the production and marketing of primary commodities, that is to say, food and raw materials, is an essential step for preventing fluctuation in industrial countries. But whatever be done to diminish fluctuations in overseas demands some fluctuation is certain to continue. The full employment policy of Britain must and can contain measures for varying home demand to meet variations of overseas demand.

42. The international implications of full employment have another aspect than that of the overseas trade of Britain. The Report made here is first and foremost a Report for Britain, and the par-

ticular policy proposed is a policy for Britain. But the central problem attacked in the Report, is the same as that which faces all advanced industrial communities which desired to win security of employment for their citizens, while preserving the democratic liberties of the citizens. Above all, the problem for Britain is in fundamentals the same as that which faces the greatest industrial community in the World—the United States of America. For Britain and for America the essential citizen liberties that must be preserved at all costs are substantially the same. The experience of recurrent insecurity through cyclical fluctuation of trade for at least a hundred years is broadly the same. The experience of the devastating unemployment and waste of men, in the last decade before the war, is the same in kind, however it may differ in degree or detail. The experience of mutual dependence of different nations that has been brought home so forcibly to all who are willing to face facts, by the Great Depression of the nineteen-thirties, should become a driving force to co-operation for mutually supported prosperity in future. The details of a full employment policy in the United States might be different from that which is suggested for Britain here. But the principle of the proposals is applicable to the United States as to Britain, that it must become the responsibility of the supreme organ of the community, the National Government, to ensure at all times outlay adequate for full employment. This is consistent with leaving the actual conduct of production and the giving of employment mainly or wholly to private enterprise, that is to say in the hands of undertakings working for profit, and tested by their success in yielding profit. But, unless outlay is maintained, mass unemployment cannot be prevented; free institutions may be imperilled in any country to which mass unemployment returns.

43. Finally, though the present Report is first and foremost a Report for Britain and is concerned with what Britain should do in her own borders, to set her house in order, this does not imply any narrow view of Britain's place in the world, or of her responsibilities to other nations. It implies no ignorance of the urgent duty that will lie upon Britain, as upon any other country which escapes wholly or largely the physical devastation of the common war, to contribute with all her strength, and seeking no reward, to the early restoration of less fortunate regions. More than that, Britain, though no longer holding or desiring the unique position which once she occupied as the leading industrial country of the world, is still a country of high standards of production and consumption. She has still, therefore, the responsibility of learning how, in future, to spread pros-

perity in place of depression, and of helping to promote industrial development and the raising of standards of living, not only among her own people but among other peoples. This is not forgotten in the Report. But Britain cannot fulfil her responsibilities abroad, and cannot be a good neighbour to other nations, unless at home she is busy, productive and contented.

THE STATE AND THE CITIZEN

44. Full employment cannot be won and held without a great extension of the responsibilities and powers of the State exercised through organs of the central Government. No power less than that of the State can ensure adequate total outlay at all times, or can control, in the general interest, the location of industry and the use of land. To ask for full employment while objecting to these extensions of State activity is to will the end and refuse the means. It is like shouting for victory in total war while rejecting compulsory service and rationing. In this Report, the new functions and powers of the State are emphasized because they are essential. This does not mean that the end can be reached through such powers alone. The underlying principle of the Report is to propose for the State only those things which the State alone can do or which it can do better than any local authority or than private citizens either singly or in association, and to leave to these other agencies that which, if they will, they can do as well as or better than the State. The Policy for Full Employment is a policy to be carried through by democratic action, of public authorities, central and local, responsible ultimately to the voters, and of voluntary associations and private citizens consciously co-operating for a common purpose which they understand and approve. The proposals in this Report preserve absolutely all the essential liberties which are more precious than full employment itself. They respect and are designed to preserve many other liberties and institutions which, though not equally essential, are deeply rooted in Britain.

45. The proposals imply, for instance, no weakening of local Government, no supersession of local authorities in their present field. The State must do some new things and exercise some controls which are not now exercised by anyone. It will set up the programme of planned outlay for attack on social evils and ensure the means to meet that outlay. But a large part of the execution of the programme —in health, housing, education and other fields—and the adjusting of the programme to local conditions will be a function of local rather than of central Government.

46. The proposals involve, again, no general change in the control or organization of industry, either on the side of management or on that of labour. They assume an expansion of the sector of industry under direct public control, but it remains a sector. The policy outlined here is put forward as something that could work and yield full employment, even though the greater part of industry continued to be conducted by private enterprise at private risk. Undoubtedly the achieving of full employment would affect the working of many industrial institutions and raise many issues; making the labour market a seller's in place of a buyer's market is a revolution which gives a new turn to every problem. Some of the most important issues, such as industrial discipline, determination of wages, determination of prices, treatment of monopolies and price associations, are discussed in Part V among the internal implications of full employment. The general conclusion is that the degree of liberty in such matters which can be left to agencies independent of the State, without imperilling the policy of full employment, depends on the responsibility and public spirit with which those liberties are exercised. There is no reason to doubt that that responsibility and public spirit will be forthcoming.

47. On the general issue of public ownership as against private enterprise in industry, the provisional conclusion reached in Part V is that the necessity of socialism, in the sense of nationalization of the means of production, distribution and exchange, in order to secure full employment, has not yet been demonstrated. This implies no judgment on the general issue between socialism and capitalism, which remains for debate on other grounds. It does not mean that the problem of full employment and the problem of the control of industry are in no way connected; they are connected in many ways. It means only a judgment that it would be possible to obtain full productive employment under conditions of private enterprise. Whether it would be easier or more difficult to obtain this under conditions of national enterprise and whether there are other reasons for socialism, it is not necessary here to decide. The problem of maintaining demand on the productive resources of the country so that they are employed productively in meeting human needs arises whether industry itself is controlled by profit-seeking individuals or by public authorities. It is also to a large extent the same problem in both cases. The policy outlined in this Report is suggested as something that could and should be accepted by people who differ profoundly as to the ultimate control of industry or as to the nature of social justice.

PLAN FOR SOCIAL SECURITY—POLICY FOR EMPLOYMENT

48. In the Report on Social Insurance and Allied Services, I set out a Plan for Social Security. The present Report sets out not a "Plan" but a "Policy" for Full Employment. The difference of wording is due, in part, to the different circumstances in which the two Reports have been prepared, one with all the help that His Majesty's Government and all the departments under their control could give me, and the other without that help. With the same help, this second Report could have dealt with many practical details which are now omitted from it.

49. But the difference of wording, between "Plan" and "Policy" does not arise simply or mainly from differences in the conditions ,under which the two Reports were prepared. It reflects also a fundamental difference between the problems to be solved. Social Security today can be made the subject of a definite Plan and of legislation to give effect to that Plan. It lies wholly within the power of each National Government; once a decision has been taken to abolish Want by comprehensive unified social insurance as the principal method, once a few issues of equity between older and newer contributors have been settled, the rest is administrative and actuarial detail: the Plan should be as definite as possible, so that every citizen, knowing just what he may expect from social insurance, can plan his personal spending and saving to suit his special needs.

50. Prevention of Idleness enforced by mass unemployment is a different task. Detailed legislation is neither needed nor useful. It is a problem of adjusting State action to the free activities of the citizens of that State and to the policies of other States. It involves one large decision of principle—acceptance by the State of a new responsibility to the individual—and the setting up of an agency of the State with powers adequate for the discharge of that responsibility. But the course which that agency should pursue cannot be laid down in advance. As is said in concluding Part IV of this Report, pursuit of full employment is not like the directed flight of an aircraft on a beam; it is a difficult navigation, in which a course must be steered among shifting, unpredictable, and to a large extent, uncontrollable currents and forces. All that can be done is to see that the pilot has the necessary controls, and an instrument board to tell him when and how to use the controls. It is necessary also that the pilot should always have the will to use the controls by which alone he can reach his destination.

Part II

UNEMPLOYMENT IN PEACE

Introduction: Understanding as basis of action (paras. 51-3).

SECTION 1: FACTS OF UNEMPLOYMENT

Unemployment before 1914 (paras. 54-60). The General Level of Unemployment between the Wars (paras. 61-2). Unemployment by Industries (paras. 63-7). Unemployment Rates and Employment Volumes (paras. 68-74). Unemployment by Localities (paras. 75-9). Unemployment by Duration (paras. 80-3). Age and Unemployment (paras. 84-9). Unemployment Compared before and after the First World War (paras. 90-4). The Old Problems in New Light (paras. 95-112). Fluctuation of Demand (paras. 96-102). Disorganization of the Labour Market (paras. 103-9). Occupational and Local Mobility (paras. 110-12). The New Problem: Deficiency of Demand (paras. 113-14).

SECTION 2: THEORIES OF UNEMPLOYMENT

Unemployment Diagnosis of 1909 (paras. 115-19). The Keynesian Analysis of 1936 (paras. 120-6). Significance of Wage Bargaining (para. 127). Offsetting of Saving by Investment or Consumption (paras. 128-30). Interplay of Theories and Facts (paras. 131-6).

SECTION 3: THE NEW FACE OF UNEMPLOYMENT

(Paras. 137-44.)

INTRODUCTION

51. This part of the Report cannot help being long. In the last forty years, since the passage of the Unemployed Workmen Act of 1905 gave statutory recognition to distress through unemployment that could not be left for general relief under the Poor Laws, Britain, in endeavouring to deal with unemployment, has acquired for the first time comprehensive accurate information about the problem. The next step is to use that information for prevention, not merely as a guide to relief or palliation. For that purpose, a review of the facts of unemployment, as they have now for the first time become available, is indispensable. The review made here begins with a survey of unemployment in Britain, as it appeared before the first World War and particularly in the diagnosis made in 1909 by the Royal Commission on the Poor Laws and Relief of Distress. It proceeds to a survey, very different in some ways, similar in other ways, of unemployment between the wars; it attempts a statistical

comparison of the relative severity of unemployment before and after the first World War. More important than this is the detailed analysis of unemployment, by industries, by localities and in other ways, based on the data provided by unemployment insurance. Only by such analysis is it possible to judge the relative importance, as factors in unemployment, of the general level of demand, of the direction of demand, of the methods of industry, and of occupational or local obstacles to movement of labour. Only by such analysis can the economic causes and the social consequences of unemployment be understood.

52. One part of the analysis of facts, dealing with the special problem of cyclical fluctuation, is set out separately in an Appendix. The length of this study of the International Trade Cycle, its statistical techniques, its use of data other than those of unemployment and, to some extent, the novelty of its conclusions, make this course convenient. The argument of this study, summarized in paragraphs 96–102 below, is that there are elements in cyclical fluctuation —first suggested by an analysis of British unemployment statistics— which have hitherto been neglected. There are facts which suggest that "one of the inner secrets of the trade cycle is to be found, not in bankers' parlours or in the board rooms of industry, but on the prairies and plantations, in the mines and oil-wells."[1]

53. With growing knowledge of the facts of unemployment, acquired through practical dealing with unemployment, has gone much hard thinking and theorizing by economists. The review of facts in the first section is followed by a review of theories in the second section, and then by a third section, showing how facts and theories converge to demonstrate the need for action and the kind of action that is needed. The new face of unemployment in Britain, as in the United States, is grimmer than the old face. But unemployment to those who will face the facts and examine the theories is no longer a hopeless mystery. The time has come for deciding to let action follow understanding.

Section I. FACTS OF UNEMPLOYMENT

UNEMPLOYMENT BEFORE 1914

54. Before the first World War, the most valuable and the only continuous record of facts about unemployment in Britain was that

[1] See para. A 42 in Appendix A.

supplied by trade unions giving out-of-work pay to their members when unemployed. The trade union returns, at their highest before 1914, covered less than a million workpeople nearly all of whom were skilled men, but they represented a considerable variety of occupations. The returns were made monthly and gave both the total membership and the members unemployed, making it possible to obtain the percentage of the membership unemployed in each union, in all the unions in a particular industry, and in all unions taken together. From these returns a general percentage of unemployment was calculated and is available for each month from 1888 to 1926; by a special enquiry whose results were published in 1904,[1] the Board of Trade, at that time the Government Department responsible for labour questions, were able to calculate annual unemployment percentages for a number of unions as far back as 1851. Out-of-work pay developed first in the engineering, ship-building and metal industries, which were particularly liable to violent fluctuation, so that the early figures related mainly to these industries, while other industries came into the returns gradually; engineering, shipbuilding and metals accounted for about three-quarters of the total membership covered by the returns in 1860–70 and about two-fifths in 1904. In order to keep the figures, so far as possible, on the same basis throughout, the Board of Trade used, as the most general indication of level of unemployment, the mean of the percentage for the engineering, shipbuilding and metal industries, and of the percentage for all other industries taken together; they described this as the "corrected" unemployment percentage. This corrected percentage is available for each year from 1856 to 1926 and is used here for all general purposes.[2] The percentage of unemployment in a particular union, or all unions, or any other group of employees will be described in future as the unemployment rate for the group.

---

[1] *Memoranda on British and Foreign Trade and Industry* (Second Series), 1904 (Cd. 2337).

[2] A table on pp. 68–9 of the 21st Annual Abstract of Labour Statistics gives general uncorrected percentages of unemployment in the trade unions for each month from 1888 to 1926, and annual uncorrected percentages weighted by the numbers covered by the returns in each trade for each year from 1881 to 1926. It shows the total membership of the unions reporting rising from 140,000 in 1881 to a pre-war maximum of 922,000 in 1913, rising further to 1,603,000 in 1920 and relapsing to 833,000 in 1926, when the returns were discontinued. There is not in most of the period covered by this table any great difference between the corrected and the uncorrected general percentages. From 1883 to 1913 both corrected and uncorrected percentages have the same average of 4·8.

55. Subtracting the unemployment rate for any group of employees from 100 gives a percentage which may be described as the employment rate, because it shows what proportion of every 100 men available for employment in that group were actually in employment at any time. The general employment rate derived in this way from the trade union returns is given in Table 22 in Appendix A for each year from 1856 to 1926, and is represented graphically in Chart I. This Chart shows employment fluctuating continually up to the first World War, in a succession of waves of unequal length. The crests of the waves, apart from the exceptional

Chart I

EMPLOYMENT RATE IN BRITISH TRADE UNIONS 1856—1926

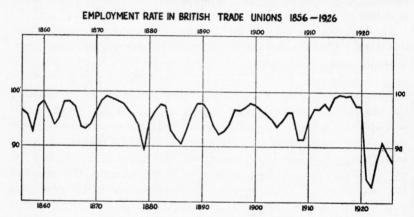

boom of 1872, are at about 98, representing 2 per cent of unemployment. The troughs, apart from the exceptionally severe depression of 1879 with more than 10 per cent of unemployment, are usually at about 92, representing 8 per cent of unemployment. As is shown in Appendix A (paragraph A6), this trade union employment rate, in spite of its narrow basis, represents with a high degree of accuracy the course of industrial activity in Britain and is of fundamental importance for the study of the trade cycle forming the subject of that Appendix. The curve on Chart I shows in its latter portion the practical disappearance of unemployment during the first World War (noted in paragraph 145), the high level of employment during the immediate aftermath of war in 1919–20 (noted in paragraph 375), and finally the catastrophic decline of employment and its lower general level from 1921 onwards (examined in paragraphs 90–4).

56. Here two general points as to unemployment before the first

World War call for notice. The first point is that unemployment, even in the years of greatest activity, never disappeared completely: after 1874 it did not in any year fall below 2 per cent. This applies not only to the general unemployment rate but also to the rates for each of the main groups of industries covered by the returns: it applies though each of these groups was growing more rapidly than the population as a whole.[1] The second point is that in most years employment was appreciably below the maximum of the best years. From 1856 to 1913 the general unemployment rate was below $2\frac{1}{2}$ per cent only in 14 years out of the 58, that is to say in about one year out of four. During the last four complete cyclical fluctuations from 1883 to 1913 it was as low as that only in five years out of 31, that is in one year out of six.

57. Though the trade union returns furnish the only continuous statistical record of unemployment in Britain before the first World War, they do not represent by any means all that was known of the facts of unemployment in those days. A contribution of fundamental importance was made by the Majority and Minority Reports of the Royal Commission on the Poor Laws and Relief of Distress, which was appointed as one of the last Acts of the Conservative Government of 1905, and reported in February 1909, to the Liberal Government which had succeeded to office.[2] Though the Commission of eighteen members presented two complete and separate Reports, the diagnosis of the problem in each Report was the same, and the remedies proposed were largely the same. The Reports agreed, first, in recognizing the reality of unemployment, in spite of the facts that the demand for labour on the whole kept pace with the supply, and that the standard of living rose continuously. "Not only is there cyclical dislocation which recurrently reduces the demand for labour and issues either in general short-time, as in collieries and the cotton trade, or in workers of all classes and grades being thrown out of employment altogether, but, going on all the time—never disappearing and only intensified by bad times—there is this normal under-employment of casual workers. . . ."[3] The Reports agreed in emphasizing, as the most serious factor in the problem, the practice of casual engagement of labour, and the

---

[1] *In Unemployment* (1909), p. 69, I gave particulars as to the irreducible minimum of unemployment even in rapidly growing industries.

[2] In this account of the two Reports of the Royal Commission on the Poor Laws and Relief of Distress I have drawn freely on Chapter XII of *Unemployment* (1930), in which I described "The Policies of 1909."

[3] *Majority Report*, Part VI, para. 202.

resulting under-employment. The Majority Report introduced the subject in a distinct section under the heading: "The New Problem: Chronic Under-employment"; they made a special analysis of dock labour as a leading case of casual employment; and they described casual labour, in this and other forms, as the greatest single cause of the production of pauperism and distress. The Minority said the same thing in almost the same words, when summing up the results of the special investigations put in hand for the Commission. "The outcome of these investigations was all the more impressive in that it was not what we anticipated. We do not exaggerate when we say that all these inquirers—numbering with their assistants more than a dozen, starting on different lines of investigation and pursuing their researches independently all over the kingdom—came, without concert, to the same conclusion, namely that of all the causes or conditions pre-disposing to pauperism, the most potent, the most certain and the most extensive in its operation, was this method of employment in odd jobs."[1]

58. In the study of unemployment which I made at that time,[2] and which appeared almost simultaneously with the Report of the Royal Commission, casual employment was treated as an acute case of the tendency of each industry to accumulate and retain reserves of labour greater than were needed to provide for local and individual changes of demand. The Report of a Special Committee on Unskilled Labour, appointed by the Charity Organization Society, summed up the position in regard to London Docks, in the following words:

> "The central evil is the maintenance of a floating reserve of labour far larger than is required to meet the maximum demands of employers. This is brought about by the independent action of the separate employing agencies each seeking to retain a following of labour as nearly as possible equal to its own maximum demand."[3]

On the analysis of unemployment made then, the men seeking to live by casual work at the London Docks were to be regarded not as extraneous to industry when unemployed, but as part of it, responding to the demand for labour in the vicious demoralizing

---

[1] *Minority Report*, Part II, Ch. IV (C), p. 195.

[2] *Unemployment: A Problem of Industry* (Longmans, Green & Co., 1909). The first edition of this work is cited later as *Unemployment* (1909). The revised edition, with a new second part, is cited as *Unemployment* (1930).

[3] Cited at p. 92 of *Unemployment* (1909).

form in which the demand was made. They were under-employed rather than surplus; the victims of an indirect form of sweating; proof of the potent attraction of the raffle. Men who would have rejected as inadequate a weekly wage of 25s. could be kept hanging about the riverside indefinitely on a gambling chance of getting 6s. a day on an average of two or three days a week.

59. But casual employment was not confined to dock and wharf labour, and the under-employment of the casual industries was only an acute case of the glutting of the labour market in each industry. The strength of the tendency to keep excessive reserves of labour varied from industry to industry, according to the numbers of separate employers, the frequency of engagements, and the methods of engaging men. In addition to casual occupations, like dock labour, the tendency was strong in industries like building in which men were continually being taken on and discharged as jobs began and ended, without any attempt to organize their movement between jobs. But the tendency was found to some extent in all industries. My analysis of the reserve of labour and explanation of the "central paradox" which made the labour market always a buyers' market rather than a seller's market, was based largely on statistics of unemployment in skilled trades.[1] The normal glutting of the labour market sprang from disorganization of the labour market, from the fact that long after exchanges had been established for every other thing needing to be bought and sold, the prevailing method of selling the most perishable and most essential good of all, the service of human beings, continued to be the medieval method of hawking it from door to door. The remedy for this evil was to replace the hawking of labour by organization of the labour market through employment exchanges, to shorten the passage from job to job in every industry, to bring the recruiting of labour by each industry into accord with its total requirements, to replace the large stagnant under-employed reserves collected in the casual industries by small mobile bodies of men adequately employed in working sometimes at one place and sometimes at another. This was the argument that, in one form or another, was put to the Royal Commission from many sources and was accepted by them. The Majority and the Minority Reports alike made the organization of the labour market by a national system of labour or employment exchanges their principal recommendation and the cornerstone of their policies for dealing with unemployment. This recommendation, known to the Government in advance, was accepted by them even before the

[1] *Unemployment* (1909), pp. 70 6.

Reports of the Commission were published. It led to the speedy passage of the Labour Exchanges Act of 1909.

60. A further source of statistical information about unemployment came into being just before the first World War through the introduction, under Part II of the National Insurance Act, 1911, of the first limited scheme of compulsory unemployment insurance. Both the Majority and the Minority of the Royal Commission had realized that, whatever was done to reduce unemployment, some unemployment must be accepted as inevitable and they had emphasized the value, as a means of preventing distress, of unemployment insurance as undertaken by the trade unions; in practice no members of trade unions giving out-of-work pay were found among the applicants for relief work under the Unemployed Workmen Act of 1905, passed to assist the unemployed without affixing to them the stigma of the Poor Law. Each of the Reports recommended, though in different ways and somewhat tentatively, an extension of unemployment insurance. The Government of the day went ahead of these recommendations by introducing in 1911 compulsory unemployment insurance in engineering, shipbuilding, construction of vehicles, building and construction of works, and one or two minor industries. By this measure—the first of its kind in the world—unemployment insurance was extended beyond the skilled organized classes covered by the trade unions. This limited scheme, covering about $2\frac{1}{4}$ million workpeople, was in operation for nearly two years before the first World War. Its working was described by the Board of Trade, which administered labour exchanges and unemployment insurance till the setting up of the Ministry of Labour in 1916, in two Reports, one published and one unpublished.[1] These Reports provide material for an interesting comparison between unemployment in 1913 and 1937, the peaks of cyclical fluctuation last preceding the first World War and the second World War respectively. The comparison is made below in paragraphs 93–4 and Appendix B, Section 3.

[1] The published Report (1913, Cd. 6965) covers the period from the passage of the National Insurance Act in December, 1911, to the end of the first Insurance year in July, 1913. The unpublished Report covers the second Insurance year, from July, 1913, to July, 1914, giving additional statistics for the whole period since the passage of the Act, and deals also with the administration of the Labour Exchanges. A copy of this Report has been made available to the students in the Library of the London School of Economics and Political Science. It is referred to below as "The Board of Trade Report, 1914."

The General Level

61. After the first World War, the limited scheme of unemployment insurance of 1911, which had received a slight extension in 1916, was made general in 1920. Thereby continuous detailed records of unemployment covering most of the population who live by employment became available. From the number of unemployment books issued each July the Ministry of Labour is able to calculate for each region and industry the number of insured persons; from the number of these books lodged during unemployment in order to claim benefit or other advantages of the insurance scheme, it is able to give, for each region and industry and for Britain as a whole, the number unemployed and by combining the number insured and the number unemployed, to calculate for each month and year an unemployment rate. This general unemployment rate for Great Britain and

Table 1

GENERAL UNEMPLOYMENT RATE, 1921–1938

Year	Percentage Unemployed		Year	Percentage Unemployed	
	Great Britain	Great Britain and Northern Ireland		Great Britain	Great Britain and Northern Ireland
1921	16·6	17·0	1930	15·8	16·1
1922	14·1	14·3	1931	21·1	21·3
1923	11·6	11·7	1932	21·9	22·1
1924	10·2	10·3	1933	19·8	19·9
1925	11·0	11·3	1934	16·6	16·7
1926	12·3	12·5	1935	15·3	15·5
1927	9·6	9·7	1936	12·9	13·1
1928	10·7	10·8	1937	10·6	10·8
1929	10·3	10·4	1938	12·6	12·9

for Great Britain and Northern Ireland is given in Table 1 for each year from 1921 to 1938. Between the two wars, from 1921 to 1938, the general unemployment rate in Great Britain and Northern Ireland among persons insured under the general scheme of unemployment, ranged from a minimum of just under ten to a maximum of just over twenty-two and averaged 14·2. The employment rate from 1921 to 1938, obtained by deducting this general unemployment rate from 100, is shown in Chart II. The later part of this chart presents a graphic record of the course in the United Kingdom of the Great Depression which lowered the employment rate from about 90 in 1929 to 78 in 1932; there came a recovery to about 90 again in 1937, after which a fresh downward move began, but was interrupted by the second World War. These figures covered

Chart II

GENERAL   EMPLOYMENT   RATE   1921 — 1938   (Great Britain and Northern Ireland)

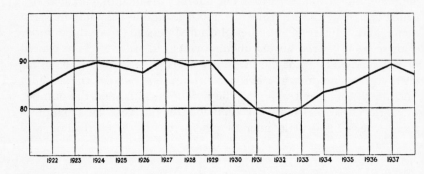

in July, 1939, just over 10 million men and boys and 4 million women and girls. They exclude agricultural workers (insured under a separate scheme since 1936), indoor domestic servants and a number of pensionable employments under public authorities and on the railways.

62. The general unemployment rate, as given above, is a single figure for each month or for each year in Great Britain as a whole. This single figure covers a great variety of facts. "The persons recorded as unemployed month by month are not homogeneous. They are persons of different ages, sexes and capacities seeking employment in different industries and districts; they have been unemployed for widely differing periods of time and they stand in different relations to the two schemes of insurance and assistance established by the Unemployment Act of 1934. The beginning of an understanding of the problem of unemployment is to break it up." This statement is taken from three articles giving "An Analysis of Unemployment," published by myself in *Economica* between November, 1936 and May, 1937. In these articles I broke up the total of the unemployed by industries, by districts, by reference to the duration of unemployment, by sex and age and in other ways. It will be sufficient here, to give a briefer analysis by industries, by localities, by duration and by ages. It is now possible to relate this analysis mainly to the year 1937, and it is advantageous to do so.

The year 1937 is of particular importance for the study of unemployment and its causes, because it marks the top of the last cyclical fluctuation.

Unemployment by Industries

63. The unemployment rate varies greatly from one industry to another. Thus in October, 1937, the mean unemployment rate for all industries taken together was 10·2, but the rates for individual industries ranged all the way from 2·8 in scientific instrument making and 2·9 in electrical engineering to 23·0 both in shipping and in port transport and 23·1 in jute. Very few of the 100 odd industries into which the Ministry of Labour divides the insured population had a rate at all close to the mean of 10·2; there was no predominant rate applying to a large proportion of the industries. This is not a result found only at that particular date. It would be found whatever the date or period chosen. This appears from Table 33 in Appendix B which, for most of the 100 or so industries shown separately in the Labour Gazette classification, gives the average unemployment rates for the years 1924, 1929, 1932 and 1937. Three of these years, 1924, 1929 and 1937 are chosen as having much the same general level of unemployment, about 10 per cent; 1929 and 1937 are the crests of the last cyclical fluctuation, with 1932 as the year of maximum depression between them. In each of the four years there is a wide variation between industries and on the whole the different industries keep their relative positions. Some industries are characterized throughout by relatively low rates of unemployment and others by high rates. Over the ten years 1927-36 the average rate of unemployment among insured males[1] ranged from 4·4 in tramway and omnibus service and 5·8 in tobacco to 32·1 in port transport and 40·8 in shipbuilding. Ten per cent of unemployment in the first two industries would mean an unexampled depression; in the other two industries it would mean incredible prosperity.

64. Table 33 has another and still more important object, that of determining how far there is any connection between the rate of unemployment in an industry and changes in the effective demand for labour in it. For this purpose another calculation made each year by the Ministry of Labour is of importance. Deducting from the numbers of insured persons, as shown by the exchange of unemployment books, the numbers unemployed, the Ministry shows for

---

[1] Statistics relating to males only are used in this comparison as the recorded unemployment among women in 1930 and 1931 was affected by administrative changes. (See para. B 14 in Appendix B.)

each industry and district and for the country as a whole, the numbers actually in employment in June of each year and expresses those numbers as relatives,[1] that is to say as percentages of the corresponding numbers in employment in June, 1924. These relatives show the change in the effective demand for labour, industry by industry, since 1924; they make it possible to set side by side with figures showing these changes of employment the unemployment

Table 2

CHANGE OF EMPLOYMENT AND UNEMPLOYMENT IN CERTAIN GROUPS OF INDUSTRIES (G.B. AND N.I.)

Group	Number of Industries	Insured Persons July 1937 (*thousands*)	Employment* June 1937 as percentage of June 1924	Unemployment Rates*	
				1924	1937
Manufacturing Industries with Employment:					
(i) Growing at more than twice average rate	17	1618.5	178.5	8.9	6.2
(ii) Growing at more than average rate	12	854.7	128.5	9.4	8.4
(iii) Growing at less than average rate	25	2231.6	111.5	12.1	7.6
(iv) Declining	19	1574.3	83.8	13.5	12.8
Service Industries	7	3407.1	153.7	7.2	9.2
Building	1	1035.3	146.0	10.6	13.8
Coal Mining	1	868.4	60.0	5.7	14.7

* The figures in these columns are the means of the figures for separate industries weighted by the numbers of insured persons in 1924 or 1937. Since the point of the table lies in the experience of separate industries, use of the unweighted means in place of one weighted by the number of persons in each industry might be the better course. Unweighted means are given in the full table in the Appendix. Use of these, in preference to the weighted means, while it would alter the wording of some of the comments made here, would not change their substance. The unemployment rates both for 1924 and for 1937 are means of 12 monthly counts.

rates in each industry at the beginning and end of the period, in 1924 and 1937. In each of those two years the general unemployment rate, taking all industries together, was much the same, while from 1924 to 1937 the effective demand for labour, taking together all industries subject to general unemployment insurance rose by 20 per cent; that is to say, the number in employment at the later date was 120 per cent of those in employment at the earlier date. But different industries showed very different changes. In Table

[1] See Explanation of Terms in Appendix D.

33 the manufacturing industries are arranged in four groups:
(i) those in which the numbers in employment rose from June,
1924 to June, 1937 at more than twice the average rate of
20 per cent, i.e. rose by more than 40 per cent; (ii) those in which
these numbers rose between 20 per cent and 40 per cent; (iii) those
with an increase less than 20 per cent; and (iv) those with an actual
decline of employment. Summary figures for each of these groups
and for certain other groups are given below in Table 2.

65. It is obvious from Tables 2 and 33 that there is no close
relation between the growth of employment in an industry and the
rate of unemployment in it or the change in the rate of unemployment. Particular industries, like electrical wiring and contracting
and silk and artificial silk manufacture, combine spectacular growth
of demand—trebling or doubling their numbers in employment—
with increases in the rates of unemployment; other industries, including marine engineering, shipbuilding, cotton, lace and pig iron,
all have less employment at the end of the period than at the
beginning and have also less unemployment. As appears from the
summary Table 2, the three groups of manufacturing industries
whose employment increased from 1924 to 1937 all had on an
average a reduction of unemployment rates, but the reduction was
greater in the third group where employment increased only 11·5
per cent than in the first group where it increased 78·5 per cent.
In the fourth group of declining industries taken as a whole, a
decrease of about one-seventh in the demand for labour left the
average rate of unemployment a little lower than before. But the
individual industries in this group show remarkable contrasts.
Industries with practically the same contraction of effective demand
for their products from 1924 to 1937, say hat and cap making and
marine engineering, have in one case a marked increase of the
unemployment rate—from 9·9 to 14·2—and in the other case a
marked decrease of the unemployment rate—from 16·9 to 9·1. Two
textile industries—linen and lace—present a similar contrast; in
each of them demand for labour declined by about one eighth from
1924 to 1937, but, while in linen the unemployment rate rose from
10·6 to 18·5, in lace it fell from 18·0 to 8·9. These contrasts are
clearly related to the way in which the labour force in different
industries re-acted to depression, that is to say to the extent to which
those engaged in the industry sought employment elsewhere or
remained in the industry in hope of better times. Of the twelve
most severely contracted manufacturing industries, six—tin-plates,
hats and caps, linen, wool, textile bleaching and jute—show a

marked increase of unemployment, while the other six—marine engineering, lace, shipbuilding, cotton, pig iron, and carriage and cart making—show a marked decrease of unemployment. In the first six taken together a decline of about 15 per cent in employment has been met by a reduction of only 9 per cent in the number of insured persons and has involved a rise of the unemployment rate from 9·9 to 14·3. In the other six a decline of about 23 per cent in employment has been met by an even greater reduction of 28 per cent in the number of insured persons, so that the unemployment rate has fallen from 18·0 to 14·3. This contrast, set out in detail in Table 34 in Appendix B, illustrates strikingly the fact that unemployment depends not simply on the demand for labour but on the way in which industry responds to changes in demand.

66. In addition to the manufacturing industries, Table 2 shows a group of industries supplying services rather than goods, and supplying them wholly or mainly to consumers. They are described henceforth as service industries. These service industries combine a rapid growth of demand for labour, by 54 per cent, with an actual rise of the mean unemployment rate from 7·2 to 9·2. The building industry has a similar experience; an increase of 46 per cent in the demand for labour is combined with a rise of the unemployment rate from 10·6 to 13·8; in this industry, while the demand for labour rose by nearly a half in thirteen years, the number unemployed nearly doubled. The last industry shown in Table 2 has a different experience; in coal-mining a catastrophic fall in demand has been accompanied by a catastrophic increase of unemployment. This illustrates industrial friction from another angle; coal mining stands apart from other industries and men do not leave it readily.

67. The facts given in Tables 2 and 33 and briefly reviewed in the last paragraphs do not mean that there is no connection between the rate of unemployment in an industry and the growth of effective demand for labour in it. But the connection is slight and uncertain. Manufacturing industries in the same group, that is to say with similar experience in regard to the demand for their products, have unemployment rates in 1937 ranging all the way from 2·8 to 11·3 in the first group, from 3·5 to 12·4 in the second group and from 3·6 to 14·8 in the third group. The dominant factor in determining the rate of unemployment in each particular industry is not the rate at which demand for labour in it is changing but the organization of the industry. All carry some reserve of labour even at the top of a cyclical fluctuation; in each of them the demand for labour may grow and fresh labour be drawn in, while some labour is unem-

ployed; in each of them the extent of the reserve varies according to the organization of the industry. In concluding in 1909 the opening chapter of my first study of unemployment, I expressed the view that "unemployment depends not so much on the volume of industry as on the methods of industry, and while the methods remain unchanged, will continue or recur, however the volume grows."[1] The detailed comprehensive record of unemployment which has become available since those words were written leaves no doubt as to the importance of the organization and methods of each particular industry as a factor in unemployment. One of the outstanding features of this record is the distinctive range and character of unemployment in each particular industry. The total of unemployment is built up of these particulars.

Unemployment Rates and Employment Volumes

68. That, however, is only one lesson of the figures just passed in review. The paradox of the simultaneous growth of unemployment and of employment in particular industries calls for further examination, for it has another lesson to teach. The paradox can be examined in detail for the period between the two wars, because from the information collected by the Ministry of Labour, it is possible to show, for each separate industry in each year, both the numbers unemployed (absolutely and in relation to the numbers insured as an unemployment rate) and the numbers employed (that is to say, the volume of employment). It is thus possible to see how a cyclical fluctuation, such as that between 1929 and 1937, affected, on the one hand, the numbers unemployed and on the other hand, the volume of employment in each industry. For the reasons explained in Appendix B (paragraph B14), it is desirable, in relation to this particular period, to use figures for males only, excluding those for women and girls, which between 1929 and 1933 are affected by administrative changes. Using the figures for males only and setting out in parallel, on the one hand, the unemployment rates and, on the other hand, the employment volumes for each industry from 1929 to 1937, two interesting points emerge.

69. The first point is that the relative severity of fluctuation in particular industries, as shown by unemployment rates and by employment volumes respectively, is by no means the same. Thus in the group of industries concerned with instruments of production, if unemployment rates are taken as the guide, shipbuilding appears as the industry in which depression from 1929 to 1932 was least

[1] *Unemployment* (1909), p. 15.

severe, while electrical engineering appears as one of those in which it was most severe. When, however, employment volumes are looked at, it becomes plain that the contraction of employment from 1929 to 1932 was greater in shipbuilding and less in electrical engineering than in any other instrumental industry. In the textile group, to take another instance, if the severity of the depression is judged by unemployment rates, it was greatest in carpets and silk, and was relatively slight in lace and linen. But, if it is judged by the volume of employment, the depression was most severe in jute and cotton, with linen suffering nearly as badly; the depression was relatively slight in carpets.[1]

70. The second and for the present purpose more important difference between unemployment rates and employment volumes relates to the generality of cyclical fluctuation. If unemployment rates are looked at, cyclical fluctuation appears in every industry. Without any exception the unemployment rates for every industry leap up from 1929 to 1930, and almost without exception they fall year by year from 1932 to 1937. So soon, however, as we turn from examining unemployment rates to examine employment volumes, the universality of cyclical depression disappears. In some important industries the employment volume, that is to say the effective demand for labour, does not decline at all in the depression. This is shown by Table 3 setting out for twelve particular industries the number of males in employment in July of each year from 1929 to 1937, expressed as relatives, that is to say as percentages of the number in 1929. These twelve industries include all the seven service industries. Four of these seven show an unbroken rise of the effective demand for labour in every year from 1929 to 1937; three show rises broken by a trifling decline in one year only, followed by renewed expansion. Apart from the service industries, the only industry showing an unbroken rise from 1929 to 1937 is electrical wiring and contracting. But electrical apparatus, printing, and tobacco show rises broken only by a barely perceptible fall in a single year, while artificial stone-making shows a substantial contraction in 1930 followed at once by rapid expansion. In all the industries named, the effective demand for labour is higher in 1932, the year of greatest general depression, than it is in 1929. Taken together the twelve industries include a substantial proportion of the whole field of employment, having in 1937 nearly a fourth of all the insured males and nearly a third of all insured persons. Their

[1] The figures cited in this paragraph are not printed in this Report. They will form the subject of a separate publication.

Table 3

EMPLOYMENT OF MALES IN CERTAIN INDUSTRIES, 1929–1937 (G.B. AND N.I.)

Males in employment in July as percentages of 1929

Industry	1929	1930	1931	1932	1933	1934	1935	1936	1937
Distributive Trades ‥ ‥ ‥	100·0	101·3	105·1	108·8	112·0	116·1	116·8	121·4	122·1
Tramway and Omnibus Service ‥	100·0	104·5	110·3	113·5	114·3	115·0	119·4	124·4	130·1
Gas, Water and Electricity Supply ‥	100·0	100·5	102·9	100·6	106·3	113·6	115·8	124·1	130·5
Professional Services ‥ ‥ ‥	100·0	102·9	105·6	108·9	114·5	120·4	123·0	127·7	133·1
Hotel, Public House, Restaurant, etc. ‥	100·0	100·9	102·3	102·0	111·3	118·7	125·0	131·3	134·8
Laundries, Job Dyeing, etc. ‥ ‥	100·0	100·2	106·1	109·7	116·2	120·2	128·4	136·3	136·4
Entertainments and Sports ‥ ‥	100·0	99·0	112·4	118·4	132·9	140·3	146·4	156·6	163·6
Tobacco, Cigars, Cigarettes and Snuff ‥	100·0	106·5	98·7	101·2	99·5	95·1	92·6	98·3	100·0
Printing, Publishing and Bookbinding ‥	100·0	101·9	101·7	103·4	103·5	104·8	105·1	107·4	110·3
Artificial Stone and Concrete ‥ ‥	100·0	92·6	99·3	103·9	111·4	119·8	132·0	146·3	169·8
Electrical Cable Apparatus, Lamps, etc.	100·0	105·3	102·6	109·8	115·0	128·8	137·2	150·2	178·3
Electrical Wiring and Contracting ‥	100·0	106·3	119·7	127·8	145·9	184·0	194·8	217·2	242·5

experience emphasizes the fact discussed in Appendix A, that cyclical fluctuation is predominantly a movement affecting industries which make durable or instrumental goods.

71. Yet while the industries set out in Table 3 experience a continuous or nearly continuous expansion of demand for their products or services from 1929 to 1937, they experience also in all cases an increase in the numbers unemployed in them. Though the demand for labour in these industries was growing, the supply was growing even more rapidly. The explanation is obvious. To some industries entry is made difficult by requirement of special skill, by trade unionism, or by marked localization; they recruit labour only to meet their demand and they are not subject to easy invasion from other industries which happen to be depressed. On the other hand, to some industries and particularly to the widely scattered service industries entry is relatively easy. In times of depression they are subject to invasion from other industries and they get more than their share of juveniles. For the industries examined in Table 3 above, the process of invasion is shown statistically in Table 4 below, which, for each of these industries, shows from 1929 to 1932 an increase in the number of males employed and also a marked increase in the number of males unemployed. In the twelve industries together from 1929 to 1932, the number of males in employment rose by 139,000 while the number unemployed rose from 110,000 to 289,000 or nearly 200 per cent. Table 4 carries the story on to 1937—showing employment rising rapidly from 1932 and unemployment falling, but not to the level of 1929. Comparing 1937, as the last crest of the cyclical fluctuation, with the preceding crest in 1929, employment of males in these expanding industries rose by 486,000 or about a quarter, while unemployment rose by 96,000 or nearly 90 per cent; there was some increase of unemployment in every industry.

72. The fact that certain industries continue to expand during a cyclical depression does not mean that they are unaffected by cyclical fluctuation. They are affected in twoi mportant ways. First, growth of the demand for labour in these industries, though it may not be stopped by the depression, is slowed down by it. The total employment of males in the twelve industries shown in Table 4 rose in the downward phase [1] of the cycle from 1929 to 1932 only by about 139,000, that is to say, at the rate of about 35,000 a year. In the upward phase from 1932 to 1937 it rose by 347,000, or nearly 70,000 a year, that is to say about twice as fast. Second, the supply of labour to these industries is affected in the opposite way, being

---

[1] See Explanation of Terms in Appendix D, under "cyclical fluctuation."

Table 4

EMPLOYMENT AND UNEMPLOYMENT OF MALES IN CERTAIN INDUSTRIES IN JULY, 1929, 1932, 1937 (G.B. AND N.I.)

Industry	Insured Males (000)			Employed Males (000)			Unemployed Males (000)			Increase in 1932 on 1929		Increase in 1937 on 1929	
	1929	1932	1937	1929	1932	1937	1929	1932	1937	Employed	Unemployed	Employed	Unemployed
Distributive Trades	1015·4	1201·7	1278·5	948·7	1033·8	1159·6	66·8	167·9	118·9	85·1	101·1	210·9	52·1
Tramway and Omnibus Service	148·0	173·0	192·6	144·6	164·2	188·2	3·4	8·9	4·4	19·6	5·5	43·6	1·0
Gas, Water and Electricity Supply	155·9	166·9	208·5	147·3	148·1	192·2	8·7	18·8	16·3	0·8	10·1	44·9	7·6
Professional Services	69·9	79·1	93·9	67·1	73·0	89·2	2·8	6·1	4·6	5·9	3·3	22·1	1·8
Hotel, Public House, Restaurant, etc., Services	121·0	140·5	172·0	111·8	114·1	150·7	9·2	26·4	21·3	2·3	17·2	38·9	12·1
Laundries and Job Dyeing	27·9	33·2	38·4	26·6	29·2	36·4	1·2	3·9	2·1	2·7	2·7	9·8	0·9
Entertainments and Sports	47·8	65·0	85·0	42·5	50·4	69·6	5·2	14·6	15·4	7·8	9·4	27·1	10·2
Tobacco, Cigars, Cigarettes and Snuff	14·8	15·8	15·0	14·3	14·5	14·4	0·5	1·3	0·7	0·2	0·8	0·1	0·2
Printing, Publishing and Bookbinding	168·6	188·0	190·3	162·3	167·9	178·9	6·3	20·1	11·4	5·6	13·8	16·6	5·1
Artificial Stone and Concrete	16·0	20·2	26·4	14·0	14·6	23·8	2·0	5·6	2·6	0·5	3·6	9·8	0·6
Electrical Cable Apparatus, Lamps, etc.	57·4	69·4	100·9	54·6	59·3	96·9	2·8	10·2	4·0	4·7	7·4	42·3	1·2
Electrical Wiring and Contracting	15·3	23·3	38·7	14·2	18·2	34·5	1·1	5·1	4·2	3·9	4·0	20·3	3·1
	1858·0	2176·1	2440·2	1748·1	1887·2	2234·4	110·0	288·9	205·9	139·1	178·9	486·4	95·9

sharply increased during the downward phase of the cycle by depression elsewhere. In the three years from 1929 to 1932 the number of insured males in the twelve industries rose by 317,000 or at the rate of 106,000 a year; in the five years of the upward phase of the cycle from 1932 to 1937 the increase was 264,000 or 53,000 a year, just half the rate in the downward phase. When, through cyclical fluctuation, demand for labour in total is weak, those industries which are least affected themselves are subject to exceptional pressure of invasion from other industries and to exceptional recruiting of juveniles. If, as in the case of most of the industries shown in Table 4, they are also open industries, easy to enter and widely dispersed, they take on additional men and boys in one place while men are being dismissed in another place. In the result the next boom leaves them, through over-recruiting, with more unemployment than before. The general unemployment rate was much the same in 1937 as in 1929, and on the whole most of the industries kept at or near their characteristic rates of unemployment. But cyclical fluctuation had done something to spread unemployment from the industries violently affected by it to those less affected by it.

73. The connection between the market for labour in different industries, shown in the foregoing examination of expanding industries, can be illustrated from the other side, by examination of declining industries. In coal-mining, the number of insured males fell from 1,069,200 in 1929 to 1,039,800 in 1932 and 864,500 in 1937; the number in employment in July fell from 867,200 in 1929 to 609,600 in 1932 and rose to 718,800 in 1937. That is to say in the three years of declining employment from 1929 to 1932 the number of miners fell by 29,400 or at the rate of 9,800 a year, while in the five years of recovery from 1932 to 1937 it fell by 175,300, that is to say at the rate of 35,100 a year. The principal textile industries (cotton, wool, linen, jute and textile bleaching) show a similar, though less striking, difference between the downward and upward phases of the cyclical fluctuation between 1929 and 1937. During the three years of the downward phase from 1929 to 1932, while employment of males in them was falling from 362,000 to 274,000, these industries lost insured men at the rate of 6,100 a year; in the following five years of the upward phase to 1937, with employment of males rising from 274,000 to 300,000, they lost men at the rate of 11,000 a year. That is to say, in each of these cases, men tend to leave the declining industry more rapidly during the upward phase of the cycle when all industries are recovering, including their own,

than during the downward phase when all industries are contracting. The same phenomenon appears in the fluctuation of numbers in the shipping industry. From 141,420 insured persons in 1929, the number rose to 161,330 in the depression of 1932 and fell again to 134,080 in 1937, to start rising again in 1938. Men are more ready to go to sea in a slump than when there is a good chance of work on land.[1] The same phenomenon appears in yet another setting in the statistics of the industrial transference given in Table 7 below, showing how the numbers of persons whom it was possible to transfer fell from nearly 44,000 in 1929 to less than 14,000 in 1933, rising again to nearly 43,000 in 1936 and falling again rapidly in the threatened depression of 1938. Movement of labour depends on there being an unsatisfied demand for labour somewhere.

74. The figures passed in review in the foregoing paragraphs illustrate and reconcile two approaches to the problem of unemployment which, in the past, have sometimes appeared to be in conflict. One approach, from a study of the facts of unemployment, industry by industry, has tended to emphasize the degree to which unemployment differed from one industry to another and the importance of friction, immobility and disorganization in the labour market as factors in unemployment. The other approach, by consideration of the general factors affecting demand for the products of industry, has treated the demand for labour and the supply of labour as a whole and has left friction out of account. The figures now presented show both the separateness of the different industries and their dependence on one another. All industries are linked together in two ways. First, unemployment in any one industry reduces the consuming power of those who seek to live in it and therefore reduces the demand they can make for the products of other industries. Second, severe unemployment in any industry causes people to try to leave it, or causes boys and girls entering life, in so far as they know the position, to avoid that industry; this sets up a strengthened flow of labour to other industries, which may be prosperous in themselves but, if they are open to invasion, with a multitude of separate employers and disorganized engagement making entry to them easy, may find that their prosperity brings to them more and not less unemployment.

[1] Changes in the numbers insured in particular industries have to be considered in relation to the change in the insured population as a whole. See Appendix B, Table 35.

Unemployment by Localities

75. As the unemployment rate differs from industry to industry, so it differs from one part of the country to another. Table 5 gives for each year from 1929 to 1937 the unemployment rate in each of the main regions into which Britain is divided for the administrative purposes of the Ministry of Labour and National Service. It shows in 1937 four relatively prosperous divisions making South Britain, with a mean unemployment rate of 6·9, and five other divisions making North Britain and Wales, with an unemployment rate more than twice as high, at 15·0.

76. The divisional unemployment rates in Table 5 show considerable variation, but are themselves averages concealing far greater local variations. From the Local Unemployment Index issued by the Ministry of Labour, it is possible to calculate unemployment rates for each of nearly 800 employment exchange districts, as well as averages for each county, and this has been done for each of the years 1934, 1935, and 1936, and on a slightly different basis for 1937; the difference of basis does not affect the substantial comparability of the figures. In Table 36 in Appendix B these rates are given for each county in Britain and for the one or two districts with highest or lowest rates in every county which has more than five districts. The wide dispersal of unemployment rates, within the same division and the same county, is the outstanding feature of this table. Thus in 1937 in the prosperous county of Berkshire there are rates of 2·8 (Didcot) and 2·9 (Bracknell) side by side with 8·0 (Abingdon) and 10·2 (Wokingham); in Somerset the range is from 2·1 (Keynsham) to 13·0 (Bridgwater); in Cambridgeshire from 1·7 (Cottenham) to 9·0 (Wisbech). In less prosperous and larger counties the range is greater still: Lancashire shows everything from 2·9 (Leyland) to 37·2 (Hindley); Yorkshire shows everything from 2·9 (Tadcaster) to 32·9 (Hoyland).

77. Nor is the local variation of unemployment rates a transient phenomenon. The differences show no sign of disappearing. The rates cited above for 1937 are means for the whole year, not for a particular day. The figures for earlier years show a general change of levels from 1934 to 1937 and a few dramatic improvements in some of the Special Areas. But the main feature of Table 36 is the persistence, year after year, of high unemployment in some districts combined with low unemployment close by. Each locality has its characteristic level of unemployment, as each industry has: the level of the local index is in general a reflection of the methods of its principal industries. There is no tendency, in any short period of

Table 5

UNEMPLOYMENT RATES BY DIVISIONS, 1929–37

	1929	1930	1931	1932	1933	1934	1935	1936*		1937
London .. : : :	5.6	8.1	12.2	13.5	11.8	9.2	8.5	7.2	7.0	6.3
South-Eastern : : :	5.6	8.0	12.0	14.3	11.5	8.7	8.1	7.3	7.2	6.7
South-Western : : :	8.1	10.4	14.5	17.1	15.7	13.1	11.6	9.4	9.4	7.8
Midlands .. : : :	9.3	14.7	20.3	20.1	17.4	12.9	11.2	9.2	9.2	7.2
North-Eastern : : :	13.7	20.2	27.4	28.5	26.0	22.1	20.7	16.8	13.5	11.0
North-Western : : :	13.3	23.8	28.2	25.8	23.5	20.8	19.7	17.1	17.0	14.0
Northern : : :	—	—	—	—	—	—	—	—	22.9	17.9
Scotland .. : : :	12.1	18.5	26.6	27.7	26.1	23.1	21.3	18.7	18.7	15.9
Wales .. : : :	19.3	25.9	32.4	36.5	34.6	32.3	31.2	29.4	29.4	22.3
Great Britain† : : :	10.5	16.3	21.6	22.2	20.0	16.8	15.5	13.2	—	10.8
South Britain† : : :	7.1	10.5	15.0	16.2	14.0	10.8	9.7	8.1	—	6.9
North and Wales† .. :	13.8	21.7	28.0	28.2	26.0	22.9	21.5	18.6	—	15.0

* The administrative divisions were re-arranged in August, 1936. Two sets of figures are given accordingly for 1936—one from the *Labour Gazette* of January, 1937, the other from the *Labour Gazette* of January, 1938.

† The figures in these rows are obtained by weighting the divisional percentages by the numbers of insured persons 16–64 in each Division as given in the 22nd Abstract of Labour Statistics, pp. 16–17. The percentages shown here for Great Britain, while strictly comparable with the divisional percentages, differ slightly from the percentages in Table 1, which are calculated on a slightly different basis and include persons under the special schemes for banking and insurance, who are excluded from the divisional figures.

time, for unemployment in different regions to reach the same or comparable levels by transfer of labour.

78. It is interesting to compare changes in the local distribution of the insured population with changes in the industrial distribution. This can be done by use of the numbers of insured persons in each of the counties of Britain, which are available from 1927 onwards. Generally changes of local distribution, as judged by these county figures, are much less marked than changes of industrial distribution. This appears from Table 6 below, showing the numbers of insured persons in 1937 as relatives, that is to say as percentages of the corresponding numbers in 1927, for those counties and industries having the greatest increases and the greatest decreases respectively. Seventeen small industries, not having in any case as many as 20,000 insured persons in either year, have been omitted from the table; the total number of separate industries covered by it is 75. For the reasons stated in the note to the table, it is necessary to combine the figures for some of the counties; the total number of county areas for which separate figures are available is 56 as compared with the 75 separate industries. The total number of insured persons in 1937 was 116·1 per cent of the number in 1927. Table 6 shows considerable differences in the growth of the insured population in different areas; there is substantial movement from one county to another. At the same time, while the county percentages do not represent quite as many separate units as the industry percentages, Table 6 leaves no room for doubt that changes in industrial distribution are markedly greater than changes in local distribution: that is to say, that labour is more fluid between industries than between counties. The industrial figures on the left-hand side of the table range from 280·8 to 64·6; the county figures on the right-hand side range only from 162·1 to 95·9. Only three counties show decreases at all, and the largest of these decreases is only to 95·9. At least twelve industries show decreases greater than that of any county. Local immobility is a greater obstacle than occupational immobility to adjustment of labour demand and supply, so long as the location of industry remains uncontrolled.

79. Another interesting comparison between industrial and local movements of labour, this time presenting a similarity rather than a difference, is afforded by Table 7, setting out from 1929 to 1938 the numbers of persons transferred by the Ministry of Labour from depressed areas to employment in other areas, under the industrial transference scheme. Under this scheme special efforts were made and financial assistance given to transfer persons for whom no

Table 6

CHANGES OF INDUSTRIAL AND LOCAL INSURED POPULATION, 1927-37

12 Industries with Greatest Increase	Insured Persons 1937 % of 1927	12 Counties with Greatest Increase	Insured Persons 1937 % of 1927
Electrical Wiring and Contracting	280·8	Bucks	162·1
Electric Cable, Apparatus, Lamps, etc.	212·3	Bedfordshire	159·7
		Oxfordshire	149·7
Entertainments and Sports ..	209·8	Herefordshire	137·4
Artificial Stone and Concrete ..	174·8	Pembrokeshire	135·1
Scientific and Photographic Instruments and Apparatus ..	157·6	Sussex	134·5
		Cambridgeshire	133·0
Tramway and Omnibus Service	155·6	Hampshire	130·0
Motor Vehicles, Cycles and Aircraft	152·8	Scotland, North and West ..	129·5
Silk and Artificial Silk	150·7	Warwickshire	129·4
Constructional Engineering ..	149·7	London and neighbouring counties	129·3
Electrical Engineering	147·4	Lincolnshire	124·7
Metal Industries not separately specified ..	145·4		
Hotel, Public House, Restaurant, Boarding House, Club, etc., Service	144·9		
Professional Services	140·7		

12 Industries with Greatest Decrease		Counties with Decrease	
Marine Engineering	93·5	Angus	99·1
Woollen and Worsted	93·0	Glamorgan..	96·1
Linen	92·1	Monmouthshire	95·9
Tinplates	91·4		
Watches, Clocks, Plate, Jewellery, etc.	89·0		
Textile Bleaching, Printing, Dyeing, etc.	88·9		
Shipbuilding and Ship-repairing	82·9		
Jute..	78·6		
Pig Iron	74·1		
Coal Mining	74·0		
Cotton	72·7		
Carriages, Carts, etc.	64·6		

In 1932 the records of insured persons for areas within a radius of about 10 miles from London were revised to represent estimates in respect of the persons resident in the areas in question, and these estimates were further revised in 1933 and 1934. The effect of the revision was to reduce substantially the figures for the administrative county and City of London (from 1,758,430 in 1931 to 1,455,290 in 1935 after which the numbers began to rise again) while increasing markedly the figures for the neighbouring counties. The figures for these counties taken separately are not comparable as between 1927 and 1937. In preparing Table 6, London, Middlesex, Herts, Essex, Kent and Surrey have been combined. North and West Scotland includes Argyll, Banff, Caithness and Sutherland, Kincardine, Moray, Nairn, Orkney, Ross and Cromarty, Zetland, as separate figures for these counties are not available before 1930. The relatively large increase shown in this area may be due to special reasons.

Table 7.—INDUSTRIAL TRANSFERENCE, 1929–38

	1929	1930	1931	1932	1933	1934	1935	1936	1937	1938
Men	36,843	28,258	17,889	8,359	5,333	6,828	13,379	20,091	17,585	11,687
Women	2,239	1,752	2,631	2,651	4,038	4,424	6,330	8,008	6,416	6,214
Boys	2,622	1,313	868	638	1,117	1,661	5,376	8,699	7,675	4,131
Girls	1,994	1,708	1,968	2,502	2,955	3,512	4,643	5,937	6,450	5,496
Total	43,698	33,031	23,374	14,140	13,443	16,421	29,753	42,735	38,126	27,478

Table 8.—DURATION OF UNEMPLOYMENT AMONG APPLICANTS FOR BENEFIT OR ALLOWANCES IN BRITAIN

Date	Last Period of Registered Unemployment					All applicants	All Insurable Unemployed*
	Less than 3 months	3 months and less than 6	6 months and less than 9	9 months and less than 12	12 months or more		
Men and Women Aged 18–64 (Numbers)							
Sept., 1929	758,800	102,900	37,250	22,750	45,100	966,800	1,132,255
Aug., 1932	1,485,152	277,783	184,518	156,443	412,245	2,516,141	2,781,019
Aug., 1936	727,863	125,307	80,549	60,219	331,635	1,325,573	1,503,558
Aug., 1937	666,625	111,326	71,894	47,295	287,821	1,184,961	1,270,752
Aug., 1938	957,069	161,705	101,770	62,159	279,840	1,562,543	1,668,145
Aug., 1939	622,408	95,772	63,104	52,819	244,000	1,078,103	1,179,587
As Percentages of All Applicants 18–64							
Sept., 1929	78·5	10·6	3·8	2·4	4·7	100·0	117·1
Aug., 1932	59·0	11·1	7·3	6·2	16·4	100·0	110·5
Aug., 1936	54·9	9·5	6·1	4·5	25·0	100·0	113·4
Aug., 1937	56·3	9·4	6·0	4·0	24·3	100·0	107·3
Aug., 1938	61·3	10·3	6·5	4·0	17·9	100·0	106·8
Aug., 1939	57·7	8·9	5·9	4·9	22·6	100·0	109·4

* Exclusive of persons insured under the special schemes for banking and finance and insurance.

employment seemed likely to be available in their own areas. The numbers whom it proved possible to transfer fell markedly from the relatively good year 1929 to the depression years 1932 and 1933 and rose again with the recovery of trade to 1936. Moreover, though all those shown in Table 7 were sent to definite employment, a substantial proportion of those transferred from August, 1928 to the middle of 1937—including a third of the men—returned to the depressed areas after being transferred out of them. On the other hand, in the eighteen months ending mid-1937, which was the period of greatest improvement of demand, in addition to the 30,000 men transferred under the industrial transference scheme, more than twice as many unemployed men moved from the depressed areas on their own initiative either to take up employment which they had found on their own account or to look for employment.[1] These figures for depressed areas present the same picture as those for contracted industries in paragraph 73. Local movement, like industrial movement, depends on effective demand.

Unemployment by Duration

80. From the point of view of effect on the unemployed person, differences in the duration of unemployment in the individual case are of first importance. Since the beginning of 1932, the Ministry of Labour have classified applicants for benefit or assistance according to the length of time for which they have been registered continuously as unemployed. Table 8 gives the results of this classification at certain dates from 1932 to 1939; the figures for September, 1929 are estimated from a sample enquiry made specially for that date. Occasional short spells of employment lasting not more than three days do not break continuity of registration but, except in so far as they may have got work for such brief spells, the persons shown in Table 8 have been unemployed for the whole of the periods stated, namely, for less than three months, three months and less than six and so on up to twelve months or more. The figures do not cover all the unemployed, but, as appears from the comparison of the last two columns in Table 8, cover all but a small proportion. The proportion omitted is smaller at the last three dates in the table than it is at the earlier dates. This results from an administrative

[1] Both these facts are given in the evidence of the Ministry of Labour to the Royal Commission on the Location of the Industrial Population, cited in para. 316 of the Report of the Commission. The numbers transferred from August, 1928 to mid-1937 included about 150,000 men and 40,000 women; the numbers known to have returned were 50,000 men and 5,600 women. Others may have returned without this being known.

change in April, 1937, admitting to assistance unemployed persons irrespective of any insurance contributions. Such persons include an exceptionally large proportion of persons subject to long unemployment, so that the change effects slightly the comparability of the percentages in the lower half of Table 8 before and after the change.[1]

81. This does not affect the main lesson of Table 8, which lies in the contrast between September, 1929, before the Great Depression, and all the later dates shown. In September, 1929, nearly 90 per cent of the applicants had been unemployed for less than six months and less than 5 per cent had been unemployed for twelve months or more. In August, 1936, the number of persons with short unemployment (less than six months) was much the same as in September, 1929, about 850,000, but they constituted only 64·4 per cent of all the unemployed: those unemployed twelve months or more were one quarter of the whole. The legacy of the Great Depression was a host of long-period unemployed—nearly 300,000 men and women in enforced idleness—for whom continuous money payments were a manifestly inadequate provision. This mass of chronic unemployment shows a decline, both absolutely and relatively, at dates after 1936, through the culmination of the trade cycle in 1937 and the re-armament programme in 1938 and 1939. But, even in August, 1939, it included nearly a quarter of a million men and women.

82. The duration figures, like the unemployment rates, differ greatly from one district to another, as appears from Tables 9 and 10 giving for each Division on 21st June, 1937, the numbers unemployed for various lengths of time and the proportions that these numbers are in the total unemployed. In London, with a mean unemployment rate during 1937 of 6·3, 83·8 per cent of those unemployed at 21st June, or five out of six, had been unemployed for less than six months, and 71·0 per cent had been unemployed for less than three months. At the other end of the scale, in Wales with an unemployment rate of 22·3, only 38 per cent had been unemployed for less than three months, and half for less than six months, while nearly two out of every five persons unemployed had

---

[1] The percentage registered as unemployed for twelve months or more jumps from 21·5 in March, 1937, just before the change, to 24·8 in April, 1937, just after it. The number of applicants from being $\dfrac{100\cdot0}{113\cdot4}$ of all insured unemployed in August, 1936, becomes $\dfrac{100\cdot0}{107\cdot3}$ in August, 1937. Actually, those brought in to assistance by the change included about 24,000 persons not held to be insured against unemployment.

Table 9

DURATION OF UNEMPLOYMENT AMONG APPLICANTS FOR BENEFIT
AND ALLOWANCES AT 21ST JUNE, 1937

ALL PERSONS AGED 16–64   NUMBERS BY DIVISIONS

Division and Estimated Number of Insured Persons 16–64 at July 1937	Period of Registered Unemployment					
	Less than 3 months	3 but less than 6 months	6 but less than 9 months	9 but less than 12 months	12 months or more	TOTAL
London 2,887,480	97,556	17,611	7,310	4,425	10,560	137,462
S. East 1,149,960	29,715	5,872	2,744	1,628	4,270	44,229
S. West 1,115,700	39,827	6,313	2,883	1,903	7,033	57,959
Midlands 2,159,560	75,807	13,996	6,958	4,304	23,807	124,872
N. East 1,500,810	111,993	13,813	7,431	5,027	27,197	165,461
N. West 2,158,260	132,581	31,108	14,843	10,449	63,800	252,781
North 808,420	47,055	14,104	8,518	7,049	51,829	128,555
Scotland 1,489,490	79,236	26,550	14,520	10,627	64,573	195,506
Wales 637,320	44,755	14,034	9,350	7,272	48,781	124,192
South Britain ..	242,908	43,792	19,895	12,260	45,670	364,522
North Britain and Wales	415,620	99,609	54,662	40,424	256,180	866,495
Britain	658,525	143,401	74,557	52,684	301,850	1,231,017

been continuously out of work for more than a year. The Northern
Division had proportions very similar to those of Wales. Yet it is
notable that even in the prosperous Divisions, in a year in which
employers were reporting inability to obtain suitable skilled workmen, there were appreciable numbers of applicants who had been
unemployed continuously for more than twelve months. Even in
London such persons formed nearly 8 per cent of the unemployed.
In South Britain as a whole they were 12½ per cent or one in every
eight of the unemployed.

83. Another distinction in regard to the character of unemployment is made by the Ministry of Labour, in classifying those who
are unemployed at any time according as they are wholly unemployed (that is out of a situation), are temporarily stopped (that is
suspended from work on the understanding that they will shortly
return to their former employment), or are persons normally in
casual employment. Table 11 below, shows for each year from 1928
to 1938 the percentages of the total numbers unemployed who were
classified under each of these three heads. Taking the eleven years

Table 10

DURATION OF UNEMPLOYMENT AMONG APPLICANTS FOR BENEFIT AND ALLOWANCES AT 21ST JUNE, 1937

ALL PERSONS AGED 16–64 PROPORTIONS BY DIVISIONS

Division	Percentage of Applicants Unemployed					
	Less than 3 months	3 but less than 6 months	6 but less than 9 months	9 but less than 12 months	12 months or more	TOTAL
London	71·0	12·8	5·3	3·2	7·7	100·0
South-East	67·2	13·3	6·2	3·7	9·6	100·0
South-West	68·7	10·9	5·0	3·3	12·1	100·0
Midlands	60·7	11·2	5·6	3·4	19·1	100·0
North-East	67·7	8·4	4·5	3·0	16·4	100·0
North-West	52·4	12·3	5·9	4·1	25·3	100·0
North	36·6	11·0	6·6	5·5	40·3	100·0
Scotland	40·5	13·6	7·4	5·4	33·1	100·0
Wales	36·0	11·3	7·5	5·9	39·3	100·0
South Britain	66·7	12·0	5·4	3·4	12·5	100·0
North Britain and Wales..	48·0	11·5	6·3	4·6	29·6	100·0
Britain	53·5	11·6	6·1	4·3	24·5	100·0

Table 11

PERCENTAGES OF UNEMPLOYED PERSONS CLASSIFIED AS WHOLLY UNEMPLOYED, TEMPORARILY STOPPED AND CASUAL WORKERS, 1928–38

	Wholly Unemployed	Temporarily Stopped	Casual Workers
1928	69·3	24·6	6·1
1929	72·1	21·5	6·4
1930	68·3	26·7	5·0
1931	73·9	21·8	4·3
1932	75·9	20·4	3·7
1933	78·7	17·6	3·7
1934	79·4	16·6	4·0
1935	81·0	14·9	4·1
1936	81·9	13·8	4·3
1937	82·5	13·2	4·3
1938	76·2	20·2	3·6
Mean of 1928–38 ..	76·3	19·2	4·5

together, a little more than three-quarters of the total number unemployed consists of persons wholly unemployed, nearly one-fifth are persons temporarily stopped, and nearly one-twentieth are casual workers. It will be seen that the onset of a depression, as in 1930 and in 1938, is marked by a great increase in the proportion of those temporarily stopped. Workpeople are put off first with the hope of returning to their work but, as the depression continues and deepens, this hope is abandoned and the proportion temporarily stopped falls as rapidly as it had risen. It seems likely that from the beginning to the end of the period covered by the table, there is a tendency for the proportion wholly unemployed to increase. Subject to this general trend, each of the peaks of the cyclical fluctuation, namely 1929 and 1937, is also a year in which the proportion wholly unemployed reaches a maximum. This, so far as it goes, tells against the idea that those unemployed at the top of the boom are an irreducible reserve of labour required in spite of there being full employment.

Age and Unemployment[1]

84. The influence of age upon unemployment is important but does not show itself in the way that is commonly supposed. In discussing this question it is necessary to begin by disposing of two popular fallacies.

85. In the first place, the assertion is often made, as if it were axiomatic, that the "speeding up" of industry is driving men into retirement at an earlier age than before: that from being too old at sixty, men are coming to be too old at fifty-five or earlier. So far as I know, there is no evidence for this assertion. The only statistical evidence known to me—derived from the age of superannuation in certain large trade unions—shows the age of superannuation rising and not falling, that is to say, it tells against the assertion. For technical statistical reasons these figures cannot be regarded as decisive. But on general grounds it can be suggested that there is no reason for assuming that technical progress puts a premium on youth; it may just as well work in favour of age, by making sheer physical vigour less important. Moreover, the general improvement of health, which is lengthening the average total life of men, must also be helping to some extent to maintain till later their working capacity.

[1] In this Section I have drawn largely on my *Analysis of Unemployment*, Part VI, published in *Economica*, February, 1937. The statistics briefly summarized here are given fully there.

86. In the second place, it is assumed by many people that an older man is more likely to lose his job than a young man. This is definitely not the case. In the period between the wars the risk of a man losing his employment was practically the same from 55 to 64 as from 45 to 54 or 35 to 44, and was actually less than at the ages 25 to 34. This was shown by two independent sample investigations of the insured population made by the Ministry of Labour and covering periods of about $7\frac{1}{4}$ and $8\frac{1}{2}$ years up to December, 1930, and December, 1932, respectively.[1]

87. But, though the risk of losing one's job is much the same at all ages from 35 to 64, the risk of being unemployed is not the same. Proportionately to the numbers in each age-group there are at any time more men unemployed between 45 and 54 than between 35 and 44, and there are still more between 55 and 64. The evidence for this is abundant. The explanation is obvious—that the older man, once he has lost a job, finds it harder than a young man to get a new job. The older man has less power of recovery industrially, from loss of employment, as he has less power of recovery physically, from sickness or accident. Once he has become unemployed, he is more likely than a younger man to remain unemployed; and he is much more likely to become chronically unemployed. Prolonged unemployment falls with crushing weight on the older men, once they have lost their niche in industry. The risk of losing one's job is much the same from 60 to 64 as it is from 35 to 44. The risk of being out of a job is half as much again at the later age than at the earlier age; the risk of becoming chronically unem-

[1] The greater liability to loss of jobs in the early years of manhood, established by these two sample investigations for the period between the Wars, undoubtedly existed before the first World War, as can be shown by two sets of data relating to 1895 and 1913 respectively. For 1895 an analysis of the out-of-work books of the Manchester and Leeds branches of the Amalgamated Society of Engineers showed that the percentage of members who lost at least three days through unemployment in the year was higher in the age-groups 25–34 than in either of the age-groups 35–44 or 45–54; the figures are given at page 441 of *Unemployment* (1930). In 1913, the unemployment experienced by men in the age-group 20–24 was more than in proportion to the numbers of men in that group in every insured industry except building, that is to say, it was higher in engineering, shipbuilding, construction of vehicles, sawmilling and construction of works; these figures are given in Table CVI of the unpublished Board of Trade Report of 1914. The fact that in this case the volume of unemployment, and not merely the number of cases of unemployment, was greater among young men is due no doubt to the circumstances of 1913; it was a boom year when those who lost a job had relatively little difficulty in finding another, whatever their age, so that the greater liability of the younger men to lose jobs led to their having more unemployment than the older men.

ployed, that is to say of being out for more than a year, is two and a half times as great.

88. The morals of this analysis of unemployment by age are three. First, men do not lose employment more readily when they are old than when they are young. If reasonable stability can be given to the economic system, most men will be able to hold down their jobs till the time comes for them to retire. Second, since some change of work is inevitable in a progressive society and must mean some losing of jobs, those who are handicapped by age in finding new jobs should have special help in doing so. In my first study of unemployment I wrote that "the adverse influence of advancing years is seen less when it is a question of retaining old employment than when it is a question of finding new employers."[1] I urged as one of the remedies for unemployment an attempt to facilitate the re-employment of these older men. "In any large single undertaking, e.g. a railway company, there is always a certain number of old men's places—light situations—kept for those who have grown grey or become injured in the company's service. In industry as a whole there are no doubt also a good many such places, yet nothing to keep them for those whom they best fit. Work which older men could do, now, perhaps, by the chances of the labour market, falls to younger men and wastes their youthful vigour and adaptability. A Labour Exchange backed by sympathetic public opinion might do much to get all the old men's places for the older men and leave to the younger generations the task of finding and forcing fresh openings for themselves. It should be noted that, though 'old' men's places are spoken of, the actual men would often be at most middle-aged and with a long character to back them might be just those whom an employer would in any case choose if he got to know them."[2] When I wrote these words, my statement as to the effect of age on unemployment was little more than an impression derived from personal dealings with numbers of unemployed men. "Since then the diagnosis has been confirmed repeatedly by statistical enquiries, covering now the whole insured population. The remedy remains to be applied. The perpetual favouring of younger men merely for their youth, in filling jobs within the competence of older men, makes for unemployment. It would not happen in a socialist community with employment unified. In an individualist community it is an anti-social act and should be recognized as such."[3]

[1] *Unemployment* (1909), p. 211. [2] Ibid., p. 121.
[3] *Economica* (Feb., 1937), pp. 16-17.

89. Third, and most important, unemployment, though worse among older men than among their juniors between the wars, was not confined to older men. In November, 1932, 400,000 men aged 18 to 24 stood idle in Britain. In July, 1935, among 362,000 men of working age who had been unemployed for twelve months or more, 38,000 were in that same age group, were young men over 18 and under 25. Failure to find any use for adaptable youth is one of the worst blots on the record of the period between the wars.

UNEMPLOYMENT COMPARED BEFORE AND AFTER THE FIRST WORLD WAR

90. The unemployment rate derived from the trade union returns averaged 4·8 over the thirty-one years from 1883 to 1913. The unemployment rate among persons covered by the general scheme of unemployment insurance in Great Britain and Northern Ireland averaged 14·2 over the eighteen years from 1921 to 1938. Does this trebling of the unemployment rate mean that unemployment was in fact three times as severe after the first World War as it had been before the war? To what extent, if at all, is the recorded increase of unemployment merely apparent, due to the different bases of the figures and to completer recording in the later period?

91. The only direct comparison that can be made between trade union figures and unemployment insurance figures relates to the first six years of general unemployment insurance from 1921 to 1926, when both sets of statistics are available. In this six years' overlap, the unemployment insurance percentages ranged from 10·3 in 1924 to 17·0 in 1921 and averaged 12·8, while the corrected trade union percentages ranged from 9·1 in 1924 to 17·2 in 1922 and averaged 13·0. The agreement could hardly be closer. So far as direct comparison can be made, it suggests that the trade union returns are a fair indication of the average level of unemployment in the working population as a whole, and that unemployment between the wars was just about three times as severe as unemployment before the first World War.

92. This comparison, however, relates to a short and abnormal period. The technical examination made in Appendix B of the bases on which the two sets of percentages were calculated, confirmed by consideration of figures derived from the limited unemployment insurance scheme of 1911–20, suggests that the trade union returns somewhat, though not greatly, under-state the true volume of unemployment before the first World War. It is impossible to be

certain as to the degree of the under-statement. But the indications are that if general unemployment insurance had been in force and unemployment had been recorded from 1883 to 1913 in the same way as from 1921 to 1938, it would have shown a mean unemployment rate, not of 4·8 as with the trade unions, but of about 6·0, though it might have been as high as 7·0 or as low as 5·0. On these figures, unemployment after the first World War was most probably nearly two and a half times as severe as before the war, but may have been not more than twice, or may have been almost three times as severe.

93. This conclusion is based in part on the experience of the first limited unemployment insurance scheme. That experience has another point of special interest for to-day. In 1913 as in 1937,

Table 12

UNEMPLOYMENT RATES BY DIVISIONS, 1912–14 AND 1937

	1912–13	1913–14	1937	Percentage of Mean for U.K.	
				1913–14	1937
London	8·7	7·3	8·2	192	79
South-Eastern	4·7	4·0	6·1	105	58
South-Western	4·6	5·1	7·1	134	68
West Midlands	3·1	3·3 }	6·0	87 }	57
East Midlands	2·5	2·7 }		71 }	88
North-Eastern	2·5	2·7	9·2	71	88
North-Western	2·7	3·3	12·9	87	123
Northern	2·9	2·4	19·1	63	183
Scotland	1·8	2·1	15·2	55	146
Wales	3·1	2·3	24·3	60	233
Ireland	6·9	7·0	26·2	184	251
United Kingdom	3·9	3·8	10·4	100	100

Note: The areas are similar but not identical, as between 1912–14 and 1937. At the earlier date the "North-Eastern" Division is described as "Yorkshire", and "Ireland" means the whole country, while in 1937 it means only "Northern Ireland." The bulk of the insured workpeople in Ireland in 1912–14, particularly those in engineering and shipbuilding, were in Northern Ireland.

The 1912–14 figures cover 2,325,598 workpeople as at July, 1914, in building (812,659), construction of works (144,231), shipbuilding (264,217), engineering and ironfounding (817,931), construction of vehicles (209,985), saw-milling (12,029) and other industries (64,546). The 1937 figures cover about the same number of workpeople, in building (1,035,300), shipbuilding (172,800) and engineering and construction of vehicles (1,173,900); divisional unemployment rates are not available for saw-milling and construction of works.

The 1912–13 figures relate to ten months September, 1912, to June, 1913; those for 1913–14 relate to twelve months July, 1913, to June, 1914.

unemployment was unevenly distributed over the country; some districts had much higher unemployment rates than others. But the distribution of good and bad fortune in the earlier year was almost the exact opposite of its distribution in the later year. This appears clearly from Table 12 above, setting out for the industries covered by the first limited scheme of unemployment insurance, the unemployment rates in 1912–13, 1913–14, and 1937 respectively in each of the main divisions of the country. London on the eve of the first World War, had much the highest unemployment rate of any part of Britain, while the south of the country generally had relatively high rates, and Scotland, Wales and the North of England had the lowest rates. Scotland, the North of England and Wales passed from about 2 per cent of unemployment in 1913 to 15, 19 and 24 per cent in 1937. London, nearly the most prosperous part of the country in 1937, had in the insured industries about as high unemployment as in 1913 when it was the least prosperous. The higher rate of unemployment in London was found in each separate industry; it applied to engineering, construction of vehicles, shipbuilding, and saw-milling as much as to building. The contrasted fate of the different regions is shown statistically in the last two columns of Table 12, in which the rate for each division is given as a percentage of the mean rate for the United Kingdom as a whole. The London rate in 1913–14 was 192 per cent of the average; the corresponding proportions for Scotland, Wales and the North of England were 55, 60 and 63 per cent. In 1937 this distribution of severe unemployment is reversed, with London well below the average and Scotland, Wales and the North far above it.

94. As in 1937, so in 1913–14, the divisional differences of unemployment rates concealed even greater local differences. There were some towns (Hastings, Bath and Portsmouth) with more than 10 per cent of unemployment in the insured industries, that is to say about three times the average for the country as a whole. There were other towns with hardly any unemployment. The table opposite is eloquent of the disastrous change that war and drift have wrought in some parts of Britain. There was a marked localization of unemployment before the first World War, as after it. If Table 12 could have been prepared not for 1913, but say for 1906, it would have shown London in a still worse position, suffering from prolonged hypercyclical depression of its largest industry of building and from the northward movement of shipbuilding and other industries. By 1913 the special causes of London unemployment were already passing off. In London, under the Unemployed Workmen Act of

Table 13

UNEMPLOYMENT IN CERTAIN TOWNS IN 1913–14 AND IN 1937

	Unemployment Rate	
	1913–14 Insured Indus- tries of 1911	1937 All Insured Persons
Aberdare	0·2	25·7
Mountain Ash	0·4	22·0
Kirkcaldy	0·5	12·2
Wallsend	0·7	16·6
Wakefield	0·8	11·3
Aberdeen	1·3	12·8
Leigh	1·3	13·9
Motherwell	1·4	20·3
Grimsby	1·4	15·1
Pontypridd	1·4	37·4
Merthyr Tydfil..	1·4	41·6
Greenock	1·6	21·4
Accrington	1·7	12·7

1905, unemployment was being relieved on a large scale in 1906; only long afterwards has it appeared from the statistics that 1906 was not a year of exceptional depression but the top of a cyclical fluctuation, as 1929 was discovered after the event to be a cyclical boom and not a depression.

THE OLD PROBLEMS IN NEW LIGHT

95. In the diagnosis of unemployment made by the Royal Commission in 1909, two main causes of unemployment were recognized, namely, cyclical fluctuation in the demand for labour and disorganization of the labour market. What further knowledge has been gained as regards each of these factors in the problem, and what developments have taken place in regard to them in the interval between the two wars? Fluctuations in the demand for labour and particularly that general fluctuation which is commonly known by the name of the trade cycle, have been the subject of innumerable studies in many countries. To attempt to review, however briefly, all that has been written about this topic in the last 30 years would far transcend the limits of this Report. The problem of the causation of the trade cycle, in spite of the attention devoted to it, cannot yet be regarded as solved. A further contribution to its understanding is given in the Appendix A, and the main results of what is written

there are summarized in paragraphs 96–102 below. As regards the organization of the labour market, the bearing of that on unemployment and the degree of importance that should be attached to mobility of labour, British experience between the two wars has much to teach. The main conclusions suggested by this experience are set out in paragraphs 103–112.

Fluctuation of Demand

96. The cyclical fluctuation of industrial activity shown in the trade union returns of employment from 1856 to 1913 can, by the use of a newly constructed index of industrial activity in Britain,[1] be traced back at least to 1785, that is to say to the earliest date for which continuous records of physical activity in the constructional industries, such as building, are available. From 1785 to 1913 this new index presents a series of waves which coincide very closely with the fluctuations of employment shown by the trade union returns when those became available. The first crest clearly shown by the new index is at 1792 with the last at 1913. In that stretch of a hundred and twenty one years, eight waves of length varying from five to eleven years can be distinguished, giving an average length of just over eight years to each.

97. This fluctuation is international in character, that is to say indices of industrial activity in other industrial countries than Britain, notably the United States, wherever they can be constructed, show the same movement, sometimes in combination with movements peculiar to each country.

98. The movement represents not a series of disconnected waves, but a continuous phenomenon, each fluctuation being marked by the same regular features. Four of these regular features are described in Appendix A, as follows :—

(a) the parallel movement of prices and production, that is to say the fact that prices rise as production rises and fall as production falls;

(b) the greater violence of fluctuation in instrumental industries[2] and in other industries making durable goods;

(c) among British industries, the greater violence of fluctuation in those dependent on overseas demand, in particular textiles;

(d) among British industries, the earlier incidence of fluctuation in those dependent on overseas demand.

---

[1] Table 22 and Chart IV in Appendix A.
[2] See Explanation of Terms in Appendix D.

99. While the first two of the foregoing special features have long been recognized, the last two have not previously been recognized, but are fully established by the facts set out in the Appendix. Though facts of British experience, they are international facts and clearly arise out of the special character of British foreign trade, as being predominantly an exchange of manufactures for primary commodities, that is to say, for agricultural products and raw materials. Taken with other facts, these two newly established features suggest that an important element in the trade cycle is the relation between primary producers of agricultural goods and raw materials and the industrial users of such products. By consequence, one of the important steps for mitigating the violence of the trade cycle lies in organizing the production and marketing of primary products.

100. The great depression of 1932, while more severe than anything previously experienced, shows all the four essential marks of the trade cycle before the first World War. The fluctuation between 1929 and 1937 is a lineal descendant of all the earlier fluctuations. After 1937 a new fluctuation began with a rapid fall of industrial activity to 1938. In this fall from 1937 to 1938, the industries in Britain most dependent on overseas demand, in particular textiles and metal manufacture, led the way, as they had led in the decline from 1929 to 1930 and in the downturn from earlier crests, from 1792 onwards. This stands out clearly in Chart III. The figures represented by this Chart are given in Table 28 in Appendix A and are explained there (paragraphs A.30).

101. Whatever the ultimate explanation of the international trade cycle, it must be regarded as something deeply rooted in the economic system of Britain, the United States and other advanced industrial countries. It has persisted, with substantially the same character though with varying degrees of violence, at least from 1785 to the outbreak of the second World War, that is to say through revolutionary changes in the monetary systems of the world and in the relative position of Britain and other countries. It has brought general instability to industry ever since industry took its modern form.

102. The movement described here as the international trade cycle is of outstanding importance, because it is both general, affecting simultaneously all or most industries in a country, and international, affecting simultaneously all or most industrial countries. But it is not the only form of industrial fluctuation. There are some movements, such as the minor business cycles of the United

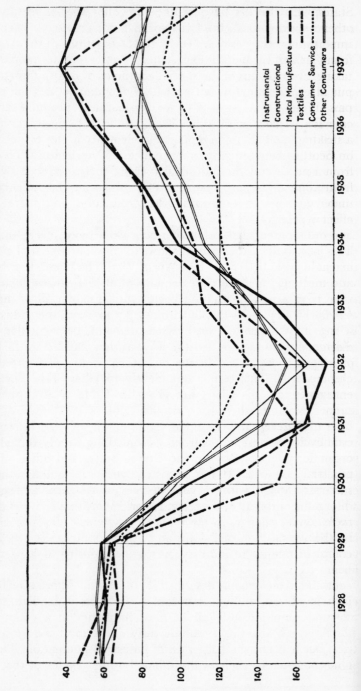

Chart III

UNEMPLOYMENT INDEX NUMBERS IN GROUPS OF INDUSTRIES 1927–38

States, which appear to occur only in particular countries. There are other movements affecting particular industries, of which the most important is the hyper-cyclical fluctuation of building activity, found in Britain and in the United States alike. This fluctuation, taking twenty years or more in Britain, and a rather shorter period, put at eighteen years, in the United States, has caused building to pass through alternations of activity and stagnation, lasting in each case for a number of years. These alternations are illustrated in a striking manner by the statistics presented recently by a Committee on Scottish Housing. The numbers of houses built in Scotland fell from a maximum of nearly 29,000 in 1876 to less than 6,000 a year from 1891 to 1893, rose to more than 21,000 in 1899 and fell to under 3,000 in each of the years 1912 and 1913.[1] The lamentable effect of such fluctuations both on employment of building operatives and on the living conditions of the population needs no underlining. This is how an unplanned market economy meets a vital need whose extent at any moment there would be no difficulty in forecasting and meeting by plan, in accord with social policy.

Disorganization of the Labour Market

103. In the diagnosis of 1909, main emphasis was laid upon the disorganization of the labour market, as involving the accumulation of excessive reserves of labour in meeting any given demand, with chronic under-employment of the industries practising casual engagement as an acute case of the general disease. The remedy proposed for this evil was the organization of the labour market by a national system of employment exchanges. Such a system was established in 1910, and since then has proved itself an indispensable organ for the mobilization of manpower in war, and for the administration of unemployment insurance in peace. How far has it succeeded in its primary purpose of substituting an organized for a disorganized labour market? The scale of operations of the employment exchanges is indicated by the total number of vacancies filled by them each year. Beginning at about 621,000 in the first year of complete operation in 1911, the number relapsed after the war boom to a minimum of 716,000 in 1922, and from then rose nearly continuously to 2,739,000 in 1938. While some of the vacancies included in this total—described officially as B Class vacancies—

[1] A graph representing these numbers of houses is given in *Planning our New Homes*, a Report by the Scottish Housing Advisory Committee published in 1944 by the Stationery Office (3s.). The poor quality of a large proportion of these houses is notorious.

represent a relatively small service, of sending back to an employer a person previously employed by him, the filling of some of the other vacancies, involving transfer from one district to another and sometimes the advance of fares to make this possible, represents a very substantial service.[1]

104. There is no doubt that, in their primary field as in other fields, the employment exchanges have conferred great benefits. But it is clear that they fall far short of having achieved in peace an effective organization of the labour market. Since the generalization of unemployment insurance in 1920 with its successive extensions, the exchanges automatically register all insured persons who become unemployed, that is to say they have on their books the whole of

Table 14

PLACING INDEX OF EMPLOYMENT EXCHANGES, 1932–38

	1932	1933	1934	1935	1936	1937	1938	Vacancies Filled 1938
Men	18·8	21·0	22·1	24·5	27·3	28·1	27·5	1,625,997
Women	32·1	36·0	37·1	36·4	37·1	36·8	31·7	572,985
Boys	36·0	43·2	38·1	30·8	28·3	27·1	28·4	258,742
Girls	42·3	46·9	37·9	29·9	29·0	26·5	28·8	247,340
All Departments ..	21·2	23·6	24·8	26·9	28·9	29·2	28·3	2,705,064

the normal supply of labour. As the unemployment books of insured persons must be lodged in making claims to benefit and are removed when the applicant obtains work in any way, the exchanges have also a record of all engagements, whether made through the exchanges or not. It is possible, therefore, to compare the number of engagements made through the exchanges with the total of all engagements, and to calculate a "placing index," that is to say to express the engagements made through the exchanges as a percentage of all engagements. Table 14 above gives the placing index in each year from 1932 to 1938 for men, women, boys and girls, and for all classes of workpeople taken together. It will be seen that the index has risen from 21·2 per cent in 1932 to 28·3 per cent in 1938, the latter figure representing a small decline from the maximum of 29·2 per cent at the top of the cyclical fluctuation in 1937. In one

[1] In 1937 nearly 200,000 vacancies were filled by the exchanges after circulation to other districts and nearly 35,000 advances of fares, totalling over £26,000, were made to workpeople to enable them to travel to employment in other districts.

respect, this general placing index exaggerates the part played by the exchanges. In four industries largely under public control—national government, local government, public works contracting, and gas, water and electricity supply—the placing index is above the average; if these industries, which contribute substantially to the total of vacancies, are excluded, the placing index for private industry, becomes appreciably lower. In another respect the general placing index understates the influence of the exchanges; a substantial proportion of all engagements are re-engagements by the same employer and, on the whole, these take place more often apart from the exchanges than through them. If these re-engagements, whether made through the exchanges or directly, are excluded, the proportion of the remaining engagements that is made through the exchanges is 35·1 in 1937 and 34·0 in 1938. That is to say, after nearly thirty years of operation of the exchanges about two-thirds of all new engagements in private industry are made otherwise than through the employment exchanges.

105. From the placing index it is possible to derive a general view of the labour market, as it stands to-day. The 2,624,798 vacancies filled by the exchanges in 1937, correspond to a placing index of 29·2, showing that the total number of engagements in that year was about 9,000,000. This refers to persons wholly unemployed. It excludes the return to work with their former employer of persons temporarily stopped, and the engagements of casual workers, forming between them nearly a quarter of all those unemployed at any moment. In the 9,000,000 engagements, about 2,700,000 are re-engagements by the same employer, and about 6,300,000 are engagements by a fresh employer. Since the total number of insured persons to whom these figures relate is little over 14,000,000, this means nearly one change of employment in the course of the year for every two persons who live by employment. Some persons, of course, have many changes of employment, but, allowing for this, it is clear that a substantial proportion of the insured persons have to find a new employer once or more often, during the course of each year. In view of the scale of labour market operations, it is obvious that the manner in which the market is organized and the degree to which it is disorganized, may be matters of vital importance; the continuance of a system which relies mainly on personal application, that is to say on the hawking of labour from door to door, is an anachronism which is socially indefensible. Yet of the total of 6,300,000 new engagements that are made each year, certainly not more than 2,300,000 are made through the official machinery of

the employment exchanges. Some of the remaining 4,000,000 are made through trade unions or through advertisements in the Press, but the bulk of them must depend upon application in person, at the place of employment.

106. It is clear from the foregoing that the employment exchanges, in spite of the great and indeed indispensable services they have rendered, have failed to secure voluntarily use by private employers sufficiently systematic to bring about the organization of the labour market. How does this show in relation to the problem of unemployment? The answer has been given above in general terms in showing how trades with an expanding demand may recruit additional labour far in excess of that demand. It can be illustrated with special reference to the two industries which in 1909 were cited as leading cases of disorganization, namely dock and harbour service and building.

107. As regards dock and harbour service, the unemployment position between the wars is shown in Table 15, giving the unemployment rates in this industry in each year from 1924 to 1938, with comparative figures for other industries of high unemployment. It will be seen that the unemployment rate in dock and harbour services averages about 30 and is seldom very far from that figure above or below. All the other industries in Table 15 show much greater variation and in all cases but one a lower average. This high rate of unemployment in dock and harbour service cannot be explained or justified by decline of demand. It is true that this industry, being dependent in the main on international trade, has been affected by the decline of international trade, but though British exports have been cut down materially, British imports in volume have been little affected. The total tonnage of ships with cargo entering and clearing from British ports was actually higher in 1937 than in 1913, and the volume of British trade, including exports and imports, was only 2 per cent lower—98 as compared with 100. The contrast between this and the experience of other industries like shipbuilding and pig-iron production, which also have been marked by high rates of unemployment between the wars, is striking. The tonnage of ships built in the United Kingdom, which was over 1,200,000 in 1913, fell to 84,000 in 1933 and even in 1937 was only 543,000, about 45 per cent of the 1913 figure. The production of pig-iron fell from 10,260,000 tons in 1913 to 3,574,000 tons in 1932 and even in 1937 was only 8,493,000 tons, or about 80 per cent of the 1913 figure. Another interesting contrast is presented by the figures in the lower part of the table, showing the proportions

Table 15

UNEMPLOYMENT IN DOCK AND HARBOUR SERVICE AND CERTAIN OTHER INDUSTRIES, 1924-38 (G.B. AND N.I.)

UNEMPLOYMENT RATE

	Dock and Harbour Service	Shipbuilding	Steel Melting, etc	Pig Iron	Coal Mining	Shipping	Jute
1924	25·6	29·4	21·1	14·3	5·7	19·5	9·9
1925	29·9	33·8	24·5	20·8	15·8	20·5	14·2
1926	30·0	39·7	41·2	46·7	9·1	20·5	23·7
1927	24·2	24·8	18·5	14·4	18·1	16·0	8·3
1928	30·5	26·5	21·2	16·8	21·9	16·2	8·5
1929	30·8	24·3	19·8	11·3	16·0	17·8	12·9
1930	35·3	35·0	36·1	24·6	20·3	25·4	37·8
1931	39·6	56·9	47·1	40·1	29·6	32·8	46·9
1932	35·0	62·1	46·8	43·9	38·9	33·9	42·1
1933	33·3	58·7	35·6	38·4	32·0	33·2	30·5
1934	31·5	48·7	29·9	24·3	27·9	30·4	31·0
1935	31·2	42·0	21·0	20·5	25·5	28·9	26·3
1936	29·5	30·1	15·0	14·1	22·5	25·2	26·7
1937	25·9	23·8	10·8	9·5	14·6	21·7	23·0
1938	26·5	21·0	23·1	17·8	15·4	24·0	28·4
Mean of 1924-38 .. .. :	30·6	37·1	27·4	23·8	20·9	24·4	24·4
In June, 1936, Percentage of unemployed on benefit	72·8	33·3	51·5	24·2	46·7	50·6	38·2
Unemployed less than 3 months ..	89·2	54·3	59·1	29·7	45·7	52·6	39·6
Unemployed more than 12 months ..	5·3	28·1	28·5	51·3	36·0	19·4	34·9
Insured Persons aged 16-64:							
1924 (est.)	184·0	245·5	199·6	28·3	1221·8	124·4	39·7
1937	166·0	172·8	181·9	17·3	868·4	134·1	30·0
Percentage change	-9·8	-29·6	-8·9	-38·9	-28·9	+7·8	-24·4

of all those unemployed at 8th June, 1936, who were on benefit, who had been unemployed for less than three months, and who had been unemployed for twelve months or more. Dock and harbour service had a much higher proportion on benefit than any of the other industries and a much larger proportion of men who had had recent employment. Men following this occupation find it easy, by getting work, if only one or two days in a week, to keep on benefit, and draw benefit very largely in their off days.

108. Dock and harbour service has a high rate of unemployment because of the way in which it is organized, rather than because of a declining demand for its services. Continuous attempts to bring about better organization of methods of employment have been made throughout the period between the wars, chiefly on the lines of registration schemes, that is to say of plans for limiting entry to the occupation so as to protect it against invasion by the unemployed of other industries. This is a step in the right direction, but so long as casual demands are met by casual engagement at many different centres of employment, the demands cannot be met except at the cost of keeping unnecessarily large unorganized reserves of labour. In the present war a great step forward to the better organization of this industry has been taken by the introduction of a guaranteed week, but if this merely means an adequate income to the dock labourer while standing idle for large parts of his time because he forms part of a stagnant rather than of a mobile reserve, it will mean the continuance of a large volume of disguised unemployment, covered by wages rather than by unemployment benefit as in the past.

109. As regards building, the results of disorganization are summed up in the fact given above that the building industry in expanding its volume of employment between 1923 and 1937 by about a half, has expanded even more the number of persons seeking to live in that industry and by consequence has doubled its volume of unemployment, in becoming more prosperous and more active. Building accounts for a larger number of vacancies filled by the employment exchanges than does any other single industry, the number reaching 273,285 in 1937; special attention has been given by the Ministry of Labour to this industry, the measures taken including the setting up of a specialized central exchange dealing solely with building and public works contracting. But the placing index in building is below the average, 26·2 in 1937 as compared with 29·2 for all industries. These figures show that the number of engagements of wholly unemployed men in the course of the year was over 1,000,000, one for every insured person.

Occupational and Local Mobility of Labour

110. The facts passed in review in this section give no support to the suggestion that, in the circumstances of Britain between the two wars, immobility of labour, in the sense of failure to change occupations or place of residence in response to demand, was a substantial cause of unemployment. The substantial cause was deficiency of demand, not friction in the labour market.[1] In physical terms, if two bodies in contact with one another do not move and there is no pull on either of them to make them move, their immobility should be ascribed to the absence of pull, not to friction between them. Friction stops or delays motion only when there is a force for motion against which friction can act. In the circumstances of Britain between the two wars, with hardly any unsatisfied demand anywhere at any time, little if any of the recorded unemployment can be described as due to friction, that is to say to insufficient fluidity of labour. Willingness to move or not to move determined upon which individuals unemployment should fall and not how much unemployment there should be. In fact, the movements of labour between the wars were very great. Table 33 in Appendix B shows that in the course of thirteen years 1924–37, the relative size of particular industries has been completely transformed, with some industries growing three- or four-fold while other industries reduced their numbers to little more than a half. Table 35 shows that of two groups of industries, each starting with about the same number of insured males—a little over 1,800,000—in 1929, one group in eight years increased by nearly 600,000, while the other decreased by 300,000. Table 6 shows that the local changes were substantial though less striking and Table 36 shows the persistence of markedly different levels of unemployment in neighbouring districts. This points to a contrast, noted in the next paragraph, between occupational and local immobility, but it does not mean that local immobility, in the circumstances of the Britain of that time, was a substantial cause of unemployment. Men move freely from occupation to occupation in response to demand. They move less freely but substantially from place to place. The real trouble between the wars was absence of demand, that is to say of any demand for labour that could not be satisfied locally. The figures of industrial transference given in paragraph 79 show clearly that local movement, like occupational movement, depends first and foremost upon the state of the demand for labour, that is to say upon the relation

[1] See "Unemployment, Frictional, Seasonal, Structural," in Appendix D.

between demand as a whole and supply as a whole. The relative mobility or immobility of labour becomes important only when there is a strong demand for labour.

111. But while the facts of unemployment, if fairly studied, give no support to the suggestion that the total of unemployment in Britain between the wars would have been materially reduced by making labour more mobile, they point to a difference between the possibilities of occupational and of local transference which will be important in happier conditions of demand. They suggest that local movement encounters, at a certain point, obstacles which cannot be overcome. This is in accord with what should be expected. The total supply of labour at any time contains a substantial proportion of boys and girls and young persons who, as far as occupation is concerned, are almost completely adaptable, but may find it difficult to leave home. Older people are in the same case. They cannot change or choose their occupations so easily as boys and girls, but they may find it even harder to change their residence. All people, practically without exception, live in families, and most families have more than one wage-earner. Apart from family feeling, each family forms an economic unit whose prosperity depends on keeping together. This expectation on *a priori* grounds of finding ultimate obstacles to complete local mobility of labour is driven home by the experience of the Industrial Transference Board, established in 1928, to bring about, if possible, a wholesale assisted transference of men and women from their homes on the assumption that work could not be brought to their homes. The Industrial Transference Board moved many tens of thousands of people but substantial proportions of these returned to their homes; the Industrial Transference Board found that in the last resort there were appreciable numbers of older people who could not be moved at all and of younger people who could only be moved with extreme difficulty. The same point is made in the Carnegie Report on *Disinherited Youth* in observing that "the crux of the training problem seems to lie in the fact that training means transference."

"The young men were apparently unwilling to accept the fact that the community in which they were born and nurtured, wherein they had built up their social life, was unable to provide them with work. They kept on looking for their luck to turn, perhaps to-morrow or next week, or next month. Some of their friends were getting odd spells of work and their turn might come. Many people appear to be unable to give the consideration of localities its due weight. A Liverpool man, when told by the officer that he had spent most of his working life in jobs away from his home, which he could visit only on holidays, exclaimed, "Good God! What kind of a home did you have, then?" This incident may serve to illustrate the folly of expecting a common-form social outlook among persons with entirely dissimilar experiences and traditions. Middle-class people, trained for the professions, expect to have to follow the job, wherever it may take them. The same holds good only to a very limited extent among the working-class people."[1]

112. Recognition of obstacles to transference of labour does not mean that steps should not be taken to make labour adaptable and mobile. If and when there is a strong demand for labour, the mobility or immobility of the supply will become a factor of real importance, and if his family circumstances permit, no individual should feel it an intolerable grievance to move for work from one part of Britain to another. But family circumstances and age make some individuals in practice immovable. And wholesale transference should be regarded as bad social policy. It involves a sacrifice of social capital, that is to say of the services for health, education and local amenities which have been built up for a community of a certain size and will be wasted if the community sinks to half or a quarter of that size. The assumption on which policy was based during the period between the wars, namely that it was impossible or undesirable to control the location of industry, unless it were industry conducted by foreigners,[2] will, to later generations, condemned to struggle with its consequences, appear a sad example of blindness leading to drift. It allowed more than one-third of the total addition to the population of Britain between the wars to be concentrated in the area of greatest congestion and strategical danger,[3] while leaving other parts of the country derelict. It sacrificed major national interests to considerations of minor importance.

[1] *Disinherited Youth*, described as "A Report on the 18 + Age Group Enquiry Prepared for the Trustees of the Carnegie United Kingdom Trust," and printed in 1943. The enquiry relates to the years 1936–39. The passage cited here is at p. 91.

[2] The location of new factories by foreigners wishing to establish themselves in Britain was brought under control in June, 1936. See Ministry of Labour Report for 1938, p. 25.

[3] See para. 224 in Part IV.

THE NEW PROBLEM: DEFICIENCY OF DEMAND

113. That the general level of unemployment between the two wars was much higher than the general level before 1914 is beyond reasonable question. The contrast extends over all years. It is perhaps most conspicuous between 1937—the best year of the 30's —and 1913, the last boom year before the World War. In 1913, less than 5 per cent of all the unemployment experienced in the industries covered by the limited scheme of insurance occurred after men had been unemployed as long as fifteen weeks. In June, 1937, even in relatively prosperous London, 29 per cent of all those unemployed had been idle for more than three months; in Britain as a whole the proportion was 46 per cent. 1937 represents the best of which the unplanned market economy of Britain was capable between the Wars. Was there in that year anywhere in Britain a substantial unsatisfied demand for labour? The number of vacancies notified to the employment exchanges always exceeds considerably the number filled by them and the difference is greater in good years than in bad years. Thus in 1932 the vacancies filled were 92·1 per cent of the vacancies notified while in 1937 they were only 83·6 per cent. But the vacancies notified to the exchanges and not filled by them do not necessarily remain unfilled and cannot be taken as a measure of unsatisfied demand; most of them get filled in other ways. As part of the study of employment and unemployment on which he and I were jointly engaged at the outbreak of the present war, Mr. J. H. Wilson made a special analysis of all the cancelled vacancies during the month of November, 1937, at eight employment exchanges in the southern part of England.[1] Taking these exchanges as a sample, the analysis yields a figure of 2,210 as the maximum of the unsatisfied demand for labour in Great Britain and Northern Ireland, as notified to the employment exchanges, in a month very near the top of a cyclical fluctuation; Mr. Wilson gives several reasons showing that this figure is an over-estimate. In the same month the number of unemployed persons was over 1,500,000.

[1] The towns selected for this examination were Banbury, Bedford, Coventry, Luton, Northampton, Oxford, Reading, and Swindon, with a total insured population of 340,830, representing 2·38 per cent of the insured population of Great Britain and Northern Ireland. They were materially more prosperous than the country as a whole, having only 5 per cent of insured males unemployed on 15th November, 1937, as compared with 11·8 per cent in the country as a whole. But they had much the same proportion of notified vacancies cancelled as the country as a whole; this in itself is an argument against treating unfilled vacancies as evidence of unsatisfied demand.

It may be said that employers probably had vacancies which they did not notify to the employment exchanges, either because they relied on other methods or because they felt it was of no use to ask for men who would not be available. There is no evidence of this unsatisfied unnotified demand[1]; on the contrary, there is evidence that employers anticipating a shortage tend to over-state rather than to under-state their needs. The employment exchanges are there for all to use freely. If employers wanting men would not even take the trouble to try the official machinery for getting them, that is a striking illustration of the difference noted earlier in this Report, between the disaster of failing to sell one's labour and the inconvenience of not being able to buy all the labour that one can use.

114. It is clear that between the two wars any unsatisfied demand for labour was trifling in quantity and transient in duration. Even the year 1937 remained for most industries a time with many times as many unemployed men as vacant jobs. In all other years, deficiency of demand in relation to total supply was greater still. The central problem of unemployment between the wars in Britain was not what it had appeared to be before the first World War. It was not a problem of cyclical fluctuation reducing demand for a time, or of disorganization of the labour market, wasting men's lives in drifting and waiting. It was a problem of general and persistent weakness of demand for labour. If the Royal Commission of 1905–9 had been asked to repeat their examination of unemployment in 1935–39, they would not have withdrawn their earlier diagnosis: they would still have described cyclical fluctuation and disorganization of the labour market as potent influences to waste human lives in idleness. But, having repeated and reinforced the old diagnosis, they would have added to it. In place of "The New Problem: Chronic Under-Employment," this hypothetical but very desirable Royal Commission on Unemployment in the nineteen-thirties would have written of "The New Problem: Chronic Deficiency of Demand." They might, approaching from a different angle the same problem as that which was examined by the Royal Commission of 1937–40 on the Location of Industry, have devoted another chapter to "Local Mis-direction of Demand." But on the facts they would have

[1] There are references in the *Labour Gazette* during the spring months of 1937 to scarcities of labour and occasionally of materials in particular industries, including engineering, shipbuilding, building and cotton. But these scarcities were nearly all confined to special types of labour, either highly skilled or juvenile; they were generally confined to particular districts; they lasted only for a few months.

given first place to general deficiency of demand, as making the bitter climate in which life was lived between the wars in Britain. Turning from facts to theories, they would then have noted a striking change in the prevailing tendency of economic thought since Victorian and Edwardian days.

Section 2. THEORIES OF UNEMPLOYMENT

UNEMPLOYMENT DIAGNOSIS OF 1909

115. In my first study of unemployment, published in 1909, I was concerned to show how and why unemployment persisted, even though the demand for labour appeared to grow on the whole at least as fast as the supply of labour. I found the explanation on the one hand in the fluctuations of the demand, seasonal and cyclical, and on the other hand in the tendency of each industry to accumulate and retain reserves of labour greater than were needed to provide for local and individual changes in demand. The strength of this tendency to keep excessive reserves of labour varied from industry to industry, according to the numbers of separate employers, the frequency of engagements and the methods of engaging men, but the tendency was found, to some extent, in all industries. The same diagnosis of unemployment was made by the Royal Commission on the Poor Laws and the Relief of Distress which reported in February, 1909. The policy of organizing the labour market, recommended by the Royal Commission and embodied in the Labour Exchanges Act of 1909, was described by me at the time as "a policy of making reality correspond with the assumptions of economic theory. Assuming the demand for labour to be single and the supply perfectly fluid, it is not hard to show that unemployment must always be in process of disappearing—that demand and supply are always tending to an equilibrium. The ideal for practical reform, therefore, must be to concentrate the demand and to give the right fluidity to the supply."[1]

116. It was not suggested, of course, either by the Royal Commission or by myself, that organization of the labour market was all that was required. The reality and the seriousness of cyclical fluctuation were fully recognized. The policies of 1909 included the regularization of employment by the use of public work; the Minority developed this idea into a proposal for a ten years' programme of work to be used deliberately to counteract cyclical fluctuation. The

[1] *Unemployment* (1909), p. 237.

policies of 1909 included also unemployment insurance, which the Majority described as of paramount importance and desired to see extended to unskilled and unorganized workmen; the Minority, while prepared to consider a partial scheme of compulsory insurance, preferred and proposed a State subsidy to voluntary insurance through the trade unions. This emphasis on unemployment insurance was a concession to the fact that the demand for labour was both fluctuating and changing in quality. It was necessary to provide workmen with the means of keeping alive, while following the changes in demand or waiting for it to recover from seasonal or cyclical depression.

117. The idea that demand for labour as a whole might be failing to keep pace with the supply of labour was raised at that time only to be dismissed. It was ruled out by the Majority of the Royal Commission on theoretic grounds. It was ruled out in my study on grounds, not of theory, but of the facts as they presented themselves up to that time: "There is no general failure of adjustment between the growth of the demand for labour and the growth of the supply of labour. The forces which constantly tend to bring about this adjustment between the growth of the demand for labour and the growth of the supply of labour have not been brought to the limit of their power." But the limitations of this cheering conclusion were carefully noted:

> "The statement that the country is not over-populated, and that its industrial system is still capable of absorbing the growing supply of labour, must always be something of the nature of a prophesy . . . Because up-to-date industry has expanded, the inference is made that it is still expanding, and capable of expansion. Because this expansion in the past has taken place through alternations of good years and bad years, the inference is made of any particular period of depression that it is only a temporary phase and will give way to renewed prosperity. All this, however, is far from inevitable."[1]

On the facts up to that time, the assumption of economic theory that demand in total could be left to look after itself appeared to be justified in practice. As the supply of labour had grown, so on the average had the demand for labour. With every pair of hands God sends a mouth. There had been a rising return to labour throughout the nineteenth century and this continued.

[1] *Unemployment* (1909), pp. 14–15.

118. But even apart from the recurrent deficiency of demand through cyclical depression, the organization of industry was such as to involve serious unemployment in responding to demand: the main positive result of my first study was to show the scale and seriousness of frictional unemployment. My object in that first study was not to show that all was well with employment but to identify what was clearly wrong so as to exclude mistaken remedies:—

> "From the beginning to the end of fifty years of unprecedented industrial expansion unemployment has been recorded continuously, and has passed at intervals of seven to ten years from a normal to an acute phase. This in itself is enough to show that unemployment depends not so much on the volume of industry as upon the methods of industry, and while the methods remain unchanged, will continue or recur however the volume grows. A falling demand for labour may come as a symptom of national decay. A rising demand for labour will be no cure for unemployment."[1]

119. This was written when the unemployment rate recorded by the trade unions was running from 2 to 8. After the first World War a different scale of unemployment, with a rate running from 10 to 20 or more had to be explained. The changed face of unemployment led naturally to new theorizing by economists about it. The first suggestion was that a general cause of the higher unemployment might be found in excessive wages. This was put forward prominently in Britain by Professor Pigou (*Economic Journal*, September, 1927) and from another angle by Professor Clay (*Economic Journal*, September, 1929).[2] The idea that high or rigid wages were an important cause of higher unemployment was substantially accepted by myself in the 1930 edition of *Unemployment*.

> "This potential effect of high wages policy in causing unemployment is not denied by any competent authority. . . . As a matter of theory, the continuance in any country of a substantial volume of unemployment which cannot be accounted for by specific maladjustments of place, quality, and time is in

[1] *Unemployment* (1909), p. 15.

[2] J. M. Keynes, in lectures given at that time in London and Manchester, and reprinted as an article on "The Question of High Wages" in the *Political Quarterly* of January, 1930, emphasized the fact that in an international system high wages in a particular country, accompanied by mobility of foreign lending, might lead to unemployment. This is quite consistent with his subsequent criticism of Professor Pigou's general thesis as to the relation between wages and employment (see paras. 125 and 127 below).

itself proof that the price being asked for labour as wages is too high for the conditions of the market; demand for and supply of labour are not finding the appropriate price for meeting."[1]

It may be recalled that long before, in 1913, Professor Pigou had carried the argument about wages to the point of saying that it was theoretically possible for wage-rates at any moment to be so adjusted in every part of the industrial field "that no unemployment whatever can exist." "In other words, it has been shown that unemployment is *wholly* caused by maladjustment between wages and demand."[2]

THE KEYNESIAN ANALYSIS OF 1936

120. A new era of economic theorizing about employment and unemployment was inaugurated by the publication in 1936 of *The General Theory of Employment, Interest and Money* by J. M. Keynes,[3] now Lord Keynes. No account, however brief, of all the changes of economic thought and language induced by this epoch-making work can be attempted here. The gist of the new approach to the problem of employment that has resulted from it can be put shortly. Employment depends on spending, which is of two kinds—for consumption and for investment; what people spend on consumption gives employment. What they save, i.e. do not spend on consumption, gives employment only if it is invested, which means not the buying of bonds or shares but expenditure in adding to capital equipment, such as factories, machinery, or ships, or in increasing stocks of raw material. There is not in the unplanned market economy anything that automatically keeps the total of spending of both kinds at the point of full employment, that is to say, high

[1] *Unemployment* (1930), pp. 362 and 371.

[2] *Unemployment*, p. 51 (Home University Library, 1913).

[3] This eminent economist has in more than one way made it inappropriate to refer to him as "Mr. Keynes." The form of reference to him which I adopt here has the advantage of differentiating between him and the present distinguished adviser to H.M. Government, and making it plain that the Government have no responsibility for the views of J. M. Keynes and may not be influenced by them. Even Lord Keynes may differ from J. M. Keynes. It should be added that the *General Theory* of 1936 (cited in that way here) was preceded in 1930 by the same author's *Treatise on Money*, in which some of the later ideas are seen in process of evolution, and expressed in a different terminology. An excellent popular exposition of the Keynesian analysis is given by Mrs. Joan Robinson, in *The Problem of Full Employment*, published by the Workers' Educational Association as a Study Outline, and the analysis is explained and illustrated by the same author in *An Introduction to the Theory of Employment* (Macmillan, 1938).

enough to employ all the available labour. Adequate total demand for labour in an unplanned market economy cannot be taken for granted.

121. According to the Keynesian analysis, the possibility of prolonged mass unemployment lies in the fact that decisions to save and decisions to invest are made by different sets of people at different times and for different reasons and may thus get out of step. The amount which any community will try to save is governed, not primarily by the outlets for saving, i.e. the opportunities for investment, but by the total income of the community and its distribution; broadly speaking, if incomes are evenly distributed, less will be saved out of the total than if they are unevenly distributed. The amount which any community will seek to invest is governed, not primarily by the amount of savings available for investment, but by expectation of profits. Savings and investment do not start with any initial tendency to march in step and there is no automatic painless way of keeping them in step or bringing them together if they fall out. The rate of interest, which was supposed to serve this purpose, of regulating automatically the processes of saving and investment, fails to do so. If savings are tending to outrun investment, the rate of interest will fall only after a severe decline in the national income:

> "Upon one thing all modern economists, of whatever school of thought, are agreed: *the amount which the community wishes to save at full-employment income levels must somehow be offset, or income will fall until the community is so poor and wretched as to be willing to save no more than can be offset.* In terms of time-period analysis, the community must return to the income stream in each period as much as it received in previous periods, or else there will ensue a cumulative downward spiral of income and employment. We are confronted with the paradox that while no one attempts to save with any thought of investment outlet, or of offsets, yet the amount which all together succeed in saving is brought into alignment by the movements of income and employment. But the alignment is performed on a cruel Procrustean bed, with employment and income being lopped off if the desire to save is excessive in comparison with available offsets, and with an inflationary straining of demand if investment is excessive."

So the position is summed up by an American economist.[1]

---

[1] Paul A. Samuelson, in *Post-War Economic Problems*, edited by Seymour Harris (McGraw-Hill Book Company, 1943).

122. The argument, it will be seen, is not that the savings of a community in total can outrun the investment. In the sense in which these terms are used in the Keynesian analysis, the total savings that a community is, in fact, able to make, can never exceed the total invested: if a number of individuals in the community together try to save more than is being invested, the income of other members of the community will be correspondingly reduced; their losses in poverty and unemployment, their spending of former savings or running into debt will cancel out some of the savings of others and will thus reduce the total savings of the community to that which can be spent in investment. "Saving," in J. M. Keynes's words, "is a mere residual. The decisions to consume and the decisions to invest between them determine incomes."[1]

123. Saving in itself is merely negative; it means not spending. Saving may be desirable from the point of view of the individual who saves, in order to ensure to him the means of spending and of independence later. Apart from this merit of securing independence, saving in itself has no social virtue. The social virtue of saving by one person depends on there being someone else who wishes to spend the savings. This is obvious when the question is asked why, in war, saving is impressed upon all citizens as a duty, hardly second to that of giving their lives and their labour to the national cause. The answer is that in war the State has an infinite appetite for spending—is ready to spend all and more than all that the citizens can save. In spite of the war-savings posters, it is not the negative act of saving by the citizen that makes bombs and launches ships against the enemy, but the positive act of spending by the State. If neither the State nor anyone else is ready to spend savings, they are not a social but a self-regarding virtue. They may be no virtue at all. J. M. Keynes wrote in a famous passage:—

> "Thus our argument leads towards the conclusion that in contemporary conditions the growth of wealth so far from being dependent on the abstinence of the rich as is commonly supposed, is more likely to be impeded by it. One of the chief social justifications of great inequality of wealth is therefore removed."[2]

On the earlier teaching of the economists, moral and technical considerations in regard to the distribution of wealth had appeared to be in conflict. Moral considerations suggested the desirability of a more equal distribution of wealth, while technical considerations

---

[1] *General Theory*, p. 64. [2] *Op. cit.*, p. 373.

appeared to require great inequality as the condition of adequate saving. On the newer teaching of the economists, as exemplified in the passage just quoted from J. M. Keynes, moral and technical considerations unite in favour of substantially greater equality of wealth than has obtained in Britain in the past.

124. But, though actual saving in the Keynesian analysis is a mere residual, the amount which the individuals of a community will try to save, i.e. will not spend on consumption out of their incomes, is a factor of immense importance. The amount which the individuals of a community will try to save under conditions of full employment, with a given distribution of income, is the most important single economic fact about the community, for it commits the community to ensuring that that amount is spent by others individually or communally, out of loans or from past savings under penalty of entering on a downward spiral of decreasing employment and growing poverty. By consequence it would be a matter of importance to have full and accurate information as to the sources from which the savings of a community come and as to the factors which influence saving. At present information on both these points is scanty; the official statistics as they stand and even the invaluable White Paper now presented annually on the Sources of War Finance throw no light upon them. Savings, their sources, form and motives would be a highly repaying subject for expert investigation with adequate resources and access to confidential information. Without such an investigation, it is possible to give only general impressions. These are to the effect that, for Britain and for the United States alike, the savings that tend to produce depression are the undistributed profits of companies and the large surpluses of a very limited class of owners of great wealth. The savings of most people are made for personal security; they merely postpone consumption; at any moment of time, while some are saving for future security, others are spending what they had saved in the past for this purpose and the two cancel out. The savings that matter in Britain and may not get offset in any way by automatic spending are not likely to derive to any substantial extent from small incomes.

125. The Keynesian analysis attacks directly and destroys one of the economic harmonies between savings and investment through the rate of interest, which according to older theory were assumed to keep the free capitalist system in prosperous equilibrium, with the demand for labour painlessly adjusted to the supply of labour. It destroys incidentally another of these harmonies also—the assump-

ion made by Professor Pigou in 1913 that wage rates could be so
adjusted as to abolish unemployment completely, and the inference
that in any given situation employment could be increased directly
by a general reduction of money wages. This question was the
subject of a spirited debate between economists in the *Economic Journal*
during 1937 and 1938. There is no need to enter here into the details
of this debate, which ended in Professor Pigou accepting the main
contention of his opponents and coming, in his own words, much
nearer than before to J. M. Keynes' general view of the inter-relation
between money wage-rates, employment, and the rate of interest.

126. The Keynesian analysis is of fundamental importance in
making clear that the adequacy of the demand for labour as a whole
to absorb the available supply should not be taken for granted.
There may be unemployment through chronic deficiency of demand
for labour, as well as unemployment through fluctuation of demand
and through friction; demand for and supply of labour in total
do not get adjusted automatically either by the rate of interest or
by bargains about money wages. Up to this point the analysis is
probably now accepted by all persons qualified to judge. It remains
not the last word on the problem, but a word which requires supple-
menting. Three comments in particular are relevant.

SIGNIFICANCE OF WAGE BARGAINING

127. First, the argument that it may prove impossible by suitable
wage bargains in money terms so to alter real wages[1] as to abolish
unemployment is valid. It does not follow that the nature of the
wage bargains as actually made may not be of great importance
for the functioning of the economic system. The responsibilities
which, in a full employment economy, fall upon those concerned
with wage bargains are examined further in Part V of this Report.
Here it suffices to emphasize the following points:—

(1) The Keynesian analysis shows that a rise in money wages
in one industry has a double effect: it raises the real wage in
that industry, but reduces real wages in other industries. The
rise on the one hand may be larger or smaller than the fall on
the other hand. Whether real wages for labour as a whole rise
or fall depends upon a great number of other circumstances.
On the whole, it may be said that a rise in money wages in
particular industries does not normally produce a gain for labour

---

[1] See Explanation of Terms in Appendix D.

as a whole; it represents merely a re-arrangement of the scale of remuneration within the wage-earning class.

(2) Such re-arrangements, however, remain necessary and important in a full employment economy. If, owing to exceptional circumstances, money wages in some industries rise out of all proportion to the wages in other industries, social unrest is the result.

(3) While the new theory demonstrates that changes in money wages do not produce equivalent changes in real wages for labour as a whole and do not directly affect the total demand for labour, it does not disprove the importance of relative changes of wage rates as between industries. Such changes may be a potent factor in directing labour to the specific jobs and places where it is wanted, that is to say, the mobility of labour may be increased by a flexible wage policy which offers an inducement for workers to leave declining industries and seek employment in expanding industries. But this should not be the only or the main method for bringing about such movements. If the demand for the products of a particular type of labour is declining, an effort by the workpeople affected to maintain their numbers by lowering their wages may lead to a progressive lowering of their standard of living and therefore of the average standard. It is better that they should keep their standards and reduce their numbers, and that labour—particularly that of young people—should be diverted to the expanding industries.

(4) The view that bargains about money wages do not affect the total demand for labour does not apply to wages in the export industries or to wages in those industries at home which compete with imported goods. A fall in these wages may increase the ratio between exports and imports, and a rise may decrease it and thus affect the total demand for labour at home. But this is true only as long as all other factors—for instance exchange rates—remain constant. Since these other factors are not necessarily constant, there is no reason for distorting the internal structure of wages merely for the purpose of affecting the foreign trade balance. The problems presented to this country on account of her relative dependence on international trade must be solved by other means, which will be discussed in Part VI.

These considerations are put forward not to question the thesis of J. M. Keynes that a general lowering of money wages is no cure of unemployment and a general increase of money wages no cause

f unemployment. They are put forward only to demonstrate that,
n a full employment economy, great responsibility continues to
est with the trade unions and employers' associations—but a
esponsibility which transcends the compass of individual unions
and industries and can be properly discharged only if every
ectional wage bargain is considered in the light of the economy
as a whole.

OFFSETTING OF SAVING BY INVESTMENT OR CONSUMPTION

128. Second, the emphasis laid in the Keynesian analysis upon
the relation between savings and investment has led some interpreters
to the suggestion that the only way of offsetting savings, so as to
maintain national income and employment, is by investment. This
is not so. If one individual saves, that is to say does not spend, the
whole of his income, the saving can be offset and total expenditure maintained by some other person or authority spending those
savings in any way whatever, whether as investment or in consumption. In practice, if the other person is a private individual or
a business concern, he will wish to invest the savings rather than use
them for consumption, because he will have to borrow the savings
with a liability for their repayment with interest. He can only secure
the means of repayment by investing the savings in some productive
undertaking. But the State is under no such restriction, since it
possesses an unlimited command over the nation's credit, and therefore can use the savings of its citizens in any way that seems good
to it. It can spend them on explosives or on milk for babies or on
salaries for civil servants and still be able to repay with interest what
it has borrowed. Whether it spends the savings of the citizens in one
of these ways or spends them on some permanent improvement,
such as a road or a bridge, the State will not as a rule have any
specific income from which to repay the loan. It will have to rely
and can rely upon taxation or further borrowing. This is one illustration only of the fundamental difference between the finance of
the State and the finance of any private individual or organization.
The necessary offsetting of savings to maintain employment can take
any form of spending, if the spending is that of the State.

129. It should be added that J. M. Keynes himself in 1936 by
no means regarded the offsetting of savings by investment as the
sole method of maintaining employment. His analysis, as he realized,
represented in some respects a throw-back to earlier theories, such
as that of J. A. Hobson which from 1889 to 1936 had been banned

as heretical by practically all academic economists, but now receive a belated restoration to the canon of orthodoxy. These theorie traced the chronic tendency to under-employment in industria societies to under-consumption, that is to say, "to social practice and to a distribution of wealth which may result in a propensit to consume[1] which is unduly low." They indicated a re-distributio of income from rich to poor, in order to increase consumption, as th main practical objective. Towards these and allied schools o thought J. M. Keynes in 1936 expressed his attitude as follows:

"In existing conditions—or, at least, in the conditions whic existed until lately . . . these schools of thought are, as guide to practical policy, undoubtedly in the right. . . . If it is im practicable materially to increase investment, obviously ther is no means of securing a higher level of employment except b increasing consumption. Practically I only differ from thes schools of thought in thinking that they lay a little too muc emphasis on increased consumption at a time when there is stil much social advantage to be obtained from increased invest ment. Theoretically, however, they are open to the criticism of neglecting the fact that there are *two* ways to expand output. Even if we were to decide that it would be better to increase capital more slowly and to concentrate effort on increasing con sumption, we must decide this with open eyes after well con sidering the alternative. I am myself impressed by the great social advantages of increasing the stock of capital until it ceases to be scarce. But this is a practical judgment, not a theoretical imperative.

"Moreover, I should readily concede that the wisest course is to advance on both fronts at once. Whilst aiming at a socially controlled rate of investment with a view to a progressive decline in the marginal efficiency of capital,[1] I should support at the same time all sorts of policies for increasing the propensity to consume. For it is unlikely that full employment can be main tained, whatever we may do about investment, with the existing propensity to consume. There is room, therefore, for both policies to operate together: to promote investment and, at the same time, to promote consumption, not merely to the level which with the existing propensity to consume would correspond to the increased investment, but to a higher level still."[2]

[1] See Explanation of Terms in Appendix D.
[2] *Op. cit.*, pp. 324-5.

130. While in this passage J. M. Keynes recognized the need to increase the propensity to consume, an object which in the last resort can be accomplished only by a redistribution of income, he laid personal and practical emphasis on increasing investment. This raises the issue as to how a market is to be ensured for the rapidly increasing products of the increased investment. The governing fact in all industrial societies is technical progress, raising productivity per head by an average which for Britain is commonly estimated at 3 per cent a year for manufacturing alone, and at $1\frac{1}{2}$ per cent for industry as a whole including services and distribution.[1] Increased productivity per head mathematically involves either increased consumption per head, or idleness, which must be taken in the form either of leisure or of unemployment. In other words, the fundamental problem of a progressive society is to distribute the results of the progress among citizens, either by shortening hours or by increasing the purchasing power of the citizens, so that they can consume more. Increase of purchasing power for citizens means either larger money incomes or falling prices. The choice between these alternatives depends on price policy. As is argued later,[2] adoption by the State of a definite policy in regard to prices, becomes an almost inevitable accompaniment of a policy of maintaining employment, in a progressive society. This is an issue which, though certainly not absent from J. M. Keynes' mind, is not treated by him at any length.

INTERPLAY OF THEORIES AND FACTS

131. The third and most general comment is that the Keynesian analysis, like any other theoretical analysis, is an instrument for interpreting facts, not a substitute for facts. The Keynesian analysis throws light upon that point in a free market economy where an essential link is missing in the mechanism: decisions to save are not automatically co-ordinated with decisions to invest or to offset savings in some other way. But this analysis, as such, does not reveal the particular economic cause which, in a given period, produced a gap between decisions to save and decisions to invest. Theoretical analysis is a guide in the search for an explanation, not an explanation in itself nor a prediction for the future. The

---

[1] These are the estimates given by Mr. Colin Clark. For the United States the estimated rate of increase is higher, according to the Day Persons index 4·3 per cent a year for manufactures alone from 1870 to 1930, and 3·7 per cent for all forms of production taken together (W. M. Persons, *Forecasting Business Cycles*, Ch. XI).

[2] In Part V, paras. 289–92.

parts which theoretical analysis and inductive study respectively have to play in the elucidation of issues vital to human welfare is well illustrated by the two main problems of employment and unemployment between the wars. One of these is the problem of the fluctuation of demand for labour in nearly all countries between 1929 and 1937. The other is the problem of why unemployment in Britain throughout the period between the wars and in the United States between 1930 and the outbreak of the second World War was so much more severe than anything experienced before.

132. As regards the first of these problems, J. M. Keynes recognized that, in so far as his theory claimed to show what determined the volume of employment at any time, it "must be capable of explaining the phenomena of the trade cycle." Like any other theory of demand for labour, it must fit the fact that demand fluctuates. J. M. Keynes himself did not give, and at the end of a long book devoted to the general problems of employment, interest and money, could not have been expected to give, a detailed theory of fluctuation. It is possible, using the Keynesian analysis as a starting-point, to argue that cyclical fluctuation of demand is not merely a possible but an inevitable feature of an unplanned market economy, arising out of the methods by which income is distributed in the community and out of the relations between the industries which make goods primarily for current consumption and the industries which make goods primarily for expanding the capital equipment of the country. This theoretical argument for the inevitability of cyclical fluctuation is set out briefly in Section 5 of Appendix B. My own different approach to the problem, through inductive study of the facts of fluctuation, is set out in Appendix A and is summarized briefly in paragraphs 96–102 above. The theoretical and the inductive approaches lead to the same practical conclusions. Whether or not cyclical fluctuation of demand is inevitable in an unplanned market economy, it has in fact occurred throughout the period for which records are available—in Britain since 1785—and has occurred with sufficient uniformity of its leading features, to prove that its causes are deeply seated in the economy and are powerful. Nothing less than total war, that is to say substitution of a planned for an unplanned economy, has sufficed to suspend the operation of these causes. And the first World War merely suspended their operation; they returned with "normalcy" in Britain as in the United States. The fluctuation from 1929 to 1937, while probably more violent than anything experienced in the past, has all the regular features of earlier fluctuations.

133. The survey of facts of fluctuation set out in Appendix A, while it leads to the same practical conclusion as theoretical analysis, that fluctuation of demand is probably or certainly inevitable in an unplanned market economy, includes new facts suggesting a need to enlarge the analysis. The facts of the greater violence of fluctuation in British export industries and the leadership in time of those industries have not entered hitherto into theoretical discussion of the trade cycle. But they must be explained by any complete theory of the cycle. And they have an important practical bearing on the search for remedies. For they suggest that planned marketing and production of primary products, both agricultural and mineral, is an essential condition for the stabilization of demand for manufacturing products.

134. As regards the second problem, of explaining the greater severity of unemployment after the first World War, that is not a matter on which the Keynesian or any other analysis throws light directly; it is a fact which has to be explained by detailed analysis of facts. But theory can help in the interpretation by suggesting which facts are likely to have most bearing on the answer. The facts are not the same for Britain and for the United States. In Britain the excess of unemployment, as compared with earlier experience, was found through substantially the whole period between the wars, and was obviously due in large measure to the falling off of overseas demand for British produce, bringing depression to the export industries on which British prosperity had depended so largely in the past. In the United States, excess of unemployment as compared with earlier experience occurred only after 1929 and had no obvious explanation corresponding to that which can be given for the experience of Britain. Why was the cyclical fluctuation which began in 1929 more violent than previous fluctuations? Why did it lead to so half-hearted a recovery in 1937? This is an issue keenly debated in the United States. One school of writers explain the "lamentable thirties" by permanent changes, such as the arrival of the United States at economic maturity; that is to say, the disappearance of the continually moving frontier, the falling rate of population growth and the special nature of recent technical progress, in being chiefly of a capital saving character. From this they draw the conclusion that permanent changes in the economic system, involving the taking of new responsibilities by the State, are necessary. Their opponents attribute the "lamentable thirties" to particular policies of labour organization or of Government as inhibiting investment. They argue that all

the permanent factors, such as the disappearing frontier, the falling growth of population, and the changing nature of technical progress are much older than the thirties. They cite from the eighteen eighties observations closely parallel to those used now by the writers who believe that, in the absence of new Government measures, the United States will enter upon a period of secular stagnation.[1]

135. The practical issue for both countries, in framing plans for the future, is to determine whether the unparalleled depression experienced between the two wars was due to exceptional and temporary causes or to causes either permanent or likely to recur. For Britain in 1936, J. M. Keynes took the view that the abnormal depression between the wars arose from a permanent change of conditions.

> "During the nineteenth century, the growth of population and invention, the opening up of new lands, the state of confidence and the frequency of war over the average of (say) each decade seem to have been sufficient, taken in conjunction with the propensity to consume, to stabilize a schedule of the marginal efficiency of capital which allowed a reasonably satisfactory average level of employment to be compatible with a rate of interest high enough to be psychologically acceptable to wealth owners. . . .
>
> "To-day, and presumably for the future, the schedule of the marginal efficiency of capital is, for a variety of reasons much lower than it was in the nineteenth century. The acuteness and the peculiarity of our contemporary problem arises therefore, out of the possibility that the average rate of interest which will allow a reasonable average level of unemployment is one so unacceptable to wealth-owners that it cannot be readily established merely by manipulating the quantity of money."[2]

[1] The argument of those in the United States who believe in the possibility or probability of secular stagnation is put by Mr. Alan Sweezy in a contribution to *Post-War Economic Problems*, edited by Seymour Harris (McGraw-Hill Book Company, New York, 1943), while a contrary view is put in the same volume by Mr. Richard Bissell. The leading American exponent of the need for Government measures, by public outlay, to maintain effective demand, is Professor Alvin Hansen. In criticizing him, in *The New Philosophy of Public Debt* (Brookings Institution, Washington, 1943), Mr. Harold G. Moulton gives some striking forecasts made in 1886 and 1887 of the imminent slackening of industrial expansion in the United States (pp. 26–7).

[2] *Op. cit.* 307–9.

On this view, the depression in Britain between the wars was not ue simply to the decline of international trade, as the result of var and its aftermath. It pointed to a permanent unfavourable hange in the working of the market economy and by consequence o the need for new policies to maintain employment. This view, s J. M. Keynes would himself have admitted, represented a judgment of probabilities rather than a demonstrated fact. But even if, ontrary to this view, the exceptional depression between the wars n Britain is attributed wholly to the special factor of decline of nternational trade, the need for new policies can hardly be questioned by reasonable men. There were serious depressions before he first World War; there was almost chronic weakness of demand. 'Except during the war," wrote J. M. Keynes, "I doubt if we have ny recent experiences of a boom so strong that it led to full employment."[1] And the trouble between the wars was not simply that lecline of international trade produced an emergency; the trouble vas that the unplanned market economy proved so little resilient, o incapable of dealing with the emergency. To frame British conomic policy on the assumption that there will be no more mergencies or shiftings of the economic structure of the world s mere wishful thinking.

136. For the United States the need of new policies to maintain teady high demand for the products of its industry is even clearer. The depression which began in 1929 cannot be explained by events utside the States or by any strictly temporary cause. It may or nay not have been intensified and prolonged by Government or abour policies, but it cannot be attributed to such policies. It certainly was intensified and prolonged by action taken in other countries to deal with their difficulties, but to a large extent these actions were a natural consequence of the depression itself and would be repeated in similar conditions. There is no ground for confidence or even for hope that the economic system which produced the depression of the lamentable thirties in the United States will, if left to itself, fail to reproduce similar depressions in future. There may be worse depressions.

SECTION 3. THE NEW FACE OF UNEMPLOYMENT

137. Unemployment before the first World War appeared as an evil calling for remedy, but not as the most serious economic problem

[1] *Op cit.* p. 322.

of its time. That it was this between two wars will be denied by few. The average rate of unemployment in Britain, that is to say the percentage of persons seeking work who could not find it, was between two and three times, most probably two and a half times, as high between the wars as it had been before the first World War. But doubling or trebling the rate of unemployment means much more than doubling or trebling the misery of unemployment. With unemployment at 5 per cent or less, the bulk of it consists of short interval unemployment of people who have not been idle long and can hope shortly to return to work. Unemployment at 15 per cent includes many who have been unemployed for long periods and have lost or are losing hope, as well as bodily vigour and the habit of work. Unemployment in Britain after the first World War had a new and grimmer face.

138. In this respect the experience of Britain accords with that of other industrial countries having similar economic systems. Though there is no direct continuous record of unemployment in the United States, authoritative and conservative estimates, such as those of the National Industrial Conference Board, show unmistakably the change that has followed the first total war. According to these estimates the year of highest unemployment in the United States between 1900 and 1914 was 1908, with 2,296,000 unemployed; in the twenties a new record was established of 4,754,000 in 1921; since 1929 the figures have run as shown in Table 16:

139. These figures are portentous. It is well to record and to remember them to-day, when in the United States as in Britain unemployment is being melted away in the heat and fury of war. What unemployment meant to each of these countries in the last time of peace must not be forgotten, in planning what each of them should do to order affairs differently and better in the next peace.

140. Nor is there room for reasonable doubt as to the direction in which the remedy must be sought. The two approaches to the problem of unemployment in my first study of 1909 and in J. M. Keynes' *General Theory* of 1936, are not contradictory but complementary. The level of employment and unemployment at any time depends on the one hand, on the demand for the products of industry, and on the other hand, on the manner in which industry responds to the demand. In 1909, I assumed, in accord with all academic economists and most practical men, that, apart from the trade cycle, demand would look after itself. I was concerned mainly with the way in which industry responded to demand; the results

Table 16

ESTIMATED UNEMPLOYMENT IN THE UNITED
STATES OF AMERICA, 1929-41 (In Thousands)*

	Total Labour Force	Unemployment	% of Labour Force
1929	—	429	0·9
1930	49,006	2,925	5·9
1931	49,597	7,065	14·2
1932	50,132	11,402	22·7
1933	50,691	11,864	23·4
1934	51,267	9,793	19·1
1935	51,769	9,116	17·6
1936	52,237	7,407	14·2
1937	52,692	6,413	12·2
1938	53,229	9,813	18·4
1939	53,788	8,795	16·4
1940	54,333	7,650	14·1
1941	54,784	3,350	6·1

* The estimates of the total labour force and of unemployment are taken from the *Economic Almanac*, 1942-43, published by the National Industrial Conference Board. The
percentages have been added by myself. Other authorities
commonly give higher estimates of unemployment than
those used here.

of that study were summed up in its title—*Unemployment: A Problem
of Industry*. The revolution of economic thought effected by J. M.
Keynes, aided by the experience of the thirties, lies in the fact that
adequate demand for labour is no longer taken for granted. The
Keynesian analysis leads to the conclusion that, even apart from
cyclical depression, there may be chronic or nearly chronic deficiency
in the total demand for labour, with full employment a rare fleeting
accident. J. M. Keynes is not concerned with frictional unemployment at all: it is excluded formally from his study. The Keynesian
analysis does not deny the importance of disorganization of the
labour market as a cause of unemployment. My first study did not
deny the possibility of deficiency in total demand for labour.

141. Both approaches are needed to-day. The reality and the
seriousness of the industrial friction deduced by me from the limited
data available in 1909, are demonstrated by the analysis of unemployment between the two wars, based on the full data now available
and summarised in paragraphs 61-89 above; this analysis shows,
as a special feature, the chronic hopeless unemployment brought
to particular regions by the shifting of demand. The error of taking

sufficiency of total effective demand for granted, on theoretical grounds, is made plain by the Keynesian analysis of 1936. Once that error is shown, the burden of proof by facts that an unplanned market economy can be trusted to maintain sufficient steady demand for its products, rests on those who maintain this and the facts are against them.

142. The new facts and the new theories of unemployment lead to the same conclusion: that an unplanned market economy is less automatically self-adjusting at a high level of employment than had been supposed in earlier times. Before the first World War there was no full record of unemployment in any country in the world. But the reality, persistence, and generality of the international trade cycle are established. For this period it is arguable though there are few, if any, facts to support the argument, that adequate demand for the products of industry was attained at the top of each cyclical boom, but, at the highest, this meant for Britain only for one year in six between 1883 and 1914. And even in this period there was structural unemployment due to the uncontrolled shifting of industry from one part of the country to another; though the general level of unemployment was much lower in 1913 than in 1937, the differences between one region and another were equally marked in the two years.

143. For the period between the two World Wars, there is a full record of severe unemployment in Britain and there are records which leave little doubt that during the nineteen-thirties unemployment was substantially more serious in the United States than in Britain, to compensate for its lesser seriousness before 1930. In this period each country experienced a particularly severe return of cyclical fluctuation; though more violent in Britain than anything experienced, at least since 1850, this fluctuation was of the same general character as former fluctuations—was a fresh manifestation of the international trade cycle. The boom which ended this fluctuation in 1937 and heralded the beginning of a new depression left 10 per cent of the labour force unemployed in Britain and about 12 per cent unemployed in the United States. As regards the United States, this high unemployment at the top of a cyclical boom cannot be explained as due to structural unemployment. If that explanation is offered for Britain, the answer is that failure for nearly twenty years to deal with structural unemployment is in itself a serious weakness of the unplanned market economy. Because such demand as was generated by this economy for the products of industry was so weak, it was not effective in overcoming industrial friction

ecause it was so badly located with reference to the supplies of
vailable labour, it made that friction abnormally strong.

144. The need for a new attack on the problem of unemployment
annot be denied to-day, except in a mood of unthinking optimism.
'he attack must be on three lines. There is unemployment due to
hronic or recurrent deficiency of demand. There is unemployment
ue to mis-direction of demand. There is unemployment due to the
egree to which the labour market remains unorganized and to the
ianner in which particular industries respond to demand. The
:duction of unemployment to a harmless minimum requires,
ierefore, measures of three kinds; measures to ensure sufficient
eady demand for the products of industry; measures to direct
emand with regard to the labour available; measures to organize
ie labour market and to assist the supply of labour to move in
ccord with demand.

Part III

FULL EMPLOYMENT IN WAR

The Melting Away of Unemployment (paras. 145–50). Economic Analysis of War (paras. 151–60). Spectacular Achievements of War Planning (paras. 161–3).

THE MELTING AWAY OF UNEMPLOYMENT

145. In the first World War the unemployment rate in the British trade unions, which for forty years had not been less than 2·0, went down to 0·4 in 1916 and was 1·0 or less than 1·0 in each of the other war years 1915–18. In the second World War, no unemployment rates have been published since October, 1940, for reasons of security, since they might throw light on the total numbers employed and so upon the numbers and equipment of the Armed Forces. In place of unemployment rates, the actual numbers of unemployed persons on the register of the employment exchanges are published. They are given for each year from 1928 to 1942 and for five dates in 1943 and 1944 in Table 17. The figures for 1942 and 1943 include persons classified as unsuitable for ordinary industrial employment; the number of such persons has fallen from nearly 28,000 in March, 1942, when their numbers were first published, to just under 20,000 in October, 1943, and January, 1944. The figures cover Northern Ireland as well as Britain; in Britain alone the total of the unemployed has been below 100,000 since April 1943.

146. The contrast between 1937—the best of the recent years before the war—with more than 1½ million unemployed and 1943 with about 100,000, is emphatic. Since the 1½ million of 1937 corresponded to an unemployment rate of 10·8 giving nearly 150,000 unemployed for every 1·0 per cent of unemployment, and since the numbers in employment now are probably more rather than less than those in 1937,[1] the rate to-day must be in the neighbourhood of 0·5. The second World War began with much heavier unemployment than the first World War and has melted it away at least as far.

147. Yet even now war has not abolished unemployment completely. The Unemployment Insurance Statutory Committee, reporting on the Unemployment Fund in 1943, set out the expen-

[1] See para. 149 below.

Table 17

AVERAGE NUMBERS OF UNEMPLOYED PERSONS ON THE REGISTERS OF EMPLOYMENT EXCHANGES IN GREAT BRITAIN AND NORTHERN IRELAND 1928-44

Year	Wholly Unemployed	Temporarily Stopped	Unemployed Casual Workers	Total
1928	869,573	309,359	75,972	1,254,904
1929	900,553	268,595	79,440	1,248,588
1930	1,347,840	527,720	98,941	1,974,501
1931	1,994,471	587,719	115,678	2,697,868
1932	2,136,052	574,315	102,675	2,813,042
1933	2,037,517	456,743	94,098	2,588,358
1934	1,763,911	369,002	88,150	2,221,063
1935	1,706,783	312,757	86,581	2,106,121
1936	1,491,051	251,568	79,081	1,821,700
1937	1,284,123	205,369	67,509	1,557,001
1938	1,433,248	380,484	67,625	1,881,357
1939	1,308,212	220,990	60,599	1,589,801
1940	829,458	165,962	39,252	1,034,672
1941	314,507	62,124	14,890	391,521
1942	151,313*	8,615	5,346	165,374*
1943 (Jan.)	135,486*	4,875	3,465	143,826*
(Apr.)	114,443*	2,221	3,212	118,160*
(Jul.)	105,416*	2,535	2,454	110,505*
(Oct.)	102,600*	1,669	2,235	106,504*
1944 (Jan.)	111,572*	2,794	1,907	116,273*

* These figures include persons who were classified by interviewing panels as unsuitable for ordinary employment. The average number of such persons who were registered as wholly unemployed during 1942 was 26,002. At the four dates shown in 1943 it was 22,815; 21,669; 19,953; 19,974 respectively, and at January, 1944, it was 19,938. The last figure is made up of 19,456 men classified as unsuitable for ordinary industrial employment and 482 women classified as unsuitable for normal full-time employment.

diture on unemployment benefit in each year from 1938, showing how from £52 millions in that year it fell to £26½ millions in 1940 and then to £9·2 millions in 1941, £3·9 millions in 1942 and £2·8 millions in 1943.[1] The Committee remark that these figures show how slow the process of full mobilization is; how many frictions have to be overcome in diverting all men and women from their peace-time tasks to that which needs to be done in war, and how even in a community working at full stretch as the British community worked in 1943, there are intervals of not working due to changes of programme and methods and other inevitable causes. Payment of

[1] *Eleventh Report of Unemployment Insurance Committee on the Financial Condition of the Unemployment Fund* (H. C. 60 of Session 1943-44).

more than 2¾ million pounds of unemployment benefit in the fourth full year of war, is not a sign of failure to mobilize the nation for war. It is merely a crowning proof that however great the demand for labour, some intervals of standing by are inevitable in any changing economic system and must be met by unemployment benefit, if they are not covered by wages. Since the middle of 1940, there have been acute shortages of labour of many kinds. There has probably been full employment in Britain in the formal sense of unfilled vacancies exceeding in number the persons unemployed for something like three years. There has been a relaxation of barriers of all kinds to the movement of men and women from one occupation to another and one district to another. There has been forced movement by direction under emergency powers. Yet it has taken two or three years of full demand to reduce unemployment to 100,000. It is clear that no similar reduction could be expected from the brief period of boom at the top of a cyclical fluctuation. A strong demand for labour takes time to produce its effects in melting away unemployment. A strong demand, if it could be maintained over many years by a full employment policy, would almost certainly lead to levels of unemployment far below that recorded in any part of Britain in 1937.

148. The figures cited are only a statistical presentation of what has now become a commonplace: that the only sovereign remedy yet discovered by democracies for unemployment is total war. Those who use war experience as an argument for the possibility of abolishing mass unemployment in peace often find themselves met by two popular objections; first, that this result is achieved only at the cost of incurring immense public debt; second, that the achievement of war proves nothing for peace, since the full employment of the civilian population depends on withdrawing millions of men and women from useful production to military service. The first of these objections is an objection not to the possibility of abolishing mass unemployment, but to the assumed cost. As is shown in paragraph 198 and in Appendix C, in dealing with the finance of a full employment policy, this objection is without substance. The second objection is also without substance, because the distinction suggested by it, between men and women in military service as doing useless things and those in industrial employment as doing useful things, is invalid. Those who use arms are neither more nor less usefully employed than those who make arms; both users and makers are engaged in meeting needs of the highest order of priority. This becomes obvious, if the question is asked:

what would happen should the nature of the war make it desirable
and possible to have, say, a million fewer men and women in the
armed forces of Britain? There can be no doubt that the whole of
that million would be absorbed in employment outside the Armed
Forces, in increasing the supply of arms and in meeting other
needs. The demand for man-power in total war is unsatiated, and
insatiable.

149. War affords, in fact, the decisive argument against the popular view that the number of jobs to be done in the world is limited,
so that each man can get a job only at the cost of displacing another
man. Though the men and women of the Forces often describe their
service pay as the alternative to the unemployment "dole," their
numbers are far greater than the numbers taken off the dole.
The total number of persons aged 14–64 in paid service or employment in the Armed Forces, Civil Defence or industry at the
middle of 1943 was 22.8 millions. This represents 4½ millions more
than the corresponding number in 1939: the absorption of 1½
million unemployed and the addition of another 3 million persons.
The division of the 22.8 millions between industry and national
service is not made public in Britain, but there is little doubt that
the former by themselves show a net increase; though the numbers
of persons in insured employment are no longer published, from
the insurance contributions to the Unemployed Fund and in other
ways they can be estimated roughly and shown to be greater than
in peace.[1] For the United States more facts are public and detailed
figures can be given. The following table taken from a publication
of the Committee for Economic Development and based on official
material compares 1940 with the estimated position at the end
of 1943.

	1940 (,000 omitted)	Dec. 1943 (,000 omitted)
Total Civilians with Jobs	46,000	52,200
Unemployed	9,000	1,000
Civilian Labour Force	55,000	53,200
Armed Forces	600	10,800
Available Man-power	55,600	64,000

[1] An article on the "Sources of Man-Power in the British War Sector," by M.
Kalecki (*Bulletin of Institute of Statistics*, Oxford, vol. 5, no. 1), puts the total
increase in the volume of insured employment from 1938 to 1941 at 1½ millions
of "1938 workers," of which 1 million represents longer working hours and
½ million a nett increase in the number of workers.

As against 8 million persons taken out of unemployment, the civilians with jobs have increased by 6,200,000 while the Armed Forces have been increased by 10,200,000, or altogether 16,400,000. These figures are the best practical demonstration that the number of jobs is not fixed, but can be expanded whenever the Government has sufficient desire to do so.

150. The only assumption which gives any plausibility to the objection examined here, is the assumption that human needs in peace have a definite limit. This is not so; the needs are there, but they are not clothed with purchasing power to make them into effective demand. It is obvious that the purely material needs of humanity are very far from being satisfied in any country of the world.[1] If and when technical progress and economic organization make it possible to satisfy all the material desires of men, the needs of peace will still remain without limit, for the needs of rational men include leisure. The repeated experience of the abolition of unemployment in war is relevant to peace. A brief analysis of what the State does and does not do in bringing about this result, is a natural step in the argument of this Report.

ECONOMIC ANALYSIS OF WAR

151. What does the State in war do that has a bearing on the problem of full employment? The answer can be given under eight heads.

First, the State substitutes its own schedule of needs and priorities in production for those of the private citizen, as interpreted by the profit-seeking undertaker, and it clothes those needs with purchasing power so as to make them into effective demand.

Second, the State secures removal of many or most qualitative restrictions on the use of man-power.

Third, the State in war does not give security to anyone in his particular job, and in fact brings about changes of employment on a vast scale.

Fourth, the State, desiring to expand its own expenditure immensely, diminishes that of the citizen by heavy taxes and by borrowing.

Fifth the State re-inforces this greatly expanded taxation and borrowing as means of transferring expenditure to itself, by rationing and other direct restrictions on consumption.

Sixth, the State replaces or re-inforces the economic motive in the allocation of labour and other productive resources by compulsory powers of conscription, direction and requisition.

[1] See note on Consumers' Needs on p. 122.

Seventh, the State controls prices of all essential articles and it controls wages to the extent at least of making arbitration compulsory and prohibiting stoppages of work through industrial disputes.

Eighth, though the State does not in Britain socialize any large proportion of production, even for the purpose of meeting its own demands, it does by taxation and price-control cut down the gains of private capital, in order to justify the demands for maximum output and abandonment of privileges which it makes upon wage-earners.

152. In this brief summary of war economics, there are some features which spring from war conditions and are foreign to peace; there are some features which spring partly from war conditions and partly from full employment as such; and there are some features directly pointing the way to full employment in peace as in war. These three sets of features will be considered in order.

153. The features foreign to peace include all the personal compulsions, the rationing, the appeals for personal saving, the astronomic increase of public debt and the extreme weight of taxation, that is to say, the measures named under the fourth and fifth heads of paragraph 151. All those measures spring from the nature of the objective in war, and from its scale and urgency. The State's schedule of needs consists largely of means of destruction—of fighting men and their arms—to be used against the enemy and those needs are indefinite in amount. The high priority given to those needs of the State involves extreme shortage of the means of satisfying the needs of private citizens, and makes necessary the various devices of rationing, heavy taxation and appeals for saving. These arise from shortage, not from full employment, and need not be reproduced in peace. Private consumption in Britain is estimated officially to have been reduced by 21 per cent from 1938 to 1943,[1] though total industrial production has increased greatly. The problem of peace is to increase both production and private consumption.

154. The features foreign to peace include also the compulsory powers of direction of labour and requisition of property, which bulk so largely in war, that is to say most of the sixth head in paragraph 151. These powers of directing labour are not wanted in peace; the power of requisitioning property is wanted but to a much smaller extent. The State in war determines the direction of practically all expenditure; as little as possible is left to the citizen except the meeting of his essential needs. The economy of war is wholly planned, with the profit-motive still used as an incentive

[1] White Paper on *War Finance* (1944, Cmd. 6520), p. 8.

but not as a guide to the allocation of resources. This allocation is made by decree of the State and is not in accord with the natural desires of peaceful men, who left to themselves desire neither to bomb or be bombed and prefer butter to guns. In a democracy at peace, even if the economy were planned, most of the spending would still be done by consumers meeting their needs from personal incomes according to their individual views; the allocation of resources would be in accord with the natural desires of the citizens, as interpreted by the planners. The interpretation might be mistaken in detail, but would not be wholly out of relation to human desires. The compulsions of war arise not from full employment but from distortion of war, from the need at all costs and without delay to make human beings do and suffer inhuman things. They are foreign to peace. The Policy of Full Employment set out in this Report dispenses wholly with direction to work, under the powers conferred by Parliament on the Government in June 1940 and with the Essential Work Order of 1941 as a means of holding men to their jobs by threats of fine or imprisonment. Whether or not conscription for military service continued in peace would depend, not on the policy in regard to full employment, but on the policy in regard to war and preparation for war. It would continue if at all, only because war is not in accord with natural human desires, and is a distortion of them.

155. The features springing partly from the nature of war and partly from full employment as such include arbitration on wages, control of prices and profits and other methods for securing output and co-operation from the wage-earners, that is to say the measures named in the seventh and eighth heads of paragraph 151. When the urgency of war is over, it is hard to believe that any need will remain for legal prohibition of strikes or lock-outs, or that such a prohibition would be accepted by public opinion, but collective bargaining about wages may need to be conducted with a wider outlook and by revised procedure. The position about control of prices and profits is similar; the conditions which necessitate almost universal control of prices in war will not continue, but there will be special reasons for price control in special cases. Most of the wartime control of prices is made necessary by acute shortage of supply in relation to demand; it is required to prevent sellers from exploiting a scarcity and to ensure that what goods are available are distributed fairly and not simply by the power of the purse. When the war is over, except in its immediate aftermath, before industry gets re-established and while gaps left by war are being made good,

this general reason for controlling prices will not apply. But other reasons are likely to lead to continuance of a large measure of price control in particular fields. One reason is the desirability of stabilizing the prices of necessaries, including food, shelter and fuel, in order to make possible a reasonably uniform wage policy under conditions of full employment. Another reason lies in the desirability of preventing the creation of artificial scarcities and undue raising of prices by monopolies and rings; it should not be possible for a strong demand for the products of industry to be met by raising prices, profits and wages to producers, rather than by increasing supply to consumers. Yet a third reason lies in the desirability of regulating the marketing, production and prices of primary commodities, whether agricultural or mineral; this may be an important contribution towards stabilizing the demand for manufacturing products. The last of the features of war economy named above is the taking of special measures to secure the co-operation of wage-earners and their maximum output free from all restrictions. Fear of dismissal and the motive that this may afford to effort are weakened by full employment in peace as in war, and in peace the patriotic motive which efficiently takes their place in war, is no longer available. How can discipline and workers' co-operation generally be ensured under full employment? All the three issues raised here—determination of wages, control of prices and industrial discipline—are discussed among the internal implications of full employment in Part V of the Report.

156. The main direct lessons from war to peace are those under the first two heads of paragraph 151: the setting up of a common objective of needs to be met and seeing that whatever money is required is in fact spent in meeting these needs up to the limit of the man-power available, and the removal of qualitative restrictions on the use of man-power. The third head also is relevant. War does not give every man security in his particular job. Full employment in peace need not give every man a freehold for life in a particular job and should not aim at doing so. The development of these points must be reserved for Part IV, in setting out the means to full employment. But something further can appropriately be said here in explanation of the economics of war, under the first, second and third heads of paragraph 151.

157. As regards the first head, the experience of war confirms decisively two theses of the economists; that employment depends on outlay and that outlay by the State which controls money is a very different affair from outlay by private citizens. The first thesis, in its general form, is no more than a truism, which becomes

interesting only when we proceed to examine the implications and sources of different kinds of outlay, on consumption and on investment, by the State and by private citizens. The significance of war in relation to employment is that the scope of State outlay is increased immensely and indefinitely and that the State formally and openly gives up any attempt to balance its budget or limit its outlay by considerations of money. The scale of wartime budgets is determined, not by considerations of finance, but by manpower. The State places orders for fighting men and their arms not up to the limit of what it believes that it can afford in money, but up to the limit of what men can be made available to fight and make arms, by squeezing the outlay of private citizens to the irreducible minimum, by contracting manpower in all occupations other than fighting and making munitions. The national budget in war becomes, in a phrase used by Mr. Ernest Bevin, a "human budget." The second thesis, as to the fundamental difference between State outlay, and private outlay, may appear to some a paradox, but is nearer to a truism. There is no financial limit to spending by the State within its own borders, as there is a financial limit, set by their resources and their credit, to spending by private citizens. This does not mean that the methods of war finance are unimportant; the choice of methods between taxation and borrowing, or between different methods of taxation may affect profoundly the distribution of income between different citizens and may thus affect both their capacity and their willingness to render service, alike in war and in the following peace. But, whatever the methods, the money for outlay up to the limits set by manpower can always be found by the State in war and is found in practice.

158. As regards the second head in paragraph 151, the effect of war in removing qualitative restrictions on the use of manpower is obvious. No one is allowed to refuse to be a sailor, soldier, or airman, on the ground that he has been brought up to some other trade or that he will be paid less than in his previous occupation. No union of existing sailors, soldiers or airmen is allowed to object to a recruit on the ground that he has not been apprenticed to that occupation. For fighting services the removal of qualitative restriction on use of manpower is absolute. It is not as complete or as automatic but is very general in regard to industrial employment, and is accepted in principle by all concerned. Discussion turns on the details and the conditions. Without this change of occupations, substantial unemployment would continue in war, in spite of an immense unsatisfied demand for manpower.

159. This leads naturally to the subject of the third head in paragraph 151. In principle men must be ready at need to change their jobs in peace as in war. Service means doing what is wanted, not pleasing oneself. In practice there need be nothing in peace corresponding to the transformation scenes of war. The immense scale on which occupations have to be changed in passing from peace to war, is due to the character of the war objective and its abnormal needs. The extent to which workpeople have to be transferred from one locality to another and change their residences is also due to war conditions; factories and munition contracts have to be located mainly with regard to security from attack and not with regard to the places in which labour is available. The passage from war to peace involves a corresponding transformation backwards. That is demobilization which, as is stated elsewhere, falls outside the scope of this Report. Once this transformation is accomplished, the rate of change in the direction of industry can and should be altogether less. Men will be able in general to follow their chosen occupations, if they desire to do so, throughout their working lives, as most of them did, subject to occasional unemployment, before the first World War. Control over the location of industry can remove all need for wholesale transfers of population and ruin of established communities. The adjustment of the labour force in particular industries to changes of demand can and should be made with less pain than in the past by influencing the flow of adaptable youth.[1]

160. Though in Britain and the United States unemployment has been abolished only in war, a similar result has been obtained elsewhere in conditions short of actual war; in Nazi Germany in preparing for war, and in Soviet Russia, in carrying through a planned industrial revolution which included as one element considerable preparation for war. In Nazi Germany between 1932 and 1939 eight million additional workers were absorbed into industry[2]; the scheme of compulsory unemployment insurance introduced after the first World War was abolished, though a scheme of assistance subject to a means test was continued. In Soviet Russia "no benefit has been provided for unemployment since 1930, on the ground that there is no unemployment."[3] In each of these two countries, with fundamental differences of spirit and final aim, there has been the common element of a centrally planned economy directed to a common objective and with finance subordinated to

[1] See para. 230, in Part IV.
[2] See *The New Economy*, p. 30, by Robert Boothby (Secker & Warburg, 1943).
[3] *Report on Social Insurance and Allied Services*, Appendix F, p. 292.

that objective. In each case, the objective involved some distortion of ordinary human desires. The rulers of Nazi Germany preferred guns to butter and used any necessary compulsion to force this unnatural preference on their subjects. The leaders of Soviet Russia, aiming at rapid industrialization of an agricultural country combined with collectivization of agriculture itself, used whatever powers were necessary to secure these objectives, against the natural opposition of individuals. In each of these cases, therefore, more direct compulsion was required than would be necessary or would be accepted easily by the British or American democracies at peace, though less than is accepted without question by all peoples in total war.

SPECTACULAR ACHIEVEMENTS OF WAR PLANNING

161. The achievements of the planned war economy are spectacular. The output of Britain in terms of 1938 prices rose from £4,360 millions in 1938 to £5,700 in 1942, that is to say by 31 per cent. or nearly a third.[1] The output of the United States in terms of 1939 prices rose from $88·6 billions in 1939 to $133·2 billions in 1942, that is to say by 50 per cent.[2] While these calculations for the two countries are not absolutely on the same basis, it is natural that the rate of increase should be greater in the United States. In each country hours of work have been lengthened, additional labour not normally seeking employment has been drawn into industry, technical advance has been accelerated, mass production has become the rule, and the hearty co-operation of the workpeople has been secured by their common interest in victory. The United States has had the advantage of not being under direct attack or the threat of it, and of escaping bomb damage, the blackout and the need to disperse factories for reasons of security. It has had the advantage, from the point of view of war, of starting with more unemployment —nearly 10,000,000 or 18 per cent of the labour force in 1938, nearly 9,000,000 or 16½ per cent in 1939, as compared with Britain's 1¾ millions or 12½ per cent in 1938.[3] With these and other advan-

---

[1] The 1943 White Paper on National Income and Expenditure, by N. Kaldor, in *Economic Journal*, June–September, 1943, p. 269.

[2] *Survey of Current Business*, March 1943, p. 11. The April 1944 *Survey* shows a further rise in 1943, to 155·3 billions of 1939 dollars.

[3] The figures for the United States are those given by the National Industrial Conference Board in *The Economic Almanac for 1942–3*, p. 155. It is likely that under some of the other heads already named as common to the United States and Britain the former country in normal times carries a larger reserve of power— a larger total agricultural population with a larger proportion of peasant subsistence farming and a shorter average working week.

tages, the United States in 1942 has been able to obtain both guns and butter, an immense output of arms and Armed Forces combined with an increase of something like 13 per cent in civilian consumption.[1] The differences between the United States and Britain in war are interesting. They are less important than the similarity in dramatic change from peace to war in both countries. Under the unplanned market economy of peace a substantial part of the productive resources of each country more often than not stood idle; in the last decade before the war the average loss of potential output through this cause was an eighth or more. Under the planned economy of war output has leapt forward by 30 to 50 per cent in three or four years.

162. The achievement of war is not merely a matter of material production. War brings about also a psychological revolution— a change of popular attitude to the problem of unemployment. This result of full employment in war is put simply and cogently by Mrs. Wootton. "No more black looks at the married woman, the old age pensioner or the refugee because they are 'flooding the labour market' and so 'taking the bread out of people's mouths.' No more defence of luxury and waste and antiquated methods because they make work. The woman no longer steals the man's job; she releases him for the war effort. All the old phobias based on the theory that one man's work is another man's unemployment are buried."[2] But, as Mrs. Wootton points out, the phobias are not dead. The change of popular opinion is for war not for peace. The economic problem is that of doing deliberately in peace that which we are forced to do in war—of creating a community in which men and women have value. The psychological and political problem is that of persuading the people that this can be done. They need no persuading that it ought to be done.

[1] Table 2 on p. 14 of the *Survey of Current Business* for March 1943, gives the total of consumer expenditures for goods and services in terms of 1939 dollars as $61·7 billions in 1939, $70·0 billions in 1941, and $69·7 billions in 1942, with many interesting comments. As the figures show, the increase of consumption took place, therefore, almost wholly before the United States was actually at war, and 1942 merely, or nearly, held the 1941 position. "The flow of goods to consumers was maintained, to some extent, out of previously accumulated inventories." The April 1944 *Survey* shows a further rise of consumption in 1943 to nearly 15 per cent above that of 1939, at 1939 prices. "Billions" here are American billions, that is 1,000 millions.

[2] *Full Employment*, by Barbara Wootton (Fabian Publications, Research Series, No. 74). The passage quoted is at p. 3. The pamphlet as a whole is an excellent brief summary of employment problems and policy, in popular language.

163. It is not necessary or desirable to attempt in peace to drive the economic machine at the pace of war. The target set in war is made deliberately too high; to stave off defeat, all that is possible must be done and more than is possible must be attempted. Hours of work are lengthened; leisure destroyed; education curtailed; the pace of work accelerated. Peace should bring back leisure and the power of using leisure. It should not bring back the misery and waste of mass unemployment. The target set for peace should be lower than that of war, related to our capacities, and not to our dangers. The target set for peace will also be different in character, in accord with the natural healthy desires of mankind, not a distortion of them to serve blind ambition and lunatic hate or to defend us against these evils. But if full employment is to be attained, the target for peace must be such as to set up effective demand for the products of labour constantly exceeding the supply. In war men and women become an asset, not a liability, because the urgency of the needs of war is effectively recognized by the people and by the Government. The bringing about of the same condition in peace depends upon a recognition of the needs of peace, which is equally effective in guiding the policy of governments. Thus and thus alone will it be possible to ensure to the people the first condition of happiness—the opportunity of useful service.

Note on Consumers' Needs

The study of *America's Capacity to Consume* published by the Brookings Institution at Washington in 1934 yields, as its most important conclusion, the statement that: "The unfulfilled consumptive desires of the American people are large enough to absorb a productive output many times that achieved in the peak year 1929. . . . The trouble is clearly not lack of desire but lack of purchasing power" (p. 127). This conclusion rests on statistical evidence of how, at each successive higher income level, the expenditures of families and individuals increase "for food, shelter and clothing, as well as for the comforts and conveniences of life." While the companion study of *America's Capacity to Produce*, published at the same time by the Brookings Institution, suggested that, even in the peak year 1929, the American productive system as a whole was operating at about 80 per cent of capacity," even full operation could not have met all the desires of consumers. "The United States has not reached a stage in which it is possible to produce more than the American people would like to consume." If this can be said of the United States, it can be said with even more emphasis about the rest of the world.

Part IV

A FULL EMPLOYMENT POLICY
FOR PEACE

Section 1. THE MEANING AND THREE CONDITIONS OF FULL EMPLOYMENT

164. In the unplanned market economy of Britain between the two wars a substantial proportion of the productive resources of the country stood idle or ran to waste. In terms of man-power this waste is measured by the 14 per cent average of unemployment throughout that period. If we could change the percentage of the normal labour force in employment from 86, as it was between the wars, to the figure of 97 that is suggested below, we should without further change add about an eighth to our production each year, and could be richer by that amount in all material goods. In war we have done this and more, have changed the 86 to more than 99, have improved in many ways the efficiency of those at work and have drawn into work many outside the normal labour force. We shall not need or desire, when peace returns, to retain all this greater production that is achieved in war, to some extent at the cost of leisure, of home life and of training for the young; we shall not want to work so unremittingly and sacrifice the ends of life to its means. But we shall need and should determine to keep the gain which comes through exchanging enforced mass idleness for full employment. If we do so, we shall end a misery of those who in unemployment are branded as useless and shall unlock a new store of wealth for all. Experience has shown that there is no need for productive resources to run to waste, if there is determination to use them for an object that is sufficiently desired by the whole community. Economic research has led to general agreement as to how this waste occurs and as to the direction in which the remedy is to be found.

165. The survey of facts and theories in Part II has shown unemployment arising in peace in three ways: through chronic or recurrent deficiency of total demand for the products of industry; through misdirection of demand; through failure to organize the labour market, involving both insufficient and excessive movement of men in search of employment. The attack on unemployment must be an an attack from three sides, aiming at the maintenance of adequate demand at all times, at the right direction of demand, and at the organization of the labour market. The first of these three is the main attack; if it does not succeed, if we cannot achieve and maintain adequate total demand for the products of industry, mass unemployment returns with certainty. Demand for the products of

industry means spending, the laying out of money to get such products made; adequacy of total demand means that total outlay is sufficient. The first condition of success in the attack on unemployment is adequate total outlay at all times. The attacks on the two other lines are subsidiary but independent, necessary to make victory complete. The misdirection of demand which can be most serious as a factor in causing unemployment is local misdirection; the stream of labour flows more readily and with less breaking of the social structure from one occupation to another than from one place to another; the second condition of success in the attack on unemployment, accordingly, is controlled location of industry. Insufficient or ill-guided movement of labour which, when demand for labour is weak, appears relatively less important as a cause of unemployment, becomes steadily more important as demand becomes stronger; the third condition of success in the attack on unemployment is the controlled mobility of labour, brought about by organization of the labour market and by other measures described below.

166. All three attacks must be made and must succeed, if unemployment is to be replaced by full employment. That is the common objective of all three attacks. In Part I this objective of full employment has been defined as meaning that there are always more vacant jobs than men seeking jobs—as meaning further, that the jobs are of a kind and so located that unemployment is reduced to short intervals of standing by, with the certainty that very soon one will be wanted either in one's old job again or in a new job that is within one's powers. This definition assumes that, even under full employment, there will be some unemployment, that on each day some men able and willing to work will not be working, as there is some unemployment even in Britain at war to-day. The definition assumes that, however great the unsatisfied demand for labour, there is an irreducible minimum of unemployment, a margin in the labour force required to make change and movement possible.

167. The need for such a margin is clear. If at any time every man and woman available for work was working, no undertaking, whether in public or private hands, could expand its labour force to meet growing needs, except by finding another undertaking which at the same moment was ready to release a workman who was qualified for the work and either was living in the right place or was able and willing to move to it. This argument is illustrated sometimes by analogies of the obstacles to change and movement that would be presented, if at any time there were absolutely no vacant houses in the country or, again, if in any town there were

no vacant rooms in hotels. The first of these conditions would mean that no man could move from his house, unless simultaneously he could find another person wishing to give up an exactly suitable house; all change of residence would become a matter of individually arranged exchanges. The second of these conditions would make travel whether on business or pleasure intolerably difficult and inconvenient, as it does in war. It is necessary that at any moment there should be a margin of empty houses, and of unoccupied rooms in hotels; in peace time there always is such a margin; at every census, however short the supply of houses may seem to be, an appreciable percentage of all the houses are empty. The rent paid for houses while they are occupied and the money paid for the occupation of hotel rooms have to be sufficient to cover the period of standing in reserve. Unemployment insurance, at its introduction, was defended as a means of providing for inevitable unemployment, by seeing that it was paid for. The need for some margin in the labour force can be shown also from another angle—that of the freedom of the worker. Employment for everybody literally all the time would mean either that there was never a change of employment and therefore no progress or that, when a job ended, everyone on it was directed forthwith to another job, whether it suited him or not; 100 per cent of employment at all times assumes the compulsory direction of labour. A margin of unemployment is not simply a business convenience; it is an incident of a free progressive society. But in order that it shall mean no hardship, two conditions must be fulfilled. First, as stated, there must by insurance be adequate maintenance as of right while standing by. Second, and more important, the demand for man-power must be such that no one ever expects to stand by for long or has any need to do so. There must always be jobs waiting to be filled. That is the test of full employment, and it means that the margin of unemployment is very small.

168. Full employment does not mean that there is absolutely no unemployment. Some margin for change and movement is needed. Is it possible to give any numerical estimate of the size of that margin? What is the irreducible minimum of unemployment in a community with adequate effective demand for labour and a fully organized labour market? It is sometimes suggested that the measure of this minimum unemployment can be found by looking at the rate of unemployment reached at the top of the cyclical fluctuation in 1937 in the prosperous parts of Britain, such as London and the South-East, and by excluding further from it such unemployment

as can be attributed mainly to personal disadvantages. For five months from June to October, 1937, the unemployment rate in London was 6·0 or a little less. Of those unemployed in June, one-sixth had been unemployed for six months or more. It is not unreasonable to assume that most persons who for more than six months were unable to obtain any kind of employment in London, in the middle of 1937, had some personal disabilities of physique, age or character, predisposing them to unemployment. By this calculation a figure of about 5 per cent is sometimes reached, as the minimum reserve of labour.[1]

169. Calculations of this character approach the matter from the wrong end. The best that could be done in the way of reducing unemployment in 1937, with deficient demand, locally misdirected demand and a disorganized labour market, is not the best that can be done by a full employment policy, and does not represent the irreducible margin of labour required to be standing by at every moment to make change possible. The right approach to the problem is along another line, by considering what factors in employment will remain beyond the control of the British community, and then allowing for those factors. The first of these factors is the British climate, involving seasonal unemployment. The actual amount of seasonal unemployment before the present war was estimated at about 2 per cent by Mr. Christopher Saunders,[2] rather more in bad years and less in good years. The same study showed that there was much seasonal unemployment—the motor industry was a conspicuous illustration of this—for which there was neither justification nor need. With proper organization and under conditions of full employment there should be no difficulty in reducing seasonal unemployment to one-half its former figure, that is to say to 1 per cent. The second factor for which allowance must be made is the margin for change of employment incidental to progress. If a quarter of the whole labour force fell out of work each year and remained out of work for an average of two weeks each, or if one-eighth of

[1] For the United States a similar or higher figure is often given. The *Report of the Technical Committee of the National Resources Planning Board on Security Work and Relief Policies* (p. 132) names an unemployment rate of 5 to 8 per cent of the available labour supply as the irreducible minimum indicated by experts, and cites the agreed finding in 1939 of "a group of some of America's best known economists and leaders in industry, agriculture, finance and politics, . . . that a condition of full employment might be considered to have arrived when 3 million persons were still unemployed."

[2] *Seasonal Variations in Employment*, by Christopher Saunders (Longmans, Green & Co., 1936).

them fell out of work each year and remained out of work for an average of 4 weeks each, that would mean another 1 per cent of unemployment. With full demand for labour and an organized labour market, it is hard to see why there should be more change of employment than this or a longer average passage from one job to the next. With seasonal unemployment at 1 per cent it would make up 2 per cent of unemployment altogether. If Britain were a closed economic system, it would be reasonable to take as an objective the reduction of unemployment to 2 per cent; in war it has proved possible to cut the unemployed margin down to $\frac{1}{2}$ per cent or less. But Britain cannot be a closed economic system, must have international trade, and cannot exclude the possibility of fluctuations in overseas demand. This problem is discussed in Part VI of the Report, where it is argued that, after everything possible has been done in concert with other countries to stabilize international trade and to develop trade primarily with countries having full employment policies, further measures will be required and can be taken in Britain to compensate for fluctuation of overseas demand by counter-fluctuation of demand at home. This, however, may involve a change of jobs for the men concerned, or at least for some of them. There will be some industrial friction making complete compensation impossible. For this it is reasonable to allow say another 1 per cent of unemployment each year on an average of all years together; this additional unemployment should be regarded as the price paid for the advantages of international trade.[1] In the light of these considerations 3 per cent appears as a conservative, rather than an unduly hopeful, aim to set for the average unemployment rate of the future under conditions of full employment. In numbers it means about 550,000 persons.[2] This margin would consist of a shifting body of short-term unemployed who could be maintained without hardship by unemployment insurance.

[1] Assuming that exports represent one quarter of our production (see para. 310) and that after they have been stabilized so far as possible, sufficient fluctuation remains to produce an average of 8 per cent of loss of employment in this quarter over good years and bad, this means 2 per cent over the whole body of workmen, requiring compensation by expansion of home demand. To allow 1 per cent of actual unemployment assumes that industrial friction is strong enough to keep half the men displaced from exports idle, in spite of home demand.

[2] The number of persons who as employees would be insured against unemployment in Class I of the Plan for Social Security in my Report on Social Insurance is given as 18·4 millions for the year 1939, in Table XVI of the Report, and as 18·1 millions for the year 1944, in the Government Actuary's Report (para. 47). This includes a substantial body of persons with practically no risk either of seasonal or of interval unemployment.

170. Three per cent of unemployment means 97 per cent of employment. If that were achieved, by how much would the material output of the community be increased? Ninety-seven per cent in employment, as compared with the 86 per cent which was the average between the wars, means raising the numbers in employment by about one-eighth. Would production rise in proportion or more or less than in proportion? There are some factors that would make production rise less than in proportion to the numbers employed; those unemployed at any time include a larger proportion of the less efficient or less steady workers than those in employment. There are other considerations which suggest that a full employment policy might increase production more than in proportion to the recorded increase of employment. In spite of the completeness of the provision made by unemployment insurance in Britain to-day, the record of unemployment does not include all the waste of labour that arises in depressions. There is disguised unemployment through short-time or lost time that does not lead to an application for unemployment benefit; through men slowing down their rate of work for fear of unemployment; through employers for a variety of motives keeping men though there is no full work for them. War has shown the possibility of increasing production more than in relation to the increase of the labour force and of the man-hours worked. Exact estimates of how much production could be increased by a policy of full employment are impossible, but it is probably fair to set the factors making for a more than proportionate increase against those making for a less than proportionate increase and to assume for the purpose of general argument, that an increase of one-eighth in employment resulting from vigorous demand for labour would lead to a roughly proportionate increase in production. In terms of output just before this war, this would have meant adding something like £500 millions a year at pre-war prices to the value of the national product. The calculations on which this figure rests are set out in Appendix C.

171. The achieving of full employment would, without any other change, add largely to our material wealth. But that is the least of the changes that it would make. It would add far more to happiness than to wealth, and would add most of all to national unity, by removing the misery that generates hate. Changing profoundly the conditions under which men live, it would affect the working of many social institutions and raise new problems, some of which are discussed in Part V among the internal implications of full employment. Three points are so important that they should be

made at once, to forestall possible objections to full employment itself.

172. The first point is that a policy designed to secure always more vacant jobs than unemployed men, does not exclude the keeping of an adequate reserve for the emergencies of war. Quite apart from the shifting force of short-term unemployed, incidental to change and necessary to make change easy, the supply of labour power can be increased or diminished by changes of working hours. To say this is not to assume that, whatever the length of the working week, production can be increased by making the week longer. This is not so. The experience of this war has reinforced the lesson of the first World War that adding to the hours of work may mean loss of production, and is likely to mean this, in proportion as the increase of hours is continued over many months or years. But it is probably fair to say that the hour which was taken off the working day of most workpeople in Britain at the end of the first World War represented an emergency reserve of power for the second World War that could be used to fill a gap at least temporarily, whether or not it was profitable to continue the longer working week indefinitely. It may be assumed that technical advance will sooner or later make possible a further reduction of the working week after this war. If some of the benefits of technical advance are taken in this way, rather than in increased material consumption, that will constitute a reserve of power for war emergencies, though it may be hoped that civilized communities will find a better reason than desire to be ready for another war for choosing this use of their technical progress. Finally, as the war has shown, there are many people not dependent on employment and not normally in the labour market, such as pensioners and married women, who can be drawn into employment at need. It may be necessary to use emergency powers of direction to get such people to work, but if that is necessary, the war emergency itself will justify the use of such powers to public opinion. Full employment at normal hours for all who are normally available for work is consistent with carrying an adequate reserve for variation in the total demand and for the emergencies of war.

173. The second point is that having more jobs than men unemployed does not mean giving to everyone security in his particular job. In some occupations there may be special reasons for giving exceptional security of tenure. But this does not apply to all occupations. Full employment does not turn all men into Civil Servants or University Professors or Judges of the High Court. It does not mean that no one will ever lose his job or have to change his job:

it means only that there will be another job to which a man who loses one job can go. Full employment does not mean the end of change, competition, initiative and risks. It means only fresh opportunity always. In order to avoid in advance a possible misunderstanding, it should be added that preservation of the possibility of change of work does not imply that all or most men would be required to make such changes continually. This point is dealt with more fully in paragraphs 236-7.

174. The third point is that setting any particular rate of employment, whether 97 or some other figure, as the goal of a full employment policy does not tie the policy rigidly to that figure, or mean that the whole policy has failed because that precise figure is not attained. Some may think 97 per cent of employment is an impossibly high figure, while others may regard acquiescence in always having half a million unemployed as a confession of failure. Acceptance by the State of responsibility for maintaining employment means, as is explained below, that the State, by influencing outlay, ensures that the economic system proceeds instead of stagnating. It does not of itself settle the pace at which the system shall proceed, and people with different outlooks may take different views on this, some favouring a lower and some a higher level of demand. The difference between the definition of full employment in the Nuffield College Statement, of slightly fewer vacant jobs than unemployed men, and that adopted here, of more vacant jobs than unemployed men, is important from the social point of view. It affects the relation of the individual and his environment and his sense of value to the community. It does not affect materially the nature of the machinery required to maintain employment. But it is necessary to name some percentage of employment, as the standard aimed at for full employment and as the criterion by which the working of the machinery may be judged. On the view of human values underlying this Report, that percentage should be as high as it can reasonably be made, not as low as will stave off revolution.

Section 2. THE FIRST CONDITION: ADEQUATE TOTAL OUTLAY

MEANING OF OUTLAY

175. Employment depends on outlay, defined as the laying out of money as demand for the products of current industry. Outlay

so defined does not include the use of money to buy property already in existence (land, houses, etc.), or rights to property (stocks and shares), or financial instruments (bonds, bills and notes). Industry in this definition is used in the widest sense, covering extraction, manufacture, construction, agriculture, distribution, finance and personal services—that is to say all forms of human activity designed to satisfy human needs. If we want full employment of our man-power in place of the under-employment of the past, we must by one means or another ensure more outlay.

176. "Outlay" means "spending," but is used here in preference to "spending" for two reasons. First, laying out money on getting a house built may appear to the person who lays out the money not as "spending," but as saving by way of investment. Second, "outlay" suggests design, as distinct from mere getting rid of money. Employment is not wanted irrespective of what it produces in goods and services. In the course of the argument it will become increasingly clear that the objective is not simply outlay but wise outlay.

177. Outlay now falls into three main classes, according to the purpose to which it is directed:

> Outlay on marketable goods and services of direct demand, i.e. marketable goods and services desired for their own sake and not merely as means to producing other goods and services (consumption outlay).
>
> Outlay on means of producing marketable goods and services of direct demand (business investment).
>
> Outlay on non-marketable goods and services, and the means of producing them, including defence, order, public health, free education, roads, drains, and other public works (communal outlay).

The first of these classes includes all goods and services which are desired for their own sake and have to be paid for; that is to say, it includes things of varying degrees of durability, such as motor cars, furniture, clothing, food, tobacco, newspapers, entertainments, personal services and railway journeys. The common feature of all these things is that they have to find a market, by free decisions of private citizens spending their own money, whether this money is derived from past or present income or is borrowed on the expecta-tion of future income. Rent for housing accommodation is consump-tion outlay, though the actual building of houses is investment.

The second of these classes includes all goods and services which are desired, not for their own sake, but as the means of producing directly or ultimately other goods and services. This class, like the first, includes goods of every degree of durability, from railways, ships and factories to raw materials of all kinds and services like transport of goods or accountancy. The building of dwelling-houses is also treated as investment, the house being regarded as a means of providing its inhabitants with the service of accommodation. The term "business investment," used for this class, is narrower than the term "investment," which applies also to outlay on durable goods of the third class, such as roads or drains. As is explained in paragraph 178 "business investment" may be either private or public.

The distinguishing feature of the third class is that the goods and services to whose production it leads do not have to find a market; their use does not depend on private citizens deciding to spend their own money. Outlay in this class is necessarily public, and no question arises of sufficient consumers' purchasing power. As is explained in the next paragraph, outlay in the other classes may in the first instance be undertaken either by private citizens or by the State, but in each case continuance of outlay depends on consumers being able and willing to lay out money of their own.

178. Each of the first two classes may be sub-divided with reference not to the purpose of outlay but to the part played by the State or other public authority. The first class, of consumption outlay, includes, on the one hand, outlay in which the State does not intervene in any way, leaving private sellers and buyers to make their contracts at market prices, and on the other hand "joint outlay" in which the State and the private citizen are both concerned, that is to say where the State buys in the first instance, with a view to re-selling later at a price which may or may not be lowered by subsidy. So, too, the second class may be sub-divided, according as it involves or does not involve the participation of a public authority. For the term "business investment" as used here does not imply that the outlay is undertaken by private enterprise working for profit. It means merely that the goods or services produced as a result of the investment have to find a market through the free spending of private citizens. A State railway and a privately owned railway both represent business investment. So does an electricity or power plant, whether publicly or privately owned. So does a house, whether built by private enterprise or by a local authority. Business investment accordingly has both a private sector which may be described as a "private business investment" and a public sector which may be described as "public business investment." These sub-divisions of

the first two classes are of great practical importance in framing a policy of full employment. In making them, the term "State" is used to cover all public authorities, whether central or local and whether departmental or organized as public service corporations; the expenditure of local authorities can be influenced by the State far more directly than can the expenditure of private citizens. This language does not pre-judge the question of the distribution of the executive functions between the Central Government and the local authorities.

179. The third class of outlay—on non-marketable goods and services—is necessarily public. For the practical purpose accordingly of considering responsibility for outlay to maintain employment, outlay, through sub-division of the first two classes, falls under five heads, which may be described as: private consumption outlay; joint consumption outlay; business investment—private sector; business investment—public sector; and communal outlay. Obviously, there are some things which may be the subject of outlay under more than one of these heads. Coal, for instance, is both a consumption good and an investment good. Some things again may be transferred from one head to another by a development of social policy, as the service of education has been largely transferred from the first head, of private consumption outlay, to the last, of communal outlay; medical service of all kinds would similarly be transferred, if the proposals of my Report on Social Insurance and of the Government White Paper on the National Health Service were carried out and there was no charge on treatment of any kind at home or in hospital.

STATE RESPONSIBILITY FOR TOTAL OF OUTLAY

180. Employment depends on outlay. Full employment cannot be attained unless outlay in total is sufficient to set up a demand for the whole of the labour that is available for employment. Where should the responsibility be placed for ensuring adequate total outlay? In view of the facts already set out, the answer is not in doubt. Outlay may be private outlay, by citizens spending their own money or credit in the ways that please them, or public outlay, by the State or other public authorities spending money which they obtain by taxation or borrowing or make available to themselves in other ways. During war a large part of the total outlay is undertaken directly by the State. During peace the bulk of the outlay can, and in a free society will, continue to be private. But the ulti-

mate responsibility for seeing that outlay as a whole, taking public and private outlay together, is sufficient to set up a demand for all the labour seeking employment, must be taken by the State, because no other authority or person has the requisite powers. No private enterprise can survey the whole field of industry or ensure at all times a demand for all that industry can produce at a price covering its costs. No private enterprise can make finance its servant rather than its master. The outlay of every person or authority other than the State is limited rigidly by the financial resources of that person or authority. The central proposition of this Report is that the responsibility of ensuring at all times outlay sufficient in total to employ all the available man-power in Britain should formally be placed by the people of Britain upon the State. That first and foremost is what is meant by adopting a national policy of full employment.

A NEW TYPE OF BUDGET

181. The instrument by which the State has influenced outlay in the past has been the annual Budget presented, usually about April of each year, by the Chancellor of the Exchequer. This Budget has determined directly the scale of public outlay undertaken by the Central Government; it has to a very large extent determined the outlay of local authorities; by the taxation proposed it has influenced both the extent and the direction of outlay by private citizens. It is through the same instrument of public outlay and of taxation that the State in future must pursue its new objective of adequate total outlay. Adoption of a national policy of full employment means a revolution in national finance—a new type of Budget introduced by a Minister who, whether or not he continues to be called Chancellor of the Exchequer, is a Minister of National Finance. The most convenient title for him and his relations to other parts of the machinery of Government and business will be considered later. The type of Budget required for full employment is new in comparison with the Budgets of peace-time: it is not altogether new if compared with what happens in war. The Chancellor of the Exchequer now presents annually to Parliament a Treasury White Paper on the Sources of War Finance, which sets out, not merely the revenue and expenditure of Government, but the estimated income and outlay of the nation as a whole. In introducing the latest Budget in April, 1944, the Chancellor of the Exchequer expressly used the occasion for a review of the economic

and financial position generally and not for a review limited to the activities of the Government. The figures given in the annual Treasury White Paper provide the basis for fiscal policy in war-time. The same type of statistical information—extended and refined—is a pre-condition for a policy designed to achieve steady full employment in peace; in the field of budgetary policy, as in other fields, experience gained in war should be used in peace.

182. What is the essence of this new budgetary policy? It is that the Budget is made with reference to available man-power, not to money; that it becomes, in Mr. Bevin's phrase, a "human budget." Man-power is a datum; it cannot be altered by State action; to take anything else as a datum and to try to fit use of man-power to it is to risk mass unemployment or mass fatigue. It follows that the Minister of National Finance has to take each year one cardinal decision: after estimating how much, assuming full employment and under the taxation which he proposes, private citizens may be expected to lay out that year on consumption and private investment, he must propose for that year public outlay sufficient, with this estimated private outlay, to employ the whole man-power of the country, that is to say sufficient to make the assumption of full employment come true. This cardinal decision involves a break with the two main principles which have governed the State Budgets of the past; first, that State expenditure should be kept down to the minimum necessary to meet inescapable needs; second, that State income and expenditure should balance each year. Each of these principles was a by-product of the assumption of full employment made by the classical theory of economics. So long as it is believed that there are economic forces which automatically ensure adequate effective demand for all the productive resources available, the State cannot prudently set out to use any of these resources for its own purposes without depriving private citizens of their use. But once the possibility of deficient private demand is admitted, the State, if it aims at full employment, must be prepared at need to spend more than it takes away from the citizens by taxation, in order to use the labour and other productive resources which would otherwise be wasted in unemployment.

183. The main elements that will enter into the formulation of the new Budget are six, which may be designated as: private consumption outlay (C); private investment outlay at home (I); the balance of payments abroad (B)[1]; the revenue account—that is to say, proposed public outlay covered by taxes or other public revenue (R);

[1] See Explanation of Terms in Appendix D.

the loan account—that is to say, proposed public outlay covered by loans (L); and the output capacity of the community, that is to say the estimated value of its output when all its man-power is fully employed (M). The term public outlay is used here and elsewhere as covering expenditure by all public authorities, whether central or local. In line with the definition given in paragraph 175, it covers all expenditure incurred for the purchase of goods and services that are being produced currently; it excludes payments made for the purchase of existing assets or for the repurchase of Government bonds or bills. It excludes also payments made out of public funds on account of pensions, unemployment insurance, the interest on the national debt, and other transfer payments.[1] The term taxation is used to cover all methods of transferring purchasing power from the private citizens to public authorities, including not only taxes and rates in their normal meaning, but social insurance contributions and other compulsory charges, though, in so far as taxation in any of these forms is required to provide transfer payments and not for outlay on goods and services, it does not appear in the table of outlay given in paragraph 186 below. The term taxation excludes funds obtained by the State through the sale of existing assets or of Government bonds or bills. The balance of payments abroad B is the difference between exports and imports, both visible and invisible. If the exports exceed imports the balance is positive, representing a net outlay giving employment in Britain. If imports exceed exports, as in Table 18 below for 1938, the balance is negative—a net dis-investment abroad, the meeting of needs without outlay giving current employment in Britain. The first five of the elements named, namely, C, I, B, R, L, together make up the total outlay O on which the level of employment depends. Full employment is reached when O is equal to the datum M.

184. The Minister of Finance will begin his Budget statement by making an estimate of private consumption outlay C—that is to say of the amount which private citizens, having regard to the taxation which he proposes, may be expected to spend on goods and services for immediate enjoyment under conditions of full employment; he will make a similar estimate of private investment outlay I, based upon information collected through the National Investment Board (see paragraphs 240-1). Both these estimates will be net, that is to say will exclude sums transferred to the State from private citizens by indirect taxes. He will then, from a review of economic conditions in the world as a whole or that part of it which is important for British

[1] See Explanation of Terms in Appendix D.

international trade, and having regard to the economic policy which
he is pursuing, estimate whether Britain is likely to have a positive or
a negative balance of payments abroad and how great a balance.
Adding to these three estimates the public expenditure which can
be incurred from the existing revenue, he will have a total of
C + I + B + R for comparison with the output capacity M. If
C + I + B + R by themselves exceed M there will be an inflationary gap and a tendency to rising prices; the private citizens and the
public authorities will be attempting between them to use more
than the total productive resources. If C + I + B + R together
add up to less than M, and there is no expenditure from loans, there
will be a deflationary gap and unemployment.

185. These are the fundamental calculations that must be made.
There is no reasonable doubt that they can be made with sufficient
accuracy, for sufficient accuracy does not mean mathematical
exactitude with no error at all, and with no power of adjusting
procedure to experience. Calculations of this character are being
made to-day in war. They can be developed and improved in peace.
The important thing is the basic design—the taking of output
capacity at full employment of our man-power as datum, taking M
and nothing else. If this calculation is made for the year 1938,
what actually happened in that year is shown opposite in the
left-hand side of Table 18. What might have happened under different forms of full employment policy, all following the basic design
of taking M as datum, is shown in the three columns on the right
of the Table. The sources and construction of the Table are described
in the Memorandum by Mr. N. Kaldor on the "Quantitative Aspects
of the Full Employment Problem in Britain", which forms Appendix C of this Report.

186. The left-hand side of Table 18 contains two elements marked
L and U calling for further explanation. In 1938 the process of
re-armament had already begun and brought about a substantial
public outlay—by central and local authorities—out of loans; this
outlay, as shown above, amounted to £75 millions. But for this,
unemployment, which at the end of 1937 had begun to rise steeply,
would have been substantially greater in 1938 than the 12·9 per
cent actually recorded in Great Britain and Northern Ireland. With
this recorded unemployment, the percentage of the labour force in
employment was 87·1 per cent. The figure for unused resources U
is got by assuming that in full employment the percentage employed
would have been 97; it is estimated, in the manner described in
Appendix C (paragraph C14) that this would have increased the

otal national output in 1938 by £500 millions. Adding this £500 millions, as resources unused through lack of employment, to the net national income of £4,675 millions, a total of £5,175 millions is reached for output under full employment, that is to say for output capacity M.

Table 18

ACTUAL AND FULL EMPLOYMENT OUTLAY IN 1938

(*£ Million*)

	Actual Outlay at 1938 Level of Employment	Outlay at Full Employment attained by:		
		Route I (Public Outlay)	Route II (Orthodox Finance)	Route III (Remission of Taxation)
Private Consumption Outlay (C) ..	3,510	3,755	3,135	4,045
Net Private Home Investment Outlay (I)	420	460	460	460
Balance of Payments Abroad (B) ..	− 55	− 130	− 130	− 130
Public Outlay on Goods and Services from Revenue (R)	725	860	1,710	460
Public Outlay on Goods and Services from Loans (L)	75	230	0	340
Unused Resources (U)	500	0	0	0
Output Capacity (M)	5,175	5,175	5,175	5,175
Total Public Outlay on Goods and Services	800	1,090	1,710	800
Increase on Actual Public Outlay ..	—	290	910	0

187. This figure of output capacity, though reached here by a calculation from actual income and unemployment, is in reality the datum. All the other six elements, including U, add up mathematically to M. From this it is obvious that, but for the £75 millions of public outlay from loans, the unused resources U would have been materially greater; owing to the multiplier effect,[1] the addition to U would have been £125 millions, that is to say, U would have been £625 millions, with the unemployment rate about 16.0 in place of 12.9, as it was in fact. It is obvious also that if, either by an increase of exports or by a reduction of imports, B had been made zero in place of being negative, while home outlay of all kinds was maintained without change, U would have been reduced: additional resources would have been used and employment given either in making the additional exports or in replacing the

[1] See Explanation of Terms in Appendix D.

missing imports. But, as is argued in Part VI, measures taken by
a particular country to improve its balance of payments, in the
absence of other measures aimed at expansion of employment
necessarily create unfavourable repercussions abroad, reducing
employment in other countries as they increase it at home. The
effect at home might be nullified if such measures led to retaliation
by other countries.

188. The five elements C, I, B, R, L together make up the total
outlay O. These five elements together, with U, add up mathematically to M. The problem of full employment is that of making
the five elements together, without U, add up to M; that is to say
it is the problem of equating O to M, so that U is nought. How
could this have been done in 1938? Obviously, it is a problem which
can be attacked in a number of different ways. One can set out to
make B zero or positive or to increase C, I, R, L, or any two or
more of them. But, though theoretically full employment can be
achieved in a number of different ways, the practical methods open
to the State of making sure that it is achieved are limited by two
considerations: first, that the State can influence some of the elements
much more directly than others; second, that all the elements are
connected, though in different ways, so that a change of one induces
changes of different orders of magnitude, and sometimes of different
direction, in the other elements.

189. On C and I in a free community the State can only act
indirectly. Private outlay on consumption C will rise when incomes
rise; it rises as a result of higher incomes, and cannot easily be made
the cause of rising incomes. Private outlay on investment I may be
stimulated by an invention; normally it rises only as a result of
rising consumption or of the expectation of a rise in consumption;
it too cannot easily be made a cause of rising incomes, except by
direct interference with the decisions of business men. Private outlay
on consumption and on investment, in other words, is determined
by the existing level of private incomes; it cannot easily be raised
by persuasion; people spend as much as—in view of their incomes
and the general state of trade—they consider it necessary or reasonable to spend. They will spend more when their incomes rise; but
their incomes will rise only if somebody spends more. Thus there
is a vicious circle—a deadlock. Sometimes expectations of an
improvement in the general state of trade are strong enough to
increase their rate of spending—but they evidently were not strong
enough in the year under consideration to give adequate outlay for
full employment.

190. On R and L, public outlay out of revenue and out of loans, which together make up the total outlay of the State and of other public authorities, the State can act directly, but must always take account of the effect on other elements. If the State spends more, from whatever source, it to that extent increases employment, wages and profits, which in turn raises private consumption outlay C, and by securing a higher degree of use of equipment stimulates private investment outlay I. Since, at the given rates of taxation, any increase in private earnings and consumption outlay raises the yield of taxes, the State's revenue from taxation rises as a result of its expenditure; from the calculations made in Appendix C, it may be estimated that at the tax rates ruling in 1938, out of every £100 increase of national income through State expenditure about £27 would have returned to the State as additional revenue, while £49 would have gone to consumption outlay and £24 to savings. These are the results of raising public outlay. If, however, to meet this additional outlay, the State simultaneously increases the rates of taxation, it reduces the spending power of private citizens and by consequence reduces C or I or almost certainly both; the precise effect on C and I depends on the nature as well as on the amount of the additional taxation. The calculations in Appendix C suggest that, at full employment levels, a proportionate change of all tax rates increasing (or decreasing) revenue by £100 millions would in the decade before this war have decreased (or increased) consumption by £73 millions and savings by £27 millions; a similar change confined to direct taxation would have decreased (or increased) consumption by £60 millions and savings by £40 millions; a similar change confined to indirect taxation including social insurance contributions would have decreased (or increased) consumption by £84.5 millions and savings by £15.5 millions. The effect of tax changes on investment is much harder to estimate; it cannot be estimated at all without specifying the length of time for which full employment is supposed to have been in operation. The special feature of L is that, as it does not increase immediate taxation, it need have no depressing effect on C and I, to counter the stimulating effect of additional public outlay. Finally, since a proportion of any increased spending in Britain, whether public or private, is certain to be directed to imported goods, an increase of national income through public outlay tends to raise imports without at the same time stimulating exports, so that, unless steps are taken to prevent this, it affects adversely the balance of payments B; in Britain, in the decade just before this war, out of every £100 of additional

spending, £15 would have been spent on imports and £85 on good and services at home.

ALTERNATIVE ROUTES TO FULL EMPLOYMENT

191. It is in the light of these and other inter-relations and reaction that any policy for full employment must be designed. As is clea from the number and variety of the elements of the problem, ther is more than one solution. Full employment is a peak up which from below one can see many alternative routes of varying degrees o difficulty. The right-hand side of Table 18 illustrates three possibl routes; it shows how the various elements in the problem woul have been affected had the State in 1938 set out to ensure ful employment by one or other of three methods of increasing the total outlay. The basis of the calculations is explained in Appendi: C, which illustrates also a number of other possible solutions a variants of the three main routes presented in Table 18. These thre main routes are as follows:

Route I. Increase of public outlay, leaving rates of taxatio unchanged.

Route II. Increase of public outlay, with all-round increas of taxation sufficient to balance public income and expenditure

Route III. All-round reduction of rates of taxation, leaving public outlay unchanged.

In all three cases, as presented in the table, it is assumed tha import and export policy are left unchanged. In all three cases als the estimate for private investment I is put at the same figure o £460 millions, as compared with £420 millions actually spent There are exceptional difficulties in estimating the effect of differen policies on this element. All that is certain is that it would have bee materially higher under any form of full employment policy in 193% than it was in fact. Route I may be called the route of public outlay Route II the route of orthodox finance, and Route III the route o remission of taxation. Each of these routes will be examined in turn

192. The column headed Route I shows that full employmen could have been obtained in 1938 by the State increasing publi outlay in total by £290 millions, while taking no action in regarc to any other element. This would have added to the deficit to bı met on loan account not £290 millions, but only £155 millions making L £230 millions in place of the actual £75 millions; thı automatic increase of private earnings and consumption unde

ull employment, without any change of tax rates, would have added £135 millions to tax revenue, and would have reduced by that sum the additional borrowing needed. On the assumption made of unchanged import and export policy, an increase of £500 millions in national income would have increased imports by £75 millions and might have raised the adverse balance of payments B from −£55 millions to −£130 millions. These assumptions (see paragraph C25) make the situation appear unduly unfavourable, for they make no allowance for the fact that 1938 was an exceptionally bad year for British exports or for the effect of additional British imports under full employment in increasing incomes abroad and almost certainly increasing demand for British exports. The figure of −£130 millions for the balance of payments in full employment in 1938 is to be regarded as a maximum rather than as probable. But an adverse balance anywhere approaching this obviously could not have been allowed to continue. It would have been possible and justifiable to prevent it by a limitation of imports, if exports could not be developed. This would have had the effect of reducing still more the addition to the State's deficit under L. Leaving this international problem on one side for the moment, Route I shows that, by increasing public outlay while making no other change, the State in 1938 could have obtained full employment, bringing £500 millions of unused resources into use, at the final cost of increasing its internal indebtedness by £155 millions. Undoubtedly in the circumstances of 1938 this would have been the simplest route to full employment. It cannot seriously be suggested that there were not in 1938 national purposes—even other than earlier rearmament—on which £290 millions with wise advance planning could have been spent to great advantage.

193. Route I, however, was not the only possible route to full employment in 1938. Route II shows what would have happened if the State had set out to cure unemployment on the principles of orthodox finance, by increasing its outlay, but at the same time increasing taxation all round so as to balance income and expenditure, making U and L both zero. As in Route I, import and export policy is assumed unchanged, so that the adverse balance of payments rises as in Route I to −£130 millions. Route II, through the adverse effect of taxation on consumption, involves a reduction of private consumption outlay from £3,510 millions to £3,135 millions; to compensate for this as well as to bring unused resources into employment, this route requires, as will be seen, a startling increase of total public outlay from £800 millions to £1,710 millions, that is

to say by £910 millions, or 114 per cent. It involves also an all round increase of tax rates, direct and indirect, of 66 per cent.

194. These figures illustrate the method of orthodox finance in its simplest form. They assume that the State decides to spend as much as is necessary to secure full employment and to cover its expenditure by raising rates of taxation evenly all round, without altering the form of taxation or the distribution of the total burden between direct and indirect taxation. It is unlikely that the State would in fact adopt this simple procedure: its aim would be to raise the additional tax revenue with the smallest possible discouragement of private outlay; this would involve increasing direct rather than indirect taxation. In Table 46 in Appendix C there is shown an alternative route, described as IIa, on the assumption that indirect taxation was left untouched and the additional revenue was obtained by raising direct taxes only. This alternative IIa, because it reduces private outlay less than does Route II, involves a smaller addition to public outlay. But the addition to public outlay is still large, £635 millions or 79 per cent of the actual outlay in 1938, while the increase of direct taxation is revolutionary; Route IIa would have meant raising the income tax in peace from 5s. 6d. to 10s. 8d. in the £. Full employment in 1938 by the route of orthodox finance, in either of the forms examined here, Route II or Route IIa, was a theoretical rather than a practical or political possibility. It involved something like a doubling of State activity as measured by spending and a revolutionary rise of taxation. Route II provides a striking illustration of one of the paradoxes of public finance. Private citizens desiring to avoid debt keep their expenditure down. The State, in pursuing a full employment policy by public outlay, has to put its expenditure up much more if it wishes to avoid debt than if it is prepared to borrow.

195. Route III presents an alternative of a different character. Suppose the State in 1938 had set out, by remitting taxation, to stimulate private outlay to the point of full employment, while keeping public outlay unchanged and meeting its loss of tax revenue by additional borrowing. On the assumptions stated in Appendix C, an all-round reduction of 31 per cent in the rates of taxation in 1938, by the stimulus given to private consumption, would have raised total outlay to a point sufficient for full employment without increasing public outlay at all; the tax revenue would be reduced not by 31 per cent but by about 23 per cent. in view of the larger yields of taxation under full employment. The resulting deficit under L is a good deal greater than in Route I: £340 millions as

compared with £230 millions of Route I, and with the deficit of £75 millions which was actually incurred, while leaving unused resources of £500 millions. But, to minds inured to war finance, a deficit even of £340 millions can hardly be described as staggering, and even that deficit is more than would be needed, if taxation was suitably adjusted. Table 18 presents the method of remission of taxation in its simplest form, assuming no change in the basis of taxation. In practice it is even less likely than in the parallel case of Route II that the State would adopt this simple procedure. If the aim is to stimulate private outlay by remitting taxation, remission should, so far as possible, be confined to taxation which falls on consumption rather than on savings; it should take the form of reducing indirect rather than direct taxation. In Table 46 in Appendix C, there is shown accordingly an alternative route, described as III*a*, on the assumption that direct taxation was maintained at the levels of 1938, and indirect taxation was reduced so far as proved necessary to bring about full employment by expanding private outlay. The reduction of indirect tax rates required for this purpose is about 50 per cent. The deficit required to be incurred by the State in maintaining its previous outlay without change is £55 millions less for Route III*a* than for Route III, and is £55 millions more than for Route I.

196. All three routes, as shown in Table 18, are worked out on the assumption that the Government adopts a purely passive attitude in regard to the balance of payments abroad, allowing a normal proportion of the increased income available to the citizens under full employment to be directed overseas, without making any attempt either to increase exports or to restrict imports. With the value of exports actually obtained in 1938, this might have meant that the adverse balance of payments would have risen from the actual figure of £55 millions to £130 millions, under conditions of full employment. An adverse balance of this scale might have been tolerable for one or two years; it would not have been desirable or even possible to submit to such a balance indefinitely. To eliminate it, measures would have had to be taken either to increase exports or, if that proved impossible, to reduce imports by restricting purchases from abroad to essential commodities for which no substitute could be found in home production. In Table 47 alternatives to each of the routes in Table 18 are shown as I*b*, II*b*, and III*b*, on the assumption that it proved possible to reduce the negative balance of payments abroad to zero, either by an expansion of exports while maintaining production for the home market, or by

a restriction of imports accompanied by equivalent increase of production at home. The practical difficulties of bringing about such a change in our balance of payments in any short time by either of these methods, are obvious and considerable, but may easily be exaggerated; they should be regarded as difficulties rather than as impossibilities. But the general lesson of these alternative routes in Table 47 is independent of the ease or difficulty of pursuing them. The general lesson is that, by achieving a balance between her exports and her imports, Britain in 1938 would have gone a long way, though by no means all the way, to full employment. The international implications of setting out to achieve full employment on these lines are discussed in Part VI; the general conclusion is that, for Britain or any other country, to balance payments abroad, as part of a full employment policy of expansion, is right and free from objection, but to make development of exports or restriction of imports into the main plank of a full employment policy, is liable to produce such unfavourable reactions in other countries as to make it a plan to be avoided; it may well appear as a policy of economic aggression. The internal implication of these alternative routes is that Britain with her output capacity of 1938 would not have found it easy to do, at one and the same time, all the things that were undoubtedly desirable for her: that is to say, she would not have found it easy simultaneously to balance her payments abroad, in place of living on overseas capital; to consume as freely as before; and to destroy the social evils of Want, Disease, Squalor, Ignorance, and malnutrition. The standard of living in Britain before this war was high, but it was by no means equal to the needs or desires of the people, and it was being maintained in 1938 in part by living on the savings overseas that had been made by earlier generations. If we are to meet all our needs, we must raise our output, by re-equipping industry so as to make it more efficient, while maintaining the health and strength of the working population, so as to make them more efficient.

THE NEW RULES OF NATIONAL FINANCE AND THE CHOICE OF ROUTES

197. The actual figures of 1938, whether as shown in Table 18 or for any of the alternative Routes in Appendix C, are not directly relevant to the post-war situation; the form which the policy for full employment should take, at any particular time, must be related to the circumstances of the time. The policy need not be the same for different countries or for the same country at different times.

But the main lesson of the variety of routes in Table 18 is relevant to all times and places. After the Government has accepted the principle of budgeting for full employment, that is to say, of budgeting to the datum of man-power, it still has to decide many further questions; as between mainly planned and unplanned outlay for maintenance of employment; as to the extent to which it shall rely upon making public outlay itself, and upon influencing private outlay; as to the division of outlay between consumption and investment; and finally as to the extent to which the means of outlay whether private or public, shall be provided by taxation and by borrowing respectively. On what grounds are these and other practical decisions to be made? In other words, what new rules of national finance should replace the old rules of public finance, named and discarded above, of reducing State expenditure to a minimum and of balancing the Budget each year? The answer lies in laying down three rules of national finance, in order of importance. The first rule is that total outlay at all times must be sufficient for full employment. This is a categorical imperative taking precedence over all other rules, and over-riding them if they are in conflict with it. The second rule is that, subject to this over-riding categorical imperative, outlay should be directed by regard to social priorities. The third rule is that subject both to the first and second rule, it is better to provide the means for outlay by taxing than by borrowing.

198. The first rule is absolute. It is better to employ people on digging holes and filling them up again, than not to employ them at all; those who are taken into useless employment will, by what they earn and spend, give useful employment to others. It is better to employ people, however the money for paying their wages is obtained, than not to employ them at all; enforced idleness is a waste of real resources and a waste of lives, which can never be made good, and which cannot be defended on any financial ground. The second rule is hardly less important. The object of all human activity is not employment but welfare, to raise the material standard of living and make opportunities for wider spiritual life. For these purposes the wise direction of outlay and so of employment, in the general interest of the community, is only less important than adequacy of outlay as a whole. The third rule is of an altogether minor order of importance. The State in matters of finance is in a different position from any private citizen or association of private citizens; it is able to control money in place of being controlled by it. Many of the mistakes of the past have arisen through failure to make this fundamental distinction. Spending in excess of current income and

borrowing have altogether different implications for the State than for private citizens. These implications of deficit spending by the State are discussed by Mr. Kaldor in Appendix C. The discussion shows that most of the objections that have been made in the past to borrowing by the State are fallacies. An internal national debt increases the incomes of some citizens by just as much as the taxation necessary to pay interest and sinking fund on the debt decreases the incomes of other citizens; it does not and cannot reduce the total wealth of the community. Nor, having regard to the actual scale of expenditure that will be needed to maintain full employment, is there any reasonable ground for fearing that national debt incurred for this purpose in peace will ever rise to a point making it necessary to raise fresh taxes. The most striking of Mr. Kaldor's conclusions is that, taking into account prospective changes in population, in productivity, and in working hours, as well as foreseeable changes of Government expenditure on pensions, education, etc., and assuming an average rate of interest of 2 per cent, the National Debt could be expanded at the rate of not less than £775 millions a year from 1948 (taken as the beginning of the reconstruction period) to 1970, without involving on that account any increase of tax rates to meet the additional charge for interest.[1] This is a rate of borrowing far in excess of anything that would be needed to sustain full employment in peace time. A policy of continuous borrowing, on a more reasonable scale adequate for all possible requirements, is consistent with a steady reduction of the burden of the debt on the taxpayer. To submit to unemployment or slums or want, to let children go hungry and the sick untended, for fear of increasing the internal national debt, is to lose all sense of relative values.

199. Nevertheless, there are good reasons for meeting State outlay, as far as is practicable, from current revenue raised by taxation, rather than by borrowing. The main reason is the objection to increasing the numbers and wealth of rentiers, that is to say of people with legal claims against the community entitling them to live at the cost of the community of the day without working, although they are of an age and capacity to work. This reason is irrespective of the purposes for which the money is borrowed; it is a ground both for keeping taxation as high as it can be kept without stifling desirable enterprise and for making the rate of interest con-

---

[1] See para. C58. The rate of interest and the burden on the taxpayer could be made still smaller by the methods described in Section 4 of Appendix B setting out a Policy of Cheap Money.

tinually lower, till in the phrase of J. M. Keynes the "euthanasia of the rentier"[1] is accomplished. A policy of cheap money should be regarded as an integral part of any plan for full employment. A subsidiary reason is that borrowing to meet State expenditure, in place of meeting it from current revenue, enables the Government of the day to avoid the unpopular task of taxing and the loss of votes from this unpopularity. In other words it increases the opportunities of general political bribery. For these two reasons, orthodox finance, so long as it does not conflict with either the first or the second of the new rules of national finance, has much to commend it.

200. But rigidly orthodox finance, in the sense of an annually balanced budget, involves, in the political and economic conditions of Britain, an impracticable route to full employment. Nor is there any need to struggle with the difficulties of such a route. A large proportion of the public outlay most needed in the near future will result in the production of durable goods—houses and their labour-saving equipment, hospitals and clinics, schools for scholars of all ages, means of transport. Few people will expect that all these should be paid for out of current revenue; they represent capital rather than current expenditure and are the natural subject of borrowing. The real problem is to decide what should be the proper relation between the tax revenue and the current expenditure of the State. And the first step in making that decision rightly is to approach the problem, not from the angle of public finance, but from the angle of social policy. Taxation in future should be looked on as a means of reducing private expenditure on consumption and thereby freeing real resources for other uses. There may be situations when the State should raise considerably more money in taxation than is needed to cover its current expenditure, not, however, for the traditional reason of reducing the national debt, but for the economic reason of securing real resources for purposes of high social priority. There may be other situations when there are no investment or other projects of high social priority, and when taxes should be reduced, so as to allow more of the national resources to be devoted to purposes of current private consumption. Decision as to the extent to which tax revenue should exceed or fall short of the current expenditure of the State depends upon the circumstances of the time. At all times, however, it should be based, not on considerations of finance and budgetary equilibrium, but on weighing of priorities, that is to say on social and economic policy.

[1] *General Theory*, p. 376.

201. This means that the decision as to how money required for public outlay should be raised depends really on decision as to how money can be spent to best advantage, by public authorities and by private citizens together. On this there arise two related issues; we have to decide between outlay which is mainly or wholly planned and outlay which is wholly or mainly unplanned, being left to the decisions of individual citizens; we have to decide (or divide) between consumption outlay, producing goods and services for immediate enjoyment, and investment outlay, producing physical equipment which will yield goods and services for enjoyment over a period of time. On each of these issues the decision has to be reached, not on general principles, but on facts of time and place, that is to say, on the circumstances of the country in which the issue arises at the time when it arises.

202. As regards the first issue, between planned and unplanned outlay, so long as there are definite common objectives which, when stated, commend themselves to the good sense of the community, planned outlay is to be preferred to unplanned outlay. So long as there are things as to which most people agree that they ought to be done, it is better to decide and to plan to do them than to take the chance that they may get done without planning. That is what happens in war; everyone is agreed as to the need of waging war successfully and the whole effort of the community gets planned to that end. The view underlying this Report is that for the country and period for which this Report is designed—Britain immediately after the transition from war to peace—there are common objectives calling for planning, as decisively as war calls for planning to-day. This period is envisaged here as a reconstruction period—twenty years or more or less—following the transition period—perhaps two or three years—that it may take to pass from war to peace after total war ends. In that reconstruction period, there are certain things which must be done. We have to bring about an even balance of our payments abroad, because we cannot live indefinitely on the savings of former generations. We have to destroy the giant evils of Want, Disease, Squalor and Ignorance, which are a scandal and a danger. We have to raise our output per head by improving our mechanical equipment, because that is the only way to the steadily rising standard of life, material and spiritual, which we desire. These are common objectives which, when stated, command general assent; all of them involve planned rather than unplanned outlay. Acceptance of these objectives leads to rejection of Route III of Table 18, with its variant Route IIIa in Table 46, in spite of their

obvious attractions. The ground for this rejection of Route III and its variants is not that they involve a constant deficit and a rising national debt. To obtain full employment that way would be better than submitting to unemployment. The first rule of national finance always overrides the third rule; any route up the peak of full employment is better than sitting in idleness and misery at its foot. The ground for rejecting Route III is that it is not the only route to full employment and is not the best route. The argument on this point is set out from another angle in paragraphs 257–62 below, in examining expansion of private consumption outlay as a means to full employment, alternative to the proposals of this Report. Briefly, private consumption outlay, even if it were high enough to set up a demand sufficient in total to absorb all the productive resources of the country, might fail in practice to absorb them because it would be directed without regard to the available labour and the need for stabilizing investment; it might be directed to purposes of low social utility; it could not secure many vital purposes which can be attained only by common action. Route III, in spite of high demand, might not cure unemployment, would do little or nothing to increase efficiency, and would leave giant social evils entrenched.

203. As regards the second issue, between consumption outlay and investment outlay, the decision is even more dependent on the special circumstances of the time. Nor can it by the nature of things be an absolute decision for one thing rather than the other. We do not want more consumption outlay only or more investment outlay only; we want some of each. We have to divide rather than to decide, and having to divide, that is to say make a quantitative decision, we must be guided by quantitative considerations. What is best to do depends in the last resort on statistical estimates of our output and our needs of various kinds. In making these estimates we have to look forward into the uncertainties of the future. The figures of Table 18, relating to 1938, have no necessary relation to the figures after the War, because the position then will be different in many ways. The productivity of our resources will almost certainly be greater. Public expenditure will be greater for social services of all kinds and, for some time at least, for purposes of defence and external order. Owing to the loss of a large part of Britain's foreign investment and of her shipping the problem of the balance of payments will be more acute. Finally, the national debt and the annual interest on the debt will be higher; though, as a transfer payment, this does not enter into Table 18, it affects the possibility of meeting public expenditure out of revenue, that is to say the division between

revenue account R and loan account L. We cannot decide upon a policy for the future without making a picture of the conditions to which policy must be adjusted.

A POST-WAR PICTURE

204. So far as it is possible to look forward into this uncertain future now and to make numerical estimates of these prospective changes, this is done in the third section of Appendix C by Mr. Kaldor, setting out the prospective national income under conditions of full employment and giving the outlines of a possible Budget, as for the year 1948. The assumption underlying the choice of this date is that total war ends for Britain some time in 1945, and in accord with the experience of the last war, is followed by a period of transition and of automatically sustained demand for two years or so to the end of 1947. This is the transition period of two or three years; 1948 is taken as the first year of the reconstruction period. The other assumptions made by Mr. Kaldor are stated and justified in detail in his memorandum. It is worth while to name some of them here, to illustrate the nature of the problem. They include the following :—

(a) That the working population and the average hours of work per week will be the same as in 1938. This assumes that half a million out of about 2½ million women not previously occupied for gain who have been drawn into industry and the Forces in the course of the war remain in industry.

(b) That average real productivity per man-hour will have risen over the period 1938–1948 by 13 per cent. This is materially below the rate at which productivity increased between 1924 and 1938 and the indications are that technical advance has been accelerated since 1938. 13 per cent represents, therefore, a conservative estimate of the rise of productivity.

(c) That the Armed Forces of the Crown will be maintained at double the strength of 1938. To some this may appear an under-estimate, but it should be remembered that in 1938 re-armament had already begun; defence expenditure in that year amounted to £380 millions as compared with about £120 millions in the preceding years. It is assumed by Mr. Kaldor that the Japanese as well as the German

War will have ended before 1948, so that there will be no hostilities anywhere.

(d) That money income from foreign investment will have fallen to 40 per cent of its 1938 amount.

(e) That the average level of prices will be 33⅓ per cent above that of 1938. Hitherto, post-war plans, such as those for Social Security in my earlier Report, have been made on the assumption of a 25 per cent increase in prices. But in view of what was said by the Chancellor of the Exchequer in his last Budget speech, and of the estimates in the latest White Paper on War Finance, this percentage is almost certainly too low. A figure of 33⅓ per cent has been assumed as better suited to present trends.

(f) That the Plan for Social Security in my Report on Social Insurance and Allied Services will have been adopted in full by the Government, with all money benefits revised upwards to allow for prices 33⅓ per cent in place of 25 per cent above 1938 level.

205. On these and other assumptions set out in his memorandum, Mr. Kaldor estimates the value of the total national output, that is to say the net national income at 1948 prices, at £7,450 millions under conditions of full employment. He puts the necessary current expenditure of the Central Government in 1948 at £1,655; this allows for interest on the national debt as it will have been swollen by the War; for the heavier expenditure on defence; for the full cost of Social Security (including the National Health Service) at the enhanced rate of benefit made necessary by the greater rise of prices; and for the cost of the new education proposals. Mr. Kaldor then proceeds to estimate how much would be yielded in 1948 by taxation at the 1938 rates and reaches a total of £1,560 millions, only £95 millions or 6 per cent less than the necessary current expenditure of the Government. Under conditions of full employment in 1948 the Government would be able to meet the whole of its necessary current expenditure, including all the new charges for debt, defence, social security, national health, and education, by taxation at rates only 6 per cent above those of 1938, that is to say, by making income-tax 5/10 instead of 5/6 in the pound, and putting up all other 1938 tax rates in the same proportion. If all tax rates were put not 6 per cent, but 18 per cent above the levels of 1938, making income-tax 6/6 in the pound, there would be a margin of nearly £200 millions, to provide for additional expenditure or to

cover error in the assumptions. With full employment, the budgetary problem ceases to be serious. All the current expenditure of the State can be met by taxation, leaving capital expenditure to be met by borrowing.

206. Full employment and the other assumptions made in Appendix C affect in a number of ways the special problem of Social Security finance. On the one hand, in allowing for cost of living 33⅓ per cent in place of 25 per cent above the level of 1938, it is assumed that the rates of benefit are raised to correspond; unless this is done, Want cannot be abolished. This increases in money terms the cost of the scheme; the increase on this account is applied in Mr. Kaldor's calculations not only to the insurance cash benefits but to children's allowances, the National Health Service and the cost of administration. On the other hand, the assumption of full employment, that is to say an average unemployment rate of 3, in place of the 8½ allowed by the Government Actuary in estimating the cost of my Plan for Social Security, materially reduces the annual cost of the scheme and, by increasing the average number of weeks of contribution each year, reduces still further the weekly contribution required from insured persons and their employers. The combined effect of these changes is that, under full employment, cash benefits and allowances adjusted to the assumed cost of living, and so about 7 per cent higher in money terms than those proposed by me, can be given in return for contributions 16 per cent lower. That is to say, in spite of higher prices, equal security against Want can be provided for a joint contribution from employer and employee of 6s. 4d. for an adult man, in place of the 7s. 6d. proposed in my earlier Report, and of 5s. for an adult woman in place of 6s. Alternatively, better benefits can be given for the same contribution.

207. There remains, as the main problem to which the post-war analysis leads, the question of how the total outlay can be divided to best advantage between consumption and investment. The issues involved in this are illustrated by Table 19 opposite, setting out the possible full employment outlay in 1948, at 1948 and 1938 prices and comparing the latter with the actual figures of 1938. The last figure of the table shows that in real terms the national outlay (which is also the net national income) would on Mr. Kaldor's assumptions be 20 per cent higher in 1948 than the outlay actually achieved in 1938, £5,600 million at 1938 prices against £4,675 millions. This increase is large enough to make it possible simultaneously to raise consumption in real terms by 19 per cent above 1938 (in contrast to the 21 per cent reduction experienced in war), to

Table 19

POSSIBLE FULL EMPLOYMENT OUTLAY IN 1948, AND ACTUAL OUTLAY IN 1938

(*£ million*)

	Full Employment Outlay 1948		Actual Outlay 1938	Column 2 as Percentage of Column 3
	1948 Prices (1)	1938 Prices (2)	(3)	(4)
Private Consumption Outlay ..	5,550	4,170	3,510	119
Public Consumption Outlay on Goods and Services*	1,135	855	760	112
Net Investment Outlay (Private and Public)	765	575	460	125
Balance of Payments	0	0	— 55	
Unused Resources	0	0	(500)	
Net National Output	7,450	5,600	4,675	120

* This is not of course the whole of the current public expenditure, since it does not include transfer payments, such as interest on national debt, social security cash benefits and allowances, and subsidies. The total expenditure of public authorities in 1948 is given in Table 55 of Appendix C as £2,275 millions, and the relation of this sum to the £1,135 millions shown above is explained in the note to Table 59. It should be added that the £800 millions of public outlay in 1938 shown in Table 18 includes £40 millions, capital expenditure on new roads, etc., which in Table 19 are included in net investment outlay, making it £460 millions, and thus leaving £760 millions for public consumption outlay on goods and services.

raise home investment in real terms by 25 per cent, and to produce enough exports to pay for our imports and reduce the balance of payments to zero. This distribution of our additional resources between consumption and investment is that which might be expected to result from the various assumptions made in Appendix C if the State raises by taxation just enough to cover its current expenditure as estimated. Whether or not it is the best distribution is a question of social policy. The main doubt is as to whether enough has been provided for investment, that is to say for improving the physical environment and the mechanical equipment of industry, so as to raise efficiency and the standard of living in the future. At the end of his section on the full employment problem after the war, Mr. Kaldor argues that it might be better social policy to increase investment in the reconstruction period more than is shown in Table 19, at the cost of having slightly lower consumption, to be brought about by taxation or other means. He suggests that the reconstruction period will represent one of those situations envisaged in paragraph 200, in which the state should raise by taxation more than it needs for current expenditure, in order to carry out a national plan of investment, public and private. He suggests also that if in practice it proves difficult, as it well may prove difficult, to balance our payments abroad as early as 1948, there would be no serious objection to allowing an adverse balance to continue for some years, that is to say to drawing on our capital abroad, so long as we were using these additional resources for investment which would increase our efficiency and make the easier the ultimate balancing of our accounts overseas. This and many other important issues remain for discussion. Mr. Kaldor's work makes it possible to discuss them with a sense of proportion and in concrete terms.

208. The calculations in Appendix C, resting on such information as is now available to private citizens, could be improved by the help of fuller information in the hands of the Government. They can be improved and refined continuously, as we approach the post-war world and can see its outlines more clearly. But they are well worth giving in their present form for three reasons. First, they illustrate the unity of the economic problem and the consequent need to study it as a whole, and not departmentally. Second, they illustrate the kind of calculations which must be made in substituting conscious concerted pursuit of common welfare for the chances and wastefulness of the unplanned market economy, in judging of priorities, in putting first things first; they show that the fundamental decision to be made for the reconstruction period is as to the appropriate rate and direction of investment as a whole, whether public or private, and they provide the quantitative material to which this decision must be related. Third, whatever the precise measure of accuracy of the actual estimates, their main lesson is not in doubt. In illustrating the great possibilities that lie in full employment, they emphasize the waste of unemployment. They make us realize by contrast, in all its blackness, the shadow which must not be allowed to return to darken the future.

THE CHOSEN ROUTE: A LONG-TERM PROGRAMME OF PLANNED OUTLAY

209. In the light of these arguments and estimates, the full employment policy that appears best suited to the conditions of Britain in the reconstruction period is one of planned outlay on a long-term programme, financed as to current items from taxation and as to capital items by borrowing at progressively lower rates of interest, with a substantial sinking fund. The programme should be inspired by realistic and imaginative appraisal of common needs

and be designed to give stability to the economic system; the practical contents are set out in the following section under a few main heads. The programme, while in the main one of public outlay, is not exclusively so; important measures included in it will be designed to influence private outlay, both on consumption and on investment. The full employment policy proposed here is not a simple adoption of Route I of Table 18; it is a combination of routes. It involves action under all the five separate heads of outlay named in paragraph 179, namely:—

1. Communal outlay on non-marketable goods and services, such as roads, schools, hospitals, defence and order;

2. Public Business Investment in a socialized sector of industry. This will include all monopolies so complete that they are taken over for administration by public corporations; inland transport and power are the leading instances. It may include other industries such as coal or steel taken over by the State for special reasons;

3. Regulation of Private Business Investment. This will take the form both of assistance by loans at low interest and of taxation policy, designed to stabilize private investment so far as possible. An essential new organ for this purpose is the National Investment Board proposed in paragraph 240–1, exercising the powers named there in order to plan investment, both public and private, as a whole. For some time to come there will be ample scope for and need of additional investment to reconstruct Britain's out-of-date capital equipment, and to raise productivity by equipping British man-power with mechanical help comparable to that used in the United States;

4. Collective demand for essential consumption goods to be supplied to private citizens through the ordinary channels of retail distribution at a price which, at need, may be lowered by a subsidy. This method of joint outlay combines the advantages of social guidance of outlay with consumers' freedom. It is also a valuable method of controlling prices and monopoly profits. The essential goods covered by it from the beginning will include food and fuel. It may, in due course, be extended over a wider field, with the State taking more and more of the general business of wholesaling;

5. Increase of private consumption outlay both as the automatic result of an increase of national income and by re-distribution of incomes through Social Security and progressive taxation.

210. The programme is one for a period immediately following the transition from war to peace rather than for the transition itself. In the transition from war to peace, say the first two or three years after hostilities cease, there may be little or no difficulty in developing total demand sufficient for full employment. In the absence of proper planning, the danger will be more of inflationary than of deflationary gaps between outlay and resources, though even thus, misdirection of demand may leave substantial unemployment. But this prospect of high demand in the transition from war to peace is no reason for delay in deciding to adopt for the future a long term programme and the new type of budget proposed here. That decision should be made now. For, without proper planning in advance of the scales of public and private outlay, the danger of fluctuations of demand will be even greater after this war, than it was between the wars; without assurance that employment will be maintained after the transition, the process of transition itself and particularly the process of demobilization will be difficult and contentious. We cannot hope for a smooth passage from war to peace, if we have no vision of that to which transition is being made.

211. A long-term programme does not mean a rigid programme. The programme, as it will be executed largely through Budget operations, will be adjusted annually in detail by the Budget, in the light of experience and to fit changing circumstances. It must include some elements on which it is possible to proceed more or less rapidly, as productive resources are or are not available. The view that public works should be kept on tap to be expanded or contracted to meet fluctuations which are allowed to continue in private investment at home is rejected for the reasons given in paragraphs 248–55 below; public outlay should be looked on as a weapon against giant social evils, not as a gap-filling device to take up the slack of private outlay. But whatever be done to stabilize investment, both public and private, at home, there are some fluctuations of demand which it will be impossible wholly to prevent, namely those arising overseas. The full employment policy must contain measures for compensating for such fluctuations (paragraphs 344–6 in Part VI).

212. A long-term programme does not mean an invariable programme or a programme for all time. It represents the general course to be steered by the ship of State, but does not dispense with steering and does not preclude a change of course as the voyage proceeds. For twenty years or so after the transition from war to peace, the energies of the British people can clearly be used to the

full in meeting proved urgent social needs and making good glaring deficiencies in their standard of life. The time may come when Want, Disease, Squalor and Ignorance have been conquered and when British industry has been equipped up to the American level.[1] When these goals have been reached or are in sight, whether in twenty years or more, new needs may arise and the quantitative setting of the problem will be changed.[2] Then the common objective will no longer present itself as the ending of gross social evils and the raising of productive power, for those ends will have been accomplished. The main objective then may be that of ensuring on the one hand, a distribution of wealth that will keep consumption level with the rising production made possible by new equipment, and on the other hand, a fairer distribution of leisure, so that leisure replaces unemployment. That is for the future. The immediate objectives are Social Security, a National Health Service, adequate and good Nutrition and supply of other necessaries, immensely improved Education and largest of all in scope for useful expenditure, Town and Country Planning, Housing and Transport.

CONTENTS OF THE PROGRAMME

213. *Social Security.* The Plan for Social Security set out in my Report on Social Insurance and Allied Services of November, 1942,

[1] An article by Dr. L. Rostas in the *Economic Journal* for April, 1943, suggests that shortly before this war productivity per head in manufacturing industry was more than twice as high in the United States as in Britain. The material used by Dr. Rostas, from the censuses of production of the two countries, has been criticized by Dr. E. C. Snow, in his Presidential Address to the Royal Statistical Society in March, 1944, as not affording a basis for accurate comparisons between the countries. Further intensive study of the figures is required. But it is hard to believe that any correction would make the great difference shown by Dr. Rostas disappear. Comparison of the United States Census of 1929 with the British Census of Production of 1930 shows an average horse-power installation per wage-earner about twice as high in the United States as in Britain.

[2] The calculations in Section III of Mr. Kaldor's memorandum relate to a particular post-war year, at the beginning of reconstruction. A plan for continuous full employment on the lines proposed here, must take into account the effects of rising productivity and of the consequent rise of the national income. Since any addition to incomes will be devoted to increased consumption only in part, while part is saved, a given rate of investment will not maintain full employment indefinitely, unless measures are taken to enable rising production to be absorbed fully in rising consumption. Increase of potential output must be matched by increasing purchasing power. This means that the State may need to increase the propensity to consume, either by bringing about a more equal distribution of incomes or by reducing taxation and the sinking fund.

will, if adopted, help materially towards the maintenance of employment by expanding and maintaining private consumption outlay. It will bring about a re-distribution of income, both horizontally within the same economic classes and vertically between different economic classes. The horizontal re-distribution, as between times of earning and not earning or between times of no family responsibilities and large family responsibilities, will come first and with the existing system of taxation will probably always be the most important. The vertical re-distribution, on the method of financing proposed in my Report, will be small at first but will rise later, as the proportion of the cost met by general taxation rises. Since the income provided by the scheme to persons who are sick, unemployed, injured or past work, will almost invariably be spent to the full, the scheme will bring about a general increase of private outlay. The actual finance of Social Security will be affected materially by the successful adoption of a policy of full employment. The finance of the Plan as submitted in my earlier Report allowed for unemployment at an average of $8\frac{1}{2}$ per cent over the whole body of insured employees, while the present Report aims at unemployment of not more than 3 per cent. The earlier Report allowed also for post-war prices 25 per cent above those of 1938, whereas it now seems prudent to allow for a greater rise to $33\frac{1}{3}$ per cent above 1938. As is shown elsewhere (paragraph 206 and Appendix C) full employment means that these larger benefits in terms of money can be provided for materially lower contributions by all parties concerned; alternatively still larger benefits can be provided for the same contributions.

214. *National Health Service*. The development of the health services of the community is one of the most generally accepted of post-war aims. Maintenance of health does not depend solely or primarily on health services, and still less on medical treatment. It depends even more on good food; on sufficiency of the other necessaries of life; on healthy homes. All these matters, falling outside the sphere of a Ministry of Health, however organized, form part of the programme of this Report and are dealt with below. But the organization of adequate health services, both for prevention and for treatment, is in itself a major task with high priority. The Ministry of Health should be a Ministry of Health and of that alone; that is to say, it should be relieved of its irrelevant duties, inherited from the Local Government Board, of supervising the finance of local authorities. These financial duties belong logically to the department described below as the Department of Control.

The Ministry of Health in England Wales and the Department of Health in Scotland, if that regional separation is maintained, will be fully occupied in bringing about a co-ordination of the whole medical work of the State, now split between several departments. Whether the medical profession is organized in part or in whole as a public service, there is room and need for a great increase of hospitals and institutions of all kinds. There are special services, such as rehabilitation after injury, or dentistry, ripe for development. The provision of comprehensive health and rehabilitation services was named as Assumption B of my *Report on Social Insurance and Allied Services*; the cost of these services, to be included in the Social Security Budget and met in part by Social Insurance contributions, was put there at £170,000,000 a year. In the recent Government White Paper on *A National Health Service*[1] the annual charge on public funds for the service proposed there is put below this, at £147·8 millions, of which £40·0 millions or 27 per cent will come from Social Insurance contributions as proposed in my Report, £54·4 millions or 37 per cent from central taxation, and £53·4 millions or 36 per cent from local rates. This, however, is not the whole cost of the health service, as the voluntary hospitals "would still be dependent on voluntary resources for a substantial part of the income necessary to balance their expenditure." While annual payments to doctors and for maintenance of institutions must be steady from year to year, the building of new institutions can proceed on a programme subject to contraction or expansion according to the urgency of other demands.

215. *Nutrition.* The war has shown the advantages of a nutrition policy based on science and designed to ensure to every person in the community a supply of essential foods suited to his special needs. For a variety of reasons the bulk purchase of supplies is likely to continue after the war, in relation to the principal articles of food, both home produced and imported. This is the way to guarantee a market and price to home farmers, in order to maintain a prosperous agriculture. It is the way to diminish the disastrous fluctuations of prices and production abroad. Finally, stabilization of the price of essential foods is necessary, if the State, as suggested in paragraphs 289–92 of Part V, accepts the general responsibility of stabilizing the cost of living at a level within the means of all citizens. On all these grounds it is reasonable to look forward to a continuance in peace of one side at least of the Ministry of Food, to stabilize the supply and price of essential foods and maintain

[1] Cmd. 6502. The finance of the service is dealt with in Appendix E.

their quality; this would not involve rationing and need not cover all foods. But if anything is done in this field, it should be done as part of a policy of nutrition, in the interest of consumers primarily rather than of producers, whether at home or abroad. The expenditure of the British people on food out of private incomes is estimated at £1,198 millions in 1938 and £1,264 millions in 1943.[1] These figures include the amounts represented by taxes and exclude the subsidies given by the State which in 1943 amounted to about £190 millions, nearly all on food. The figures exclude money spent on alcoholic drink and tobacco, which amounted to £1,053 millions in 1943.

216. *Fuel and other Necessaries.* In addition to housing and food, the necessaries of life include fuel, on which about £240 millions was spent in 1943, and clothing, on which about £447 millions was spent. What is to be done about coal? Is the production of coal to be left as it is or nationalized in one way or another? Decision on that issue lies outside the direct scope of this Report, though not wholly outside its implications; this point is discussed further at the end of Part V. It is clear, however, that the direct way of maintaining any desired level of employment in mining is by guaranteeing a demand up to that level, that is to say a market and price. For that purpose alone, nationalization of production is unnecessary, as nationalization is unnecessary for the purpose of guaranteeing a market and price for the fruits of agriculture. On the other hand, even with nationalization, the problem of marketing the output remains. Socialization of demand for staples like coal is wanted in any case, with or without socialization of production. The executive departments should include accordingly, in any case, a Coal Marketing Corporation, which would place orders for coal for six months or a year ahead sufficient to employ the desired total of men in the industry. If the Corporation found difficulty in disposing of that quantity of coal, it would cut down its order for the future, while steps would be taken to reduce the supply of labour (see paragraph 230 below). If the Corporation found demand tending to outrun output, it might increase its orders. Management of demand for coal in this way presents practical problems. But they are problems which have to be solved on any assumption as to how the production of coal is organized. The principle and technique of Government wholesaling, suggested here for coal, can be extended to other essential commodities, such as clothing and furniture.

[1] White Paper on War Finance, Cmd. 6520, p. 5.

217. *Education.* The introduction of the new Education Bill and its imminent passage into law have opened the way for a large programme of public outlay. It remains only to ensure that execution of the programme is as rapid as the productive resources of the country allow and that the programme covers fully adult education as well as the teaching of youth. Though development of education is not the most urgent of reconstruction tasks, it is ultimately the most important. One cannot teach children who are hungry or ailing, and children who return to squalid homes each night may lose there much that they have gained in school; the foundations of learning must be laid in physical well-being. But that foundation comes first in time only, not in value. Expenditure on education is the communal investment which in the end may bring the best return. It does more than any other expenditure to make material progress both possible and worth while. Improvement of the standard of life should not and does not mean solely an increase of material satisfactions. It has meant in the past a growth of leisure; it should mean that still more so in future. Education needs to grow with leisure, to teach the best use of leisure. For that purpose adult education should rank with school education as an essential interest of the community.

218. *Town and Country Planning, Housing and Transport.* Adequate and healthy housing presents the largest single objective for desirable outlay after the war and affords the largest scope for raising the standard of life, health and happiness. Housing involves the setting up of a long-term programme of building to approved designs with the maximum of economy. The scale of the programme must be determined not arbitrarily but with reference to the total labour available; some forms of building and construction can be used as the balancing factor in the national man-power budget. The prospective importance of housing makes it vital to secure, by new methods if necessary, the maximum efficiency of the building industry. It is even more important to secure that national planning of town and country is made a reality, before permanent housing begins. National planning of town and country involves at least three things:

(*a*) Clearing the ground of compensation-betterment obstacles in the way recommended in the Report of the Uthwatt Committee[1] or in some other way that is not less effective;

[1] The full title of this Committee, of which Mr. Justice Uthwatt was Chairman, is the Expert Committee on Compensation and Betterment. The Report is Cmd. 6386 of 1942.

(*b*) making and administering the plan, i.e. setting up machinery which can promptly and rightly give or withhold consent to any proposed use of land;

(*c*) developing and administering transport facilities to fit the plan, with a suitable policy of rates.

There is here a complex of difficult problems—land, planning, housing, transport—which will need to be treated together, probably, as suggested by the Uthwatt Committee, under a Minister of National Development, who, though subject financially to the Minister of National Finance, would be hardly less important.

219. There falls for mention here yet another problem which in itself is worthy of a separate Report. Planning means country planning as well as town planning. It raises not merely the question of location of urban industry, but the question of the importance to be attached to agriculture and of the methods for giving agriculture in future its right permanent place among the progressive and successful occupations of Britain. Agriculture should be regarded not as a Cinderella among industries, but as one possessing advantages which have long been unduly neglected. It is nearly certain that the gradual development of manufacturing in other countries, and the necessity in future of paying by current exports for a larger proportion of Britain's imports, will make it desirable to diminish the dependence of Britain upon food from overseas. This should be done, not by protecting old-fashioned methods and not by maintaining a low-paid agricultural population, but by putting at least as much capital, ability, and research into agriculture as in the past have been put into manufacturing.

220. The actual execution of a housing programme may be devolved to a large extent to local authorities and must in any case be carried through in close co-operation with them. The executive functions of the Minister of National Development in relation to housing will be primarily financial, directed to making houses cheaper and rents lower, on the one hand, by use of State credit to reduce the rate of interest, and on the other hand by bulk buying of standard equipment to make it available to consumers at lower cost. On a £500 house the difference between money at $4\frac{1}{2}$ per cent interest and money at $2\frac{1}{2}$ per cent represents £10 a year or nearly 4s. a week of rent; on a £1,000 house it represents nearly 8s. a week. If a policy of cheap money is adopted and pursued firmly[1] it should be possible to reduce the rate of interest well below

---

[1] See note on *A Policy of Cheap Money* in Appendix B.

2½ per cent; this change, desirable and justifiable on many grounds, is the simplest route to lower rents. As regards bulk buying, it is obvious that washing machines, sinks, refrigerators and all the other equipment that can and should be used to save needless labour in the home and to improve health and welfare can be made far more cheaply if made in bulk for a guaranteed demand.

221. But the financial problem in the field of planning and housing will not be confined to this issue of lowering the total cost. There is also a problem of distributing the cost fairly. The wide varieties of local need and the strength of local sentiment make it essential that steps to improve the physical environment of the nation by planning and housing should be taken largely through local authorities or with their co-operation. But a national plan cannot fairly be executed at the cost of particular localities. This will force the issue of a re-casting of local finance, as no longer adequate to the requirements of national planning. The housing programme as a whole will be settled by the Central Government, in the light of the general economic situation; in the light of a plan for the location of industry and population; in the light, possibly, of strategic considerations. The local authorities must operate within the framework thus set. It is not reasonable to expect them to engage in the activities envisaged by the national plan, as long as a substantial part of the cost is likely to fall upon local rates. Such costs must be borne centrally, inasmuch as the plan which gives rise to them is determined centrally. It has been a frequent experience in the past that "distressed areas," which needed most urgently an influx of industry, were burdened with such a high load of local rates that this alone was sufficient to deter industrialists. It has also been a frequent experience that the level of local taxation was lowest in the most prosperous areas—those where a further concentration of industry was least desirable from a national point of view. Nor is it desirable, once there is a plan for national development, that the ability of local authorities to collaborate fully should be dependent upon their credit status. Just those regions where development is most desirable often find it most difficult to raise the necessary capital and have to pay the highest rates of interest when they do so. This burdens local finance still further. Finance should be provided centrally, at the rates of interest at which the Central Government is able to borrow. If subsidies are required, it should be for the Central Government, not the local authority, to provide them.

222. A revision of local taxation is necessary also because local

rates fall heavily upon private consumption and form an integral part of taxation as a whole. They are a part of "Revenue," as defined in paragraph 183, and the incidence and scale of local rates will have to be taken into account by the Minister of National Finance in framing his budget. He may need some powers of influence or control over them. This need not interfere with the freedom of local authorities to enlarge the field of their communal activity. An increase in local rates due to the voluntary expansion of free services will still be possible. But those activities—such as a housing programme—which are the result of a central decision must not burden local finance. And arrangements should be made so that even voluntary activities, if approved by the central authority, can be financed at rates of interest as low as those paid by the State.

Section 3. THE SECOND CONDITION: CONTROLLED LOCATION OF INDUSTRY

223. The main instrument of a full employment policy has been described above. It is a new type of Budget based on man-power, rather than on the assumed limits of taxation. But this by itself would meet only the first of the three conditions of full employment named in paragraph 165. It would provide total outlay. It would not ensure the second of the three conditions—that outlay was wisely directed with reference to the location of available labour. In war, full employment is obtained largely without this condition. Fighting men and serving women go where war calls them. New factories and war contracts have to be located in the main by strategic considerations. But this involves a local disturbance of the population and breaking of local associations that is accepted only because of the necessities of war and is carried through by use of compulsory powers that would not be tolerated in peace. Failure to direct locally such new demand as arose between the two wars contributed to the persistence of structural unemployment, wasted the social resources of the derelict areas, and led to all the evils of bad living conditions and transport conditions that are laid bare in the Report of the Royal Commission on the Distribution of the Industrial Population.[1]

[1] Signed in December, 1939, published in 1940 and reprinted in 1943, Cmd. 6153.

224. The Report of this Commission of thirteen members, which is known usually by the name of its Chairman, Sir Montague Barlow, begins by describing briefly two outstanding features of population growth in the past two centuries. One is the astonishing expansion of the nations of the Western civilization. The other is "the even more rapid proportional rate at which the great urban centres of Western civilization have spread, overflowing their boundaries and forming sprawling agglomerations of humanity." There are now about fifty "millionaire" cities in the world, that is to say cities of more than a million inhabitants.[1] Concentration of population into great cities is a world-wide phenomenon under industrialization. It is most marked in Britain which led the way in industrialization. In 1937 more than two-fifths of the population of Britain were in seven millionaire conurbations, while the corresponding proportion in the United States was about one-fifth. More than one-fifth of the people of Britain—nearly ten millions—were in London, which has grown more rapidly than any other centre of population, taking in the ten years 1921–31 34 per cent and in the six years 1931–37 35·4 per cent of the increase of the whole population. The British in Britain have become a nation of great city dwellers. The Commission, having examined the social, economic and strategical consequences of this situation, came to the conclusion that many of the consequences were harmful and called for remedy. "It is not possible from the evidence submitted to us to avoid the conclusion that the disadvantages in many, if not in most, of the great industrial concentrations, alike on the strategical, the social and the economic side, do constitute serious handicaps and even in some respects dangers to the nation's life and development, and we are of opinion that definite action should be taken by the Government towards remedying them."[2] This is a unanimous finding.

225. The Commission, as they were unanimous in their diagnosis of serious evils calling for remedy, were in effect unanimous in their main recommendation of a remedy; that is to say, the setting up of a new central authority, national in scope and character, to plan the location of industry and population. They differed only as to the nature of the new authority and of the powers that should be given to it immediately. The main Report of the Commission, signed by 10 members (three of whom made an important reserva-

[1] These cities are so described by Professor C. B. Fawcett, in a book with that name, published in 1935.
[2] Cmd. 6153, para. 413.

tion noted below), proposed a National Industrial Board, not apparently directly responsible to Parliament, with (1) immediate executive power to refuse consent to the establishment of industrial undertakings in London and the Home Counties, that is to say, immediate negative control of industrial location applied to an area containing about a quarter of the whole population; and (2) the duty of reporting what further powers they wanted. Three members who made a reservation and the three who signed the Minority Report agreed in effect in wanting a great deal more than the rest of the Commission. They desired a negative control of the location of industry to apply throughout the country and not merely to the South-Eastern corner, and in addition a positive policy of development to apply simultaneously with the negative control. The whole Commission agreed also in pointing out that one of the problems to be solved, before national planning of the distribution of the population could become a reality, was the problem of the shifting of land values that would result from such a policy. They recommended the establishment of an Expert Committee on Compensation and Betterment. The Committee was duly appointed in January, 1941, under the Chairmanship of Mr. Justice Uthwatt, and reported in August, 1942.[1] This Committee, again with unanimity on all its essential recommendations, proposed a plan for the acquisition by the State, on payment of a global sum as compensation, of the development rights in all undeveloped land, combined with more effective and simpler procedure for acquisition of land already developed. They made these proposals, in their own words, on the assumptions "that planning is intended to be a reality and a permanent feature of the administration of the internal affairs of the country, and that the system of planning assumed is one of national planning with a high degree of initiation and control by the Central Planning Authority, which will have national as well as local considerations in mind, and that such control will be based on organized research into the social and economic life of the country and be directed to securing the use of land to the best advantage."[2]

226. The Barlow Commission were concerned mainly with evils falling outside the scope of this Report. They were concerned with the disadvantages in the great cities to which population flowed, rather than with the damage to the districts which were left derelict. They summed up the disadvantages of the growing towns under four main heads: the higher mortality of the towns; the congestion

[1] Cmd. 6386.   [2] Cmd. 6386, para. 359.

and discomfort of the living conditions in them; the congestion
and discomfort of the travelling conditions of them; the cost of
measures to mitigate each of the first three disadvantages. All these
are different forms of waste of human life and energy—different
ways of throwing away the advantages of growing power over
nature. As set out in the Commission's Report they make an unanswerable case for that national planning of the location of industry which the Commission proposed. They are reinforced by
the evidence collected here, showing the disadvantage of the uncontrolled movement of industry in its other aspect of leaving
particular areas without a demand for their products and causing
mass unemployment. These evils are even more acute if less general.
When, through decline of industry in a particular place, a third or
two-thirds of its working population become simultaneously unemployed, to say that they must move in order to find employment
is equivalent to destroying the community and wasting the social
capital that it represents. To say that this must happen because,
though demand for new industrial products is arising, business men
prefer to place their works elsewhere, is to lose sense of proportion.

227. The matters just discussed raise the issue of how far, in
pursuit of a full employment policy, the State should be guided by
consideration for producers and how far by consideration for
consumers. The main consideration must clearly be that of consumers; employment is wanted not for the sake of employment
but for the sake of consumption. Yet to ignore producers is futile
and cruel. It is of no use to set up a demand for non-existent labour;
it is foolish and wasteful to set up a demand for labour which cannot
be made available or can only be made available at excessive
social cost. Both in the transition from war to peace, and immediately
thereafter, while the occupational and local distribution of the
population and its housing are still affected by the disturbances
made by war, deliberate direction of demand, with reference both
to the industries and the places in which the workpeople can be
found, will be an essential measure for prevention of unemployment.
But this is a temporary problem. In the long run there is, on the
facts, no real conflict between the interests of producers and consumers. The remarkable figures as to the growth of particular
industries set out in Part II show that there is no difficulty in
diverting the supply of labour into those industries in which there
is effective demand. Difficulty arises not in regard to movement
between occupations nearly so much as in regard to movement
between localities. Here technical advance comes to the rescue.

There is no longer any necessity for industry to be concentrated near the source of power which it uses, for power can be distributed. There is equally no reason and no sense in using the vast developments of transport in order to throw an increasing burden of travel on human beings rather than on goods. It is possible for industry to move from one part of the country to another. It has done so in Britain, first moving North and West up to the outbreak of the first World War then moving back again South and East, moving as a sluggish tide which in bringing prosperity to particular areas brought many evils and inconveniences, which in other areas caused evils unredeemed by prosperity. There can be no question to-day of the need for the community to control and direct this movement.

228. Most of the questions dealt with both by the Barlow Commission and by the Uthwatt Committee fall outside the scope of this Report, but the practical conclusion is the same. For an effective attack upon mass unemployment, as much as for an effective attack on the evils of urban congestion, control over the location of industry is indispensable. This control must be both negative, prohibiting undesirable location, and positive, encouraging desirable location. The control must be exercised ultimately by a central authority, making a national plan for the whole country but using local authorities for the local execution of the plan and the adjustment of the plan to local conditions. In relation to a full employment policy the Minister of National Development proposed in paragraph 218 will be much more than one of the executive agencies for public outlay. He will be the main agency for securing, through control of location of industry, the second condition of full employment: that the total outlay of all kinds shall be wisely directed, having regard to the labour available.

SECTION 4. THE THIRD CONDITION: ORGANIZED MOBILITY OF LABOUR

229. The survey of unemployment in peace made in Part II has shown unemployment resulting not simply from deficiency or misdirection of demand but also from the way in which industries are organized to meet demand, in particular from their methods for engaging men. The review of war conditions, in Part III, has shown that the almost complete disappearance of unemployment in war is made possible by two things not one. Unlimited demand for

man-power is one. The abolition of nearly all qualitative restrictions on the use of man-power is the other; men and women by the million have changed their occupations of their place of work. Demobilization and the transition from war to peace—with which this Report is not directly concerned—will call for industrial migration on a scale comparable to that which has occurred during the War. A peace economy does not require movement on anything like that scale. If, however, it is to be an economy combining a minimum of unemployment with change and progress, it does require a reasonable flexibility of response by industry to the demand set up by the State, and it requires organization of the labour market to avoid misdirection of labour and the accumulation and maintenance of needless reserves of labour. In achieving this, the State, the managers of industry, and the workpeople themselves all have their parts to play.

230. The State in Britain has already done its part towards the organization of the labour market by setting up the national system of employment exchanges. As was shown in Part II, the use of the system by employers falls far short of what is needed to reduce the intervals between jobs to a minimum; too many employers still cling to personal application at the place of employment, that is to say, to the hawking of labour. During the war the use of the employment exchanges has been made compulsory in many industries as a means of directing the supply of man-power in accordance with national policy. The suggestion is sometimes made that the compulsory use of employment exchanges for all engagements should continue in peace as in war. In regard to one particular class of work-people, boys and girls up to the age of eighteen, the case for imposing such a requirement is clear. Under the new educational system such persons will still be subject to the care of the community, citizens in process of formation not yet fully formed. But it is idle to train them in schools and allow them to be misplaced and misguided in work. For themselves and for the nation, it is important that boys and girls should be fitted into occupations adapted to their capacities, and should receive the best possible advice in choosing their careers; that they should not be tempted into "blind-alley" occupations, or declining industries. Controlling the flow of adaptable juveniles is the simple, painless way of adjusting the total supply of labour in each industry to changes in demand; in all normal cases it should enable a contraction of demand in a particular industry to be met by checking new entrants without displacing existing workmen.

231. It is clear also that, in one other special field, return to the old ways of engaging labour should be definitely made impossible Industries like dock and harbour service, which by practising casual engagement have been the main generators of chronic under-employment in the past, have been transformed in the war. I may be assumed that the main principle of the transformation will remain in peace, that the men following such occupations will have guaranteed weekly wages, and that this will lead in due course to the organization of regular work as well as of regular wages, with men working for a single employing agency or for groups of employers, in place of taking their chance with single employers at a number of separate taking-on places. It may be hoped that in many other industries the former position in regard to the engagement of men will be transformed by the substitution of weekly for daily or hourly engagements.

232. Whether or not a general requirement on employers to use either the national employment exchanges or an approved alternative system, such as a trade union exchange, for engagements of workpeople should be imposed in peace, is a question which it is perhaps unnecessary to decide now. It is desirable to put an end to the aimless, unguided search for work which is involved in the hawking of labour from door to door, and since all workpeople are in practice required to be registered at an exchange when unemployed as a condition of obtaining benefit, there can be no objection of principle to requiring corresponding notification by employers of every vacancy to an employment exchange, or going further and requiring the actual engagement to be made either through the exchange or an approved agency, such as a trade union. But the use of exchanges by employers is likely to grow naturally and automatically as a consequence of full employment, as it has grown in the past during the upward phase of the trade cycle and declined in the downward phase. Compulsion may prove to be unnecessary at least it may seem reasonable to wait to see whether full systematic use of an organized labour market can be brought about without it

233. Fluidity of labour depends not simply on organizing the labour market. It requires also the removal of obstacles to movement. Such obstacles may be of two kinds—arising from the unwillingness of the individual to change his job or place of residence or arising from restrictions on entry to particular trades. In war obstacles of both kinds have been levelled to the ground. Individual men and women have been more ready than in peace to turn to unfamiliar tasks; often they have welcomed tasks because they were

new. There is no reason to contemplate such a wholesale change of occupations in peace. Change will be exceptional not normal. But it should be accepted as a general citizen duty that if there is a demand for labour at fair wages, men who are unemployed for any substantial period should be prepared to take that work and not to hold out indefinitely for work in their own trade and place; service means doing what is wanted, not just pleasing oneself. This does not imply that there should be continuance in peace of the powers of direction exercised in war by the Ministry of Labour and National Service. No man should be subject to criminal penalties in peace for refusing work however unreasonably. But he should not be assisted to be unreasonable by provision of an insurance income. A just consequence of a full employment policy would lie in the stiffening of the conditions of unemployment benefit as regards individuals whose unemployment continues for any length of time. A man who has only just fallen out of work might be presumed to have a good chance of being wanted again in his own trade and place, and should be allowed to decline a move that would diminish that chance, without being held to have refused suitable employment. But if his unemployment continued, that would be growing evidence of his not being wanted in his trade and place; after a certain time had elapsed, employment at a distance or in another trade would be held to be suitable for him, that is to say, to be employment which he could not refuse without losing benefit. Such a stiffening of conditions for benefit would probably be accepted as reasonable by public opinion. It is now practised informally by many Courts of Referees. It would become even more reasonable if, under a full employment policy, the State provided not only facilities for training but the practical certainty of a job at the end of training.

234. As the reluctance of individual men and women to take new jobs has vanished in war, so have many or most of the difficulties that in peace time might have been placed in their way by others. Trade·unions have by agreement surrendered, for the period of the war, many rules and customs which they valued, as to methods of work, demarcation of trades, types of labour and entry to occupations, and which might have prevented or delayed full mobilization of the nation's strength in war. This surrender has naturally and rightly been made only for the period of the war. But it is clear that if, with peace, industrial demarcations with all the restrictive tendencies and customs of the past return in full force, a policy of outlay for full employment, however vigorously it is pursued by the

State, will fail to cure unemployment and may encounter difficulties in raising the general standard of living. It is of little use
for the State to set up, as it easily might, a demand for houses and
their equipment that would improve out of all knowledge the
conditions of life and health in Britain and would use in the process
every man that could be spared for this work, if demand runs up
against a wall of restrictive rules and customs. It will be tragic to
throw away in peace all or anything that we have learned in war
of new and simpler methods of work and training, and of the signal
capacity of women for many tasks hitherto treated as beyond their
powers. The undertaking of new responsibility by the State for full
employment of all man-power in meeting needs according to a
scale of social priorities may fitly be made an occasion for reviewing
rules and customs as to use of man-power. Undoubtedly fear of
unemployment in the past has been the source and justification for
many restrictions, formal or informal, on types of labour, on methods,
and on output. With the removal of that fear, the way should be
opened to reconsideration of the restrictions.

235. Reconsideration of restrictive rules does not mean that they
should all be abandoned. Many of the rules and practices evolved
by organized labour, by professional bodies and by organized
business are essential to a progressive society. They serve to maintain
or to promote high standards of skill, professional ability, integrity,
efficiency and quality. They are the only way in which private
interests—of labour, of the professions, or of capital—can bring
order out of disorder and can co-ordinate activities which, if unco-
ordinated, may lead to social waste and needless acrimony. It is
useless to criticize them unless it is shown at the same time that
the same positive functions could be more easily or more efficiently
fulfilled by a public agency. But many of these rules and restrictions
are of a purely negative character. Demarcation rules by trade
unions, restrictions on entry into trades and professions, price
maintenance agreements between business firms, and so forth, are
all born largely out of a spirit of self-defence against the large
disruptive forces which make effective demand too small to take up
the full output of industry. They are manifestations of one of the
social evils of unemployment, that it makes each man appear the
enemy of his fellow instead of his helper in a common task, as he is
and appears to be in the full employment economy of war. They
will become unnecessary defences under full employment in peace.

236. Reconsideration of restrictions, as it does not mean abandonment of standards of training, does not mean the unregulated

ntry of fresh labour into contracting or stationary industries, so as o threaten the livelihood of those already there. On the contrary, he suggestion made above for the compulsory use of employment xchanges in respect of young people is intended to make it possible o direct the flow of flexible juvenile labour away from such in-lustries into expanding industries. So long, moreover, as an industry practises casual employment, taking on and dismissing men con-inually without giving any of them a prior claim to engagement, egistration schemes such as those in force in most British ports before the war are the necessary defence of the men following that occupation. The third feature of a full employment policy is not mobility of labour but organized mobility. That means preventing or discouraging needless movement, as well as promoting movement where it is needed. It means diminishing aimless movement in chase of jobs which are not there.

237. Finally, emphasis on the view that full employment depends on flexibility of the labour supply as well as on sufficiency of demand, does not imply the view that in peace all workpeople will be under continual necessity to change their jobs and places of work. If demand is directed wisely—with regard to the labour available and its location—there is no reason why most people should not continue normally in their chosen occupations and their settled homes so long as they desire. When we give up playing musical chairs with not enough seats to go round we don't have of necessity to play general post with enough seats for all but with no one allowed to keep his seat. Mobility of labour does not mean perpetual motion. Mobility of labour means merely that labour should be capable of moving and ready to move if necessary. Organized mobility means that men do not move if movement is futile and do move rapidly and directly to the job when there is a job.

Section 5. CHANGES OF GOVERNMENT MACHINERY

238. What changes of Government machinery are required to carry out such a programme as that outlined above? The answer to that question is best introduced by naming the three distinct functions to be performed in securing the chief condition of full employment, namely the adequacy of total outlay. There is, first, the function of ensuring that total outlay, public and private, is sufficient but not more than sufficient to employ all available man-power. There is, second, the function of ensuring that the best

possible value is obtained for outlay, by efficiency and economy of administration. There is, third, the function of actually making outlay for the various purposes included in the national programme. Consideration of these three functions points to departmental organization in three tiers: a Ministry of National Finance to determine outlay; a department for control of public expenditure to ensure good value for outlay; a number of executive departments undertaking outlay up to the amount fixed by the Ministry of National Finance and under the supervision of the department of control. Outlay, however, must not only be sufficient in total; it must also, as the second condition of full employment, be directed rightly in relation to the available productive resources. Here two departments have important parts to play. One is the new Ministry that should become responsible for controlling the location of industry; it is suggested above that this should be a Ministry of National Development, covering the whole field of town and country planning, housing and transport. The other is the Ministry of Labour, whose administration involves a continuous survey of employment and unemployment; its experience must be the basis of man-power planning; it is also the instrument for securing, by its own action and by the co-operation of employers and employees, the organized mobility of labour which is the third condition of full employment.

239. The first of the functions named in paragraph 238 is new and calls for a Minister of the highest authority. It would be in accord with British practice, while introducing the revolutionary change of substance involved in budgeting by man-power rather than money, to give the new Minister an inappropriate historic title, such as Chancellor of the Exchequer or First Lord of the Treasury. But it is necessary to realize that each of these titles is inappropriate and that the functions to be performed by the new Minister are antipathetic to the spirit which has rightly animated the Treasury in the past. The Treasury has been concerned very largely with the second function—of control of public spending—in order to get good value for money. Finance in the sense of this Report has hardly been undertaken at all. So far as it has been undertaken—as in attempting to counter cyclical fluctuation by adjusting rates of interest or by open market operations—it has in peace been left largely to a private corporation outside the Treasury, that is to say the Bank of England. The Treasury of the past is the natural matrix of the Department of Control rather than of the Ministry of National Finance.

240. The Minister of National Finance will be concerned not only with the outlay which the State can control directly, that of the State itself and other public authorities, but with the outlay of private citizens for consumption and in business investment. Consumption outlay will be influenced by taxation and price policy. As regards investment, the division between private and public enterprise and between private and public borrowing, is a matter of expediency rather than principle. Execution of the long-term programme for full productive employment requires—(i) that in all the main spheres of economic activity (such as housing and town-planning, public utilities, transport and agriculture and each of the major industries) plans of reorganization and reconstruction should be worked out under the initiative and guidance of the State and in co-operation with the industries concerned; (ii) that if in any particular case private enterprise proves unwilling to embark on a major project that the Government considered to be necessary for the national interest, the State should undertake it under public auspices by providing the funds or, if necessary, being responsible for its execution; (iii) that sufficient investment projects should be elaborated to provide for the needs some years ahead, but that the timing of their execution should be under public control, so as to ensure a steady flow of capital expenditure for the national economy as a whole; (iv) that the investments undertaken by the Central Government, the local authorities, public utilities and private industry should be co-ordinated in accordance with the scale of priorities in a single national plan.

241. The responsibility to Parliament for these matters will rest with the Minister of National Finance. For execution there will be needed a new organ described as a National Investment Board. This Board will have powers of obtaining intelligence, of giving assistance and of regulating investment by public and private enterprise alike. The Board will exercise these powers in pursuance of a national plan prepared by itself and approved by Parliament. For intelligence it should obtain information of important investment plans, before they are carried out, by returns which would be compulsory on all undertakings above a certain size; the Minister of Finance must be able to make his programme of public investment with full knowledge of the probable course of private investment. Under the conditions envisaged in this Report, probably not more than 25 per cent of the total national investment will be accounted for by private manufacturing industry, and half of this 25 per cent is controlled by about three thousand firms, numbering less than 2 per cent of all

firms.[1] Assistance would take the form of ensuring, by a Governmen guarantee, a lower rate of interest on investments for approve purposes. The National Investment Board would not provide financ out of its own or out of public funds. By pledging the credit of th State it would enable approved borrowers to obtain funds from established financial institutions on terms otherwise unobtainable this would be of critical importance in relation to housing schemes For the regulation, that is to say the stabilization, of private invest ment, the Board should have some power, suitably safeguarded, o direct control of investment—that is to say power to stop or reduce by order a proposed private investment plan. To what extent i would need to use such a power is uncertain. It should be added that, so far as any revision of stock exchange rules and method seemed desirable and called for Government intervention, this, too would fall within the purview of the National Investment Board.

242. The banking system must clearly function in accord with th general financial policy of the State. This implies that the Bank o England should become in peace as it is in war an agency of th State, to give effect to the national policy, and with the Governo of the Bank formally appointed by the Government. It does no involve anything that can be described as nationalization of th joint-stock banks. The Bank of England, by its control over the casl basis of the banking system, possesses full control over the rate o interest. A direct control by the State over the banks, whether o not it is desirable for other reasons, is not necessary for the purpose of controlling credit and the rate of interest.

243. The Ministry of National Finance will be concerned not only with outlay at home but with outlay abroad, that is to say with the international problems discussed in Part VI. The various agencie which may be needed in that field—a Monetary Fund, an Inter national Investment Board, and an Exchange Control—clearly fall within the purview of the Ministry of Finance. So too does impor and export policy, even i the actual administration is left to a subor dinate executive department such as the Board of Trade.

244. The second function named in paragraph 238, of seeing that good value is got for outlay in all its forms, will be of even greater importance in the future than in the past, as public expenditure grows and as the significance of monopolies and trade associations is recognized. The new Budget is an expression of a new social responsibility which no Government can any longer fail to discharge —the responsibility for full employment. But employment is not an

---

[1] This estimate is derived from the Census of Production in 1935.

end in itself: it is a means to an end. The end is the abolition of great social evils which, in spite of the existence of idle resources, have been allowed to survive. In view of the magnitude of these evils, the nation cannot afford any unnecessary waste. The State is called upon to enlarge the scope of its activities and to enlarge its spending. But such spending must be wise spending—expenditure that yields the highest possible results. Our economy, even when fully employed, is still too poor to afford a wasteful use of man-power—the limiting factor to advance. It must be the responsibility of some organ of the State, adequately staffed and with sufficient power, to ensure good value for outlay. This organ has been named above as a Department of Control, rather than a Ministry. It has no strictly ministerial function of policy; its work would be to a large extent technical, like that of the Comptroller and Auditor-General, and for political purposes it might be represented by the Minister of National Finance. But its authority within its technical sphere must be strong; it might be a Board with power of independent Report to Parliament. Whatever the precise form of this organ, its function and the need for it are clear. While the Ministry of National Finance fixes the outlay to be incurred by the various executive organs, outlay itself, on whatever scale, should be under effective independent expert supervision. The Treasury has in the past been largely concerned with this function, and should exercise it in future over a wider field.

245. The department which in the interests of efficiency and economy supervises the spending of other departments of State should also naturally supervise the spending of local authorities; that is to say, the financial side of the Ministry of Health, as successor to the old Local Government Board, should pass to the Department of Control. Supervision of spending by Government Departments and local authorities depends on inspection and cost accounting. These same techniques will be required in connection with wage settlements and the control of monopolies. That is to say, supervision of monopolies, assistance in wage arbitration and price control generally might become the duty of the Department of Control.

246. The precise form of the machinery that will be required for the supreme conduct of public affairs in peace cannot be outlined here. It involves many considerations falling outside the scope of this Report. But it is fair to suggest that the problems of peace are likely to be more, not less, complicated than those of war, while their handling will not be simplified, as the handling of nearly all problems is simplified in war, by the self-denial of the democracy. The supreme direction of the country must be in the hands of men

with leisure from the daily routine of vast departments, men able to decide quickly, but with time to read, think and discuss before they decide. In addition to a Prime Minister, freed from every departmental care, two Ministers seem clearly designated for this supreme Cabinet, a Minister of National Finance described above and a Minister of External Affairs.

Section 6. SOME ALTERNATIVES EXAMINED

247. The policy outlined here is of planned outlay directed by social priorities, including both consumption and investment, on a long-term programme. Both the nature of the policy and the reasons for it can be illustrated by examination of alternative approaches to the problem. It will be sufficient for this purpose to examine two such alternatives, which may be described as stabilization of total investment, and expansion of private outlay.

STABILIZATION OF TOTAL INVESTMENT

248. A common approach to the problem of full employment today, is from the side of investment. It is pointed out by those who use this approach that the main recurrent cause of mass unemployment is cyclical fluctuation, which affects primarily investment industries, namely those making instruments and materials of production. The activity of the consumer goods industries is relatively stable, while the activity of capital goods or investment goods industries is highly unstable; such instability as appears in the former is mainly induced by the instability of the latter. From this the inference is often drawn that the primary objective of a full employment policy should be the stabilization of investment.

249. This point of view is set out ably and clearly in the pamphlet on "The Problem of Unemployment," issued by Lever Brothers and Unilever Limited. The pamphlet outlines a programme for stabilizing the total of investment by measures of three types:

(1) Measures to stabilize so far as possible private business investment. These may include direct subsidies, loans at low rates of interest, tax remission when stimulation of private investment is desired; and action in an opposite sense when private investment is ample or excessive.

(2) Extension of public business investment into new fields,

by substituting public monopoly for private ownership in particular industries, such as those connected with transport or power, yielding marketable goods and services.

(3) Much greater planned activity of communal outlay in its established field of roads, schools, hospitals and the like, yielding non-marketable goods and services.

The intention in regard to the second and third of these measures is that public investment not for profit should be used as a means of compensating for the fluctuation which private investment is still expected to show, in spite of all efforts to make it more stable. It is pointed out that those measures involve a complete change of budgetary policy. There should be a "double budget," that is to say a budget split into two parts "one containing the standing expenditure that should be met annually out of current revenue; the other containing normal capital expenditure and all such emergency measures as should be taken in times of depression to fight unemployment or stimulate trade." The "ordinary" budget should be balanced annually and it should remain the principle that any rise in its expenditure be covered by raising taxation. The "extraordinary" budget should be covered—or over-covered—only in times of prosperity. The pamphlet contemplates a lower level of employment than that aimed at in this Report, assuming the maintenance of a substantial reserve of labour. This difference does not affect the arguments that follow.

250. Full employment clearly involves stabilization of investment as of outlay generally, and many of the measures just named would find a place in a full employment policy. But on the view taken here they cannot be the whole or the main part of that policy. They represent treatment based on an incomplete diagnosis of the disease. Full employment cannot be attained simply by efforts to stabilise the trade cycle by revised financial budgetary methods for dealing with private investment, reinforced by public investment whether for business or for communal purposes. To a programme limited in this way there are many objections.

251. First, quantitative fluctuation of demand, whether cyclical or otherwise, is not the only cause of long-term unemployment. In Britain, between the two wars, structural unemployment was far more serious. Nor was structural unemployment simply or mainly a problem of demobilization, of transition to peace in the immediate aftermath of war. It resulted mainly from the decline of international trade, that is to say from the changed economic structure

of the world.[1] Fear of failure to find jobs of any kind after this wa
is the main anxiety of most people to-day. It will not be allayed
by promise of attempts to control the trade cycle.

252. Second, the general trade cycle is not the only form o
fluctuation which may lead to long-term unemployment. The
hyper-cyclical fluctuation of building, common to Britain and the
United States[2] though not simultaneous in the two countries, as i
the general trade cycle, requires measures specifically directed to
the building industry. These measures can only take the form of a
long-term programme of effective demand for building construction
guaranteed by the financial power of the State.

253. Third, it is far from certain that measures of the kind now
proposed—variation of taxation and offer of cheap loans—would
be materially more effective for the control of the trade cycle than
the methods of the past, such as variations of the rate of interest and
"open market" policy. All such financial inducements to invest are
apt to prove too weak for their task. It is one thing to take the horse
to the water, and quite a different thing to make him drink. Most of
those who make control of the cycle in private investment their main
proposal look forward to no more than partial success. They assume
that some fluctuation of private investment will continue and they
propose that the State should compensate for this by a counter
fluctuation of public works, that is to say by a de-stabilization of
communal investment. This leads to the next objection.

254. Fourth, the idea of keeping communal investment on tap to
fill gaps in private investment is practicable only for a very small
fraction of communal investment. It is true that road construction
or house building can, theoretically, be slowed down or speeded
up at will. But the demand for roads and houses, as well as for most
other forms of publicly controlled investment (sewerage, public
utilities, schools, hospitals, etc.) is intimately linked with the general
economic activity of the nation. If private enterprise erects a new
factory in some part of the country, public enterprise must follow
suit and create the social capital required by those who are to work
in that factory. It is not practicable to build factories one year and
to postpone to a later year, when there might be a slump in private
investment, the provision of houses for the workers, schools for their
children, hospitals, civic centres and other communal services

---

[1] See *Unemployment* (1930), pp. 355–7, showing that the industries subject to
heavy unemployment in 1929 included hardly any war industries.

[2] Described for Britain in *Unemployment* (1930), pp. 335–9. For the United
States see paras. A 47–8 in Appendix A and the authorities cited there.

What is said here of houses and of communal investment, providing goods or services without charge, applies equally or with even greater force to public business investment, providing goods and services such as light, power or transport, for which a charge is made to the consumers. The reason for desiring a large extension of the public sector of business investment is not in order to de-stabilize it to fit the instabilities of private investment, but in order to make steady development on a long-term programme possible over a larger field. It is true that a considerable proportion of total investment was under public control even before this war and the proportion is likely to grow. But investment does not become any more postponable because it is public. Only investment of low social utility is postponable. The amount of public investment which on any just view of social priorities can be regarded as postponable to fit fluctuation in other fields is likely at highest to be sufficient to compensate for such fluctuation of overseas demand as cannot be prevented (see paragraphs 344-6 in Part VI). Public investment should not be given the additional task of compensating for fluctuation of private investment at home.

255. Fifth, merely to stabilize investment at about its present average rate, by cutting off booms and slumps, even if that could be accomplished under conditions leaving the bulk of investment to private enterprise, would be manifestly inadequate. Since the first World War, the booms at the top of the trade cycle in Britain have been accompanied by more than 10 per cent of unemployment, while the boom of 1937 in the United States left more than 12 per cent of the labour force unused. Even before the first World War anything approaching full employment, with unfilled vacancies comparable in number to persons unemployed, was attained, if at all, only for a few months at the top of each cyclical fluctuation. The idea that the booms of the past represented an excess of industrial activity and employment which must be cut off in order to cure the slump cannot survive an examination of the facts of unemployment. The boom of the past consisted in large part of making good deficiencies of equipment resulting from the slump. If, without any other change, investment were stabilised at the average level achieved in the past, a substantial proportion of labour would always be unemployed; cyclical fluctuation would be replaced by a condition of permanent semi-slump. Stabilization of investment not at the average of good and bad times, but at the level of the best times means much more investment than at present. But the growing stock of productive capital which continuous private

investment activity at a boom rate would bring into being would be unprofitable unless the market for the goods produced by this growing stock of capital grew continuously. Such a growth of market, however, pre-supposes an equal growth of consumers' real purchasing power. There is nothing in these proposals to show where the additional purchasing power is to come from, once the desired level of employment has been attained and no further unemployed men are being restored to a full wage. Private investment can grow only with the growth of population and with a type of technical progress that demands more capital per head. Loans at low interest, increases in depreciation allowances, and so forth, may help to stabilize private investment, but they alone cannot raise it sufficiently to fill a deflationary gap of the dimensions which we have experienced in the past. This is not to say that intelligent State planning and particular schemes of industrial re-organization may not increase private capital investment—at least for a certain period of time. Such planning and re-organization, however, which ought to be the task of the National Investment Board, go far beyond the scope of Government activity envisaged in the proposals here under review.

256. The last of the objections set out above raises difficult economic issues. The broad results of the argument does not depend on technicalities. A full employment policy worthy of the name cannot limit itself to curbing the boom slightly and slightly mitigating depression. Its aim is the abolition of booms and slumps and the maintenance of a level of employment hitherto not even attained during booms. It is not a policy to be applied intermittently, but continuously. It is a policy of consciously and continuously steering the economy on a steady course of progress.

EXPANSION OF PRIVATE CONSUMPTION OUTLAY

257. Some expansion of private outlay, brought about by a redistribution of income increasing the propensity to consume, should be part of a full employment policy. Several of the measures included in the programme of spending set out above, in particular those for Social Security, would have this consequence. The proposal to be examined here goes further. It is that the placing of adequate purchasing power in the hands of the citizens, so that they will spend more, should be the main instrument of a full employment policy. It is argued that in this way full employment might be achieved with a minimum of State interference and planning. To a proposal of this character there are several serious objections.

258. First, the citizens' outlay might not be wisely directed, having regard to the quality and location of the available labour. The waste of resources occasioned by unemployment is not evenly spread over the whole of industry. As is shown in Part II, some industries are far more severely affected than others. The industries which produce for popular consumption at home—and would thus be the direct beneficiaries of an increase of popular spending—are not the ones most severely hit by unemployment in peace-time. Allowing more purchasing power to remain in the hands of the public will certainly increase the demand for a great variety of goods and services; but there is no certainty or probability that this additional demand will exert itself just in those directions in which unemployment is to be found. Money spent on drink does not give employment to the miner, but to the brewer; money spent on milk does not help to solve the problem of the unemployed engineer. It may be said that consumers' demand should be supreme, and that, if the consumer so ordains, the miner should become a brewer and the engineer a dairy farmer. While the argument can be accepted for the long run, it is impracticable for the short run. There must be time for such a change. But full employment cannot wait. The outlay which is designed to produce full employment cannot be indiscriminate outlay; it must be directed to those industries and localities where idle labour and idle capacity can be brought together; it must be designed to correct the instability of investment. Moreover, general stimulation of private outlay—attained by a remission of taxation—may to a large degree set up a demand for foreign instead of home produced goods, and thus give employment to foreigners rather than to people unemployed in this country. This would raise difficult additional problems as to how payment for such imports is to be made.

259. Second, the additional citizens' outlay might not be directed to those forms of consumption which were socially most desirable; it might go to luxuries rather than to the necessaries—good food and good housing. In a free market economy, consumers can buy only that which is offered to them, and that which is offered is not necessarily that which is of most advantage to them. It is that which appears to give the best prospect of profit to the producer. In a free market economy under pressure of salesmanship the negroes of the Southern States of America have, to a large extent, obtained automobiles and radios and have not obtained good housing, sanitation and medical service. In the free market economy of Britain under pressure of salesmanship the citizens have devoted appreciable

parts of their increasing resources to funeral benefits of little social importance furnished at excessive cost or to the waste of football pools and other frivolous amusements.

260. Third, and most important, there are many essential services which individuals either cannot get for themselves or can get only at excessive cost, compared with the cost of collective provision. Even if individual parents want to do the very best they can for their children, they cannot individually secure nursery schools, play-grounds, hospitals, libraries; they cannot individually secure good housing in healthy surroundings. There are great economies in large-scale spending and there are many vital needs which can be met only by collective action. In Britain, by full employment, we might without any other change raise our production one-eighth above the levels reached before the war. Would the best use of the whole of that increased productivity to-day be to increase the free spending power of consumers? The spending power of the community rose by nearly one-third in the thirty years up to the present war. That rise no doubt conferred great benefits but it did not abolish Want. It left the giant evils of Squalor, Disease and Ignorance still strongly entrenched.

261. The third of the foregoing reasons, as is stated, is the most important and for the present the decisive reason. Against the first reason it is arguable that, given adequate control over the location of industry, occupational mobility is sufficient to enable the labour supply to follow any change of demand resulting from consumers' choice. Against the second reason it is arguable that freedom of citizens to spend their money well or ill is an essential citizen liberty and that, in so far as bad spending results from high pressure sales-manship, the remedy is not to restrict the liberty of citizens but to control the methods of salesmanship, by such measures as regulation of hire purchase or conversion of industrial assurance into a public service. The third reason remains untouched by such arguments. There are vital things needing to be done to raise the standard of health and happiness in Britain which can only be done by common action, which in a community where democracy is so well established as in Britain will be secured in accord with the wishes of the citizens by the democratically controlled State.

262. Some re distribution of private incomes, increasing the propensity to consume should be part of a full employment policy. But it cannot be the whole of that policy or its main instrument. For technical and for moral reasons alike, the State, if it undertakes the responsibility of ensuring sufficient total outlay for full employ-

ment, must concern itself also with the direction of outlay. The right division between the scope of the State and of the private citizens in this matter may well be found in the application of the principle of a social minimum. In the total outlay directed to maintain full employment, priority is required for a minimum for all citizens of housing, health, education and nutrition, and a minimum of investment to raise the standard of life of future generations. The democratic state must be guided, and can safely be guided by social priorities up to that minimum. The scope for free action by the citizens is in spending above that minimum.

SECTION 7. A FULL POLICY FOR FULL EMPLOYMENT

263. Examination of each of two alternative approaches to the problem of full employment—by stabilization of total investment and by increasing the purchasing power of consumers—leads to the same conclusion. Each of these policies has elements of value, but each is incomplete; neither can stand by itself. Many of the measures proposed as part of these incomplete policies fall naturally into place as part of a larger adequate programme. It is necessary to increase consumption, but not only or mainly by increasing purchasing power in the hands of consumers. It is necessary to stabilize investment, but not at a level of inadequate consumption and under-employment, and not by leaving private investment to pursue an erratic course, while de-stabilizing public investment to fit that course.

264. Full employment means ensuring that outlay in total is sufficient. Only the State can ensure that. Full employment at the rising standards of life made possible by technical progress means that the outlay is wisely directed. The State cannot escape ultimate responsibility for the general direction of outlay by reference to social priorities, however much it may be guided in its direction by the preferences expressed by citizens, in buying as well as in voting. The State cannot undertake the responsibility for full employment without full powers. It must adopt neither the consumption approach nor the investment approach exclusively, but must be free to adjust policy according to circumstances, over the whole range of possible subjects of spending.

THE PROSPECTS OF SUCCESS

265. If the State in Britain adopts the policy outlined here, can it make certain of success in conquering unemployment? The

answer to this question has to be given in stages. There are some
things of which the State can make certain. It can, by incurring
expenditure, raise the total demand for labour to any desired point
that is to say the State can make certain that there is always a demand
for labour quantitatively exceeding the supply of labour. This is
the most important step required, and will make impossible such
mass unemployment as occurred between the Wars. But it will not
reduce unemployment to a harmless minimum, unless demand for and
supply of labour are related qualitatively as well as quantitatively
This means either (a) ensuring that the demand for labour, besides
being sufficient in total, is in each of its main types stable, so that
men are not thrown out of work by fluctuation in particular industries, or (b) making the supply of labour so fluid that even if men are
thrown out of work of one kind they are able to turn to other work
without delay. In a totalitarian self-sufficing community the qualitative adjustment of demand and supply is simple. The demand in
each industry can be kept stable or alternatively men can be directed
from one industry to another. In a free community the problem is
more complicated, in proportion to the degree of freedom and independence which it is desired to preserve for the citizens. In a community which trades largely with other independent communities
the problem is more complicated still. In Britain under the policy
proposed, even assuming adequacy at all times of the total demand
for labour, change in particular demands involving a risk of unemployment may come about in three ways.

266. First, there may through technical progress be change in the
kind of labour demanded. Clearly no attempt should be made to
stop technical progresss. It may involve some change of employments and by consequence some unemployment, but if by control
of location of industry violent local mis-direction of demand is
prevented and if the entry of youthful labour into industries is
controlled, while training facilities are provided for older persons,
experience suggests that the resulting unemployment can be reduced
to a point at which it represents no serious evil, and is a small price
to pay for progress.

267. Second, there may be fluctuation in private business investment at home. So long as any substantial part of industry is conducted by private enterprise, there remains the possibility that the
process of equipping and re-equipping it with machinery and other
means of production will be irregular, and by consequence the
demand for labour in making the means of production will fluctuate.
How serious this is likely to be as a factor in causing unemployment

depends in part upon unsettled theoretical considerations as to the causation of cyclical fluctuation of investment, and in part on the practical possibility of bringing about, by suitable measures of control, a greater stability of business investment, while still leaving it in private hands. In this matter it will only be possible to proceed experimentally. If the State fails by lesser methods to bring about sufficient stability in private investment, even though consumption is expanding steadily, the case will be made out either for bringing a larger part of industry into public ownership, or for stronger controls over private investment generally.[1]

268. Third, there may be fluctuation in demand coming from countries overseas. This is discussed in Section 4 of Part VI where a distinction is drawn between countries engaged in supplying the primary products, that is to say food and raw materials, which form the bulk of the imports to Britain and constitute the main demand for British exports, and industrial countries engaged like Britain mainly or largely in producing manufactures and liable like Britain to cyclical fluctuation. It should prove possible, by appropriate common action, greatly to diminish the violence of these fluctuations, particularly in the first class of country. In relation to those countries Britain by herself, as one of the largest buyers of their products, can do much to secure their prosperity and her own

[1] Investment includes addition to stocks. Fluctuations in the volume of stocks carried have been important factors aggravating economic instability in the past. In so far as fluctuations of stock-holding arise from fluctuation in other factors, such as the rate of interest or the rate of adding to capital equipment, they will be reduced automatically by stabilizing those other factors. But there have also been spontaneous changes in the desire to hold stocks, through speculative influences, i.e. expectation of rising or falling prices, whether justified or unjustified. If these are allowed to go unchecked they gather momentum and may cause serious instability; the volume of stocks held is usually estimated at about half the annual output, so that a decision to reduce stocks by, say, 20 per cent in a particular year would cause a 10 per cent reduction in total outlay, even if secondary influences are ignored. It would be inappropriate and impracticable to offset such changes by opposite variations in the rate of long-term investment, or to rely on countering them by indirect methods, such as playing about with the rate of interest, which might be both ineffective and dangerous. If speculation in stocks seems likely to continue as a serious disturbing influence, the remedy is for the State to retain permanently some of the controls over stocks and working capital established in war-time, continuing to act as wholesaler in relation to the principal food-stuffs and raw materials; it may find itself driven into that position automatically in dealing, by long-term collective contracts, with the instability of overseas demand from primary producers (see para. 268). In the management of stocks as in other matters, private enterprise can be allowed to continue only so long as it serves public interests.

prosperity together. In so far as overseas demand for British products cannot be stabilized completely, it will still remain possible for the State in Britain to expand home demand to compensate for falling off of overseas demand, reducing unemployment to that which results from friction, that is to say from inability of the men thrown out by depression abroad to turn over without delay to meet the increased demand at home.

269. Adequacy of total demand for labour implies also general stability of demand. The State by ensuring outlay can achieve both these things. But except in a totalitarian community, there remains the possibility of particular instabilities which, through friction, may cause unemployment. The three forms of particular instability noted here stand on different footings. The first, being a condition of progress, will persist in any progressive society, but need not and should not produce permanent or large scale unemployment; it is allowed for in the 1 per cent of interval unemployment named in paragraph 169. The second is the price of leaving a substantial part of business investment in private hands; if it proves serious, it can be reduced by extension of the public sector of business investment; it does not exist in war. The third is beyond the control of the British national State, but not beyond its influence; compensation for it by home demand is completely within the power of the State; the frictional unemployment that may remain in spite of compensation is allowed for in another 1 per cent of unemployment in paragraph 169. Exactly how much of a problem will be presented by each of the three forms of particular instability cannot be determined in advance. But the State has resources for dealing with all these types of fluctuation. Given adequacy of total demand, given control of location of industry, given the organization of the labour market and a reasonable readiness of men on proved need to change their trades rather than stand indefinitely idle, there is every reason for believing that the policy proposed here could rob unemployment of nearly all its terrors, by reducing it to a harmless minimum that could be fitly and honourably covered by unemployment insurance. An adequate scheme of unemployment insurance is in part a price which a free community may rightly pay for freedom, and for the advantages of international trade.

SOCIAL DEMAND

270. The policy of full employment outlined here is a policy of socializing demand rather than production. It attacks directly

the central weakness of the unplanned market economy of the past—failure to generate steady effective demand for its own products. It makes possible the retention of competition in meeting social demand. It makes possible the retention of private enterprise to discover and develop the best technical methods of production, so long as private enterprise appears to be the most efficient agency for that purpose. At the same time it does not block the way to socialization of production in general or in any particular industry. It is a policy of doing what must be done under any economic system which aims at full employment, namely the adjustment of total outlay to the datum of man-power. That has to be done, and it can be done, whether production itself is socialized or not. It could be done in a United States which remained capitalist as in a Soviet Russia which was wholly collectivized or in a Britain which took a middle course. Nationalization of the means of production in every industry would not be an alternative to the policy of ensuring outlay for full employment; it would only change the conditions under which that policy had to be pursued. Nationalization of particular industries may be useful as part of this policy, but is even less of an alternative to it; the adjustment of total outlay to total manpower is meaningless, except as a global policy covering the whole of industry.

271. The policy of this Report, while suggested by economic analysis, is direct and practical and in accord with the lessons of experience. It is direct and practical, because giving employment to building operatives, coal miners, agriculturalists, or any other class of persons depends on directing outlay to their products; ensuring employment up to any given amount depends on guaranteeing a market and price. It is in accord with the lesson of repeated experience of war that full employment is achieved, not by socialization of production which even in war is still left largely in private hands, but by socialization of effective demand, determined by a scale of priorities. That, with a different scale of priorities, to suit peace rather than war, with no limitless demand for war material requiring rationing and restrictions elsewhere, with a restoration of all essential citizen liberties, including free spending of personal incomes, is the essence of what is proposed here.

272. The policy outlined in the Report by-passes the socialist-capitalist controversy. It can be accepted by persons holding many different views on that controversy—by those who desire socialism at once, by those who oppose socialism at any time, and by those who are prepared to judge private enterprise and public enterprise

on their merits in the light of experience. This does not mean that the adoption of a full employment policy does not affect the debate between socialism and capitalism. It does affect that debate in many ways. It places the old issues of efficiency, enterprise, and social justice in a new setting. It gives a fresh turn to every controversy.

273. The policy is not proposed as a solution of all social problems, as a settlement of all issues of social justice or a satisfaction of all human desires. It is not proposed on the assumption that employment itself is an end. It will not deprive Britons of the future of the duty and pleasure of political controversy, conducted with vigour but with a sense of fundamental unity and leading usually to practical compromises sanctioned by voting. The policy is proposed only as a next step which must be taken and on which all parties might agree whatever their views on steps to follow.

274. The proposals of this Report do not pre-judge any unsettled issues. They place on the State the responsibility for maintaining full employment in a free society, and they give to the State all the necessary powers for that purpose. How the State should exercise those powers, how much it should undertake directly and how much should be done by private citizens, can be left to be settled later in the light of differing views as to the advantages and disadvantages of central planning and individual action respectively, and also in the light of growing experience of those advantages and disadvantages.

275. What is proposed here is a policy rather than a cut-and-dried programme. In the field of Social Insurance it is possible and desirable to define rights and duties clearly and completely. It is possible to be precise because Social Insurance deals with measurable risks and action to provide for them is within the power of the community. It is desirable to be precise, so that knowing the minimum that is guaranteed to them by Social Insurance, individuals can with confidence plan their lives and actions above that minimum. The adventure of full employment in a free society is different. It is an adventure, because it has never been accomplished in the past. It it an adventure, because the State in this field is not wholly master of events so long as it desires to preserve the freedom of individuals, and so long as it must adjust its actions to the actions of other communities. It is an adventure which must be undertaken if free society is to survive. It is an adventure which can be undertaken with confidence of ultimate success. Success, however, will come not by following any rigid formula but by adapting action to circumstances which may change continually. The adventure of full em-

ployment in a free society is not like the directed flight of an aircraft on a beam. It is a voyage among shifting and dangerous currents. All that can be done is to see that the craft is well found, and that the pilot has all the necessary controls, and instruments to guide his use of them.

Part V

INTERNAL IMPLICATIONS
OF FULL EMPLOYMENT

Industrial Discipline (paras. 277–82). Determination of Wages (paras. 283–8).
Price Policy (paras. 289–92). Monopolies and Trade Associations (paras.
293–5). Full Employment and Private Enterprise (paras. 296–300).

276. To abolish chronic or recurrent deficiency of demand, and
bring it about that there are always more vacant jobs than unemployed men seeking jobs, will change the conditions of life for
all men and will affect the working of many institutions. It will
give a new turn to all social relations. Here a few only of all the
implications of established full employment can be examined. It
will be convenient to take in order the problems of industrial
discipline and efficiency; of the determination of wages; of the
determination of prices; and of the treatment of monopolies and
trade associations. The last of these topics leads naturally to the
general issue of the control of industry, that is to say, of the function
of private enterprise and of public enterprise or public control,
respectively, under conditions of full employment.

INDUSTRIAL DISCIPLINE

277. Some people anticipate that if a policy of full employment
becomes effective, industrial discipline and efficiency resting on
discipline will be destroyed or diminished. This point of view finds
expression in an article appearing in the *Banker's Magazine* :[1]

"... And is there not also a tendency in much of this modern
planning—not forgetting the Beveridge Plan—to overlook the
fact that, human nature being what it is, the workers of the
future, capitalists and wage-earners alike, will require the old
spur of rewards and punishment (good profits and good wages,
fears of losses and bankruptcy, and, yes, fears of unemployment and poverty) to ensure the necessary drive in this world
of internal and international competition."

[1] *Banker's Magazine*, August, 1943, pp. 76–7.

The possibility that under conditions of full employment, industrial discipline and private enterprise may be found to be mutually incompatible is faced frankly from another standpoint, in one of the articles on full employment that appeared in *The Times*:

> "Unemployment is not a mere accidental blemish in a private-enterprise economy. On the contrary, it is part of the essential mechanism of the system, and has a definite function to fulfil.
>
> "The first function of unemployment (which has always existed in open or disguised forms) is that it maintains the authority of master over man. The master has normally been in a position to say: 'If you don't want the job, there are plenty of others who do.' When the man can say: 'If you don't want to employ me, there are plenty of others who will,' the situation is radically altered. One effect of such a change might be to remove a number of abuses to which the workers have been compelled to submit in the past, and this is a development which many employers would welcome. But the absence of fear of unemployment might go farther and have a disruptive effect upon factory discipline. Some troubles of this nature are being encountered to-day, but in war-time the over-riding appeal of patriotism keeps them within bounds. In peace-time, with full employment, the worker would have no counterweight against feeling that he is employed merely to make profits for the firm, and that he is under no moral obligation to refrain from using his new-found freedom from fear to snatch every advantage that he can."[1]

The inference drawn by the writer of these words is not that mass-unemployment should be continued in order to preserve discipline under private enterprise, but that full employment involves a further change in the status of the workpeople and a greater share by them in industrial management.

278. There is no doubt of the tendency in the past for bad time keeping and other signs of industrial discipline to become more prominent in times of good trade. This was shown statistically many years ago in a Board of Trade Memorandum on Fluctuations in Employment. Loss of working time amongst engineers through unpunctuality in the morning was found to be considerably greater on the average in times of active trade than in years of depression.[2] The same tendency appears unmistakably in the administration of

[1] *The Times*, 23rd January, 1943.
[2] *British and Foreign Trade and Industry*, Second Series, p. 100.

unemployment insurance covering all industries. Table 20 below sets out the numbers of cases coming before Courts of Referees for refusal of benefit on the ground that the workman has been dismissed for misconduct or has left his work voluntarily without good cause, and shows these numbers rising and falling regularly with the employment percentage in the trade cycle.

Table 20

DISALLOWANCES OF UNEMPLOYMENT BENEFIT, 1930–39

Year	Employment lost through Misconduct	Employment left Voluntarily without just cause	Failure or refusal to apply for or accept suitable employment or carry out written directions	Total of cols 1-3
1930 (est.)	50,200	85,800	45,500	181,500
1931 (est.)	50,600	79,400	54,100	184,000
1932	40,821	58,232	29,470	128,523
1933	38,169	61,386	29,555	129,110
1934	42,029	78,265	31,636	151,930
1935	46,535	91,883	32,118	168,536
1936	54,241	119,157	37,498	210,896
1937	58,380	144,468	39,936	242,784
1938	62,004	141,294	36,982	240,288
1938 Jan.–Jul.	35,296	79,646	21,353	136,295
1939 Jan.–Jul.	33,962	80,925	23,950	138,837

The Unemployment Insurance Act, 1930, which came into operation on 13th March, 1930, made extensive changes both in the conditions for receipt of benefit and in the procedure for consideration of claims, so that numbers of disallowances before and after that date cannot be compared. In the *21st Abstract of Labour Statistics* (p. 64), figures are published from 13th March, 1930 to 8th December, 1930, and from 9th December, 1930, to 31st December, 1931. The estimates given above for 1930 represent an addition of one-third to the figures for 13th March to 8th December; those for 1931 represent a subtraction of 5 per cent from the figures for 9th December, 1930, to 31st December, 1931. These proportions are based on the experience of 1937 and 1938. The estimates are approximations only, but are sufficient to leave no doubt of the large fall in disallowances in the depression of 1932. No figures have been published after July, 1939. As appears from the last two lines of the table, disallowances were at much the same level in the first seven months of 1938 and 1939 respectively.

279. The figures in Table 20 are interesting in several ways. First, they show that disallowances of benefit were nearly twice as numerous in the relatively prosperous year 1937 as they were in the depression of 1932–33. Second, they show that the number of disallowances, though not negligible, is small in proportion to the total number of claims to benefit, even in 1937 not more than 2½ per cent, for the number of claims in that year exceeded 10,000,000.

It is important to realize also that the increase of disallowances, in good years as compared with bad years, does not arise simply from relaxation of the sense of discipline in the same individuals. It is in part due to a change in the composition of the labour force. Men of unsteady character are the first to lose their situations when trade declines and to be wholly unemployed in a depression; in times of good trade they are better able to obtain employment; they form thus a larger proportion of those who are liable to lose employment.

280. Undoubtedly a change from chronic unemployment to full employment will affect the problem of industrial management. But it is easy to exaggerate the difficulty of the new problem, and it is unimaginative to be blind to the new opportunities. In the first place, full employment does not mean that men will have no motive to retain their present jobs; full employment does not mean that everyone has security in his present job even if he behaves well in it; still less does it mean that he has security if he behaves badly. Full employment means only that, if a man loses one job, he has a chance of finding another. That does not make it of no importance to the individual to preserve his present job, if he has one which suits him and uses his capacities. He will not get unemployment benefit, if he leaves his job without just cause or is dismissed for misconduct. He will have a better prospect than now of getting another job, but he may have to change his trade and place of residence to get it. Dislike of doing that will in all normal cases continue to be a motive for steady work and good performance. In the second place, against any loss of efficiency that may come through lightening the fear of unemployment must be set the gain that will come from the same cause. Fear of unemployment in the past has been the fertile source and justification of resistances to technical change and of restrictions on output, open or covert. To remove this fear from all the steady men who want nothing but a steady job and to take pride in their work, would bring advantages infinitely outweighing any loss through indiscipline of the few idlers and shirkers. In the third place, it is a test of good management in any industrial establishment to promote the right feeling among those employed there. Workmen have no love for idlers. If the conditions of employment are recognized as just, if by participation in management and in discussion of their common interests the general body of workpeople are made to feel themselves partners in enterprise, the public opinion of each man's mates will be a strong and effective motive to keep him up to the mark.

281. The challenge to management that will be presented by full employment is a challenge that enlightened employers will welcome. The essence of civilization is that men should come to be led more by hope and ambition and example and less by fear. The essence of democracy is that men of ability and integrity should be able to rise to leadership and greater responsibilities, irrespective of their first occupation and their parentage. It is not civilized that a man should feel bound at all costs and in spite of bad treatment to stick to the job he has, because he has no chance of ever finding another. It is not democratic that a man should feel bound to suppress criticisms and comments on matters that concern him and his work-mates, for fear of being punished with lasting unemployment.

282. Whatever the bearing of full employment upon industrial discipline one thing is clear. A civilized community must find alternatives to starvation for preservation of industrial discipline and efficiency. But a free community cannot look for those alternatives by increasing the list of forbidden actions and making new crimes. Special obligations may be attached to the the performance of particular tasks of critical importance to the community. But in general, in a free country at peace men must not be subject to penalties of fine or imprisonment simply for refusing to work or for working badly. It is an essential condition of freedom, and one of the marks distinguishing war and peace, that in peace each individual should be able to choose between leisure and more earnings, as he may choose between available occupations. The Essential Work Order as a method of controlling labour is for war, not for peace.

DETERMINATION OF WAGES

283. The problem of how wages should be determined under conditions of full employment is more important and more difficult. The article already quoted from *The Times* names as a second function of unemployment in a private enterprise economy the function of preserving the value of money:

> "If free wage bargaining as we have known it hitherto is continued in conditions of full employment there would be a continuous upward pressure upon money wage rates. This phenomenon also exists at the present time and is also kept within bounds by the appeal of patriotism. In peace-time the vicious spiral of wages and prices might become chronic."

There is here an implication of full employment which calls for careful consideration.

284. The right of wage earners to combine for the purpose of negotiating wages, hours, and conditions of work is generally regarded as an essential British liberty; the tradition that they should bargain sectionally, each craft and trade for itself, is old and strong. Making the labour market generally a seller's market rather than a buyer's market will increase permanently and markedly the bargaining strength of labour. In so far as this leads to labour, as a whole, gaining a larger share of the total product of industry, it leads to a desirable result. But, given the sectional structure of trade unionism, that is not the only possible result. Particular wage demands which exceed what employers are able to pay with their existing prices and which force a raising of prices, may bring gains to the workers of the industry concerned, but they will do so at the expense of all other workers, whose real wages fall owing to the rise in prices. The other workers will naturally try to restore the position, by putting forward demands of their own. There is a real danger that sectional wage bargaining, pursued without regard to its effects upon prices, may lead to a vicious spiral of inflation, with money wages chasing prices and without any gain in real wages for the working class as a whole.

285. It is necessary to face this possibility. Irresponsible sectional wage bargaining may lead to inflationary developments which bestow no benefits upon the working class; which spell expropriation for the old-age pensioner and the small rentier; and which endanger the very policy of full employment whose maintenance is a vital common interest of all wage-earners. How real is this possibility cannot be decided on theoretical grounds. Employers, under full employment in peace time, will not find it as easy to raise prices in response to increased wage costs as they find it when working on war contracts on a "cost plus" basis. Thus they will resist unreasonable wage demands more strenuously. Since peace-time demand, moreover, is more flexible than war-time demand, some industries at least will be able to raise prices only at the cost of a loss of trade to other industries. But the fact remains that there is no inherent mechanism in our present system, which can with certainty prevent competitive sectional bargaining for wages from setting up a vicious spiral of rising prices under full employment.

286. Two suggestions may be made for dealing with this problem. First, the central organizations of labour, such as the Trades Union Congress General Council, should devote their attention to the

problem of achieving a unified wage policy which ensures that the demands of individual unions will be judged with reference to the economic situation as a whole. If prices are kept stable, as is suggested below, rising productivity will make possible a continuous, if not spectacular, rise of money wages, even if the share of the total product that goes to the wage-earner remains no higher than at present. If that share can be increased, wages may rise still more; such a development is desirable from the economic as well as from the moral point of view. But the attempt to bring it about must be a co-ordinated attempt; it must not be a blind groping and pressing by numerous groups, each of which sees only its own sectional interest and tries to exploit its particular strategic advantages, and none of which attempts to judge the position of the whole economy. Organized Labour in Britain has sufficiently demonstrated its sense of citizenship and responsibility to justify the expectation that it will evolve, in its own manner, the machinery by which a better co-ordinated wage policy can be carried through.

287. The second suggestion relates to arbitration. In the new conditions of full employment, wages ought to be determined by reason, in the light of all the facts and with some regard to general equities and not simply by the bargaining power of particular groups of men. This suggests, not that there should be continuance in peace of the compulsory arbitration which has been accepted in war, but that collective bargains in each industry should in general include a clause for arbitration by an agreed arbitrator, in default of agreement between the parties. The employers' association and the union would thus be pledged in advance to accept the arbitration and to give no support of any kind to lock-outs or strikes in defiance of arbitration. But just as it has been argued above that, in a free society in peace, mere refusal to work by an individual should not be the subject of criminal proceedings, the same should apply to refusals which are not individual but collective. In other words, in peace in a free society, men should not be imprisoned for striking, though they may rightly be deprived of all support if the strike is contrary to a collective bargain or an agreed arbitration.

288. So long as freedom of collective bargaining is maintained, the primary responsibility of preventing a full employment policy from coming to grief in a vicious spiral of wages and prices will rest on those who conduct the bargaining on behalf of labour. The more explicitly that responsibility is stated, the greater can be the confidence that it will be accepted. But both the State and the managers of business have their part to play. The part of the

State lies in the adoption of a definite policy of stable prices, as suggested in paragraphs 289-92 below; it is unreasonable to expect from trade unions a reasonable wage policy, unless there is a reasonable price policy, just as much as it is impossible to have a price policy without a wage policy. The part of business managers lies in accepting the need for making available to others than themselves full information as to the financial condition of industry. Wages ought to be determined by reason, not by the methods of strike and lock-out. Ordeal by battle has for centuries been rejected as a means of settling legal disputes between citizens. Strikes and lock-outs, though they cannot in a free society be forbidden by law, are anachronisms as indefensible as ordeal by battle. They should give place to reason, but reason cannot work in practical affairs without facts. The correlative to acceptance by trade unions of an arbitration clause in all collective bargains would be acceptance by employers in all important industries of standardized accounting practice and their readiness to put all facts as to profits, costs and margins unreservedly at the disposal of the arbitrator and an expert staff for criticism.

PRICE POLICY

289. Adoption by the State of a price policy is a natural and probably an inevitable consequence of a full employment policy. This has been shown under full employment in war, when the price level has been a primary consideration in framing the National Budget. It is as necessary under a full employment policy in peace. One of the first and most obvious signs that total outlay was tending to be excessive in relation to the productive resources available would be a rapid rise of prices.

290. Inflation is almost as much an evil as deflation. It expropriates all those whose incomes are fixed in terms of money, not only the numerically unimportant group of rich rentiers, but also great numbers of small rentiers and particularly the growing class of old-age pensioners. There need be no fear that inflation might be the result of the Minister of National Finance overestimating the size of the deflationary gap, when he draws up his annual statement. Enough is known about the behaviour of consumers, as a group, to allow for sufficiently accurate estimates of their outlay. The behaviour of investors is less predictable, since the appearance of new technical processes, calling for new investment, is largely unpredictable. But, even if there are fluctuations in this field, they are not likely to be of great quantitative importance when compared

with the total of national outlay. The National Investment Board, moreover, would have certain powers of veto, to be used if private investment activity threatened to get out of hand. Even a fully employed economy, finally, possesses sizeable reserves of productive capacity; there is always the possibility of working overtime in some sectors, if the pressure of demand is temporarily increased. Inflationary tendencies, however, may appear from an altogether different source, that is to say, from the bargaining strength which full employment gives to organized labour, leading to demands for wage increases which business can satisfy only by an increase in prices. Such a development might upset the calculations upon which the Minister of National Finance has based his estimates. The successful working of a full employment policy, if free collective bargaining for wages continues, will depend ultimately on the degree of responsibility with which bargaining is conducted. But it would be unreasonable to expect the trade unions to abstain from using their bargaining strength to the full, unless the Government can give them some assurance that it is pursuing a policy of stable prices. This is the reason why price policy must be an integral part of a full employment policy.

291. Nor is there room for practical doubt as to what that policy should be. It should be a policy of maintaining a stable value of money in terms of necessaries, with wages rising both in money terms and in real terms as productivity per head increases. In the prospective circumstances of Britain, the ingenious arguments which have been advanced in the past, on the one hand for a policy of gently falling prices and on the other hand for a policy of gently rising prices, lose their validity. A falling price level increases the share of the total income going to rentiers. This, in view of the inevitably large national debt, is a grave disadvantage. But it does not justify the opposite suggestion that the right policy is one of rising prices, so that the claims of rentiers are cut down automatically. In future, with the vastly increased proportion of aged persons in the total population, the numerically most important class of rentiers will be old-age pensioners. If it is desired to cut down the gains of rentiers, or any particular class of them, that should be done directly through taxation—by death duties, by differentiation between earned and unearned incomes, and in other ways. Letting the price level rise is a clumsy form of taxation.

292. The need for a control of prices is greatest with regard to all goods and services which enter heavily into the cost of living of the average citizen. It is also great with regard to all essential

goods which are temporarily in scarce supply. As far as luxury articles or goods in ample supply are concerned, the need for price control is less pressing. Price control, therefore, does not have to cover the whole range of goods and services currently produced; it will concentrate upon essential goods and services and upon those in the supply of which there is a temporary scarcity. When concentrated in this fashion, the problem of price control presents no insuperable administrative difficulties. The faster the productivity of industry develops under the stimulus of a full employment policy, the smaller will be the difficulty of preventing prices from rising. Industrial progress tends to lower prices, while the bargaining of labour tends to increase prices. These two opposite tendencies can be held in balance in a progressive society, if all classes co-operate willingly.

MONOPOLIES AND TRADE ASSOCIATIONS

293. The problem of the right treatment of monopolies and trade associations arises under conditions of unemployment and full employment alike. It is a general question of the control of industry, arising from the constant efforts of all private enterprises to escape in one way or another from the pressure of competition and to organize barriers against it. This general problem cannot be discussed here; the control of industry would require another Report of its own. All that can be done is to note some of the ways in which passage from unemployment to full employment will affect the problem and the nature of the measures required for dealing with it.

294. In some ways the change to full employment might reduce the problem of monopoly practices. Many of the restrictive practices of business in the way of parcelling out markets, fixing minimum prices, making difficult the entry of new competitors, are like the restrictive customs of trade unions, in being measures of defence against deficiency of demand. The justification for these measures will be destroyed and the principal motive to adopt them will be weakened under conditions of adequate sustained demand. In some industries, if demand were strong and it was not supposed that a depression was immediately ahead, it is possible that the present tendency to associate would be reversed and that the natural individualism of British business men would assert itself. But in other ways, a full employment policy might work in a different direction. The response of industries already strongly organized to the setting up of a high demand for their services might take the

form of endeavouring to exploit the demand by raising prices, rather than of meeting the demand by increased production. It is essential that a full employment policy should be protected against such risks of exploitation. This protection is needed alike in the interest of consumers and in the interest of full employment itself. The successful working of any full employment policy depends upon the co-operation of the work-people, in maintaining discipline and a reasonable attitude in wage-bargains. That co-operation cannot be expected, unless the work-people are satisfied that exploitation of the position by their employers has been made impossible.

295. How can this be secured? As a general principle it may be laid down that business competition must be free, not forced. If in any industry a strong tendency develops towards collaboration between independent units or towards their amalgamation, the part of the State should be, not to try vainly to stop that tendency but to bring it under control. Amalgamations and large scale enterprises have many advantages to set against their dangers. There are three possible stages of control. The first stage is supervision; the starting-point of any treatment of the problem of control of industry, under full employment or under unemployment, must be the arming of some Government department with the duty of supervision, with the right to information and with a highly developed technique of cost accounting. These powers of supervision, that is to say of obtaining information, should apply to all businesses above a certain size, as well as to all trade associations. Every such association should be required to be registered and to give all necessary information as to its actions. The second stage is regulation. The supervising department should have power to disallow any price fixed by trade associations or any restrictive regulation as unreasonable and should be able, as the ultimate sanction, to cancel registration. Whether or not trade associations should be given any statutory powers of controlling their own industries, raises a wide question which cannot be discussed here. All that is certain is that if any statutory power is given to an industry in the management of its own affairs, the use of that power must be subject to effective control by the State, exercised through an independent Department with powers of veto and disallowance. The third stage of control is public ownership. If an industry is by nature a monopoly, or if it becomes a monopoly, it is essential that it should be conducted in the public interest and not in the interest of a section. The simplest way to secure that is to make it a public service under a public corporation.

FULL EMPLOYMENT AND PRIVATE ENTERPRISE

296. Examination of the internal implications of full employment leads at its close to a general issue. Can a policy of full employment be carried through and yield its full benefits under a system in which production is controlled in the main by private enterprise? The policy, as it has been set out here, is primarily one of socializing demand rather than production. It may be found convenient, as a subsidiary measure, to transfer particular industries from private to public ownership, in order to increase the power of the State directly to stabilize demand in a specified sector and in order to bring monopolies under assured control. It will certainly be necessary for the State, by inspection and supervision, to protect the community against risk of exploitation by monopolies and trade associations, in all industries. And it will be necessary for the State, in planning its own outlay, to have full continuous information as to the outlay plans of all large undertakings and to have some power of modifying those plans. But all this is far short of the nationalization of production generally. In particular it leaves the small, independent enterprise, in factory or shop or farm, unaffected. The "little man" can respond to demand under full employment, as under other conditions. So long as he remains little, he remains subject to competition and the interests of consumers need no further official safeguards.

297. The policy set out here is one which might be adopted by a community which held firmly to private enterprise, and accepted the principle laid down by an American economist: "Private industry can and will do the job of production. It is the responsibility of the Government to do its part to ensure a constant demand."[1] Full employment is achieved in war by State control of demand without socialization of production. There is every reason for hoping that full employment could be secured in peace by the policy outlined here, while leaving the major part of industry to private enterprise. Apart from the problems of international trade, discussed in Part VI, the only significant doubt that arises on this is as to the possibility under such conditions, of bringing about a sufficient stability of private investment, and preventing its cyclical fluctuation. It is reasonable to let that doubt be resolved by experience.

298. It can be argued, nevertheless, that under such conditions a policy of full employment, even if it gave full employment, would

[1] Professor Alvin Hansen, in *Post War Economic Problems*, edited by Seymour Harris, p. 14.

fail to yield its full benefits and might lead to dangerous consequences. It can be urged that all that is proposed here is insufficient,
without the socialization of production in all its more important
forms. This position may be supported by a variety of arguments.
In the first place, as has been pointed out above, the smooth working
of a full employment policy involves the co-operation of workpeople,
in enforcing industrial discipline on the unruly, in securing maximum
efficiency and removal of restrictions on output, in refraining from
pressing unreasonable claims that might set up a vicious spiral of
wages and prices. Can that co-operation, it is asked, be secured
under conditions of enterprise conducted for private profit? It is
argued, in the second place, that a State policy of full employment
will always be liable to sabotage by capitalists desiring to make
difficulties for the State. It is argued, in the third place, that substitution of national for private ownership of the means of production
is necessary to prevent the piling up of wealth which may be used
to manipulate the political machine. It is argued finally, that full
employment will not by itself bring about the more equal distribution of income which is essential to social justice.

299. These arguments raise large issues, economic, political and
moral, which fall to a large extent outside the scope of this Report.
The importance of these issues is obvious. They are not prejudged
in what is written here. The proposals of this Report are designed
for one essential practical purpose—to bring to an end the mass
unemployment and the fear of unemployment which, next to war,
have been the greatest evils of modern times. The proposals take us
round the next corner ahead—a corner which must be turned, if
we desire to preserve free institutions. The problems that lie beyond
that corner will become clearer when that corner has been passed;
they can, if we so desire, be left to be dealt with when they are
reached.

300. The basic proposals of this Report are neither socialism nor
an alternative to socialism: they are required and will work under
capitalism and under socialism alike, and whether the sector of
industry conducted by private enterprise is large or is small. A
conscious control of the economic system at the highest level—a
new type of budget which takes man-power as its datum—adequate
sustained directed demand for the products of industry—organization of the labour market—these are required in any modern
society. These things the State must provide in any case, if the
citizens want full employment. What else the State may be called
on to do has to be determined on other grounds, or can at need be

lecided later. From the point of view of full employment, the
lecision depends largely on how private citizens use their liberties.
f trade unions under full employment press wage claims unreasonably, maintenance of a stable price level will become impossible; wage determination will perforce become a function of the
State. If the private owners of business undertakings under full
employment set out to exploit consumers by organizing monopolies
and price rings, or abuse their economic power for political purposes,
or fail, with all the help of the State and in an expanding economy,
to stabilize the process of investment, the private owners cannot
for long be left in their ownership. If the people of Britain generally
under full employment become undisciplined in industry, that will
show either that they are not sufficiently civilized to be led by
anything but fear of unemployment and are unworthy of freedom,
or that the control of industry must be changed. All liberties have
their responsibilities. The greater the sense of citizen responsibility,
the greater can be the measure of liberty and the scope that is
left for agencies independent of the State.

Part VI

INTERNATIONAL IMPLICATIONS OF FULL EMPLOYMENT

SECTION 1. INTERNAL POLICY AND INTERNATIONAL EFFECTS

301. The international implications of a full employment policy are dealt with last in this Report, not because they are unimportant, but because that is their logical place. International trade has fundamentally different aspects for a country with full employment and for a country which, through deficiency of effective demand

or the products of its industry, is liable to chronic or recurrent mass
unemployment. For a community enjoying full employment, international trade is a means of raising the standard of life by international specialization and exchange; exports are desired only as
a means of paying for imports; they confer no advantage unless they
are exchanged for imports either immediately or later. For a community suffering from mass unemployment, exports may be advantageous even though they are given away, or, what comes to the
same thing, though they are made on loan to a country which later
repudiates the debt or are exchanged for a relatively useless token,
like gold, while useful imports are refused. This is because of what
is known to economists as the multiplier effect: the employment
given and the wages paid to the persons engaged on additional
exports set up an internal demand for other labour, so that the
exports, even though they are themselves given away, may increase
the production of useful things and add to prosperity at home.[1]
This is a particular aspect of the general proposition put by J. M.
Keynes, that, in a community suffering from deficient demand, even
useless employment like pyramid building, or digging holes and
filling them up again, or unproductive employment in making
armaments, may increase real prosperity. In default of a better policy
directed to production of useful things, any of these may be better
than doing nothing at all.

302. The dependence of the classical argument for the advantages
of free international trade and the disadvantage of almost all forms
of protection upon the assumption of full employment is a point
also emphasized by J. M. Keynes.[2] A country in which this assumption is realized, that is to say a country in which there is sufficient
effective demand for all its available man-power, may seek to develop
its foreign trade as a means of raising the standard of living. It may
lend abroad and for that purpose may export for a time without
requiring payment in imports; but it will do so only in hope of
getting imports later in payment of interest. It will have no motive
for restricting imports and can only lose by doing so. But a country
suffering from depression and unemployment may want a surplus
of exports over imports as a way of getting out of depression, and
in order to secure this export surplus, it may by tariffs and in other
ways, restrict drastically its current imports. This is a policy of each
country helping itself at the expense of others which, if practised by

[1] See *Export Policy and Full Employment*, by E. F. Schumacher (Fabian Publications, Ltd., 1s.).
[2] *General Theory*, pp. 333–4.

all countries, can lead to no positive result for any of them. But for every depressed industrial country, the temptation to such a course is strong, and may often be irresistible. In the great depression of the nineteen-thirties, it proved irresistible for nearly every country in the world.

303. Avoidance of mass unemployment is an assumption of uncontrolled international trading, in a much more important sense than it is an assumption of Social Security. In relation to the Plan for Social Security set out in my earlier Report, Assumption C— that mass-unemployment is prevented—means merely that, if there is mass unemployment, Social Security by income maintenance does not meet the needs; unemployment benefit is adequate treatment only for short interval unemployment. In relation to international trade, avoidance of mass unemployment in each of the main industrial countries is an underlying assumption in a much fuller sense; the whole economic relationship of different countries to one another depends primarily on the success which each of them achieves in securing a high stable level of employment at home. Plans for international trade must be different, according as we do or do not expect the chief industrial countries of the world to be successful in avoiding mass unemployment. Exactly what this means in practice will become clear from the discussion in Section 3 of bilateralism and the conditions of multilateral trade. Before proceeding to that discussion, it will be convenient to consider the special position of Britain in the world economy.

Section 2. BRITAIN'S NEED OF IMPORTS

304. For Britain international trade is vital. The structure of the home economy, and the benefits obtainable through a full utilization of home resources, will be profoundly affected by what happens in the international field. Britain needs foreign foodstuffs and raw materials; this need may be reduced by suitable policies at home, but it can never be abolished. To what extent it may have to be reduced will depend on factors largely outside Britain's control. Her ability to import depends upon her ability to export, and her ability to export depends in turn upon the willingness and ability of others to import manufactured goods. If depression abroad destroys that willingness or reduces that ability, then Britain is forced, by necessity and not by her own predilection, to make herself less dependent on foreign supplies. If she be forced into such a policy, her standard

of living may be lower than it might have been under conditions of flourishing international trade. This would mean that a full utilization of her home resources would become even more vital than before. Her own desire to participate in world trade and obtain the general advantages that flow from it will not be reduced by her pursuit of a full employment policy at home: it can be reduced or frustrated only by the failure of other countries to pursue a similar policy. Thus the choice—so often posed—of either pursuing a full employment policy at home or participating fully in international trade, is a false choice. The virtue of international trade is that it saves labour; the virtue of a full employment policy is that it uses labour. It would be senseless to save labour through international trade only in order to waste labour in unemployment. A vigorous demand at home and development of international trade are not alternative policies but the two halves of one policy.

305. Each half of the policy calls for the guidance and interest of the central Government. A strong sustained internal demand for labour, as has been argued in earlier portions of this Report, cannot be ensured by any power less than that of the State. But if, through successful use of that power, the home market is always buoyant, there is at least a possibility that the eagerness of British industrialists to find markets abroad may be reduced. The industries which most need imports of raw materials are not always the industries which produce exports to pay for them. Maintenance of exports, in order to ensure adequate purchasing power for imports, is a national interest, rather than the interest of any particular industry. It must be regarded as one of the responsibilities of the State. If buoyancy of the home market should cause British industrialists to neglect the foreign market, it would be necessary for the Government either to create sufficient inducements for private traders to export or itself to take a hand in the export business. This possibility of the need for direct Government action to maintain overseas trade makes it all the more necessary to put exports in their right place, by first ensuring full employment at home. Only so can it be made clear to the world that exports are wanted by Britain, not for the sake of full employment, but primarily as the means of paying for essential imports from other countries, and, in the second place, as a means of giving help to other countries where help is needed, for their relief and rehabilitation after the war and for their industrial development. This is the problem of Britain's need of international trade, in general terms. What does it mean in actual figures of imports and exports?

306. The net annual value of British imports just before the present war, on the average of the three years 1936–8, was £866 millions, after deducting £66 millions for goods re-exported in the same form as that in which they had entered. In addition, raw materials to the value of about £100 millions included in the total of £866 millions were re-exported after having undergone one or more processes of manufacture.[1] The "net retained imports," accordingly, which entered directly into the British standard of living may be put at about £770 millions. Only about £85 millions or 10 per cent of the total of £866 millions consisted of finished products;[2] £402 millions, or 46½ per cent were food, drink and tobacco; £240 millions, or 27½ per cent were raw materials; and the remaining £142 millions, or 16 per cent were goods which, though classified as "manufactured," had gone through some processes of manufacturing only and needed further treatment before being ready for use or consumption.

307. How were these imports paid for? The answer is given in general terms in the following table based on the average of three years, 1936–8:

	£ millions
Exports (excluding re-exports)	478
Earnings by Shipping Services	105
Earnings by Financial Services	40
Earnings on Foreign Investments	203
	826
Disinvestment, i.e. sale of British foreign assets or borrowing abroad	40
	866

If the value of the £100 millions or so of raw materials re-exported after manufacturing is excluded from imports and exports alike, the following table shows roughly how the net retained imports of about £770 millions were paid for:

	£ millions	Per cent
Visible Exports	380	49·3
Invisible Exports (Shipping and Finance Services and Investment Income)	350	45·5
Disinvestment	40	5·2
	770	100·0

---

[1] The average "import content" of British exports is probably about 20 per cent. Applying this percentage to the total of £478 millions of exports yields a figure of just under £100 millions.

[2] Two small items of "animals not for food" and "parcel post" representing together about £6 millions are included here as finished products.

That is to say only half the net retained imports were paid for by visible exports;[1] the other half were paid for by invisible exports and disinvestment.

308. That was the pre-war position. What may we expect to find when peace returns? That question naturally cannot be answered except, for the most part, in terms of conjecture, and is answered very differently by different authorities. It is certain, for instance, that we have parted with some of our overseas investments and have incurred some overseas debts, and shall have less net income under that head. Some talk as if we are likely to have lost the whole £203 millions shown in paragraph 307. To others, "it does not seem too sanguine to assume that we shall retain about £100–120 million net income from foreign investment after the war."[2] It is almost certain also that we shall end the war with a smaller merchant fleet of our own than that with which we began it. Some talk as if most or the whole of £105 millions of earning from shipping services would disappear. But ships need men and shipping is a skilled occupation. It is needless defeatism to suppose that the British will ever cease to be one of the most important seafaring nations in the world, whether the ships in which they start unconvoyed sailing again immediately after this war have been built in Britain or elsewhere. The financial services include not only finance in the narrow sense but insurance. Both of these will continue to be required. Britain will be almost the only country of Western Europe not shattered by war, and will have to take a leading share in re-establishing Europe financially and otherwise. When the time comes for financial and insurance services to be paid for, why should Britain not be able to earn in this way in the future as in the past? Taken as a whole, our invisible exports for some time to come will be materially less after this war than the £350 millions shown in paragraph 307. But whether they will be reduced by half or by more or by less than that is free for guessing. If we want to import as much as before the war, we shall have to export more in visible form, but how much more no man can say.

309. How much shall we need to import? Here, too, we are in the region of conjecture. Hardly any of our imports before the war can be described as luxuries. We could not have dispensed with them as imports, without lowering the standard of life of the general population, unless we replaced them by home production. More

[1] See Explanation of Terms in Appendix D.

[2] N. Kaldor in *Economic Journal*, July–September, 1943, p. 262. A later calculation by Mr. Kaldor in Appendix C puts this income at £80 millions at pre-war and £110 millions at post-war prices.

than that, adoption of a full employment policy would increase our imports of food and of raw materials alike. On the other hand, the proportion of our total food supply that is grown at home has been much increased in the war. This increased reliance on home production can continue with advantage as part of a policy of better nutrition, though it may be hoped that this policy will be directed mainly to producing at home those foods which can be produced there at less cost in human toil or which cannot readily be transported or stored. It is certain also that modern science opens the way to increasing self-sufficiency in relation to more things than food. The first World War led to the development in many countries of substitutes—chiefly water-power—for the British coal from which they were cut off. The present war has compelled Britain and America to find substitutes for rubber and other articles the supply of which has been destroyed or reduced drastically by the Japanese onslaught in the Far East. If such a course proved to be necessary, it is hard to believe that Britain could not replace imports of materials and food by home production, at least up to the extent of the diminution of her purchasing power through loss of some invisible exports. If, further, Britain seeks full employment in the first instance less by increasing free purchasing power, which consumers might use for imports, than by physical improvements at home, she may avoid much of the rise of imports that would follow otherwise through full employment itself.[1] Even under full employment, the problem might become one of regaining pre-war exports rather than one of increasing them by 50 per cent or 100 per cent or some other proportion.

310. On any alternative, the quantity of exports required is well within the capacity of the British industrial system. The proportion of total production exported, which was nearly 33 per cent in 1907, fell to somewhere between 21 and 24 per cent in 1924 and between 13 and 16 per cent in 1935. To double these exports would not mean making them 30 per cent of the total production after the war; total production will be increased both by technical progress and by full employment.

[1] The "import content" of objects of local authority expenditure, such as housing, educational buildings and public health (other than sewerage) has been estimated at 12 per cent to 13 per cent, while that of roads is negligible (see *Public Investment and the Trade Cycle in Great Britain*, by R. F. Bretherton, F. A Burchardt and R. S. G. Rutherford, Oxford, 1941, p. 302). On the other hand the import content of cotton piece goods consumed at home is about 33 per cent, while the average import content of all goods and services consumed or invested in Britain in 1938 was about 20 per cent.

SECTION 3. BILATERALISM AND THE THREE CONDITIONS
OF MULTILATERAL TRADE

THE MEANING OF BILATERALISM AND MULTILATERALISM

311. Britain must have imports; she must have exports to pay
for the imports. She must have international trade up to a certain
minimum; she has an interest, in common with other countries,
in re-building international trade not merely to that minimum but
to a maximum, so that all may benefit to the largest possible extent
from the saving of toil and effort which can be achieved through
the international division of labour. How should Britain proceed
in this matter? The first point to realize is that Britain's chances
in international trade are not unfavourable. There is a problem to
be solved, but it is a problem which has a solution. The countries
which produce food and raw materials need markets and have
largely developed their economic systems to supply markets of which
Britain is, for many articles, the largest and most important. They
are not only willing but anxious to sell to us. Should we then try
to make specific bargains with them—bargains advantageous to both
parties—so that we shall take their goods and they ours? Should
we confront them with the clear-cut alternative: we give you a
stable market here, if you give us a stable market for our exports;
but if you are not prepared to do the latter, you cannot have our
custom? This type of arrangement is normally called "bilateralism";
it is a form of barter, although all actual transactions are made in
the currency of the countries concerned. But the currency which
either country surrenders in payment for its imports is a blocked
currency; it cannot be used for purchases in countries outside the
bilateral arrangement; it can be used only to pay for the purchase
of goods of the country from which it was issued. Should we on the
other hand, attempt to return to a "multilateral" system—to a
system along the lines of the Gold Standard, under which countries
make their purchases wherever they find them cheapest and sell
their exports wherever they can, and do not attempt to balance
the purchases from one particular country against the sales made
to that particular country? Under a multilateral system, the currency received for exports to one country can be spent on imports
from any other country. No one can say: "you must now buy from
me, since I have bought from you." No one can say: "the currency
I have given you for your goods must be considered as blocked;
you can spend it or keep it; but if you want to spend it you must
spend it on my goods and on nobody else's."

312. Strict bilateralism means that the goods and services supplied as exports by country A to country B must be paid for by exports of equivalent goods and services from country B to country A. The international accounts of every pair of countries must balance.[1] In multilateral trade there is no need for the accounts of any pair of countries to balance and in practice none of them do. Country A may habitually sell to country B more than she buys from B and may habitually buy from country C more than she sells to C. Thus the United States on the average of the three years 1936–8 sold to Britain goods to the value of $499 millions a year and bought from Britain only to the extent of $174 millions a year. On the other hand, in the same three years, the United States bought from British Malaya goods, chiefly rubber and tin, to the value of $174 millions a year and sold to British Malaya less than $8 millions worth a year. This means that British Malaya from her sales to the United States had more dollars than she needed to use for her purchases in the United States—had a dollar surplus of $168 millions a year—while Britain had a dollar deficiency of $225 millions. What happened was that some of the surplus dollars of British Malaya were made available to Britain for buying from America. In goods British Malaya exported to Britain in those three years about as much as she imported from Britain, but she had also to pay Britain for services, like shipping, and to pay interest on British investments. In effect British Malaya transferred her surplus dollars, or some of them, to Britain to pay for imports from Britain and by that means Britain was able to pay for some of her imports from the United States. This is one illustration only of what happens all over the world under multilateral trade.[2] From one set of countries the United States imports normally less than she exports to them, so that they have dollar deficiencies; in addition to Britain, these countries in 1936–8 included France, Germany, Holland, Canada, Mexico, Venezuela. From another set

[1] Actual arrangements of a bilateral nature between two countries are seldom completely and strictly bilateral in the sense of the foregoing definition. The actual arrangements may merely specify a proportion of country A's imports from B as requiring to be balanced by exports to it; sometimes country A expects to be able to pay for the imports not covered expressly out of its general foreign balances. Sometimes the arrangement may be formally trilateral rather than bilateral. The essence of bilateralism lies in excluding the general interchangeability of all currencies.

[2] A yet more important source for Britain of the dollars which she needs to balance her accounts with the United States is South Africa. British exports of goods to South Africa as a rule greatly exceed her imports of goods from South Africa and are paid for either in gold which can be turned into dollars or by transferring dollars paid to South Africa for gold shipped to the United States.

of countries the United States imports normally more than she exports to them, so that they have dollar surpluses; in addition to British Malaya these countries in 1936–8 included the Dutch East Indies, China, Brazil and Cuba. As will appear later, the different trading relations of all these countries to one another and to the United States are of great importance in considering measures to deal with depressions; here they are given simply as illustrations of the nature of multilateral trade.

313. It is obvious that a multilateral system has great advantages. Bilateralism is akin to barter, with some of the limitations of that primitive system; it is workable but clumsy. Multilateral trade is trade with convertible money, a common medium of exchange. All currencies are freely exchangeable into all others, which means in effect, that there is a common denominator for all currencies, whether that denominator receives a special name or not. Gold used to play the part of international currency in the past, and it was the common purpose of the "Proposals for an International Clearing Union," published as a Treasury Memorandum by the British Government in April, 1943 (Cmd. 6437), and of the "United States Proposal for a United and Associated Nations Stabilization Fund," published by the United States Government at about the same time, to recreate an international trade and exchange system with an international currency, called in one case "bancor" and in the other case "unitas." A third plan was shortly afterwards put forward by the Canadian Government. These separate memoranda have now been followed (in April, 1944) by a proposal representing "the consensus of opinions of the experts of the United and Associated Nations," entitled "Joint Statement by Experts on the Establishment of an International Monetary Fund."[1] All these proposals aim at providing the machinery for multilateral trade without discrimination,[2] that is to say without one country treating the export offers of any other country differently from those of the rest of the world.

314. It is unnecessary here to make a detailed or technical examination of these proposals. Their basic design is this: every country is to be given a certain quota of international purchasing power which it can use, in addition to the gold already in its possession, to make payments abroad whenever its total income from abroad (from visible and invisible exports and from borrowing) fails to cover its total expenditure abroad (on imports, visible or invisible, or—with certain safeguards—on loans given to foreigners). There is no doubt that, by furnishing all countries with a reserve of inter-

[1] Cmd. 6519.   [2] See Explanation of Terms in Appendix D.

national purchasing power, it would be possible to start international trade after the war on a free multilateral basis; the larger the reserves, the greater is the freedom of action of each nation and the initial impetus given to world trade. The question to ask about all of these proposals is whether the initial impetus given by them to multilateral trade would renew itself, so that the system lasted. Would the engine keep running after it had been started? The answer to the question is that the continuance of multilateral trade depends, not on the scale or form of the initial reserves or on the technical details of international clearing and currency, but on suitable economic policies being adopted by all the countries taking part in multilateral trade. What constitutes a suitable economic policy?

315. A suitable economic policy obviously cannot mean that all nations must have the same domestic economic structure. Trade must be made possible between countries, some of which are socialist while others are capitalist; some of which are democratic while others are authoritarian; some of which favour free trade or low tariffs while others are highly protectionist. A suitable economic policy can only mean a policy which is free from sudden and unpredictable changes; a policy which does not put undue strains and stresses upon the rest of the world; in short, an economic good neighbour policy. General multilateral trading, as practised under the Gold Standard and as envisaged in the expert proposals for establishment of what is for practical purposes an international currency, is possible only if three conditions, or assumptions, are fulfilled: first, each of the participating nations must aim at full employment within its borders and must do so without relying on export surpluses as the principal means to full employment. Second, each of the participating nations must be prepared to balance its accounts with the rest of the world; for that purpose any nation which, for any reason, systematically sells abroad in goods or services more than it buys from abroad, and so has an export surplus, must be prepared to grant long-term loans sufficient to enable the rest of the world to pay for those exports, without losing gold or other reserves essential for international liquidity.[1] Third, each of the participating nations must aim at a certain stability of economic behaviour—continuity in tariff, subsidy, foreign exchange and other economic policies—and must refrain from introducing important changes in these policies without prior consultation with the other participants. These are the three conditions of multilateral trade; they will be considered in turn.

[1] See Explanation of Terms in Appendix D.

THE FIRST CONDITION: FULL EMPLOYMENT AT HOME

316. The first condition, that all participating countries pursue a full employment policy at home, is suggested by the general consideration set out in paragraph 301, namely that international trade has a different significance for a country with full employment, and for a country suffering from unemployment through a deficiency of demand at home. Only when nations can look upon international trade as a means of mutual advantage, and not as a means of exporting unemployment, is their co-operation likely to be fruitful and stable, and free from fear. But the need for this first condition does not rest on general considerations. It rests upon analysis of how a system of uncontrolled multilateral trade reacts to acute depression in one of the participating countries. This analysis can be presented most simply, not in general terms, but by reference to recent history, that is to say to the events of the decade before the war and what happened to multilateral trade in the Great Depression which began in 1929. These events are recorded from the standpoint of the United States of America in a remarkable State paper recently published by the Government of the United States.[1]

317. The depression which began in the United States with the Stock Market collapse of September, 1929, in three years reduced American industrial production at home to little more than half of its 1929 level. In relation to the rest of the world its effect was to cause American imports to contract sharply and American lending abroad to cease. While the combined effect of America's buying of goods from abroad and of American investors lending abroad in 1929 had been that the rest of the world received 7,400 million dollars wherewith to make payments for American exports and on their debts to the United States, the combined effect of depression on these activities was that the supply of dollars to the rest of the world shrank to 2,400 millions. In 1932, as in 1929, $900 millions were required to meet fixed debt-service payments to the United States, so that the supply of dollars available for purchasing American exports in fact declined from $6,500 millions to $1,500 millions, i.e. by 77 per cent. The authors of the United States Department of Commerce study, from which these figures are taken, make the following comment:

[1] *The United States in the World Economy*, published by the Department of Commerce in 1943, with a Foreword by Wayne C. Taylor (Under Secretary of the Department). This paper has been reprinted in Britain by H.M. Stationery Office.

"Curtailment in the supply of dollars resulting from our reduced imports and cessation of investment activity presented a readjustment problem of unparalleled dimensions. . . .

"The abrupt fall in the dollar supply by some $5,000,000,000 . . . over the short space of three years necessitated vast changes in the foreign use of dollars and in the economic systems from which the demand arose. . . .

"Although several of the primary producing countries including Australia and Argentina, quickly abandoned the [gold] standard, it was given up only reluctantly and under the inexorable pressure of events by most nations. The initial endeavour to defend their exchange parities and reserve positions let the task of re-adjustment in their external demand fall full force on their internal economic life, thus strengthening the forces of depression and deflation throughout the world generally.

"One can only speculate as to how much deflation other countries would have had to enforce and endure—if the adjustment had been carried all the way through in this manner. The degree of deflation that would have been required was possibly even greater than that experienced by the United States and certainly far more severe than that which actually occurred abroad. . . .

"Other countries could halt the drop in their economic activity and institute measures for domestic expansion only by freeing themselves from external deflationary pressure."[1]

318. This argument does not mean that the rest of the world would have had no depression, if there had been no United States. Cyclical fluctuation is older than the emergence of the United States to economic importance. What would have happened without the United States is free for guessing. What actually happened is clear. The immensely powerful economic system of the United States generated its own unparalleled depression; the supply of dollars to the world economy came almost to an end; world-wide devastation followed; in the words of the United States Department of Commerce, vast changes in the economic systems of nearly all countries in the world were necessitated by what had happened in North America. Whether or not the other countries would have had a depression on their account, they could not escape plunging into depression with the United States. It is important to realize just why, under the multilateral system of that day, the other countries had to follow this lead.

319. A sum of $5,000 millions, though large in itself, is small in

[1] *Op. cit.*, pp. 5 and 6.

comparison to the total outlay and income of the world in 1929. United States imports in that year were only 12 per cent of world imports and world imports account only for a few per cent in the total income of the world. Why should such great results be attributed to the cutting out of $5,000 millions from the world economy? The answer to this question is of great significance for the future, because only by understanding the process by which depression travels from one country to all the others, is it possible to learn what must be done to prevent such a spreading of destruction.

320. It is obvious that a reduction in the supply of dollars by 77 per cent was bound to cause a reduction in foreign purchases of American goods. Actually, the reduction in the value of American exports between 1929 and 1932 amounted to a little less—70 per cent as against 77 per cent—which is largely explained by the fact that many of America's debtors defaulted on their interest and dividend obligations and used the available dollars partly for buying American goods instead. Thus American exports fell by 70 per cent—by almost exactly the same percentage as American imports. The rest of the world did not curtail its purchases from the United States of its own free choice; it curtailed them because there were no dollars to pay for them. But why did the whole of world trade slump by a similar percentage? It is clear that a reduction in the supply of dollars abroad must entail a reduction in American exports; but why should a reduction in the supply of dollars entail a slump in the trade which the countries of the rest of the world carry on with one another? Why was it that 70 per cent reduction in the value of American trade brought with it a 64 per cent[1] reduction in the value of all international trade—seeing that American trade accounts for less than one-eighth of all such trade? The answer is found by studying the mechanism of any multilateral trading system. If all currencies are freely exchangeable into all other currencies, a shortage of dollars does not immediately become visible as a shortage of dollars. It becomes visible as a general shortage of foreign exchange, or under the Gold Standard, as a loss of gold reserves. Thus, under a non-discriminatory system, the other countries do not react to a shortage of dollars by curtailing their purchases from the United States; they react by curtailing their purchases generally, from all countries alike. The reduction of purchases from the United States is achieved only incidentally by the general reduction of all purchases. The effect

[1] This is the figure for 1934. There was a certain time lag between the reduction in the supply of dollars and the shrinkage of world trade. The figure for 1932 is 60·9 per cent.

of a shortage of United States dollars upon the Argentine may be that the Argentine cuts its imports by 10 per cent all round, but nine-tenths of the goods thus excluded from the Argentine market may come from other countries whose currency is not in short supply. These other countries, in consequence, suffer an unnecessary and purposeless reduction in their exports and are forced into a similar general curtailment of their purchases from abroad. Never has a system been devised by which a small cause can have such disproportionately large effects.

321. That is how a free multilateral trading system without discrimination may work when one of the principal partners in the system falls into a major depression. It sets up a vicious spiral of contraction. Can nothing be done to stop this process? Two possible remedies call for examination.

322. The first of these possible remedies is discrimination by selective control of imports. If when one major country, in this case the United States, falls into a depression, all the other countries in the world, in place of continuing to treat trade with that country on exactly the same lines as trade with other countries, discriminate and cut down purchases from the depressed country in accord with the supply of that country's currency, while continuing to trade with one another as before, it is in theory possible to isolate the depression. In defence of such a policy of discrimination, it can be urged that though it may appear an unfriendly act to the country in depression, it cannot, in reality, make the final condition of that country worse. In the depression of the thirties purchases by the rest of the world from the United States were bound ultimately to be reduced to the level allowed by the number of dollars supplied. The question was merely whether this reduction of purchases should be brought about directly and consciously by discrimination, so that it remained confined to the world's trade with the United States or whether it should be brought about indirectly and incidentally by a general reduction of trade between all countries. When a major country falls into depression, if all the other countries act together at once to cut down their purchases from it, they can isolate the depression and make their own position better, without making the ultimate position of the depressed country worse; partial abandonment of multilateral trade may enable multilateral trade among all the other countries to continue.

323. But the limitations on this method of dealing with major depressions are such as to make recourse to it a theoretical rather than a practical possibility. First, it deals only with the spread of

the depression and not with its immediate effects. Countries which normally export largely to the United States and normally have a dollar surplus are hit at once by a depression there. British Malaya and the Dutch East Indies lose their main markets for rubber and cannot be saved from that by any discrimination against American exports. Second, drastic instantaneous curtailment of imports from the United States is not a practical policy for a type of country such as Britain, which normally obtains from the United States not luxuries but essentials. Most of Britain's imports from the United States, as elsewhere, are things essential for her industry; no doubt, given time, many or most of them could be obtained from other sources, but an instantaneous change over to other sources on the scale involved is not a practical possibility. Third, the practicability of discrimination against a depressed country as a means of isolating the depression depends on common action being taken by the rest of the world as a whole. If, as appears to be contemplated in the joint proposals for an International Monetary Fund, the rationing of a currency which becomes scarce, say dollars, affects solely the countries which have to apply to the Fund for dollars because they use more dollars than they earn directly, the whole of the scarcity is concentrated on them and in a severe scarcity any rationing becomes a mockery. It is like rationing meat to the townsman while leaving the countryman to eat as much as he likes, even though there is much less meat than before in total. In view of the number of different countries and the variety of their trading relations, it is unimaginable that they would in fact act together with the requisite speed and unison when depression hits one of the major countries. Discrimination, that is to say, selective control of imports, may be useful and necessary for adjusting minor discrepancies in the balance of payments between particular countries. As a means of isolating major depressions it is a theoretical possibility, rather than a measure on which practical reliance can be placed.

324. The second measure that may be suggested for mitigating the international consequences of depression is international lending. When, through a depression and contraction of imports, a country ceases to supply its currency to other countries for purchases from it, it can still maintain the supply of its currency by increasing its lending abroad. This gets over the difficulty of other countries not being able to buy from the depressed country things which they must have; they buy on credit, since their exports are no longer wanted by the depressed country. But lending does not get over the difficulty of diminished demand from the depressed country, causing

unemployment among those who have lived by making exports to meet the demand that has vanished. Increased lending of dollars by the United States, when in depression, obviously would do nothing directly for British Malaya which always has more dollars than are necessary for her. It would do something for countries like Britain, but would meet only part of the trouble. Borrowing of dollars which she could no longer earn by exports would enable Britain to get her essential imports of raw materials. It would not make good her loss of export markets. It is true theoretically that, by suitable financial measures, a country which loses employment in working for overseas demand can expand home demand in compensation. But this will not prevent unemployment, unless the new demand is such that the men displaced from exports can turn over to it. No country can change the whole direction of its industry over night. International lending, as will appear in a moment, has its place—a very important place—in a system of multilateral trade. But international lending is relevant to the second rather than to the first condition of multilateral trade. No country can hope to escape unemployment, if another country with which it has developed a large trade falls into major depression.

325. The problem is essentially a quantitative one. In a minor depression or a depression affecting a small country, discrimination supported by international lending may solve the problem of international trade, may localize the depression, and enable a multilateral trading system to continue working with reasonable smoothness, while compensatory expansion of home demand, as suggested in paragraphs 344-6, substantially maintains employment in other countries. For a major depression in a major country there is no remedy under a multilateral trading system. From 1929 to 1930 imports into the United States fell from $4,399 millions to $3,061 millions or 30 per cent; $1,338 millions of effective demand was withdrawn from the rest of the world between one year and the next. From 1937 to 1938 there was a similar though even greater proportionate fall, from $3,084 millions to $1,960 millions or 36 per cent; $1,123 millions of effective demand was withdrawn from the diminished international market. This withdrawal of demand in 1938 was spread throughout the world; it meant that from one year to the next $200 millions fewer were being spent in Canada, $160 millions fewer in South America, $250 millions fewer in north-western and central Europe, $400 millions fewer in Asia. No economic system can be expected to stand such shocks. On the first occasion, after 1929, the shortage of purchasing power was spread and multiplied throughout

the world in the manner described above and issued in the Great Depression. On the second occasion, in 1938, the certain coming of another world depression was stopped by a World War.

326. To ensure the continuance of multilateral trading it is necessary that all the major participating countries should not merely aim at full employment, but should in practice secure it or secure something like it. This illustration of the first condition of multilateral trade has been couched in terms of the United States and of dollars, because of the historical importance of the United States in the depression of the thirties. But the moral is of general application. The nations taking part in multilateral trading are partners, each affected by the economic health or sickness of the rest; depression is an infectious disease. All who propose to take part in such a system may rightly be asked to inoculate themselves against depression by adopting a policy of full employment at home. The general reason given in paragraph 301 for a full employment policy in each participating country as the first condition of multilateral trade, is strengthened by further examination: only if all the participating countries provide one another mutually with reasonably stable markets, can trade between them proceed smoothly and freely to common advantage. The practical conclusion is that a country which aims at full employment, in making plans for international trade, must have regard not merely to the external economic policies but to the internal economic policies of those with whom it plans to trade: must consider whether these internal policies are or are not likely to lead to stable full employment. International trade can be arranged in one way if all important industrial countries have policies of full employment; it must be arranged in another way if any important industrial country does not have such a policy.

THE SECOND CONDITION: BALANCE IN INTERNATIONAL ACCOUNTS

327. The second condition of multilateral trade is that every country taking part should undertake to balance its accounts with the rest of the world. This condition applies even if all the countries have full employment. It applies particularly to countries which tend to have an export surplus, by selling more than they wish to buy. Even with general full employment some nations may wish to export more than they import and others may wish to import more than they export; if the former are highly developed industrial countries with an ample supply of savings, and if the latter are countries in the course of industrial development, continuing export

surpluses from the former to the latter are wholly desirable and conduce to a raising of living standards in both types of country. But the countries with the export surpluses must be prepared, in one way or another, to engage in long-term lending abroad sufficient to offset their surpluses. Otherwise, sooner or later, the bulk of the international currency of the world, on which it relies for liquidity, will find its way to the countries with an export surplus and will stay there, out of action. That happened between the wars with gold. It would have happened with the "bancor" or the "unitas" of the original British and American proposals, if the export surplus countries maintained their pre-war economic policies. It would happen in the same circumstances under the new joint proposals: the currencies of the export surplus countries would become scarce to the deficit countries; unable to rely on buying from the surplus countries, they would be forced to seek safety in bilateral arrangements. International lending is only indirectly relevant to the first condition of multilateral trade. It is essential in order to secure the second condition.

328. To ensure that the necessary amount of long-term lending from the surplus countries is actually taking place, there must be some international authority with the requisite powers. One of the most important lessons to be learned from the international experiences of the inter-war period is that long-term foreign lending cannot be safely left entirely to private initiative. Nothing has so much aggravated the international currency crisis of the early thirties as the refusal of American investors to continue to lend at a time when American traders continued to try to export on a scale that always tended to exceed imports. If export surpluses are not matched by long-term lending, the countries receiving the exports are forced into illiquidity, and no escape is open to them but the restrictionist policy of cutting down imports. If the future is to see, in the words of the original British Treasury memorandum, the "substitution of an expansionist, in place of a contractionist, pressure on world trade,"[1] it is not enough merely to create an international currency; it is necessary to create a mechanism by which long-term lending can be relied on to maintain permanent equilibrium.

329. What do we mean by having an expansionist policy rather than a contractionist policy? We mean that, so long as any human need remains unsatisfied, difficulties of finding a market are attacked not by restricting supply but by expanding demand, by clothing needs with purchasing power so as to make them into effective

[1] Cmd. 6437, para. 10.

demand. This is the basis of a full employment policy, nationally and internationally. In each field it involves positive rather than negative action, enabling consumers to buy more cloth, in place of ploughing in cotton crops. Positive action in the national field must be taken by national authority; particular industries can only try to save themselves by restriction. Positive action in the international field requires an international authority. One country, made illiquid by the export surpluses of another country, can only take negative action to save itself—can cut its imports, thus cutting the exports of others. Positive remedial action must be international. The various proposals for the creation of an international currency system are expansionist at the outset in virtue of the positive international action of creating and distributing international purchasing power. But this is a strictly temporary service. The normal activities of the International Monetary Fund are little more than book-keeping. There is no machinery in any of these proposals to secure expansionist rather than contractionist policy in dealing with difficulties which arise later.

330. From this there follows the practical inference that, for continuing equilibrium on an expansionist rather than on a restrictionist basis, an international currency system should be accompanied by a plan for international lending. On this point the interesting proposal is made in the Oxford University Institute of Statistics pamphlet on *New Plans for International Trade*[1] that the Clearing Union, as envisaged under the original British proposals, should have the power of creating additional international currency for long-term lending to countries needing loans, and the power, if necessary, to direct purchases made with those loans to particular deficit countries. The principle of the proposal, as it is put by one of its authors, is that "if we can make foreign long-term lending independent of the initiative and sanction of the surplus countries our problem is very nearly solved."[2] The principle is, in effect, that for continued expansionism in international trade we need an international and not a purely national authority. Whether in this way or in some other way, it seems clear that we must proceed beyond the creation of an international currency or a Monetary Fund to the creation of a mechanism for international lending if we are to return to the multilateral trade of the period before the World Wars.

[1] Bulletin, Vol. 5, Supplement No. 5 of the Institute of Statistics, Oxford (August 1943).
[2] *Export Policy and Full Employment*, by E. F. Schumacher, p. 19.

331. The third condition of multilateral trade is that the countries participating should have a reasonable stability and continuity of foreign economic policy. This is necessary because international trade is not simply a matter of spending, receiving, or creating purchasing power: it is a matter of production, consumption and investment, which involves the lives and happiness of large numbers of human beings. No fruitful economic existence is possible in the face of sudden, violent, and unpredictable changes. No country that has developed a certain line of production in response to a demand coming from abroad should find itself suddenly confronted with new tariff walls which at a day's notice render this line of production redundant. General multilateral trading, to be of benefit to all participants, pre-supposes that no substantial changes of tariff policy are made by any member without previously consulting the exporting countries affected and without giving due notice of the intention. The same applies to alterations in exchange rates, to subsidies, and to other governmental measures affecting the flow of trade.

332. This third condition does not mean that, in order to participate in international trade, the different nations have to surrender freedom to frame their own economic policies. They may be high tariff or low tariff countries. They may have tariffs directed to favour production of one sort rather than another—to prevent Australia from becoming a sheep-run or to prevent Britain from becoming a country of factory and office workers without agriculture. It may be hoped that some of the reasons which have inspired tariff policies in the past—the desire to prepare for war or to be safer in war—will have less force in the future. It may be hoped also, with growing security both against war and against unemployment, that the way will be open to a steady progressive lowering of all artificial obstacles to trade. But this is not essential. The one essential is a reasonable continuity of policy. An unpredictable neighbour cannot be a good neighbour or one with whom it is prudent to have many dealings.

ECONOMIC POLICIES AND MONETARY PLANS

333. The analysis made here of the conditions of uncontrolled multilateral trading between nations took as its starting-point the disaster of the early thirties which brought such trading so largely

o an end. The analysis was illustrated by facts from the survey of
world economy made by the United States Department of Commerce. It cannot be completed better than by a citation from the
foreword to that survey by Mr. Wayne C. Taylor.

"Although numerous salutary lessons are to be drawn from
the experience of the past, the conclusion that emerges most
emphatically from the survey is the fundamental importance of
maintaining conditions conducive to a more stable and ample
flow of dollars in our transactions with other countries. The
most essential of these conditions lies not in the field of foreign
economic policy as such but in the attainment of a more fully
and more smoothly operating domestic economy—the major
determinant of the volume and course of our purchases of
foreign goods and services. In addition, a more adequate supply
of dollars should entail both a freer flow of imports and a
renewed and sounder participation of American capital in
international investment.

"Of even greater importance than the general level of the
flow of dollar payments to foreigners is the need for continuity
and regularity in the foreign economic policy of the United
States and in the actual behaviour of our international transactions. It would be tragic indeed if the United States, after a
period of renewed full participation in the world economy, were
to permit another abrupt fall in the supply of dollars to disturb
the recreated international commercial and financial mechanism, whether through increased trade restrictions, through the
misbehaviour of foreign investment, or through the improper
functioning of the domestic economy. Commercial and investment policies, however, are susceptible of intelligent determination and should no longer constitute such disturbing
elements as in the past. The functioning of the American
economy as a whole presents some of the most baffling problems.
On the solution of these problems, through maintenance of a
high and reasonably stable level of economic activity in the
United States, the interests of this country and of other countries
are most clearly and indisputably united.

"A world economic structure organized on the basis of equal
treatment and with large scope for free enterprise cannot be
maintained in the face of such reductions in the supply of
dollars as have occurred in our international transactions in
the past. Unless the supply of dollars is more adequate to meet
foreign requirements, other countries will assuredly insist on

their rights to exercise a close selective control over the use of the amounts available and to promote more intensive relations with third countries under preferential trading arrangements. Unless dollars are made available with greater regularity than in the past, it would be both unjust and unwise to demand the removal of restraints and controls largely designed to protect the internal economies of other countries against external shock and pressure."[1]

334. These are remarkable words from a remarkable State paper. Authoritatively and dispassionately they set out the indispensable conditions of multilateral trade. All the three conditions of the preceding analysis are there. "A more fully and smoothly operating domestic economy" is the first condition: full employment at home. A "supply of dollars more adequate to meet foreign requirements" is the second condition: balancing accounts abroad. "Continuity and regularity in foreign economic policy" is the third condition, almost in the words in which it has been set out above. If the teaching of this paper can be translated into the practical policy of the United States, the prospects of general multilateral trading are bright.

335. It is acceptance of these economic policies that is needed, rather than further elaboration of monetary plans. Multilateral trade involves an international currency or, what comes to the same thing, the interchangeability of the currencies of all the countries participating in such trade. It is necessary, therefore, for nations which desire a restoration of multilateral trade after the war to frame monetary plans. Invaluable service has been done by the experts who have produced the alternative plans already noted, and finally have agreed upon a single plan. But the best laid monetary plans are of no avail, unless the economic policies of the principal participating countries are suitable. Monetary plans can provide an initial impetus, as a self-starter does; they can provide lubricant for the machinery of multilateral trade. But the machinery cannot be kept running on the self-starter or the lubricant. It cannot be kept running except on the basis of substantial acceptance by all the important nations taking part of the three conditions of multilateral trade that have been named above. Each of these conditions is so much in the interest of each particular nation, so long as its aim is peace, that, once these conditions are understood, they should be accepted. But understanding must come first.

[1] U.S. Department of Commerce, *The United States in the World Economy* Re-printed by H.M. Stationery Office, London, 1944, pp. v, vi.

Section 4. THE NEED FOR COMMON ACTION

336. The economic clauses of the Atlantic Charter represent not vague idealism but plain business sense. No nation can enjoy high and rising standards of life without some trade with other nations. No two nations can trade with one another without becoming linked in a partnership for prosperity or adversity. All nations which wish to trade together for economic advancement with security must pursue full employment together. The united military war of the freedom-loving nations against tyranny and barbarism needs to be followed by common action, embracing more and more nations, against the economic instability which has spelt insecurity to so many millions in the past. What form should this common action take? In considering this problem, it is convenient to consider, first, instability in the production and marketing of primary commodities, that is to say food and raw materials of industry, and, later, instability in manufacture and trade.

337. Since the primary commodities satisfy, in the main, basic human needs which do not change rapidly, they might have been expected to show exceptional stability of production and price. They show in fact astonishing instability, particularly of price. Striking figures were given by J. M. Keynes for ten recent years before the war, in an article on "The Policy of Government Storage of Foodstuffs and Raw Materials."

> "Thus for these four commodities—rubber, cotton, wheat and lead—which are, I think, fairly representative of raw materials marketed in competitive conditions, the average annual price range over the last ten years has been 67 per cent. An orderly programme of output, either of the raw materials themselves or of their manufactured products, is scarcely possible in such conditions."[1]

Another illustration is given in a pamphlet issued by the World Trade Alliance. In twelve months of 1937–38 wheat fell in price from 7s. 5d. to 3s. 4d. per bushel; copper fell from £75 to £35 per ton; cotton fell from 8d. to 4½d. per pound; wool fell from 170d. to 48d. per pound. It is idle to expect that the demand for British exports can become stable if the prices of British imports and by consequence the purchasing power of Britain's supplier customers continue to vary as violently as in the past.

[1] *Economic Journal*, September, 1938, p. 451.

338. Full diagnosis of the causes of instability in primary products and prescription of detailed remedies would unduly extend this Report. But it is hard to dissent from the general conclusion in a recent study of some typical commodities by Mr. Lamartine Yates that the root of the trouble lies in "what economists call the in-elasticity of supply, i.e. supply's irresponsiveness to changes in price." In many cases, indeed, to describe the trouble as irresponsiveness is understatement; the real trouble is the wrong response, multiplying the original maladjustment instead of correcting it.

> "In the first place, a large number of primary products are produced mainly by peasants or natives whose object is to maintain their cash incomes at a stable level and who, therefore, when prices fall, try not merely to maintain but actually to increase their production. Because they have not the capital resources of an industrialist, they cannot afford to close down their plant (i.e. their farms) and wait for better times; they must keep on producing or else starve. Nor can they easily move into other occupations. In most raw material producing countries the agricultural alternatives are few and poorly paid, and manufacturing industries are comparatively undeveloped."[1]

To this first cause of continuing maladjustment, Mr. Lamartine Yates adds many others and concludes: "When one contemplates the cumulative effect of all these resistances—the peasant's attempt to maintain his income, the time-lag in production and the pro-tective assistance afforded by governments—it is small wonder that price has proved a singularly ineffective weapon for achieving reduction in output, and it is not surprising, therefore, that even small diminutions in price or in demand have produced gluts of quite astonishing proportions."[2]

339. Measures to introduce more stability into the production and marketing of the primary products which Britain uses, should be an integral part of any full employment policy for Britain. But such measures fall only to a limited extent within the power of Britain. It is true that Britain can propose long-term contracts stabilizing her price for particular articles from particular countries. But Britain is only one—although a very important one—amongst a number of purchasers. If the raw material and food imports of other countries continue to show large fluctuations in volume, even a complete steadiness of British purchases and a complete stability

[1] P. Lamartine Yates, *Commodity Control*, p. 214 (Jonathan Cape, 1943).
[2] *Op. cit.*, p. 216.

of British prices will not assure steadiness of purchasing power to the primary producers. The problem of extreme and irrational instability in primary products can only be solved completely by international action, embracing both the primary producers and their principal industrial customers. No attempt can be made here to define the practical form which such action should take in regard to particular commodities. Full discussion of the various alternative policies—of long-period global contracts covering the whole supply of each country, of "buffer stocks" and of quota systems, would occupy another volume or several volumes. Different policies would no doubt be required for different commodities.[1] The central problem in all cases is that of ensuring reasonable stability in production as well as in price, without stopping change and technical progress.

340. In helping to stabilize the production and marketing of primary commodities, the advanced industrial countries will be helping themselves no less than the primary producers. The new facts as to the international trade cycle which are set out in Appendix A point clearly to the significance for cyclical fluctuation in industrial countries of instability in primary production. But this is one element only in cyclical fluctuation of industry. The main attack on such fluctuation must come within the industrial countries, by the adoption of a policy of internal full employment, setting up an expanding demand for consumption and steadying the process of investment. The argument returns to its central proposition.

341. The first and necessary contribution to world prosperity that every large industrial country should make is to adopt for itself a policy of full employment and stable activity. Depression is contagious in proportion to the size and strength of the national economic system from which it comes. To-day the strongest and most productive national economy in the world—that of the United States—is also the least stable.[2] The adoption of a policy of full

[1] The principal alternative policies are discussed by Mr. Lamartine Yates, with reference to the eight leading commodities of wheat, sugar, coffee, cotton, rubber, tin, copper, and mineral oil, in the book already cited.

[2] According to the Department of Commerce Memorandum already quoted, in the depression of the early 30's, "as compared with 1929 levels the fall in economic activity in the United States was greater than that in other countries and was somewhat more prolonged." As is shown by the figures in para. 325, the percentage contraction of imports in the United States was actually greater from 1937 to 1938 than it had been from 1929 to 1930. In each of the two downward movements, the initial contraction of the British imports was markedly less than contraction of United States imports: in 1929 to 1930 from £1,221 millions

employment by the United States would be the most important
economic advance that could happen in the whole world and to
the benefit of the whole world. In solving, as they only and only
in their own way can solve, the "baffling problems" of their home
economy, more than by the most generous outpouring of gifts or
loans, the American people can confer immeasurable benefits on
all mankind. Full employment in the United States can be combined
with preservation in full of all the citizen liberties which all English-
speaking peoples hold to be essential. Full employment, on the view
taken here, can be attained while leaving the actual conduct of
industry in private hands, if that course commends itself. Full
employment, finally, is attainable by several different routes. The
route suggested for Britain in this Report is not likely to be that
which would best suit the United States, with her sparser population,
her higher standard of capital equipment and her different structure
of Government. Each country must work out its own full employment policy, but no great country should be without one. No
great country should submit to defeat by unemployment.

Section 5. THE CHOICE FOR BRITAIN

342. All nations which propose to have trade with one another
should pursue full employment and economic stability. This does
not mean that no nation can do anything in this matter except in
agreement with all the other nations. Still less does it mean that
Britain must wait and do nothing till she knows the minds of
all mankind. There are some respects in which Britain can frame
her economic policy only in alternatives, to suit the alternative
policies of other nations. But she should frame these alternatives
as soon as possible and explore the views of other nations on
them; the main alternatives for international trade, as they arise
out of the preceding discussion will be reviewed briefly in concluding this Part. There are some things which are Britain's
sole responsibility and on which she can and should take decisions
now. The chief of these is the decision in any case to pursue a policy
of full employment at home, by ensuring at all times outlay adequate
to require use of all her productive resources. This decision is irrespective of the form which international trade may take. Full
employment comes first. There arise from this decision three or

to £1,044 millions, or 14 per cent; in 1937 to 1938 from £1,028 millions to
£919 millions or 11 per cent.

four practical issues relating to overseas trade which may be noticed briefly.

343. In the first place, since a considerable overseas trade is indispensable for Britain, the maintenance of this trade should be regarded as a vital objective of national policy. This is partly a general question of industrial efficiency, of regaining for Britain by technical research some of the leadership in invention and ways of material progress which came to her historically at the beginning of the Industrial Revolution. It is partly a question of how the actual business of importing and exporting can best be undertaken. In the circumstances in which this Report had to be prepared, it did not seem worth while to attempt any detailed study of this problem, involving examination of each separate industry and discussion of its possibilities with the leaders of that industry. But as a guide to the practical problems and their scale, it may be convenient to set out the values of the principal classes of British exports in each of the last three years before the present war.

Table 21

EXPORTS OF BRITISH PRODUCE OR MANUFACTURE

(£ *million*)

	1936	1937	1938
Food, Drink and Tobacco	35·6	38·8	35·9
Coal	29·3	37·6	37·4
Iron and Steel and Manufactures thereof..	36·0	48·4	41·6
Non-Ferrous Metals and Manufactures thereof	12·1	15·7	12·3
Machinery	41·2	49·7	57·9
Vehicles (including Locomotives, Ships and Aircraft) ..	32·2	39·9	44·6
Electrical Goods and Apparatus	10·0	12·5	13·4
Cotton Yarns and Manufactures	61·5	68·5	49·7
Woollen and Worsted Yarns and Manufactures	32·2	35·5	26·8
Other Textiles	18·6	21·8	16·2
Chemicals, Drugs, Dyes and Colours	21·1	24·7	22·1
Other articles wholly or mainly manufactured	75·9	88·0	80·7
Other raw materials and mainly unmanufactured ..	22·0	27·0	19·5
Parcel Post and Animals	12·9	13·3	12·7
Total Exports..	440·6	521·4	470·8

It is assumed, for reasons indicated above, that an increasing proportion of British imports, mainly food and raw materials, will come under collective management. What will or should be the position in regard to exports? The answer will differ from one industry to another, and will be affected by decisions as to the organization of the industry. If, for instance, the coal or the iron and steel industries were brought under unified control by a public corporation, the business of exporting would presumably be undertaken as a whole. If, without unifying production of coal, demand for coal were made collective in the first instance through a marketing corporation, as suggested in Part IV, paragraph 216, the corporation would be responsible for finding a market abroad as well as at home. But apart from these special cases it may be convenient in other industries for export organizations to replace, to co-ordinate, or to assist the individualism of the past.

344. In the second place, since some international trade is indispensable to Britain, some of the demand on which productive employment in Britain depends will come from overseas. Whatever be done in other countries or by co-operation between Britain and other countries to reduce fluctuations of overseas demand for British goods and services, some risk of fluctuation will remain. A full employment policy for Britain must include plans for expanding and contracting home demand to meet fluctuations of overseas demand. The power of the State, controlling the money machine, to maintain the total demand for labour in Britain at any desired point, is not affected by the fact that some of the labour is normally employed in meeting an overseas demand. In purely quantitative terms any fluctuation of overseas demand, however great, can be offset by an expansion of home demand. The problem is practical rather than financial. Its solution depends on detailed study of British exporting industries and of the extent to which and the methods by which men engaged on making exports for a particular country, can, if the demand from that country fails, find alternative productive employment in working for a new demand either at home or in some other country.

345. Even if adequate alternative demand is established, industrial friction is likely to make it impossible to avoid some increase of unemployment. An allowance for this has been made in assessing in paragraph 169 the irreducible margin of unemployment. That is part of the price of international trade and the raising of the standard of living by international exchange. How completely industrial friction can be overcome in expanding home demand to compensate for declining overseas demand, it is impossible to say in advance. What is certain is that the unemployment due to this cause will be smaller, if careful plans are made ahead, than if no plans are made. But the necessity of being able, at need, to compensate

INTERNATIONAL IMPLICATIONS OF FULL EMPLOYMENT 237

at home for fluctuations of demand overseas is an additional reason for not placing upon the State the further responsibility of adjusting public outlay to fluctuations of home investment. Business at home must learn to put its own house in order and not trust to compensatory fluctuation of outlay by the State.

346. Expansion of home demand to meet the falling off of overseas demand, even if it maintains employment, does not solve the problem of the balance of payments. If outlay in dollars is replaced by outlay in pounds the exchange between dollars and pounds is affected. Here the two measures discussed above, of discrimination and of international lending, enter. Disturbance of the balance of payments by industrial fluctuation in different countries can always be fully compensated by suitable international lending. But such lending must be of strictly temporary character to tide over short-term fluctuations. It should not enable any country to incur trade deficits over a long period. The other measure available for adjusting the balance of payments in face of minor fluctuations of overseas demand is discrimination.

347. In the third place, whatever the machinery for adjusting the balance of payments between different countries and for international clearing in multilateral trade, there is one cause of breakdown against which this machinery must be protected. There is general agreement that the uncontrolled movements of capital from one country to another, or in more popular terms the panic flights of "hot money," which reached such a disastrous violence between the two wars, represent a danger against which safeguards must be provided. This is fully recognized in the Joint Proposals for an International Monetary Fund and is cogently argued in the British Treasury Memorandum of April, 1943:

> "There is no country which can, in future, safely allow the flight of funds for political reasons or to evade domestic taxation or in anticipation of the owner turning refugee. Equally, there is no country that can safely receive fugitive funds, which constitute an unwanted import of capital, yet cannot safely be used for fixed investment. For these reasons it is widely held that control of capital movements, both inward and outward, should be a permanent feature of the post-war system." [1]

It is difficult to see how, in practice, this control of capital movements can be secured without a general system of control over all

[1] Cmd. 6437, paras. 32–3.

exchange transactions, though this need not involve a postal censorship.

348. In the fourth place, a problem arises from the fact that the course of international trade in a number of articles is now determined or influenced by international cartel agreements. Such cartels may serve a good purpose in stabilizing trade and production. The whole trend of the argument of this Part of the Report is towards a management of international trade, in place of leaving it to unregulated competition. That is to say, it is towards that for which the cartels stand. To attempt to destroy or stop cartellization would, therefore, be a contradiction of policy. But it is equally essential that, whatever policy in regard to international trade is adopted by the Government of Britain, that policy should not be liable to defeat or deflexion by the extra-governmental decisions of cartels. The latter should act in accord with national policy and as agents of that policy, not in disregard of that policy. The first step to securing this is full information as to the operation of cartels. They should work always under the scrutiny of the Government. But this is a first step only. It will not be sufficient for the formal arrangements of cartels to be recorded and supervised while substantive policy is determined by "gentlemen's agreements" which do not get recorded. It will not be sufficient to have scrutiny on behalf of the Government exercised by Civil Servants of no technical knowledge. What is wanted is that those who have the responsibility of conducting great and highly organized industries should come to regard themselves as the agents of a wider policy than that of their business. Just under what forms and by what institutions this can best be accomplished can probably be learned only by experience.

POLICY IN ALTERNATIVES.

349. These particular problems for Britain arising in the working out of a full employment policy in the international field have been mentioned because they must not be forgotten. But they are all secondary. The central problem is that of securing, by co-operation with other nations, the maximum of economic stability abroad as well as at home, and the greatest and freest development of international trade that is consistent with stability. A full employment policy for Britain must, on its international side, be framed in alternatives, to suit the most probable different lines of economic policy that may be adopted by the United States, by Soviet Russia and by other countries. The three main alternatives for Britain's

foreign trade, in the order of desirability, are general multilateral trading, regional multilateral trading and bilateralism.

350. The most desirable alternative for Britain and the whole world is restoration of general multilateral trade. But such a system is based on the assumption of reasonably full employment in all important industrial countries. Multilateral trading spreads adversity as certainly and as widely as it spreads prosperity. As the experience of the nineteen-thirties has shown, depression at home is practically certain to lead to beggar-my-neighbour policies abroad, to export drives and import restrictions. The direct consequences of a depression in any one country become multiplied by the unco-ordinated attempts of each of the other countries to save itself, whatever happens to its neighbours.

351. On the assumption of the Atlantic Charter, that all the larger countries will announce and adopt a policy for maintaining employment at home, international trade can be based on the most desirable of the three alternatives. That is to say, the first aim should be a world-wide trading and clearing system, with international arrangements providing adequate lasting liquidity for multilateral trading, without requiring individual countries to subordinate domestic economic policy to international exigencies. Subject to the adoption by all countries of suitable economic policies, such a system could have been developed out of the first British proposals for international clearing by adding thereto machinery for directed international investment. It could be developed out of the recent joint proposals for an International Monetary Fund. But, even under such a system, Britain, with other countries, must retain and exercise powers not used before the first World War, including:

(a) Control of capital movements. This appears to involve control of all exchanges.

(b) Making of long-term contracts for the purchase of essential raw materials and food.

(c) Making of long-term contracts for the planned supply of exports to develop backward areas.

352. The second of the three alternatives for international trade is regionalism. This means multilateral trading not throughout the world but between a group of countries, sufficiently complementary to one another, and sufficiently alike in their economic policies, including the pursuit of full employment, to make it easy for them to work together. All that is said in the last paragraph would apply

not to all countries but to the region. Britain might become the financial centre, of a sterling full employment area, as before the first World War she was the financial centre of the world. This would not, of course, prevent trade between countries in different regions, but such trade would take place subject to special controls.

353. A policy of regionalism applied in Europe or in the British Commonwealth or both together should not be regarded as in any way unfriendly to the United States or to Soviet Russia. Room must be kept in the world for a variety of economic policies in different countries. Soviet Russia will certainly continue to have a completely managed economy; the United States is likely to return, at any rate for some time to come, to a large measure of freedom from Government action. It should be open to Britain, and countries which like her desire to follow the middle course of full employment in a free society, to do so, without being charged with pursuing selfish or national aims.

354. It is difficult to believe—in truth it is incredible—that, if a general multilateral system could not be established throughout the world, Britain would fail to find other countries, sufficient with her to make up a region of stable prosperity, ensuring to her the essential imports in return for her exports, ensuring to them markets and capital. But if for any reason this could not or could not immediately be secured, there remains the last certain recourse of bilateralism. This for Britain would mean the making of specific bargains with individual countries to ensure the supply of imports of food and of raw materials indispensable for British industry, including in such bargains provisions as to means of payment and the exchange between their respective currencies.

355. The first of the three alternatives is, as has been emphasized before, the most desirable in itself and most in accord with Britain's role and traditions in the past. To realize it Britain should do everything possible, except surrender the right to fall back on the other alternatives, if the first one could not be attained in full and satisfactory measure. It is better to secure multilateral trading in a limited region where it has good prospects of success and can be made the basis of wider trading later, than to aim at multilateral trading in the world at large, without effective agreement on its fundamental conditions.

356. That it would be possible either under the second or under the third alternative to ensure the imports required for our prosperity, if we are prepared to take the necessary steps, is not open to reasonable doubt. Nor is it doubtful that strong central planning of Britain's

internal affairs will make her more, not less, useful as a partner in world affairs. International trade, both for imports and for exports, will on the whole have to come under public management, in place of being left to market forces either competitive or monopolistic. The organs which serve for planning at home will serve also for planning in a wider sphere.

357. The need to face and solve problems of international trade after the war is inherent in Britain's position. It is not due to the adoption of any particular economic policy, whether of full employment or not. It should not be made the excuse for postponing adoption of such a policy. The greatest contribution that Britain by herself can make to confidence in the possibility of world prosperity is to show confidence in herself and in her power of managing her own economic affairs better. The still greater contribution she should seek to make, with others, is to work for a full international system, covering both current transactions and investment, and ensuring both short and long-term equilibrium. Before the first World War, the gold standard, as administered from London, kept sufficient though imperfect economic order, as the British Navy kept peace. Now for both purposes international authority is needed. To make internationalism adequate in a limited field of arms and of money is the way to preserve the maximum of self-government and individuality for nations in their national fields. To this task of making the new world order, in economics as in politics, we must come with clean hands and single hearts, seeking no advantage for ourselves, save the advantage of order which we share with all others. But while hoping for the best, that is success in our efforts for world-wide economic order, we must be prepared for failure and must retain for that event all necessary powers to ensure the second or third best.

358. In terms of convenience for traffic, world-wide multilateral trade may be likened to an elevator, speedy but capable of going out of action. Regional multilateral trade may be likened to a staircase, less speedy but consistent with reasonable comfort. Bilateralism is the fire-escape, clumsy but certain. We may hope that the world after this war will be equipped with all modern conveniences for bringing men together for their common advantage. We should do our full share to bring such a world into being. But, in constructing the new edifice, we cannot prudently leave out the fire-escape and the staircase, until we are sure that there will be no fire and that the elevator will always be in action.

FULL EMPLOYMENT AND SOCIAL CONSCIENCE

UNEMPLOYMENT AND THE INDIVIDUAL

359. Statistics of unemployment are not just statistics. Economic arguments about unemployment are not arguments in the air. In my first study of unemployment thirty-five years ago, I illustrated the statistical record and the economic argument by an extract from the life story of one of the early labour leaders and Members of Parliament, Mr. Will Crooks.[1] The story is so little out of date while fear of unemployment remains, that it may fitly be repeated here. It tells how, after tramping in search of work from London to Liverpool and back again, Crooks decided to try to find work outside his own trade of cooper. He went down to the docks, where by the aid of a friendly foreman he got occasional jobs as a casual labourer.

"One typical day of tramping for work in London he described to me thus:

'I first went down to the riverside at Shadwell. No work to be had there. Then I called at another home and got two slices of bread in paper and walked eight miles to a cooper's yard in Tottenham. All in vain. I dragged myself back to Clerkenwell. Still no luck. Then I turned homewards in despair. By the time I reached Stepney I was dead beat.

'That year I know I walked in London till my limbs ached again. I remember returning home once by way of Tidal Basin, and turning into Victoria Docks so utterly exhausted that I sank down on a coil of rope and slept for hours.'"

·   ·   ·   ·   ·

[1] *From Workhouse to Westminster: The Life Story of Will Crooks*, M.P., by George Haw (Cassell & Co., Ltd., 1907).

"Work came at last in an unexpected way. He was returning home after another empty day when he hailed a carman and asked for a lift.

" 'All right, mate, jump up,' was the response.

"As they sat chatting side by side, the carman learned that his companion was seeking work.

" 'What's yer trade?' he enquired.

" 'A cooper.'

" 'Why, the governor wants a cooper.'

"So instead of dropping off at Poplar, Crooks accompanied the carman to the works. . . . That work was a stepping-stone to another and better job at Wandsworth. . . . Crooks was never out of work again in his life."

. . . . . .

"Nothing wearies one more than walking about hunting for employment which is not to be had. It is far harder than real work. The uncertainty, the despair, when you reach a place only to discover that your journey is fruitless are frightful. I've known a man say: 'Which way shall I go to-day?' Having no earthly idea which way to take, he tosses up a button. If the button comes down on one side he tracks east; if on the other, he tracks west."

In repeating this story, in 1909, I added the comment, "Nothing can better illustrate the waste of time, energy and shoe leather involved in the personal search for employment. This is the lottery which industrial disorganization makes of the workman's life. This is the process as to which comfortable ignorance has so often assured us: 'The men know where to look for work all right, they know. Lord bless you! *they* know!' "[1]

360. To-day the same or worse statistics could be illustrated by countless human tales, from many sources:

"The depression and apathy which finally settles down in many of the homes of these long-unemployed men lies at the root of most of the problems which are connected with unemployment. It is one of the reasons why they fail to get back to work.It is one of the reasons why the majority of them 'have not the heart' for clubs or activities of other kinds, and it is one of the reasons why their homes seem so poverty stricken. 'I don't know how it is,' said a young married woman in Blackburn,

[1] *Unemployment* (1909), pp. 265–6.

'but these last few years since I've been out of the mills I don't seem able to take trouble, somehow; I've got no spirit for anything. But I didn't use to be like that.' One of us who saw her had little doubt 'how it was.' The woman looked thin and ill, and it was clear that what food there was was going to the children."[1]

.　　.　　.　　.　　.

"My chief trouble is the monotony of a long spell of un-employment . . . monotonous and insufficient food and having nothing to do all day after the garden is done, kill all a man's interest in life. . . . Perhaps I miss cigarettes most, and I hate being chained to the home most. There is no substitute for work. . . . There is nothing I can do to keep myself efficient; odd repairs in a house are no substitute for constructional work on a steam engine."

(A skilled millwright aged 49.)[2]

.　　.　　.　　.　　.

"The wife works while I look after the home. . . . I earned good wages (£4 a week) for years and we had saved fifty pounds when I lost my job. We have none of that fifty pounds to-day. . . . Any long spell of unemployment leaves you with little to be proud of and much to be ashamed of. Our child is still too young to realize that it is her mother who works. We carefully keep her from knowing it."

(A skilled wire-drawer aged 32.)

.　　.　　.　　.　　.

"My husband is a good man and he does a lot for me in the house. . . . But he is a changed man these last two years. He never complains, but I wish he would. It makes me unhappy to find him becoming quieter and quieter, when I know what he must be feeling. If I had someone to talk to about my troubles I should feel much better. But having to keep them to myself, as my husband does, makes everything so much worse. We quarrel far more now than we have ever done in our lives before. We would both rather be dead than go on like this. . . . He has been out of work so long now that I do not think that

---

[1] *Men Without Work*, a Report made to the Pilgrim Trust, pp. 148–9 (Cambridge University Press, 1938).

[2] This, and the two passages following, are from *Memoirs of the Unemployed*. Introduced and edited by H. L. Beales and R. S. Lambert (Gollancz, 1934).

he will get his Old Age Pension when he is sixty-five for he will
not have enough stamps on his Health Insurance Cards. . . .
That will be our greatest disappointment."

(A Derbyshire miner's wife aged 66, he being 62.)

361. The passages just quoted describe people past their first
youth or with domestic ties that might limit their availability for
work. But the statistics of unemployment are not confined to such
people. They cover many tens of thousands in the first flush of
manhood and womanhood. From a survey of *Disinherited Youth*,
made under the auspices of the Carnegie United Kingdom Trustees
during the years 1936–9, the following passages are taken:

"From the very start of their industrial life, at fourteen,
they had experienced unemployment, so that even the youngest
of them at age eighteen, were personalities that had matured,
during those very important and impressionable four years
against a background of unemployment, in some cases slight,
in other cases entirely devoid of any pattern of work as a part
of life." (Page 65.)

"One young man described his feeling while unemployed as
'living death.' Many more may have felt this, but could not
express it. Unemployment due to conditions of world trade, or
technological changes in industrial organization, meant nothing
to them. Such explanations left them cold. What mattered to
most of them was that they were fit and able for work and
wanted it badly, not so much as an end in itself as a means to
an end. They needed the money, their homes needed the
money, and it would be money earned by their own effort.
One young wife put it thus: 'Somehow when it's money that
your man has worked for, it goes further.'

"Unemployment was a new and strange feature in the lives
of a few. They were anxious and alert. They expressed their
youthful impatience with the slow moving queues and hurriedly
left the Employment Exchange after 'signing on.' Others,
however, had acquired the art of patience. They had longer
and more frequently recurring experiences of unemployment.
With drooping shoulders and slouching feet they moved as a
defeated and dispirited army. They gave their names, signed
the necessary forms and shuffled out of the Exchange. This,
twice a week, was the only disciplined routine with which they
had to comply." (Pages 5–6.)

.   .   .   .   .

"I am still unemployed and have no prospects. I have come to the stage when I think I will never find employment. I am glad you still take an interest in me as it is good to know someone is interested in the welfare of the unemployed." (Page 6, W. B., aged 22.)

．　　　　．　　　　．　　　　．　　　　．

"I was an apprentice engineer and during the depression (1931) I was paid off. I got the offer of my job back but I was working then as a labourer and getting 30s. a week. I just couldn't go back to my apprentice's wage of 15s. I'm sorry now that I didn't." (Page 13.)

．　　　　．　　　　．　　　　．

"To tell you the truth I don't look for work now. You've got about as much chance of picking up a job nowadays as of winning the Irish Sweep." (Page 14.)

．　　　　．　　　　．　　　　．　　　　．

"A number of the men married during the period of the Enquiry. One talked with them first as single men and then, later, as married men, and the urge to make fresh attempts 'for the wife's sake' was noticeable. But one or two short spells of temporary or casual employment soon brought about a change of attitude. The young wife soon found that this fluctuation between a few days' wages and a few days' unemployment allowance instead of a regular, if minimum, weekly sum for total unemployment, upset any plan of expenditure she might make. One young mother told how, when her husband got the offer of a job, she had immediately to go and get him a pair of heavy working boots and pay them up by instalments. He thought the job would last at least a fortnight and with two weeks' pay she could manage to pay them up in full. The job lasted four days. It took her many weeks to return to her planned budget. Such a simple happening as this throws light on part of the reason for the married man's unemployment." (Page 27.)

．　　　　．　　　　．　　　　．　　　　．

"The central problem of the lives of most of these young men is one of maintenance of self-respect. Rightly, they feel a need to take their places in society, achieving in their own right the means of living. Much of their conduct, irrational and unreasonable to outward seeming, becomes understandable if regarded in its perspective, as part of a struggle for the retention of self-respect. The attitude of many men who refuse training—a problem discussed in a later chapter—has its origin here; similarly, their resentment at being 'messed about' can be understood for what it really is—an essay in self-respect. They have no function in society. They are the unwanted hangers-on of a community in the life of which they are unable to play their full part." (Page 80.)

362. The facts that in certain parts of Britain even young adaptable people could find no employment and the disastrous effects upon them of prolonged idleness have been described already as among the worst blots on our record between the two wars.[1] In the United States the position was no better: "The difficulty of youth in finding jobs has emerged as one of the most serious problems of depression. It is estimated that youth constituted a third of all the unemployed during the thirties and that at least one-third of all the employable youth were unable to find jobs.[2] This estimate of wasted youth in the United States is no hasty judgment; it is confirmed by numerous local surveys. The record of where youth stands in free democracies in times of peace is in poignant contrast to what is required of youth in war, and to the call to youth made by the German dictator in preparing war. By this judgment of uselessness that it passed so widely on adaptable youth, the unplanned market economy of the past in Britain and in America must itself be judged and stands condemned.

363. Statistics of unemployment mean rows of men and women, not of figures only. The three million or so[3] unemployed of 1932 means three million lives being wasted in idleness, growing despair and numbing indifference. Behind these three million individuals seeking an outlet for their energies and not finding it, are their wives and families making hopeless shift with want, losing their birth-right of healthy development, wondering whether they should have been born. Beyond the men and women actually unemployed at any moment, are the millions more in work at that moment but never knowing how long that work or any work for them

[1] Para. 89.

[2] *Report of the Technical Committee of the National Resources Planning Board on Security, Work and Relief Policies*, p. 21.

[3] The highest number registered as unemployed was 2,979,425 in January, 1933, but 1932 in general and particularly in its second half had higher figures than 1933. No doubt even in 1932 there was some unemployment which escaped registration.

may last. Unemployment in the ten years before this war meant unused resources in Britain to the extent of at least £500,000,000 per year. That was the additional wealth we might have had if we had used instead of wasting our powers. But the loss of material wealth is the least of the evils of unemployment, insignificant by comparison to the other evils. Even with that loss, Britain was still one of the richest countries of the world. If that unemployment could have been divided evenly over the whole people as leisure, we should have been as rich and altogether happier; we should have had a standard of living with which few countries could compare. The greatest evil of unemployment is not the loss of additional material wealth which we might have with full employment. There are two greater evils: first, that unemployment makes men seem useless, not wanted, without a country; second, that unemployment makes men live in fear and that from fear springs hate.

364. So long as chronic mass unemployment seems possible, each man appears as the enemy of his fellows in a scramble for jobs. So long as there is a scramble for jobs it is idle to deplore the inevitable growth of jealous restrictions, of demarcations, of organized or voluntary limitations of output, of resistance to technical advance. By this scramble are fostered many still uglier growths—hatred of foreigners, hatred of Jews, enmity between the sexes. Failure to use our productive powers is the source of an interminable succession of evils. When that failure has been overcome, the way will be open to progress in unity without fear.

365. The necessity of preventing the return of mass unemployment is a recurrent theme in nearly all that has been written on reconstruction problems in Britain after the war, from whatever angle it is written. "Unemployment such as darkened the world between the two wars, must not recur."[1] "There must be no return to the disastrous waste of man-power which characterized the period between the wars."[2] "This is the issue which in the years after the war, more than any other, will make or break the reputation of any minister of any government. Yet, as Sir John Anderson remarked exactly a year ago when discussing Assumption C of the Beveridge Report, "There is no question whether we can achieve full employment; we must achieve it. It is the central factor which will determine the pattern of national life after the war, including, perhaps, the fate

[1] *Work: The Future of British Industry* (being a Report by the Conservative Sub-Committee on Industry), para. 3.

[2] *Nuffield College Memorandum on Employment Policy and Organization of Industry after the War*, para. 4.

of democratic institutions."[1] The same thoughts find utterance in America: "Never again will doles and subsistence levels be tolerated."[2] "The liberty of a democracy is not safe if its business system does not provide employment and produce and distribute goods in such a way as to sustain an acceptable standard of living."[3]

366. The necessity of preventing after this war a return to the mass unemployment between the two wars is formally admitted by all. The possibility of doing so, if we are prepared to will the means as well as the end, is not open to reasonable doubt. Depressions of trade are not like earthquakes or cyclones; they are man-made. In the course of relieving unemployment, all industrial countries, but particularly Britain, have acquired much knowledge as to its causes. Though there remain some unsolved problems, the conditions without which mass unemployment cannot be prevented are known and the main lines for remedial action are clear. Finally, the experience of the two wars has shown that it is possible to have a human society in which every man's effort is wanted and none need stand idle and unpaid.

SOME OBJECTIONS ANSWERED

367. The doubt is not as to the possibility of achieving full employment but as to the possibility of achieving it without the surrender of other things that are even more precious. Some things which are more precious than full employment, that is to say, some of the essential British liberties, are surrendered in war. But it can be shown that this surrender is required by the special nature of the war objective, and not by the full employment which is incidental to war. This surrender of essential liberties would not be required for full employment in peace and should be refused. The Policy for Full Employment set out in this Report preserves all the essential British liberties; it rejects rationing, which forbids the free spending of personal income; it rejects direction of men and women to compulsory tasks; it rejects prohibition of strikes and lock-outs. The policy preserves also other liberties which, if less essential, are deeply rooted in Britain, including collective bargaining to determine wages, and private enterprise in a large sector of

[1] *The Times* (Editorial), 16th February, 1944.

[2] From a leaflet by the Committee for Economic Development—an organization financed by business firms to assist and encourage industry and commerce in the United States to plan for maximum employment after the war.

[3] President Roosevelt in Message to Congress, 29th April, 1938.

industry; it preserves these lesser liberties, subject to the degree of responsibility with which they are exercised. The policy preserves possibility of change, the springs of progress and the way to rising standards of life. It is not open to the criticism that it would destroy essential liberties or lead to stagnation. Is it open to any other serious objection? It will be convenient to name some of the possible objections and give brief answers.

368. There are some who will say that full employment, combined with unemployment insurance, will remove the incentive of effort which depends on fear of starvation. The answer is that for civilized human beings ambition and desire for service are adequate incentives. It may be that cattle must be driven by fear. Men can and should be led by hope. The policy set out in this Report is not one of stagnation or forced equality. It does not give security for life in a particular job; it gives only the opportunity of exercising one's gifts and energies in generous rather than in ungenerous rivalry with one's fellows.

369. There are some who will say that the great development of State activity involved in the policy proposed here will destroy the "little man," that is to say the small, independent business. The answer is that the policy does nothing of the sort, unless risk of bankruptcy in trade depressions is essential to the existence and happiness of the "little man." The policy is simply one of setting up sufficient demand. It involves, as an implication, control of monopolies to prevent exploitation of the demand and supervision of large concerns in order to plan investment. It does not touch the "little man" at all; he can work to meet the demand like any other. He will find more scope than before, once strong demand has eliminated the slumps in which so many small businesses in the past have come to grief.

370. There are some who will object to the proposals of this Report on the ground that they involve an extension of the activities of Government and a consequent increase in the number of civil servants. That the proposals do involve action by Government in fields which in the past have been left wholly to private enterprise is true; the justification for this lies in the failures of the past. In certain industries men may find themselves working directly for the community in place of being the employees of a monster business corporation. In all industries, the managers of large undertakings may find themselves both regulated and assisted in keeping what they do—in investment, in the location of industry, in price policy— in accord with national interest. But there is nothing in all the pro-

posals of this Report to involve greater interference in the private lives of the mass of the people. On the contrary, not only will all the war-time restrictions on consumption and choice of work vanish with war, but many of the previous interferences with private lives will be ended. There will be no unemployment assistance subject to a means test; the 8,000 officials of the Unemployment Assistance Board in 1938 will become unnecessary for that work. So, too, a substantial proportion of the 28,000 peace-time officials of the Ministry of Labour, that is to say, those engaged in paying or calculating unemployment benefit, will find that occupation gone, though it may be hoped that most of these will render still better service in preventing unemployment by organizing the labour market. A full employment policy involves more public control over a limited class of business undertakers, and less control over the private lives of the mass of the people. It may in the end mean fewer bureaucrats, not more.

371. There may be some who will say that in the emphasis laid in this Report on the need for organizing the labour market the Report treats labour as a commodity, in conflict with the opening declaration of the Charter adopted by the International Labour Conference in Philadelphia in May, 1944. There is no conflict. The Philadelphia declaration that labour is not a commodity cannot mean that men should not be free to sell their labour as men sell commodities. In a free community the right to sell or to refrain from selling one's labour by hand or brain and to bargain as to the terms on which it should be used is essential. This makes important the question of how those who desire to sell their labour and those who, whether for private profit or as representatives of a public authority, desire to buy the labour, shall be brought together. In concerning itself with these matters, the Report does not treat men themselves as a commodity; it treats them, as the Philadelphia declaration demands, as an end and not as a means; it proposes a fundamental difference to be established between the position of those who desire to sell their labour and the position of all other sellers. Only for labour should the market always be a seller's market. It should not be that always for any particular commodity.

372. There are some who will say that the policy of this Report subordinates the individual to the State. The answer is that this criticism directly reverses the truth. If the State is regarded as more important than the individual, it may be reasonable to sacrifice the individual in mass unemployment to the progress and prosperity of his more fortunate fellows, as he is sacrificed in war by the dictators

for their power and dominion or that of the race. If, on the other hand, the State is regarded as existing for the individual, a State which fails, in respect of many millions of individuals, to ensure them any opportunity of service and earning according to their powers or the possibility of a life free from the indignities and inquisitions of relief, is a State which has failed in a primary duty. Acceptance by the State of responsibility for full employment is the final necessary demonstration that the State exists for the citizens— for all the citizens—and not for itself or for a privileged class.

373. There are some who will say that the policy of this Report is a mere palliative which will block the way to further reforms like socialism or communism. The answer is that the policy does not block the way to these or other reforms, if they are good in themselves. It is a policy directed against one particular evil and includes steps which must be taken under any economic system which preserves essential liberties, in order to deal with that evil. The case for socialization of the means of production must be argued in the main on other grounds, of efficiency of production or of social justice. The Policy for Full Employment is in essence that the State takes responsibility for seeing that while any human needs are unsatisfied, they are converted into effective demand. This leaves open to argument on its merits the question whether production to meet that effective demand should be undertaken under conditions of private enterprise guided by profit, or of social enterprise working directly for use, or of a combination of these methods.

374. There are some who will say that the introduction of this or any other policy for Britain must wait for international agreement. Undoubtedly any economic policy for Britain must take account of the world of which Britain is part. It should be inspired by recognition of community of economic interest between different nations. It must be framed in alternatives to suit the alternative policies that may be adopted by other nations; it must include means of off-setting, so far as possible, fluctuations of overseas demand. But Britain must have her own policy; will do better for the world and herself by leading, rather than by waiting and following. The subordination of British policy to supposed international exigencies has been one of the major mistakes of the period between the wars, the period of disastrous appeasement, political and economic. Britain is in the world and cannot escape from the world or her responsibilities for world order and world prosperity, but she cannot meet those responsibilities unless she puts her own house in order.

375. There may be some, finally, who feel that what is left out of this Report—the problem of demobilization and of transition from war to peace—is the most urgent practical task of all. That problem undoubtedly is both practical and urgent. It is not covered in this Report, because it cannot be covered effectively by any unofficial enquiry. To deal with the problem of demobilization would have required help and information from Government sources which were not available to me. In any case it is a different problem from that which forms the subject of this Report. After the end of hostilities in the first World War employment in Britain remained at boom levels for nearly two years.[1] This war has already lasted longer and has been more total; the gaps in material equipment and resources needed for peace that will be left by the war in nearly all countries of the world are likely to be greater, not less, than last time. It does not follow from this with certainty that last time's experience of automatically sustained demand for one or two years after the end of total war will be repeated this time. The conditions when total war ends this time will be different in many ways from those of the last war. It would be foolish in the extreme to make no plans for action to ensure adequate demand, even in the demobilization period. But there is at least a possibility that no special action will be needed; there is the possibility of something like a post-war boom and automatic excess of demand in the transition from war to peace. From this two practical morals emerge. First, we must not be deceived by a passing flush of demand, if it should come, when total war ends. Knowing that it may come and will pass, we must make plans beforehand to deal both with the flush and with what will follow after the transition from war to peace has been completed. Second, unless plans are made now and are known to be made for maintenance of employment after the transition from war to peace there can be no hope of a smooth transition.

376. While it is impossible to forecast with certainty the conditions of demobilization in the present war, the probabilities are that the process must be more gradual than in the last war and may be divided into stages, as the ending of the war is divided into stages. That is to say, it will be necessary to require some of the men and women of the country to continue in military service while others are being set free. Selection will raise difficult questions of equity

[1] The general unemployment rate in British trade unions, as given on page 69 of the *21st Abstract of Labour Statistics*, averaged 2·0 from November, 1918, to September, 1920.

and the principles on which this selection is made will need to be most carefully defined. However well defined and just in themselves, they will not be accepted, if those who are retained in service feel that they are thereby losing, not merely another year or so of civilian life, but their place in a coming scramble for jobs. Those who, in the common interest, are required to continue in national service after their fellows are set free, must have the assurance that when they in turn become free they will still be wanted. Adoption by the Government of a full employment policy to follow demobilization, and confidence that the Government will pursue that policy to the end, are essential for success in demobilization. The problems of demobilization and of full employment thereafter are different but they are connected.

SOCIAL CONSCIENCE AS DRIVING FORCE

377. Twice in this century the onset of cyclical depression has been arrested by the outbreak of war, just after the culmination of an upward movement of the trade cycle. After the boom of 1913 employment had already begun to fall in 1914. After the half-hearted boom of 1937 employment fell in 1938. In each case an incipient depression was stopped or reversed, but it needed a war to bring this about. The test of statesmanship in the near future lies in finding a way to avoid depressions without plunging into war.

378. That is the aim and hope of this Report. We cure unemployment for the sake of waging war. We ought to decide to cure unemployment without war. We cure unemployment in war, because war gives us a common objective that is recognized by all, an objective so vital that it must be attained without regard to cost, in life, leisure, privileges or material resources. The cure of unemployment in peace depends on finding a common objective for peace that will be equally compelling on our efforts. The suggestion of this Report is that we should find that common objective in determination to make a Britain free of the giant evils of Want, Disease, Ignorance and Squalor. We cure unemployment through hate of Hitler; we ought to cure it through hate of these giant evils. We should make these in peace our common enemy, changing the direction and the speed rather than the concentration and strength of our effort. Whether we can do this, depends upon the degree to which social conscience becomes the driving force in our national life. We should regard Want, Disease, Ignorance and Squalor as common enemies of all of us, not as enemies with whom each

individual may seek a separate peace, escaping himself to personal prosperity while leaving his fellows in their clutches. That is the meaning of social conscience; that one should refuse to make a separate peace with social evil. Social conscience, when the barbarous tyranny abroad has ended, should drive us to take up different arms in a new war against Want, Disease, Ignorance, and Squalor at home.

379. Want, arising mainly through unemployment and other interruptions of earnings, to a less extent through large families, is the subject of my earlier Report on Social Insurance. It could, without question, be abolished by the whole-hearted acceptance of the main principles of that Report. The worst feature of Want in Britain shortly before this war was its concentration upon children. Wages were not and probably could not be adjusted in any way to family responsibilities; the various social insurance schemes for providing income when wages failed either ignored family responsibilities entirely—as in health insurance or workmen's compensation —or made inadequate provision for them—as in unemployment insurance. By consequence there followed a sinister concentration of Want on those who would suffer from it most helplessly and most harmfully. Nearly half of all the persons discovered in Want by the social surveys of British cities between the wars were children under fifteen. Nearly half of all the working-class children in the country were born into Want. It is certain on general principles and can be shown by experiment that the bodies and minds of children respond directly and automatically to better environment, that the citizens of the future will grow up taller, stronger, abler, if in childhood all of them have had good feeding, clothing, housing and physical training. Want and its concentration on children between the wars represented a destruction of human capital none the less real because it did not enter into any economic calculus.[1] The decision to destroy Want should be taken at once, for its own sake, to free Britain from a needless scandal and a wasting sore. That decision would deliver at the same time the first blow in the war against Idleness. The redistribution of income that is involved

---

[1] 52·5 per cent of all children under one year of age in York were found by Mr. Rowntree in 1936 to be in families with incomes below his standard of human needs (*Poverty and Progress*, p. 156). York was certainly not less prosperous than Britain as a whole, with less than the average of unemployment. The effects of environment on the height and weight of school children have been demonstrated repeatedly by the statistics published by the Corporation of Glasgow. Uniformly, for both sexes and at all ages, the children from larger homes are heavier and taller than those from one and two-room homes, and keep their advantage, while children of all classes improve with rising standards of life.

in abolishing Want by Social Insurance and children's allowances will of itself be a potent force in helping to maintain demand for the products of industry, and so in preventing unemployment.

380. Disease is in part a subject of my earlier Report on Social Insurance and Allied Services. But on this side the Report is limited to proposing that medical treatment of all kinds should be secured to all persons, free of all charge on treatment, and to discussing some of the general issues involved in the proposal. The acceptance of this proposal, announced by the Government in the Parliamentary Debate on that Report in February, 1943, forms the starting-point of the White Paper on the National Health Service which was published in March, 1944. This White Paper, outlining for discussion with the medical profession, the hospitals and the local authorities concerned, a scheme for the organization of a comprehensive health service free for all, opens the way to a revolution in the health of the people. Removal of any economic barrier between patient and treatment is an essential negative step for bringing avoidable disease to an end. But while essential, it is only a small part of all that is required. There is needed an immense positive extension both of preventive treatment and of curative treatment, through more and more hospitals, more and more doctors, dentists and other practitioners. There is needed, as an essential part of the attack on disease, a good policy of nutrition carried through by the wisdom of the State in using science. Here is a large field for communal outlay, using resources for purposes of high priority, in preserving the health and vigour of all.

381. Ignorance is an evil weed, which dictators may cultivate among their dupes, but which no democracy can afford among its citizens. Attack on it involves an immense programme of building schools, training and employing teachers, providing scholarships to fit opportunity to young ability wherever it is found. The first essential steps for that have been taken in the framing and introduction of the new Education Bill; there remains the task of pressing the attack on Ignorance with vigour and speed on all fronts. Learning should not end with school. Learning and life must be kept together throughout life; democracies will not be well governed till that is done. Later study should be open to all, and money, teaching and opportunities must be found for that as well. In the development of education lies the most important, if not the most urgent, of all the tasks of reconstruction. The needs of civilized men are illimitable, because they include the wise, happy enjoyment of leisure.

382. Squalor means the bad conditions of life for a large part of our people which have followed through the unplanned disorderly growth of cities, through our spoiling more and more country by building towns without building good towns, through our continuing to build inadequate, ill-equipped homes that multiply needlessly the housewife's toil. The greatest opportunity open in this country for raising the general standard of living lies in better housing, for it is in their homes and in the surroundings of their homes that the greatest disparities between different sections of the community persist to-day. Better housing means not merely better houses but houses in the right environment, in the right relation to places of work and recreation and communal activity. Town and country planning must come before housing, and such planning, as one enquiry after another has shown, is impossible, until we resolve justly but firmly the problem of land values. Here is the greatest urgency of all. The attack on Squalor cannot wait, but it must be a planned attack. The war will leave a yawning gap, which must be filled without delay by building more homes. We must have housing at once but we must have town and country planning before housing.

383. The Policy for Full Employment outlined in this Report is a policy of spending and doing. It is a policy of common action. If we attack with determination, unity and clear aim the four giant evils of Want, Disease, Ignorance and Squalor, we shall destroy in the process their confederate—the fifth giant of Idleness enforced by mass unemployment. The carrying out of the policy depends on the positive acceptance of a new responsibility by the State, that of ensuring adequate demand for the products of industry, however industry itself may be organized. The policy preserves all the essential British liberties; it uses Britain's political advantages to carry through a task which can be carried through only by the power of the State. These political advantages are great and should be used. The constitution of Britain concentrates in the Government of the day the great power without which the problems of a great society cannot be solved. It makes the use of that power subject to continual scrutiny by the citizens and their representatives, and the power itself subject to re-call; the essence of democracy is effective means of changing the Government without shooting. Finally, Britain has a public service, central and local, second to none in the world for efficiency, integrity and devotion to duty. Through these advantages, Britain has a chance of showing, sooner and more easily than any other large nation, that democracy can

order peace as well as war better than the dictators do. The British people can win full employment while remaining free.

384. But they have to win it, not wait for it. Full employment like social security, must be won by a democracy; it cannot be forced on a democracy or given to a democracy. It is not a thing to be promised or not promised by a Government, to be given or withheld as from Olympian heights. It is something that the British democracy should direct its Government to secure, at all costs save the surrender of the essential liberties. Who can doubt that full employment is worth winning, at any cost less than surrender of those liberties? If full employment is not won and kept, no liberties are secure, for to many they will not seem worth while.

POSTSCRIPT:

THE GOVERNMENT'S EMPLOYMENT POLICY

ON the 26th of May, 1944, a few days after I had sent this Report for printing on the 18th of May, 1944, a White Paper on Employment Policy was published by the Government.[1] It has seemed best to let what I had written stand as it had been written, without significant change. The White Paper and this Report are independent contributions to the same problem, representing Coalition Government enterprise and private enterprise respectively. The slower processes of private publication in war make it possible for me to add this Postscript,[2] recording briefly the salient points in the White Paper and comparing its approach to the problem with my own approach.

As an official document and declaration of policy the White Paper is epoch-marking in several ways.

First, the Paper, with its comprehensive though brief survey of employment problems in the transition from war to peace and thereafter, is the practical proof that the central machinery of Government in Britain at last includes an organ capable of expert study of general economic problems, as the basis of orderly foreseeing treatment of them. That is to say, the machinery of Government includes what a Committee of Economists appointed to consider reconstruction problems in 1917 propounded as their first and most emphatic recommendation—an Economic General Staff. The same recommendation has been urged on many occasions since then by many people, including myself in 1924 in a spirit of unwarranted

---

[1] The White Paper is Cmd. 6527. One part of what is printed in this volume—Appendix C and the paragraphs directly arising out of it in Part IV (paras. 201-11)—was not completed at this date, as it involved the use of official statistics which became available to my colleagues and myself only when published on the introduction of the 1944 Budget; this material needed elaborate statistical handling. But this part of the Report was not and could not be influenced by anything in the White Paper, which attempts no similar calculations.

[2] The Postscript represents the substance of an address given to the Royal Economic Society on 22nd June, 1944, and is printed with minor changes in the *Economic Journal* for September, 1944.

hopefulness about the first Labour Government. Now after a quarter of a century and the outbreak of a second World War it has been accepted. Whatever be thought of the name "Economic General Staff," the thing is there, has produced an admirable first product, and is to continue. "The Government intend to establish on a permanent basis a small central staff qualified to measure and analyse economic trends and submit appreciations of them to the Ministers concerned."

Second, the Paper disposes finally and officially of the economic fallacy whose pious acceptance by the British Treasury in the past has stood firmly in the way of action by the State to maintain employment. As Mr. Winston Churchill, in his capacity of Chancellor of the Exchequer, told the House of Commons in his Budget speech of 1929, "it is the orthodox Treasury dogma steadfastly held that, whatever might be the political and social advantages, very little additional employment and no permanent additional employment can, in fact, and as a general rule, be created by State borrowing and State expenditure." This dogma was attacked at the time by a formidable variety of economic authorities, including J. M. Keynes, Mr. H. D. (now Professor Sir Hubert) Henderson, Professor Pigou and Professor Clay.[1] By the renewed experience of full employment it has been consumed completely in the fires of war, and the White Paper may be regarded as a ceremonial scattering of its ashes.

Third, the Paper announces that the Government accept "as one of their primary aims and responsibilities the maintenance of a high and stable level of employment after the war." This means having "a policy for maintaining total expenditure." This is the critical decision which must be taken to prevent mass unemployment.

The White Paper on Employment Policy is a milestone in economic and political history. It remains to examine the practical measures proposed for fulfilling the responsibility for total expenditure and to consider whether they are likely to be adequate.

---

[1] The issue is discussed briefly by myself at pp. 413–16 of *Unemployment* (1930). The case against the dogma was stated in popular unanswerable language by J. M. Keynes and H. D. Henderson in a pamphlet *Can Lloyd George Do It?* and the gist of this is printed in *Essays in Persuasion* by J. M. Keynes (Macmillan, 1933). Professor Clay's views were given in his volume on *The Post-War Unemployment Problem*, pp. 132–3 (Macmillan, 1930), and Professor Pigou's in an article on "The Monetary Theory of the Trade Cycle" in the *Economic Journal* of June, 1929. The only economist of comparable standing supporting the dogma was Mr. R. G. Hawtrey in *Trade and Credit*, Ch. VI (Longmans, 1928).

PRIVATE INVESTMENT AND PUBLIC WORKS

The principal measure is that of expanding and contracting public investment, on plans prepared beforehand, to offset contraction and expansion of private investment. The White Paper assumes the continuance of fluctuations of economic activity, and by consequence of periods "of depression," (§ 60) or "of sub-normal trade" (§ 74) or of "trade recession," which, it argues, "provide an opportunity to improve the permanent equipment of society by the provision of better housing, public buildings, means of communication, power and water supplies" (§ 66). This attitude follows on the recognition of what is described in § 47 as one of two "highly inconvenient facts," which form "the most serious obstacles to the maintenance of total expenditure," namely that "those elements in total expenditure which are likely to fluctuate most—private investment and the foreign balance—happen also to be the elements which are most difficult to control."

The first comment to make on this is that the two elements, of the foreign balance and private investment, are not on the same footing. The foreign balance or rather one factor in the foreign balance, namely the demand from other countries for British goods and services, is beyond the control of the British Government, though by no means beyond its influence, as will be suggested below. But investment at home is beyond the control of the British Government only so long as the British Government chooses not to control it. Treating the foreign balance and private investment on the same footing is equivalent to treating British industry as if it were a sovereign independent State, to be persuaded, influenced, appealed to and bargained with by the British State.

That in fact is how industry is treated in the White Paper. The Government in § 82 "appeal with confidence to industry" to provide the statistical information essential to an employment policy: obviously the Government, in place of appealing, can and should require this information. The section on stabilization of private investment contains nothing effective. "The possibility of influencing capital expenditure by the variation of interest rates will be kept in view" (§ 59). This is the possibility explored with negative results throughout the nineteenth century; how it is to be reconciled with the altogether more desirable policy of cheap money is not explained. It is recognized, however, in the next paragraph that "monetary policy alone will not be sufficient to defeat the inherent instability of capital expenditure" (§ 60); and accordingly "the Government propose to supplement monetary policy by encouraging privately owned enterprises to plan their own capital expenditure in conformity with a general stabilization policy" (§ 61). The only form of encouragement to which the White Paper is rash enough to commit itself is the giving of good advice. It points out that "to a strong and well-established business, confident of its long-run earning powers, there are obvious attractions in executing plans for expansion or for the replacement of obsolete plant at times when costs are low." This is open to two criticisms: first, experience of a hundred years of the trade cycle shows that lowness of costs in a depression does not encourage investment, so long as expectation of profits is as low or lower; second, the assumption that costs, which must mean wages and prices, will fluctuate, conflicts with the emphasis laid elsewhere (§§ 49–54) on stability of wages and prices. Apart from giving good but far from new advice and re-exploring an avenue which has already been found to be a *cul-de-sac*, the White Paper, in regard to private investment, does nothing but hold out hope of still more explorations. "A further inducement (to stabilize private investment) would be provided if it were found to be practicable to adopt a device similar to that of the deferred tax credits mentioned in paragraph 72 below and calculated to stimulate capital expenditure at the onset of a depression. This and other possible methods of influencing the volume of private investment will continue to be studied as knowledge and experience of the new technique for maintaining total expenditure are accumulated" (§ 61).

The White Paper, when critically examined, is seen to propose no serious attack on the instability of private investment. It pins its faith to the expansion and contraction of public investment to compensate for contraction and expansion of private investment. It does so without enlarging the scope of public investment and without daring to propose increased powers for the central Government in relation to investment by local authorities. The policy of the White Paper is a public works policy, not a policy of full employment. It amounts to little more than always having ready a five-year plan of public works of the established kind to be put in hand by the existing authorities, not when those works are most needed, but when private enterprise is slack. The White Paper does not go so far even as the Lever pamphlet, which in addition to public works contains definite budgetary proposals for influencing private investment as well as proposals to increase the scope of public investment. The criticism in paragraphs 248–56 above, of the Lever Pamphlet and stabilization of total investment as an inadequate approach to full employment, applies even more to the White Paper.

The practical difficulties of a public works policy are not unknown to the authors of some parts of the White Paper. In § 47 they name as the second of the highly inconvenient facts to be faced in seeking to maintain total expenditure the fact that "an increase in one part of total expenditure can only within limits offset a decrease in another. For if, through a decline in private investment, the construction of new factories is discontinued and building labourers are thrown out of work, it may be useful to stimulate the purchase of clothing but it would be idle to expect the building labourers to turn up next day ready to handle sewing machines in the clothing factories." In § 62 they recognize that the capital expenditure of public authorities meets urgent needs and cannot readily be postponed or accelerated to fit the vagaries of private investment. But four paragraphs later in the White Paper, in § 66, composed perhaps by another hand, a different, less critical note is sounded. In § 66 "the Government believe that in the past the power of public expenditure, skilfully applied, to check the onset of a depression has been under-estimated." If this means that this power was under-estimated by the Treasury in the days of the orthodox dogma, it is undeniable. If it means that public works are an effective policy for full employment, it represents no more than wishful thinking.[1]

VARIATION OF SOCIAL INSURANCE CONTRIBUTIONS

Apart from public works the only practical measure proposed, though even this is offered with some reservations, is that social insurance contributions should be varied, being raised in periods of good trade and lowered in times of bad trade, with a view to making consumption more stable. This interesting and novel proposal was brought to my notice during the preparation of my Report on Social Insurance and Allied Services and is mentioned there. It does not appear in my present Report, which proceeds on the basis of planning for continuous steady expansion rather than on the basis of mitigating fluctuations. The practical and psychological difficulties of the proposal are considerable. So far as I can judge, it would involve changing the price of insurance stamps upwards or downwards without notice, in the same way as that adopted for

[1] In the House of Commons Debate (*Hansard*, 22nd June, 1944, cols. 412–13) Sir John Anderson, in a curious passage, recognised the objections to de-stabilising public work to fit vagaries of private work. "What I feel is that we have to develop a technique which, in regard to industry, whether privately owned or publicly owned, will enable influence to be exercised and directions to be given, within limits, which will conduce to the maintenance of a high level of employment. That is by the way . . . " It certainly is not in the White Paper.

changes of the bank rate; employers would learn on a Saturday that the stamps which they had been buying for 7s. 6d. would, as from next Monday, cost them (say) 9s. or 6s.; workpeople would need to be persuaded that it was reasonable to make them pay more for unemployment when there was less unemployment, and pay less when there was more unemployment. The advantages are not very great: this device would, at highest, mitigate the secondary rather than the primary effects of fluctuation. The addition to personal consumption that might, after an interval, result from it, in face of an increase of 4 per cent in unemployment above the assumed average of 8 per cent, is put in the White Paper at £70–£80 millions. This is named as a minimum but appears in fact to be an optimistic maximum; it would be attained only when unemployment was as high as 12 per cent, representing unused resources, at 1938 prices, of £500 millions a year. If further serious consideration is given to the proposal by the Government, two suggestions may be made. First, if it is good for social insurance contributions it is even better for general taxation, and under the pay-as-you-earn system could presumably be applied to income tax; the social insurance fund is simply one of the Government banking accounts. Second, the case for varying the employer's contribution is by no means the same as that for varying the contribution of the employee. Variation might with advantage be confined to the employee's contribution. If in a slump the employer finds the cost of his insurance reduced he may not spend more, but may add to his reserves.[1]

FINANCIAL INHIBITIONS

The White Paper is still far too inhibited in regard to central finance, too fearful of increasing the national debt.[2] The section on this subject starts off with a sentence to reassure the old school:

[1] It is theoretically possible of course that employers, when their contributions were reduced, might lower prices, or might distribute higher dividends in which case in due course consumption would be stimulated. But the chance of any employer being induced to do either of these things by a lowering of contributions which was strictly temporary and would be reversed as soon as employment improved is so small as to be negligible. In any case neither of these actions has the possibility of results so immediate as to make them of any significance for anti-cycle policy.

[2] Sir John Anderson in the House of Commons (*Hansard*, 22nd June, 1944, col. 415) said that §§74–9 dealing with central finance "owe their origin entirely to the Treasury." This was obvious from their character. The penetrating and brilliant analysis of those paragraphs, made in the *Economist* of 17th June, under the title "Balanced Budgets?", leaves little to be said in the way of exposing their ambiguities and their inconsistency with an effective employment policy.

'None of the main proposals contained in this Paper involves deliberate planning for a deficit in the National Budget in years of sub-normal trade activity." "The authors of the White Paper," as Professor Hicks has pointed out, "are evidently well aware that unemployment cannot be tackled without public borrowing, but they are prepared to resort to any subterfuge in order to ensure that the debt does not fall directly on the shoulders of the Central Government."[1] Thus they are prepared to contemplate lowering social insurance contributions and increasing the debt of the social insurance fund in time of depression: but they do not favour the lowering of ordinary taxes. They are prepared to encourage additional borrowing by the local authorities but not by the State. This is the old Treasury attitude, with self-deception added. There are reasons for meeting outlay of all kinds so far as possible from current revenue rather than by borrowing; the policy of doing so is named by me as the third rule of national finance. But the main reason for this policy—objection to creating and enriching rentiers—applies to borrowing of every kind, by the social insurance fund, by local authorities and by private business as much as to borrowing by the Central Government. And the rule itself is of minor importance, not able to stand for a moment against major rules. The whole section on central finance is based on a wrong sense of values which comes to the surface in paragraph 79. "Both at home and abroad the handling of our *monetary* problems is regarded as a test of the general firmness of the policy of the Government." Again, "in controlling the situation . . . the Government will have *equally* in mind the need to maintain the national income and the need for a policy of budgetary equilibrium such as will maintain the confidence in the future which is necessary for a healthy and enterprising industry." I have italicised the words to which objection must be taken. The policy of the Government in future will be judged by its handling of economic, i.e. real, problems, not "monetary" problems. Maintenance of the national income and maintenance of budgetary equilibrium are not "equally" important. The former of them is fundamental—the first rule of national finance. The latter is subordinate, a local bye-law as compared with an Act of Parliament.

LOCATION OF INDUSTRY

The location of industry is dealt with in Chapter III of the White Paper under the heading of The Balanced Distribution of Industry

[1] *Manchester Guardian*, 5th June, 1944.

and Labour. Power will be taken to prohibit the establishment of a new factory in a district where serious disadvantage would arise from further industrial development. The Government will use financial and other inducements "to steer new factory development into areas which call most urgently for further industrial diversification." All this is to the good, but the Government's policy, as interpreted in the Parliamentary Debate of 7th June, 1944, appears to fall far short of the national planning of the location of industry and consequent distribution of population that is envisaged in the Barlow Report and is among the assumptions of the Uthwatt Report. The Barlow Commission's recommendation for checking any further development in the London area has been rejected. There is no mention of the Uthwatt Report or of any alternative method for the solution of the problem of shifting land values which the Barlow Commission rightly regarded as the essential preliminary to effective town and country planning.[1] In dealing with the possibility of structural unemployment there is a welcome statement of principle that "where a large industrial population is involved, the Government are not prepared either to compel its transfer to another area or to leave it to prolonged unemployment and demoralization." But it is not clear what action the Government could or would take to give effect to these brave words, if need arose. They will not themselves, under the White Paper policy, control directly anything except public works, and an industrial population cannot be employed indefinitely in these. They contemplate disposing of all war factories to private enterprise. Will they be prepared to prohibit the establishment of new factories in one area, not on the ground of any disadvantage to that area but because there is some other area where additional employment is needed?

In this matter everything depends on the general policy and outlook of the Government. In the Debate of 7th June on the location of industry, this was expressed by the Parliamentary Secretary to the Board of Trade in winding up the Debate in the following terms: "Our policy is not a coercive policy . . . we are confident that the business men of the country are best able to judge the

---

[1] Since this was written, the Government have published a White Paper on the Control of Land Use, which after rejecting the Uthwatt Committee proposals, after a somewhat cursory statement of reasons, sets out an alternative scheme of compensation-betterment. The point of most general interest in this latest White Paper is the express rejection, in the concluding paragraph, of national planning of the use of land.

usiness needs of the country, and we feel it to be our bounden
uty to render all the help we can to them." In one who had pre-
umably read the Report of the Barlow Commission and its account
f how between 1932 and 1936 the business men of the country
udged the needs of the country in locating five-sixths of the new
actories in the area of greatest congestion and strategic danger,
uese are truly remarkable words.

THE INTERNATIONAL ASPECT

On the international side the White Paper is indefinite. As regards
ther nations it has not been found possible to say more than that
ue Government are "seeking to create, through collaboration
etween the nations, conditions of international trade which will
uake it possible for all countries to pursue policies of full employ-
uent to their mutual advantage." As regards our export trades, the
ecessity of expanding these is stressed, but "while the Government
ill spare no effort to create, in collaboration with other Govern-
uents, conditions favourable to the expansion of our export trade,
is with industry that the responsibility and initiative must rest for
uaking the most of their opportunities to recover their export
uarkets and to find fresh outlets for their products"; the only
efinite action promised by the Government is that of giving high
riority to the export trades in allocation of materials, labour and
uctory space in the period immediately following the end of the
uar. It is clearly not easy for the British Government, at this stage
f international discussion, to make any definite pronouncements as
u international trade. Here private citizens have an advantage;
uey can write more freely and can seek to form public opinion in
ll countries. The White Paper's treatment of the international
roblem suggests the following comments:—

First, the White Paper concentrates too much on increasing
exports and not sufficiently on stabilizing them. "To avoid an
unfavourable foreign balance, we must export much more than
we did before the war." Is this certain? There is the alternative
of cutting down imports and becoming more independent; the
figures given recently by the Minister of Production show how
great are the possibilities of self-dependence, even for Britain.[1]

[1] "The imports of raw materials, that is the raw materials for industry in
u43, were down to about 40 per cent of the average pre-war year, say 1938,
ud yet the total industrial production of the United Kingdom was about 40 per

This is said not to suggest that self-dependence is to be preferred to expansion of international trade. But the stability of international trade is as important as its scale. Indeed instability of international trade is one of the principal factors in reducing its scale, as has been shown by bitter experience between the wars.

Second, while stability of international trade depends on other nations as well as Britain, this does not mean that there is nothing which Britain can do about it. Steady employment in British export industries depends on steady demand from overseas. By a policy of long-term contracts for primary product from overseas Britain can guarantee a market for these product and promote stability of demand for her exports.

Third, it is not clear that adequate development of export must or can be left to the chance that business men will develop them. Exports up to a certain minimum are a vital national interest and it is the duty of the State to ensure, by direct action, if needed, that this interest is not neglected.

COMPARISON OF DIAGNOSES

What are the main differences—in diagnosis and in prescription—between the White Paper and what is written in this volume?

The main diagnosis in each is on the same lines, representing the general agreement of economists that employment depends on expenditure, so that the fundamental condition for avoidance of mass unemployment is maintenance of total expenditure. This is common ground, as it is common sense. But the diagnosis in my Report, as it is much fuller, brings out several important points which appear in much weaker form or not at all in the White Paper.

First, the analysis in Part II of my Report, showing the marked differences of unemployment rates between industries and localities emphasizes the heterogeneity both of demand for and supply of labour, and the degree of friction in the labour market. Second, the analysis of cyclical fluctuation in Appendix A emphasizes a factor in fluctuation which has been unnoticed hitherto, that is to say the important part played by demand from primary producers of food and raw materials in initiating fluctuations of manufacturing in

cent higher than it was in 1938. I think this is the most striking testimonial to the intensive work, the conservation of raw material and the use of our home grown products. It is a striking achievement." Mr. Oliver Lyttelton, addressing the Cambridge University Conservative Association, 19th May, 1944.

lustry. Third, apart from the transitional problems dealt with in its Chapter III, the White Paper diagnosis treats fluctuation of demand as the main or sole problem. It is concerned almost wholly with the timing of demand, and proposes nothing for its expansion. The analysis of facts and theories of unemployment in Part II of my Report shows, as the central weakness of the unplanned market economy, chronic deficiency or weakness of demand, with full employment as rare as total wars.

The first of these three differences is in the main a difference of emphasis. The economist authors of most of the White Paper realize the existence of industrial friction, if not its strength. My fuller diagnosis reinforces the doubts expressed by them as to the practicability of offsetting decline of demand for one sort of labour by increasing the demand for another sort. It emphasizes the need for stabilizing the demand for labour, not merely in total, but in each of its main categories. Stability does not mean stagnation, that is to say absence of change and progress. It is right that men should move from declining to progressive industries to meet a permanent change in demand and should be helped by training to do so. It is not reasonable or practicable to expect men in great masses to move into and out of public works according as their own industry is slack or busy. Stability means absence of meaningless unprogressive fluctuation.

The second of these three differences arises through discovery of new facts. These facts make not merely desirable but essential the taking of steps to stabilize markets and prices of primary products. Full stabilization involves international action. But Britain in any case must be prepared by long-term collective contracts to ensure for primary producers the prosperity on which her own prosperity depends.

The third of the three differences of diagnosis is the most important, as it is also that which may raise the greatest economic and political controversy. The White Paper does not face up at all to the problem of chronic deficiency of demand, or draw the moral clearly pointed by its own study of the transition period, in which there will be no unemployment because "it will be a period of shortages." So long as any human needs are unsatisfied there are shortages. The problem is that of clothing these needs with purchasing power, either by redistribution of income or by social demand for things needed in the common interest.[1]

[1] There is yet another respect in which what is said in the White Paper about the transition period should be applied generally. In § 17 the Government

DIFFERENCE OF PRESCRIPTIONS

The differences of diagnosis are substantial. They lead up t
prescriptions for treatment whose difference is fundamental. Th
substantive policy of the White Paper is one of public works, to b
expanded or contracted to compensate for contraction or expansio
in private investment. Apart from the half-hearted influencing c
location of industry and the plan for varying social insurance con
tributions which the Government favour for adoption at som
future time, there is nothing more than this, except several promise
of further exploration. There is nothing to stabilize private invest
ment; there is no increase of the sphere of public outlay; there i
nothing to cause the steady expansion of demand on which fu
employment depends.

In relation to the strictly limited problem with which it is con
cerned—namely cyclical fluctuation of demand—the White Paper
read in conjunction with my Report, raises two critical questions
(1) Can business investment be stabilized sufficiently, so long a
the whole or the greater part of industry is in private hands; (2) I
this cannot be done, can a high and steady level of employment b
maintained by using public investment to offset fluctuations c
private investment?

The White Paper in effect answers the first question negatively
In laying down in § 48 as the second of the guiding principles of th
Government's policy in maintaining total expenditure, that "every
thing possible must be done to limit dangerous swings in expenditur
on private investment"—it adds the warning that, "success in thi
field may be particularly difficult to achieve." Practically, as ha
been shown, the White Paper contains nothing effective for stabilizin
private investment and really gives up the hope of doing so. It pin
its faith to giving an affirmative answer to the second question.

My Report answers this second question in the negative an
proceeds to consider the conditions on which the first question ca
be answered affirmatively. It accepts the view expressed by J. M

announce their determination that in the transition period "the most urger
needs shall be met first"; in § 18 they recognize the possibility that "productio
of unessential goods may interfere with the production of essentials" and th
consequent need to establish broad priorities for the guidance of productio
This is justly and cogently said, but why is it limited to the transition period
Should not essentials always have priority over unessentials? Should the securin
of better housing, or better power and water supplies depend on the "oppo
tunity" named in § 66 of a slump in private investment directed without regar
to priorities?

Keynes in 1936 "that the duty of ordering the current volume of investment cannot safely be left in private hands."[1]

It may be objected that my Report, in so far as it contemplates the continuance of private enterprise, leaves open the possibility that private investment will fluctuate. This is true, but does not mean that my Report accepts this fluctuation as inevitable or proposes no definite measures to prevent it. The measures directly relevant include the following:—

1. A long-term programme of expanding consumption demand, social and private, which should lead to maintaining investment.
2. Stabilization of marketing and production of primary commodities, by international agreement so far as possible and by British action in any case.
3. Stabilization of private investment through a National Investment Board, which would plan investment as a whole, using powers of control and loan and taxation policy.
4. Expansion of the public sector of business, so as to enlarge the area within which investment can be stabilized directly.

Finally, in so far as these measures do not bring about sufficient stability of investment of all kinds, it is recognized that the case for further measures will be established. My Report, in place of accepting the inevitability of fluctuation and aiming merely at offsetting it, accepts the necessity of stability not merely in total expenditure but in each main section.

How far the measures named above will succeed in stabilizing the process of investment is open to argument. Some economists appear to hold that steady expansion of consumers' demand in Britain will, by itself, abolish cyclical fluctuation of investment, even if investment remains largely in private hands; in effect they hold that the first of the four measures named above will do the trick. This appears to me unduly optimistic, and to ignore the significance of overseas demand and its fluctuations, as shown in my Appendix on the International Trade Cycle, and the tendency to competitive over-investment, that will persist so long as any important industry is not under unified control. In my view, the second, third and fourth measures named above are needed in addition to the first.

The first of the four measures, whether or not it is sufficient, is indispensable. But it does not fall within the purview of the White Paper and its omission is the most serious weakness of the Paper.

General Theory, p. 320.

This weakness reflects in part the incomplete diagnosis of the problem as wholly or mainly one of fluctuation. It is even more a result of financial inhibitions. The importance attached to balancing the Budget, in the long run though not in a particular year, excludes continuous deficit spending by public authorities. Yet, either this or a drastic redistribution of income to increase the propensity to consume is in the last resort essential to a permanent policy of full employment.[1]

THE POLICIES COMPARED

The Government's Employment Policy is a policy of public works planned five years at a time and kept on tap to mitigate fluctuations. It is an anti-cycle policy, not a policy of full employment; the term "full employment" does not occur in the White Paper, except, somewhat oddly, in two passages in each of which the Government are thinking rather of what others ought to do than of what the Government ought to do: in the passage already quoted from the Foreword as to the pursuit of full employment by "all countries," and in § 54 when emphasis is being laid on the duty of workers to examine their trade practices and customs.

The Policy of my Report is a Policy for Full Employment, defined as meaning always more vacant jobs than idle men. The Policy consists of setting up and carrying out a long-term programme of planned outlay, directed in the first instance against the giant social evils of Want, Disease, Squalor, and Ignorance and towards the raising of productivity by improvements of our capital equipment. The immediate programme includes:—

> Abolition of Want by Social Security and Children's Allowances increasing and stabilizing consumption.
>
> Collective Outlay to secure good houses, good food, fuel and other necessaries at stable prices for all, and a National Health Service without a charge on treatment.
>
> Encouragement and Regulation of Private Investment by a National Investment Board, to rejuvenate and expand the mechanical equipment of the country while stabilizing the process of doing so.
>
> Extension of the Public Sector of Industry so as to increase the scope of direct stabilization of investment and to bring monopolies under public control.

[1] See the article on the White Paper contributed by Mr. Kalecki to the *Bulletin of the Institute of Statistics*, Oxford.

A National Budget based on the datum of man-power and designed to ensure year by year total outlay sufficient to set up demand for the whole productive resources of the country.

Control of the Location of Industry with full powers, including transport, on a national plan.

Organized Mobility of Labour to prevent aimless movement, the hawking of labour and mis-direction of juveniles, while facilitating movement when it is desirable.

Controlled Marketing of Primary Products, so as to stabilize overseas demand to the utmost.

International Trading Arrangements based on acceptance of the three fundamental conditions of multilateral trade: full employment, balancing of international accounts, and stability of economic policy.

When the goals set in this immediate programme have been reached or are in sight, new goals will come into sight. The planning of adequate outlay will continue, but outlay may be directed to new aims of steadily rising consumption and of growing leisure, more fairly distributed and used for the free development of all men's faculties.

ECONOMICS AND POLITICS

In the last resort the differences between the two documents compared in this Postscript represent differences of social philosophy. The economics of the White Paper are better than its politics. The Government in the White Paper treat private ownership of the means of production as fundamental; my Report treats it as a device to be judged by its results. The Government in the White Paper are conscious of the need for giving confidence to business men by monetary stability and budgetary equilibrium. They appear to be unconscious of the still greater need of giving confidence to the men and women of the country that there will be continuing demand for their services, so as to secure their co-operation, individually and collectively, in reasonable bargaining about wages, in working for the maximum of production without fear of unemployment, in relaxing restrictions, formal and informal, on the full use of resources. This confidence will not be given by a promise to undertake public works whenever unemployment threatens to become serious. It will be given only when the steady expansion of demand, for investment, as for consumption, has been ensured and when it is proved by experience that though technical progress may sometimes involve a change of jobs, there are always more vacant jobs than idle men, in the planned economic war against social evils and for rising standards at home, as there are more vacant jobs than idle men in the military war against barbarism and tyranny abroad.

This is the root of the matter. The Government in the White Paper are fighting unemployment. They ought to be planning for productive employment. But one cannot do that unless there is something that one desires passionately to see accomplished. Employment is wanted not for its own sake but as a means to an objective. Experience in peace has shown that the desire of men who are already above want to increase their profits by investment is not a strong enough motive or sufficiently persistent in its action to produce a demand for labour which is strong enough and steady enough. Experience of war has shown that it is possible to have a human society in which every man has value and the opportunity for service, when the motive power and direction of economic activity are given not by private interest but by collective determined pursuit of a common good.

The Government have not faced the implications of this experience either of peace or of war. Within the limits set by its social philosophy, the White Paper is a sincere attempt to deal with the disease of unemployment. But its brief diagnosis, admirable up to a point, understates the seriousness of the disease, that is to say the extent of the past failure of the unplanned market economy. And its practical proposals are inadequate, not only through deficient diagnosis, but even more because action is inhibited by a sense of values that is wrong in two respects: of treating private enterprise as sacrosanct—a sovereign power independent of the State, and of treating maintenance of budgetary equilibrium as of equal importance with full employment. It is necessary to declare war on unemployment, as it was necessary to declare war on Germany in September, 1939, and to give, in April, 1939, the guarantee to Poland which showed where Britain stood and made war certain. But, as experience has shown, it is possible to make such declarations without being prepared for war and for all the changes of economic and social habits that are necessary for success in war. The time calls for total war against unemployment and other social evils, not for a war with inhibitions.

Appendix A

THE INTERNATIONAL TRADE CYCLE AND OTHER FLUCTUATIONS

1. The economic activity of nearly all industrial countries is subject to fluctuations of several different types, varying in generality, length, violence, and other respects. One type of fluctuation is of outstanding importance and forms the principal subject of this Appendix; use of the term "international trade cycle," to describe this fluctuation implies two definite views as to its character which will be explained in due course. There are other types of fluctuation which call for briefer notice.

2. The phenomenon described here as the international trade cycle can be identified most simply by saying that it is the fluctuation of economic activity which, in relation to Britain, is reflected in the new index of industrial activity from 1785 to 1938, given in

figures in Table 22 on pages 310–13 and set out pictorially in Charts IV and VI. The construction of this index must first be described briefly.[1]

A NEW INDEX OF INDUSTRIAL ACTIVITY IN BRITAIN

3. The index numbers in Table 22 are based on series of annual figures recording for various industries, in terms of number, weight or volume, their output, their consumption or import of raw materials, or, in one or two cases, the shipment of their produce; transport industries themselves, such as shipping or railways, are represented by statistics of clearance or traffic. Nearly all the series used have a marked upward trend, reflecting the growth of the population and the development of industry. To allow for this, a curve representing the trend[2] has been fitted to the data, and the actual figure for each year has been expressed as a percentage of the trend ordinate; the curves fitted are in most cases curves of the second degree, but in some cases a curve of the third degree or a straight line has been used and in one or two cases it has been necessary to fit separate curves to different sets of years. The percentage shows how the actual activity of the industry in each year compares with what would have been its activity if it had developed steadily from beginning to end of the period covered; that is to say, they are indices of fluctuation. Combination of these indices gives a general index of fluctuation for all industries. In this combination weights have been assigned to the separate industries roughly in accord with the assumed number of persons employed in them, or represented by them. In addition to the general index, indices have been calculated for each of three main groups of industries, described as construction and instruments, textiles, and other industries.

4. The index records deviations in particular years of the degree of industrial activity from the general level of the period. When the index is above 100, that means that the activity of trade and industry was above the average and that employment was more than usually easy to obtain. When the index is below 100, it means the contrary of these things. The index contains no element of money or of

---

[1] The material and sources used for the period 1785–1859 are described in an article on "The Trade Cycle in Britain before 1850," published by me in *Oxford Economic Papers*, No. 3 (February, 1940), and in a postscript in *O.E.P.*, No. 4 (June, 1940). These articles explain the weighting of the different series and correlate the movements of the new index with other financial and social series. The material for the periods from 1860 to 1913, and from 1921 to 1938, comes from well-known published sources, mainly official.

[2] See Explanation of Terms in Appendix D.

prices. It is based on data of physical quantities, weights or numbers. The index, of course, is representative only. It cannot include all

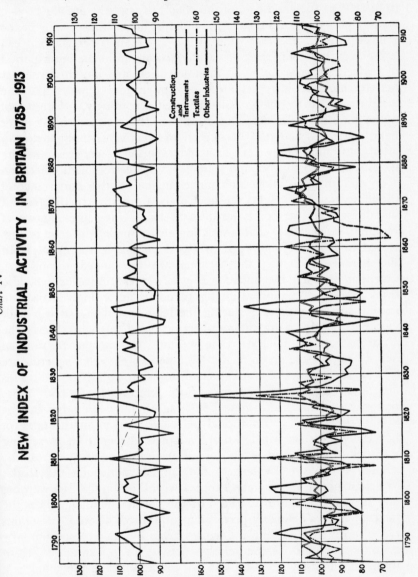

Chart IV

NEW INDEX OF INDUSTRIAL ACTIVITY IN BRITAIN 1785~1913

industries, for data are available only for some industries, and the material available differs in detail from one end of the one hundred and fifty years covered to the other. The industries included, the nature of the data and the weights assigned to each are set out in Table 23 on page 314. The material used is substantially unchanged from 1785 to 1849 and again from 1860 to 1913; the decade 1850–9 forms a period of transition in the records, dealt with specially in the postscript in *O.E.P.*, No. 4, June, 1940. The main difference between 1785–1849 and 1860–1913 lies in the absence from the latter period of any series corresponding to those for bricks and tiles in the earlier period; building is represented only by timber imports and the weight assigned to this series is increased accordingly. A number of minor industries also drop out at or just before 1850; on the other hand, coal, iron and steel become more effectively represented soon after that date. The weight assigned to cotton is increased and the weights assigned to wool and leather are decreased steadily between 1785 and 1814, to allow for changes in the relative importance of the industries. All weights are unchanged from 1815 to 1849 except in adding the two points for tiles to bricks (as representative of building) after 1822. The weighting, with some adjustments described in *O.E.P.*, June, 1940, is based on the census of 1841. In the period 1860–1913 the weights are unchanged throughout, except in treating the data for iron as representative of steel also from 1860 to 1874 and assigning 12 points accordingly to iron in those years. In weighting during the later period regard was had, in the first instance, to the numbers occupied in each trade in the United Kingdom in 1891. The weights used in the transitional decade 1850–9 are those of the later period, though the series are for the most part continuations from the earlier period. This weighting, as is explained in *O.E.P.*, June, 1940, is both more reasonable in itself and gives better agreement with other indices in this decade. The transitional period is marked in the table of figures by the plan which I have adopted elsewhere in presenting statistics of prices and wages, of a line drawn half-way across the column. This is equivalent to the familiar notice on the roads: "Reconstruction in Progress: Proceed with Caution." It is a warning not to press the figures too hard at the particular point, but at the same time, it is definitely permission to proceed. There is no serious risk of error in regarding the figures given by me as a substantially continuous record of the relative activity or slackness of British trade and industry from 1785 to 1913. The index is presented as a substantive record of fluctuation only for that period.

5. In fact it is possible to continue the index by the same methods over the interval between the two World Wars, from 1920 to 1938. This has been done in order to test the value of this index by com-

paring its course with those of the more elaborate indices available since 1920. For the period 1920–38 the series used and the weights are the same as from 1860 to 1913, with two small exceptions; that silk imports by quantity are not available and have been omitted, and that passenger traffic figures are not available before 1928 on a basis comparable to the figures thereafter and have therefore been omitted for the years 1920–7. Substantially the index covers the same ground before and after the first World War. The new index numbers in this period are based on the average of 1920–38 = 100.

6. The index of industrial activity in Britain presented here is a new addition to historical statistics. For the latter part of its course it can be compared with other indices of equally general character. From 1860 to 1913 this other index for comparison is provided by the general employment rate among trade unionists, that is to say, the percentage of trade unionists desiring employment who were successful in obtaining employment. This rate has hitherto been treated as probably the best single index of cyclical fluctuation available for Britain. This general employment rate and the new index of industrial activity are set out together in Chart V.[1] The shape of the two curves is different, in so far as the employment curve, particularly in its upper portions, tends to be more rounded. The agreement of the two curves in timing is remarkable; the correlation coefficient[2] between them is 0·86. The data represented by the two curves are independent and entirely different in character. The agreement of results is evidence of the soundness both of the original data and of the methods of construction.

7. In its experimental continuation from 1920 to 1938 the new index can be compared with the index of industrial production prepared by the London and Cambridge Economic Service. The trend of the two indices is different. That of the London and Cambridge Economic Service, covering a wide range of industries,

[1] In Chart V the trade union employment rates are shown as relatives, that is to say, as percentages of the mean rate for the whole period from 1860 to 1913. The actual rates from 1856 to 1926 are shown in Chart I in para. 55, and are given in the last column of Table 22. The employment rate is the corrected rate, described in para. 54. The curve in the lower half of Chart V, described as "U.S.A. Business Index," represents an index number, constructed by Miss Dorothy S. Thomas and published in the *Journal of the American Statistical Association* for September, 1922. Its composition is described briefly in para. A46 below, where it is used to illustrate the minor business cycles characteristic of the United States.

[2] See Explanation of Terms in Appendix D.

Chart V

BRITISH INDUSTRY AND EMPLOYMENT 1860–1913 AND U.S.A. BUSINESS

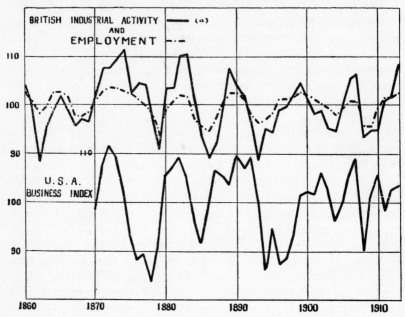

Chart VI

INDUSTRIAL ACTIVITY IN BRITAIN 1920–38

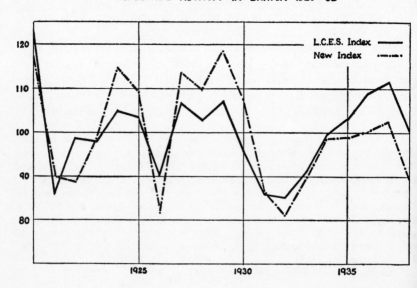

shows an upward trend. The new index with its narrower basis gives a much larger relative representation to textiles and to other trades dependent on export; it shows no definite trend from beginning to end of the interval between the wars. As records of fluctuation from year to year the two indices show remarkable agreement. If the London and Cambridge Economic Service index numbers are expressed as deviations from a straight line representing their trend,[1] the two indices show practically the same movement, as appears from Chart VI. The coefficient of correlation between them is 0·87.

CYCLICAL FLUCTUATION IN BRITAIN

8. The new index, as pictured in Chart IV, shows a succession of waves, of crests alternating with troughs. Some of the crests or troughs are more clearly marked than others, but there is no serious difficulty in singling out years of boom and years of depression as set out below. The earliest of these crests is at 1792, the last before the first World War, is at 1913. That stretch of one hundred and twenty-one years covers fifteen fluctuations, giving an average length of just over eight years.

CYCLICAL FLUCTUATION IN BRITAIN

Crests	Troughs
1792	1797
1803	1808
1810	1816
1818	1821
1825	1832
1836	1842–3
1845–6	1849–50
1853	1858
1860	1862
1865	1867
1874	1879
1882–3	1886
1889	1893
1899	1903–4
1906–7	1908–9
1913	—

9. What is implied in giving to the succession of waves that appear in the record of British industrial activity the name of "the international trade cycle"? This title, as is said above, implies two definite views as to the nature of the phenomenon described. One

[1] The L.C.E.S. figures represented in Chart VI are given in the last column of Table 22 from 1920 to 1938.

is that it is international, common to a number of different countries. The other is that the fluctuation represents more than a succession of disconnected accidents—that its successive waves have more in common than the mere fact of being waves, and are marked by uniformities sufficiently important to justify a unifying title.

THE TRADE CYCLE IS INTERNATIONAL

10. The international character of trade fluctuation hardly calls for much emphasis in a generation which has experienced the events of 1929 to 1937, and the world depression included between those years. No summary, however brief, of all the data upon this subject can be attempted here. The community of suffering of nearly all nations, whether industrial or agricultural, in that period is a commonplace. As will be shown later, this fluctuation from 1929 to 1937, while more violent than anything experienced in the past, has all the essential features identifying the trade cycle before the first World War. It is a lineal descendant of past fluctuations, and it is manifestly international. To illustrate the international character of the earlier fluctuation it is sufficient to place upon the same Chart VII the index of British industrial activity and three curves for other countries, based on readily available material drawn from the recent work of an American statistician, Dr. Simon Kuznets.[1] One of these curves represents cyclical fluctuation in the

[1] In his study of *Secular Movements in Production and Prices* (Houghton Mifflin Company, 1930), Dr. Kuznets gives for each element two series of index numbers of fluctuation, in columns III and V respectively, of his statistical tables. Column III shows the deviation of the datum for each year from the primary trend lines for the whole period covered, usually a logistic curve: that is to say, the datum for each year as a percentage of the corresponding trend ordinate. Column V shows the deviation of these percentages from their running average of seven, nine or thirteen years: that is to say, the percentage in each year as a percentage of the running average. Column III shows the total fluctuation, including both what Dr. Kuznets describes as secondary secular movements and the cyclical fluctuation. Column V is cyclical fluctuation after elimination both of primary trend and secondary secular movements. In preparing the new index of industrial activity for Britain from 1785 to 1913, I followed Dr. Kuznets in calculating two series; one (a) showing the datum for each year as a percentage of the corresponding trend ordinate and corresponding to Dr. Kuznets' column III: the other (b) showing this percentage for each year as a percentage of a running average, usually of nine years and corresponding to his column V. In view of the significance attached by Dr. Kuznets to his column V, I have used that column in presenting the American curves in Chart VII and have used my series (b) for the British curve which accordingly differs from the figures in Table 22. But I am doubtful as to the general utility of this attempt to eliminate secondary secular movements and for all other purposes have used the figures of Table 22.

Chart VII

INDUSTRIAL FLUCTUATION IN U.S.A., BRITAIN AND EUROPE

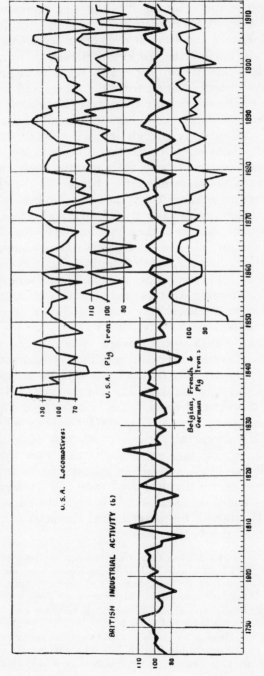

production of American pig iron; another represents the mean of
corresponding data for three countries of Continental Europe—
Belgium, France and Germany; another represents the activity of
the Baldwin Engineering Works in Philadelphia from 1835 to 1913.
It is obvious that, though each of these curves at times shows individual movements, varying from the others and from the British
fluctuation, there is a large measure of agreement between them.
The agreement of the curves, as measured statistically by the correlation coefficient, is enough in each case to establish beyond
reasonable doubt a real connection, that is to say, to demonstrate
a common factor underlying the phenomena that they record.[1]

11. This is the more interesting because of the character of the
series compared—that is to say, their freedom from money or prices.
Professor Pigou, in his work on *Industrial Fluctuations*, illustrated the
international character of these movements by the close parallelism
in the course of prices in the chief European countries and in the
United States. I myself, in my first discussion of cyclical fluctuation,
used statistics of export values to establish the same point. It is not
surprising, however, that prices, i.e. the wholesale prices of the
principal commodities, should move together in different countries;
the commodities covered by these statistics are for the most part
commodities with a world market. It is even less surprising that
the values of goods exported from different countries should move
together; they are knit together not only by prices but by being
exchanged for one another. The curves presented here are of a
different character—free from the price element and representing
industrial activity as a whole, not for export only. There is no
direct link between the pig iron production of different countries,
making it natural that when production rises (or falls) in one
country it should rise (or fall) in another; on some views it might
have been expected that increase in one country would have meant
a decline, under competition, elsewhere. The curves presented in
Chart VII establish the international character of the trade cycle
empirically and beyond question.[2]

[1] British industrial activity from 1860 to 1913, as shown on Chart VII, has
correlation coefficients of 0·65 with U.K. pig iron production, of 0·53 with the
pig iron production of Belgium, France and Germany taken together, and of
0·45 with U.S.A. pig iron production. Figures for French pig iron production
are available from 1824, and from 1824 to 1859, and have a correlation coefficient
of 0·42 with British industrial activity.

[2] The *U.S.A. Business Index*, constructed by another authority (Miss Dorothy S.
Thomas), and represented in Chart V and described in para. A46 below, shows
the same general agreement with the course of cyclical fluctuation in Britain.

12. Perhaps the most interesting of the three curves, because of its length, is that which deals with the production of locomotives in the works of the Baldwin Company at Philadelphia, covering nearly eighty years from 1835 to 1913. Except in the ten years 1894-1903, the agreement between the waves of this curve and the British curve is remarkable; the correlation coefficient over the whole period is 0·44. The range of fluctuation of the Baldwin curve is much greater than that of the British curve; engineering is one of the more fluctuating industries and the activity of a single firm may well be more fluctuating than that of many firms.[1] But these details are secondary. The main point standing out from the juxtaposition of these two curves—prepared in independence of one another from totally different materials—is the community of economic experience which has linked the United States of America and Britain, certainly for a hundred years, probably throughout the time of their political separation. They have swung from prosperity to adversity and back again together; they have a common interest in discovering the causes of cyclical fluctuation and then inventing a cure.

FOUR UNIFORMITIES IN THE TRADE CYCLE

13. The term "cycle," as used here, does not imply the recurrence of similar events at equal intervals of time. The intervals from one industrial boom to another, or one industrial depression to another, are not equal, as are the intervals from one summer solstice to another summer solstice; the crests of the curve in Chart IV are separated by periods ranging from five to eleven years. Some dictionaries and some writers limit the use of the term "cycle" to recurrence in equal periods. But etymologically the term "cycle" does not include that connotation; it means return—that the wheel comes round; it does not require or suggest that each revolution of the wheel takes the same time. For recurrence at uniform intervals of time the word "periodicity" is available. It is a waste of words to keep two words for one and the same thing, particularly when a word is urgently needed to describe recurrence without implying equality in the length of each revolution. The term "cycle" is used here for this purpose. Use of this term is meant to imply a

---

[1] There is also some tendency for the Baldwin Company figures to move in advance of the British figures, as is shown by the fact that the correlation coefficient is actually a little higher—at 0·46—if the Baldwin figures are taken a year in advance.

great deal more than that business fluctuates, that one wave succeeds another. It implies similarities between the different waves; in each some common features; in each a recurrence in the same order of the same phases. "Cycle" is used here as it is used when we speak of the "life cycle" of a species—the succession of phases of birth, growth, adolescence, maturity, and decay through which every individual passes, though the timing of these phases is not always the same. The use of a single unifying title—such as "trade cycle," in place of such a title as "industrial fluctuations" in the plural as used by Professor Pigou, has to be justified—it can be justified—by showing in all the waves uniformities so important as to make a similar pattern for each of them and point to a persistent underlying cause.

14. No attempt can be made in the limits of this Appendix to give all the evidence justifying this position, that is to say, to describe all the regular features of the trade cycle. It will be sufficient to deal with four of them: the parallel movement of prices and production; the greater range of fluctuation in certain industries either as making durable goods or producers goods; the greater range of fluctuation in British export industries; and the earlier incidence of fluctuation in British export industries. These do not by any means exhaust the list of uniformities, but they are sufficient to establish the case.

(i) The Parallel Movement of Prices and Production

15. The first regular feature of the trade cycle, in the words of Professor Haberler, is, "that the cyclical ups and downs of production and employment are accompanied by a parallel movement of the money value of production and transactions."[1] As stated by Professor Haberler, this feature implies not necessarily a rise of prices in the upward phase of the fluctuation, but only that prices should be maintained or should not fall so far as to compensate for the increase in production or transactions: the statement is made in this form to cover the case of the American expansion before 1929. "The case of constant or even falling prices (in the upswing of the cycle) has occurred, so far as I know, only once; that is to say, during the last boom in America and elsewhere. Even in this case it was only true of commodity prices: factor prices and stock-exchange prices rose."[2] An actual rise of prices accompanying the rise of production is the normal feature of the upswing, occurring always unless prevented by exceptional causes.

[1] *Prosperity and Depression*, p. 180.   [2] *Op cit.*, p. 180 note.

16. Rise of the general level of prices with the upward swing of production, followed by a fall of prices with the downward swing, implying a fluctuation of money in quantity or velocity greater in range than the fluctuation of production, is one of the most familiar features of cyclical fluctuation. It is the basis of Mr. R. G. Hawtrey's doctrine that the trade cycle is "a purely monetary phenomenon" arising from the inherent instability of credit. It is used by Mr. R. F. Harrod as an empirical fact about the trade cycle, not discoverable by introspection or deduction from first principles. The evidence for the existence of this feature in Britain and elsewhere since the middle of the nineteenth century is abundant and need not be repeated here. With the new index of industrial activity it is possible to carry enquiry as to this feature in Britain back to earlier periods, and to get an interesting result. From 1815 to 1849 the new index and commodity prices show parallel movement; from 1785 to 1814 they do not.[1] This negative result for the earliest period is not surprising. That was a period of nearly continuous war, with prices distorted by inflation and other political expedients It is the kind of exception which proves the rule.

(ii) Greater Range of Fluctuation in Producers' or in Durable Goods Industries

17. The second of the regular features of cyclical fluctuation named by Professor Haberler is that such fluctuations "are more marked in connection with the production of producers' goods than in connection with the production of consumers' goods."[2] Evidence is given by him covering the United Kingdom, United States of America, Germany, Sweden, and Australia. To the statement of the feature he adds an explanation: "When we speak of consumers' goods we mean perishable consumers' goods (such as food) and semi-durable goods (such as clothing, shoes and furniture). Durable consumers' goods (such as apartment houses) show very wide fluctuations, and belong rather to the category of capital goods, for reasons which will be discussed later." Professor Haberler elsewhere (in the index to his book) treats "producers' goods" and "capital goods" as synonymous, and as covering two distinct conceptions of durability of the product and of place in the productive process. In this, he follows a common, but unfortunate, practice.[3]

[1] *Oxford Economic Papers*, February, 1940, pp. 86–7.

[2] *Prosperity and Depression*, p. 180.

[3] Mr. R. F. Harrod treats "capital goods" and "durable goods" as synonymous and formally includes residential houses among capital goods. Professor Pigou treats "producers' goods," "production goods" and "instrumental goods" as synonymous.

"Producers' goods," i.e. goods used by producers in the process of production, are by no means all durable; it is necessary only to mention explosives, chemicals, fuel and lubricants, which are perishable, and rubber, paper, leather, which are at best semi-durable. "Consumers' goods," equally with "producers' goods," exhibit every variety of durability from houses to tobacco and services. Durability, and the feature of making goods not for consumers directly but to be used in production, are different characteristics, with no necessary connection between them. To identify them verbally, is bound to lead to confusion. To ignore the possibility that they are not only different characteristics in themselves but may each have an independent influence in cyclical fluctuation is to risk missing a clue to the secret of the trade cycle.

18. There is no doubt of the special violence of fluctuation in recent times in industries making instruments of production, such as engineering, ship-building and vehicles, with constructional industries like building also showing marked, though usually smaller, fluctuation. The evidence on this point is abundant and there is no need to add to it here. The difficulty is that instrumental goods are both producers' goods and very durable, while the products of constructional industry are also largely producers' goods and even more durable. To which of these features—of durability or of place in the productive process—the greater liability to fluctuation should be attributed cannot be determined from these industries alone.

19. The material collected here makes it possible to add to knowledge in two ways. First, as is shown in paragraph A27 below, by use of the new index of industrial activity, this feature of greater violence of fluctuation in instrumental and constructional industries can now be carried back into the eighteenth century. Second, by use of unemployment insurance records it is possible to throw light on the question whether durability of the product as such or place of the industry in the productive process is the principal factor making for greater violence of fluctuation.

20. The effect of durability of the product can be tested by comparing, so far as possible, industries occupying the same place in the productive process but supplying products of different degrees of durability. Looking first at consumers' goods, there is no doubt as to the greater violence of fluctuation in industries making for consumers durable goods like houses or motor cars. But apart from these, and leaving out the textile industries because of their exceptional dependence on export, there appears to be clear evi-

lence of a connection between the life of the product and the range of cyclical fluctuation in consumer industries generally. This is shown by Table 24 for the depression beginning after 1929. The table classifies the consumer industries, other than those making durable goods like houses, or textiles, according to the durability of their product and shows the percentage decline of males in employment in each industry from the boom of 1929 to the ensuing depression. It will be seen that there is a steady decline in the severity of the depression from the semi-durable to the perishable goods and an actual increase of employment in the industries supplying consumer services.

Table 24

CONSUMER INDUSTRIES: CONTRACTION FROM 1929*

Semi-durable goods		Semi-perishable goods		Perishable Goods		Services	
Musical Instruments	37	Hats and Caps	18	Cocoa ..	11	Gas, Water	
Leather..	35	Tailoring ..	14	Grain Milling	10	Electricity	+ 1
Oilcloth ..	22	Dress	13	Oil-Glue Soap	7	Hotels ..	+ 2
Pottery	19	Boots, Shoes ..	12	Drink ..	7	Distributive	+ 9
Watches, Clocks	16	Hosiery ..	7	Other Food..	3	Professional	+ 9
Scientific instruments	12	Glass bottles ..	7	Bread ..	1	Laundries ..	+ 10
Furniture ..	8	Shirts ..	7	Tobacco ..	1	Trams and	
		Stationery requisites ..	7	Printing ..	+ 3	'Buses ..	+ 13
		Toys, Games..	7			Entertainment ..	+ 18
		Brushes ..	5				
Means:							
Unweighted	21·3		9·7		4·4		+ 7·3
Weighted by insured males in 1929 ..	16·0		10·2		2·4		+ 8·3

* The numbers represent the percentage fall or rise of the number of males in employment from July, 1929 to 1932 or other year of maximum depression. Numbers without a sign indicate a fall; + indicates a rise. Textiles are excluded.

21. It is not easy to make a similar comparison between producers' goods industries, uncomplicated by other factors, but so far as such a comparison can be made, it points in the same direction. The industries making producers' goods other than instrumental, extractive, constructive and metal manufacturing show a materially smaller fall of employment from 1929 to the depression than do the instrumental industries—engineering, shipbuilding and vehicles; the essential difference between these groups of industries lies in the

durability of their products. Again, within the "other producers'
goods" group, the industries making semi-perishable goods like
glass, rubber, leather, paper, appear to experience a milder fluctuation
than those making semi-durable goods, such as wood boxes, brass-
ware, stoves, grates and pipes, and hand tools.

22. The comparisons in the last paragraphs relate only to the
latest cyclical depression between 1929 and 1937. There is no
material for an equally detailed comparison in earlier periods.
But from the trade union returns it is possible to compare the range
of fluctuation as between woodworking and furnishing, on the one
hand, and printing and bookbinding, on the other hand, from
1860 to 1913. These two groups of industries are mainly engaged
in supplying consumers. In practically every cyclical depression
throughout that period, the first group, making semi-durable
goods, shows a greater rise of unemployment than the second
group, whose products are largely perishable.

23. While the connection between durability and fluctuation
seems to be established, the evidence for believing that to occupy
an early place in the productive process, apart from durability,
increases the range of fluctuation, is weaker and less abundant than
might be supposed from the emphasis that has been laid on this
factor in most studies of cyclical fluctuation. It is for Britain at
least a question of probabilities rather than of rigorous proof. But
it is highly probable. Thus, building has a large element of work
for consumers; in spite of the durability of its product, it shows
normally a much smaller contraction in the course of a cyclical
fluctuation than does the instrumental group. So, too, the motor
vehicle, cycle and aircraft industry, working largely both for producers and for consumers, has a smaller contraction than engineering.
The transport industries, other than trams and omnibuses, in the
main render producer services; they show greater fluctuation than
the consumer services.

24. It should be added that for building from 1923 to 1938, it is
possible to distinguish between dwelling-houses and other types of
building in the returns of plans approved by one hundred and
forty-six local authorities in Great Britain. The estimated cost of
buildings of various types whose plans were approved each year is
shown in Table 25 on the following page.

All the different types of building show a marked upward trend
and the building of dwelling-houses is clearly affected by changes of
public policy. Taking only the years 1927–38 and eliminating the
trend, the range of fluctuation in plans for dwelling-houses, as

Table 25

BUILDING PLANS APPROVED, 1923–38—BY TYPES OF BUILDINGS

Estimated Cost of Buildings £000

Year	Dwelling Houses	Factories and Workshops	Shops, Offices and other Business Premises	Churches, Schools, and Public Buildings	Other Buildings and Additions and Alterations to existing Buildings	Total
1923	31,778	3,632	4,218	2,992	8,081	50,701
1924	37,667	3,785	4,865	3,307	8,558	58,182
1925	45,358	4,354	4,411	3,920	8,404	66,447
1926	46,209	3,752	5,075	4,691	7,903	67,630
1927	39,889	4,978	5,667	5,014	8,734	64,282
1928	40,124	5,427	6,633	6,113	9,138	67,435
1929	44,260	6,243	5,878	7,657	9,056	73,094
1930	46,764	4,581	5,475	8,402	9,383	74,605
1931	40,492	2,734	5,214	7,198	7,372	63,010
1932	46,888	3,072	4,748	4,668	6,878	66,254
1933	62,308	3,697	4,376	5,969	7,332	83,682
1934	69,586	6,073	5,021	5,872	9,011	95,563
1935	78,429	7,670	7,911	9,028	11,270	114,308
1936	75,062	10,061	8,753	10,809	12,347	117,032
1937	67,638	9,276	10,324	10,900	12,783	110,921
1938	60,004	7,469	9,495	9,498	11,134	97,600

measured by standard deviation[1] from trend, is only half the range for factories and other business premises taken together, and is materially less than that for churches, schools and other public buildings. The depression between 1929 and 1937 is far more marked in relation to factories and workshops than it is in relation to dwelling-houses. So far as this goes, it is direct evidence of greater range of fluctuation in making for producers rather than for consumers but it relates to an exceptional time.

25. The greater violence of cyclical fluctuation in instrumental industries must be attributed primarily to the greater durability of their products, and secondarily to their place in the productive process. Whatever the cause, the fact of greater fluctuation is certain and has long been recognized. It remains to consider two features of cyclical fluctuation which are in fact as regular as the parallel movement of prices and production and the greater range of fluctuation of instrumental industries, but which have not been recognized hitherto. These are, on the one hand, the greater range of fluctuation, and, on the other hand, the earlier incidence of fluctuation in British export industries.

[1] See Explanation of Terms in Appendix D.

(iii) Greater Range of Fluctuation in British Export Industries

26. Dependence on overseas trade as a factor increasing violence of fluctuation in the period 1929–37 appears most clearly from Table 26, setting out figures for textiles in the same way as those for consumer industries in Table 24. The products of textile industries are for the most part consumers' goods of no great durability, yet six of the industries—jute, cotton, linen, silk, textile bleaching, and wool—show severe contraction of employment from 1929 to 1932— more than twice the mean for all industries taken together; all but one of the six (silk) are largely dependent on exports. By way of contrast, hosiery, which of all British textile industries is least dependent on exports, has the smallest contraction of employment. The textile industries as a whole show a contraction of employment nearly twice as severe (28·6 per cent) as that of the consumer industries making semi-durable goods (16·0 per cent). Dependence on exports is probably a factor also in the relatively high degree of contraction shown by all the metal manufactures, and by some of the "other producers' goods" and "other consumers' goods" industries, such as hand tools, chemicals, explosives and musical instruments. In any case, the significance of overseas trade as affecting the range of cyclical fluctuation in the period 1929–37 is established by the textile industries. It appears also in both the earlier fluctuations, 1907–13 and 1900–6, for which trade union returns of unemployment in textiles are available.

Table 26

TEXTILE INDUSTRIES: CONTRACTION FROM 1929*

	To Year	Percentage fall from 1929
Jute	1932	69
Cotton	1931	34
Linen	1932	32
Silk	1931	31
Textile Bleaching	1931	27
Wool	1931	22
Hemp, Rope, etc.	1932	19
Carpets	1931	17
Lace..	1931	16
Textiles unspecified	1932	12
Hosiery	1931	7
Mean: Unweighted		26·0
Weighted by insured males in 1929		28·6

* The numbers represent the percentage fall in the number of males in employment from July, 1929, to the year of maximum depression.

27. It is not necessary, however, for the period before the first World War to rely on the trade union returns for evidence of marked fluctuation in the activity of the textile industries. That is provided by the new index of industrial activity, in which separate figures are given for each of three main groups—construction and instruments, textiles, and other industries. These separate figures are plotted in Chart IV, while in Table 27 below standard deviations for each group and for all industries together are given for each of our sub-periods from 1785 to 1913 and for 1920–38.

Table 27

RANGE OF CYCLICAL FLUCTUATION IN VARIOUS PERIODS*

	Construction and Instruments	Textiles	Other Industries	All Industries
1785–1814	12·4	9·8	4·9	6·7
1815–1849	19·0	10·0	5·7	9·2
1860–1886	10·8	6·6†	4·8	6·4
1887–1913	8·5	5·5	4·2	4·9
1920–1938	22·0	10·2	12·0	11·3

* The figures in this table are the standard deviations of the series shown in Table 22.
† Omitting 1860–5.

The construction and instruments group of the index covers, so far as the data are available, both industries making instrumental goods or the materials largely used therein (shipbuilding, engineering, iron) and building (represented by bricks, tiles, and timber), which is an industry engaged largely in making durable goods for consumers. In each of the four sub-periods before 1914 the range of fluctuation is greatest for the construction and instruments group and least for the other industries, with textiles intermediate. In the period 1920–38 the construction index fluctuates much more violently than either of the other groups; between these two there is no substantial difference. This approximation between textiles and other industries appears in Table 27 as the end of a continuous process by which fluctuation in textiles, from being at the outset nearly as violent as that in construction and twice as violent as that other industries, has fallen steadily in relation to the former and has come nearer to the latter. Whether this represents a real change or is due to change in the basis of the index cannot be decided without further enquiry. But the greater range of fluctuation in textiles up to the first World War can hardly be due to anything but their dependence on overseas demand. Their products in general are less durable than those of the other industries and are to a larger extent consumer's goods. Since, in spite of this, textiles fluctuate more than other industries. Table 27 gives clear evidence of the influence throughout the period covered by it of dependence on overseas demand as a factor increasing the range of cyclical fluctuation. This—the third of the facts named in paragraph A14—is added to the uniformities of the trade cyelc.

28. Table 27 yields another result of great interest. The violence of fluctuation, as measured by standard deviation, increases from the first to the second sub-period and decreases thereafter to the first World War. Since this applies to each group separately as well as to all industries in combination, it represents presumably a real change in the trade cycle itself. This is a fact which may be important in throwing light on the cause of the trade cycle. The last line of the table shows in the period between the wars return to a much greater violence of fluctuation. The new index in this period is less fully representative than in earlier periods, but the very comprehensive index prepared by the London and Cambridge Economic Service has from 1920 to 1938 a standard deviation from trend of 9·4 per cent, a little less than the 11·3 shown by the index in this period and practically the same as the 9·2 per cent given by the new index for 1815–49. The broad result is that industrial fluctuation between the two World Wars was much more violent than it had been since the middle of the nineteenth century, but was comparable to the fluctuation experienced from 1815 to 1849.

(iv) Leadership in Time of British Exports

29. The fourth persistent feature of cyclical fluctuation is the leadership in time, into and out of depression, of those industries in Britain which are dependent largely upon exports. This is not, like the first two features named above, a long established and familiar fact. It is a recent discovery; I do not know how far it has been accepted as established by other students of the trade cycle. But there is, I believe, no doubt about it. It came to my notice first in an analysis of unemployment statistics from 1927 to 1938, showing textiles and metal manufactures leading the way into and out of the depression of 1931–2 and in the downward movement of 1938 which has now ended in war in place of depression. Analysis of trade union unemployment statistics gave similar results, so far as data were available, for earlier fluctuations between 1872 and 1913. I gave my results first in a paper read to Section F of the British Association at Cambridge in August, 1938, and briefly in

n article in the *Economic Journal* of March, 1939. Mr. D. G.
Champernowne, who was working at employment and unemployment at that time, partly with me and partly independently, came
independently on the same feature—of the early incidence of
fluctuation in textiles—and was due to read a paper at the same
British Association meeting, which would have made the same point.
He was prevented on that occasion by illness, but gave his results,
emphasizing the significance of exports, in an article in the *Review
of Economic Studies* for 1938–9. Further investigations, some by
myself and some by my colleague, Mr. J. H. Wilson, not yet published, and so far as he is concerned now interrupted by Government
service, have gone far enough to establish beyond reasonable doubt
the connection of this leadership in time of certain industries in
recent cyclical fluctuation with their dependence on demand for
British exports. With the new index of industrial activity it is possible
to carry the enquiry to an earlier period, with the same results.

30. The timing of cyclical fluctuation by industries in the most
recent period is shown compendiously in Table 28 below, which for
each of 12 groups of industries sets out unemployment rates from
1927 to 1938 as index numbers, that is to say, as percentages of
the mean rate over the ten years, 1927–36. Chart III, printed in
paragraph 100, shows the index numbers for some of the groups. For
reasons already explained, the figures relate to insured males only,
since in some of the critical years from 1930 to 1933, unemployment
insurance statistics for women and girls are affected by administrative
changes. The industries included in each group are identified in
Table 33, in Appendix B, where all the industries are set out
separately, though in a different order. Here it will be sufficient to
say that the instrumental group includes engineering in its various
forms, shipbuilding and construction of vehicles. The constructional
group, in addition to building, includes the making of building
materials and one or two industries ancillary to building. In the
'other producers' goods" group, the principal industries are
chemicals, stove grate and pipe-making, electrical cable and apparatus, tanning, coke ovens, paper, rubber and unspecified metal
trades. In the "other consumers' goods" group, the most important
industries are printing, furniture, oil soap ink etc., pottery, and
musical instruments. For each group the figure for the year of
maximum depression—1931 or 1932—is shown in heavy type. The
'miscellaneous" group is included for completeness, but in each of
these industries, for one reason or another, the insurance statistics
give an incomplete picture.

Table 28

UNEMPLOYMENT INDEX NUMBERS BY GROUPS OF INDUSTRIES, 1927–38

(Male Unemployment Rates weighted by Insured Persons in 1929.   1927–36 = 100)

Numbers and Groups of Industries	Insured Persons July 1929 1,000's	1927	1928	1929	1930	1931	1932	1933	1934	1935	1936	1937	1938
						Unemployment Index Numbers							
8 Instrumental	1,280	59	61	58	103	165	**176**	148	98	80	53	37	49
7 Constructional	1,029	58	70	70	97	130	**166**	136	105	92	78	80	83
6 Metal Manufacturing	324	64	67	64	123	**167**	164	126	90	79	57	39	81
11 Textiles	1,317	46	59	63	150	**160**	136	111	107	95	74	64	110
6 Food	467	62	67	71	94	125	**135**	127	116	109	93	80	82
5 Clothing	580	55	66	68	99	129	**137**	128	116	108	96	89	99
7 Consumers' Service	2,661	55	61	65	92	119	**133**	130	121	119	106	91	97
15 Other Consumers' Goods	816	59	56	58	93	142	**155**	137	112	102	86	75	84
17 Other Producers' Goods	847	63	64	60	107	159	**161**	132	98	88	66	53	78
5 Transport	651	65	75	75	100	121	**136**	131	106	103	89	75	85
1 Coal Mining	1,075	73	85	63	82	120	**138**	130	113	104	91	60	63
6 Other Extractive	108	43	51	54	90	137	**172**	153	115	104	79	67	71
6 Miscellaneous*	939	56	60	68	88	112	**129**	126	126	124	111	113	101
100 All Industries	12,094	58	65	65	101	135	**146**	131	111	103	86	73	86

* Fishing, Public Works, Commerce, National Government, Local Government and "Other Industries."

31. The table illustrates two of the other features of cyclical fluctuation already noted, namely, the greater range of fluctuation in instrumental and constructional industries, as compared with other industries, and the greater range of fluctuation in textiles, as compared with other consumer industries. The special significance of Table 28 is in relation to the timing of cyclical fluctuation. Whereas all other groups of industries reach their maximum of depression in 1932, two groups, namely metal manufacturing and textiles, reach their maximum a year before in 1931 and textiles in particular show a marked recovery in 1932; in other words, these two groups lead out of the depression. In this respect the group averages shown in Table 28 represent fairly the experience of each of the individual industries in the group. The two groups which lead out of depression are also those which move into depression most rapidly. The proportionate increase of unemployment rates from 1929 to 1930 is greater for textiles and for metal manufactures than for any other group. That is to say, these two groups lead into depression as well as out of it. As is noted later (paragraphs A43-4), this leadership into depression by these groups is repeated in 1938.

32. It may be suggested that the early recovery of the British export industries from the Great Depression was due to special circumstances, namely, the departure of Britain from the Gold Standard in September, 1931. This, however, is not the case. Detailed examination of the course of cyclical fluctuation quarter by quarter in these industries shows that recovery had begun before Britain left the Gold Standard. Cotton, linen, tin-plate and steel-melting all reached their maxima of unemployment in the last quarter of 1930; jute, chemicals, explosives and dock and harbour service—all industries with large dependence on export—reached their maxima before the middle of 1931. The leadership in time of this particular group of industries out of the Great Depression was due to permanent and not to exceptional causes.

33. Discovery of these facts as to the timing of cyclical depression between the two wars, led to an enquiry whether the same thing happened before the first World War. By use of the trade union returns, it has proved possible to construct unemployment index numbers by groups of industries for each of five earlier fluctuations, namely, 1907-13, 1900-6, 1890-9, 1883-9, 1872-82. Tables 29 and 30 for two of these periods—1907-13 and 1890-9—are given below and are illustrated by Charts VIII and IX; in the earlier of these periods, the figure for textiles is based not on trade union returns, but on raw cotton consumption. It will be seen that in both these

Table 29

UNEMPLOYMENT INDEX NUMBERS, 1907–14

(Mean of 1907–13 = 100)

Industrial Group	1907	1908	1909	1910	1911	1912	1913	1914*
Instrumental	73	191	**201**	105	53	41	34	43
Constructional	98	155	**157**	115	68	55	51	60
Metal Manufacturing ..	58	**187**	147	102	78	68	52	73
Textiles	68	**169**	110	110	101	77	72	76
Other Producers' Goods	107	148	**163**	109	72	55	61	55
Other Consumers' Goods	92	**127**	125	105	91	89	70	61
Coal Mining†	72	119	**135**	116	116	83	62	77

* January–June only.

† The figures given here for coal-mining take account both of the average number of days worked per week and of the unemployment of individual men as recorded by their trade unions.

Chart VIII

UNEMPLOYMENT INDEX NUMBERS 1907—14

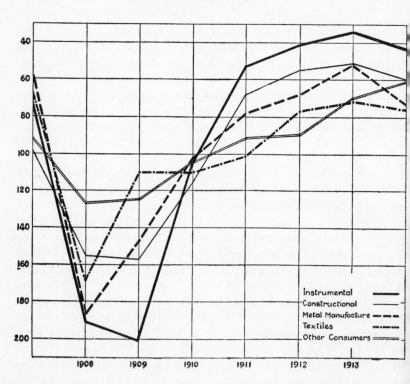

Table 30

UNEMPLOYMENT INDEX NUMBERS, 1890–9

(Mean of 1890–9 = 100)

Industrial Group	1890	1891	1892	1893	1894	1895	1896	1897	1898	1899
Instrumental ..	41	71	134	177	**182**	134	62	79	72	47
Constructional	84	95	115	146	**159**	148	72	64	55	63
Metal Manufac-turing ..	24	124	122	**206**	89	106	94	95	113	22
Textiles (Cotton)[1]	(73)	(74)	(120)	**(137)**	(102)	(100)	(109)	(114)	(85)	(85)
Other Con-sumers' Goods	51	94	110	124	**146**	122	89	87	86	92

[1] Based on raw cotton consumption.

Chart IX

UNEMPLOYMENT INDEX NUMBERS 1890—1899

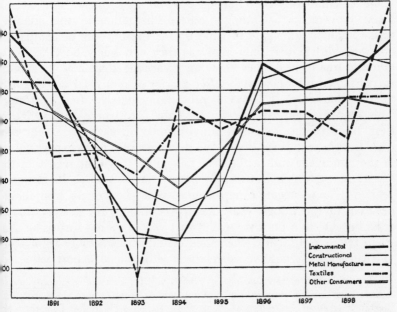

periods the same two groups of metal manufacturing and textiles
take the lead, having their maximum depression a year before the
other groups. The tables for the other fluctuations between 1872
and the first World War all give, with minor variations, the same
result. The leadership in time in cyclical depression of the metal

manufacturing and textile groups of industries in Britain is establishe
from 1870 onwards. The metal manufacturing group is engage
almost wholly in making producer goods of a high degree of dura
bility. The textile group is engaged mainly in making consume
goods of low durability. The only thing common to the two grouf
is the large measure of their dependence on overseas demanc
That this is a factor explaining their common leadership in depres
sion, is made clear by detailed examination of the groups. In eac
group, so far as information is available, the industries which ar
most dependent on overseas demand, such as tin-plates, cotton an·
linen, show a tendency to move into depression even earlier tha.
the other industries of the group.

34. With the new index of industrial activity, the enquiry ca·
be carried back to an earlier period, taking the form of a compariso·
of the new index with the course of British exports as valued offi
cially. These official values—the only ones available before 180
and continued to 1857, though "declared" or true values were als·
being calculated—were changed only at rare intervals, if at al.
Their movements accordingly reflect fluctuation in the quantit
rather than in the value of exports; for the purpose of comparin·
one year with a neighbouring year they can safely be taken as
guide to quantities.[1] They show an invariable tendency for export·
to fall violently immediately after a crest of industrial activity an·
to rise markedly, if less violently, immediately after a trough
This tendency appears clearly in Table 31, where the deviatio·
from trend of the industrial activity index in each crest year an·
each trough year is set beside the deviation of official export value
in the same year and in the year following. It will be seen that th
export index, which has usually been a large positive in the cres
year, is a large negative in the next year; conversely from bein·
negative in the trough year the export index rises sharply, in al
cases but one to a positive, in the next year. It is not surprising tha
when tested statistically, the index of industrial activity from 178·
to 1849 shows a positive correlation with official export values c

[1] The official rates of valuation for exports and imports are commonly state·
to have been fixed in 1694 or 1696 and not to have been changed since that tim·
(Porter, *Progress of the Nation*, 1847, p. 358). It seems clear that changes wer·
sometimes made in the valuations and in any case the great changes in th
relative importance of different exports (e.g. of cotton and wool manufactures
would make the use of official export values unmeaning or dangerous as a guid·
to export volumes, in comparing distant dates, say fifty years apart. But thi
does not affect the significance of these figures for indicating changes of quantit·
from year to year, in a period of ten or twenty years.

ie same year and a negative correlation with official export values
ɔf the following year. The negative correlation coefficient is high
nough to be proof of a real connection, that is to say, of a tendency
ɔf export quantities to be low in the year following a boom and to
e high in the year following a depression.[1] The unemployment
atistics of 1870–1938 and the official export statistics of 1785–1849
ell one and the same story about cyclical fluctuation in Britain,
nat exports lead into depression and out of it.

Table 31

INDUSTRIAL ACTIVITY AND OFFICIAL EXPORT VALUES

Crest Year	Deviations from Trend			Trough Year	Deviations from Trend		
	Industrial Activity	Official Export Values			Industrial Activity	Official Export Values	
		Same Year	Following Year			Same Year	Following Year
1792	+ 12·0	+ 13·0	− 17·9	1797	− 14·9	− 15·1	− 4·7
1802	+ 7·4	+ 13·9	− 8·9	1808	− 15·4	− 5·9	+ 20·2
1803	+ 7·8	− 8·9	− 5·4				
1810	+ 14·8	+ 16·5	− 21·7	1816	− 16·6	− 7·4	+ 3·7
1818	+ 7·6	+ 9·5	− 15·2	1821	− 8·1	− 1·0	+ 4·4
1825	+ 33·4	+ 0·3	− 16·4	1832	− 7·0	− 0·6	+ 1·7
1836	+ 8·1	+ 5·9	− 14·5	1842	− 12·4	− 8·4	+ 2·6
				1843	− 13·4	+ 2·6	+ 9·1
1845	+ 11·4	+ 0·4	− 0·3				
1846	+ 12·6	− 0·3	− 4·3				

35. Table 31 deals with official export values, which represent
uantities rather than true values and are available only until the
niddle of the nineteenth century. The new index and declared
xport values can be compared throughout that century and to the
utbreak of the first World War. This comparison, made in a table
ɪ my postscript of June, 1940,[2] reveals an interesting difference in
he relation of the new index and declared export values as between
he early part of the nineteenth century and later. In the period
867–1913 there is high positive correlation coefficient (+ 0·74)
etween the new index and exports taken simultaneously, and the

[1] The co-efficients are given in *Oxford Economic Papers*, No. 3, p. 88 as − 0·33
ɔr 1785–1814, and − 0·59 for 1815–49.
[2] *Oxford Economic Papers*, No. 4, p. 72.

correlation coefficient remains substantial and positive (+ 0·50
even when exports are taken a year behind. On the other hand, i
the period 1815–59, though there is a significant positive correlatio
coefficient (+ 0·50) between the new index and declared expor
values taken simultaneously, the coefficient becomes negative whe
export values are lagged a year and in respect of one group c
exports, namely textiles, is high enough to be almost certainl
significant (− 0·35). This contrast between the earlier and th
later period is well worth further examination, with a view t
determining whether it arises through a change in the character c
British exports, from being predominantly textiles to including larg
proportions of other articles, or to a change in the character of th
countries to which exports were sent, from being almost wholl
agricultural to being largely industrialized with a cyclical rhythn
parallel to that of Britain. It should be added that the table referre
to in my Postscript gives separate correlations for the main group
of exports and shows that throughout the period covered by i
from 1815 onwards, textiles move relatively early in the trad
cycle, while iron and steel, coal and machinery move late. This i
in accord with recent experience and underlines the substantia
identity of cyclical fluctuation throughout the time for which it i
known to have existed.

THE NEW FACTS AND THEIR MORAL

36. The fact that in Britain industries dependent on export mov
early in cyclical fluctuation must be taken as established and as ye
another uniformity justifying the title of this Appendix. The ex
planation of this fact still lies in the region of hypothesis. Yet ther
is little doubt as to the direction in which the explanation will mos
probably be found. The overseas trade of Britain consists substantiall
of the exchange of manufactured goods for primary products–
agricultural and mineral. This exchange, which in other countries
notably the United States, takes place mainly within the nationa
boundary, for Britain takes place across national boundaries. The
leading part played by British export industries in the trade cycl
suggests that one of the important elements in the cycle is the relatior
between primary producers, and industrial communities using thei
products, whether food or raw materials. This suggestion is supportec
by further facts as to cyclical fluctuation in Britain which, if no
yet as well established as those given above, are highly probable.

37. The first of these probabilities is that the turning-points o

the fluctuation in Britain, both upwards and downwards, as recorded in the monthly unemployment rates, have a tendency to occur at particular seasons of the year. This apparent seasonality was named by me as a second new fact about cyclical fluctuation at the Cambridge meeting of the British Association in 1938. In the *Economic Journal* of March, 1939, the crests and troughs of cyclical fluctuation —as deduced from monthly unemployment rates after elimination of seasonal fluctuation—were set out in the following table:—

Table 32

CRESTS AND TROUGHS OF CYCLICAL FLUCTUATION IN BRITISH UNEMPLOYMENT RATES, 1890–1932

CRESTS		TROUGHS	
Single Month	Three Months Running Average	Single Month	Three Months Running Average
January, 1890	January, 1890	December, 1892	December, 1892
December, 1899	November, 1899	December, 1904	December, 1904
September, 1906	August, 1906	October, 1908	October, 1908
December, 1912	December, 1912		
July, 1929	July, 1929	August, 1932	August, 1932
August, 1937	August, 1937		

Whether judged by single months or by running averages of three months (taken to avoid chance disturbances) all the turning points but one fall into two groups: from July to September or from November to January. The exception falls in October 1908 between the two groups. None of the ten turning points occurs in any of the months from February to June. It is difficult to believe that this concentration of the turning points of the trade cycle in Britain on certain months of the year and their avoidance of other months can have come about by chance; according to a calculation made for me by Mr. D. G. Champernowne the odds against getting by chance the result shown in Table 32 are about 22 to 1. But if the result is not due to chance, the trade cycle itself must contain a seasonal element, and seasonality in this connection can hardly mean anything but the influence of agricultural production. The two seasons selected for turning points—July to September and November to January—point suggestively to the harvest seasons of the Northern and Southern hemispheres respectively. It must be taken as highly probable, though not finally established, that the trade cycle has an agricultural root.

38. The second of these probable facts is the tendency of the purchasing power of overseas buyers of British exports, as measured by the relation between import values and export prices, to turn both upwards and downwards, ahead of export quantities, and to turn at particular seasons of the year. This is one of the first results of an investigation on which my colleague, Mr. J. H. Wilson, was engaged with me when his work was interrupted by war.

39. Another result of Mr. Wilson's may be given here in further support of the hypothesis that the undoubted special significance of British export industries in cyclical fluctuation is due not to their exporting, i.e. meeting demand across an international boundary, but to their supplying manufactures in exchange for primary products, largely agricultural. In cyclical fluctuation, while the total values (quantity multiplied by price) of British imports and of British exports both vary largely, the variations are different in character; imports change more in price than in quantity, while exports change more in quantity than in price. The same difference appears in the experience of agriculture and of industry in the United States. From 1929 to 1932 farm prices there fell much more than industrial prices; the quantity of agricultural marketings fell much less than the quantity of industrial production.

40. Yet another suggestion from Mr. Wilson's work, which it seems worth while to mention now as a clue to further enquiry, relates to the exceptional position of textiles as being normally ahead even of other British export industries in cyclical fluctuation. Mr. Wilson suggests that this is probably due to the principal textile industries, notably cotton, using imported raw materials. A downward turn in the price of these materials leads to an immediate decline of buying of raw cotton and curtailing of production of cotton goods in anticipation of a further fall of material prices, even before the diminished purchasing power of the overseas consumer begins to affect export industries generally. An interesting sidelight on this is afforded by the fact that the hosiery industry, which exports relatively little but depends ultimately on imported raw materials, appears to agree with the other textile industries in moving early in the fluctuation, though it does not have anything like the same violence of fluctuation.

41. The new facts, established and probable, as to the international trade cycle, that are set out above, have important bearings both on theory and on practice. They make it necessary to enlarge previous theories of cyclical fluctuation, in order to accommodate these facts. They point to a new direction in which preventives of

fluctuation must be sought by practical men and they emphasize the need of joint action by many nations in this field. It is difficult to avoid the conclusion that an important and hitherto almost wholly neglected element in the causation of the trade cycle is the relation between primary producers and the industrial users of their products; that a fundamental cause of the trouble has been the conditions under which primary production has been carried on, making its volume singularly irresponsive to changes in price, and therefore unmanageable in an unplanned market economy.

42. If there is any substance in the suggestions made here—and the main facts cannot be denied—one of the inner secrets of the trade cycle is to be found, not in bankers' parlours or the board rooms of industry, but on the prairies and plantations, in the mines and oil-wells. The new sign-post points clearly to the need for joint action by many nations to bring order into the production and marketing of primary commodities. This is one of the practical problems discussed among the international implications of full employment in Part VI (paragraphs 337-9).

HISTORY REPEATS ITSELF FROM 1793 TO 1938

43. The leadership in time of the British export trades in cyclical fluctuation since 1785, however it be explained and whatever its counterpart in other countries, is a fact of great importance. For though it is a fact of British experience it relates to an international experience. With the other and more familiar, though not more certain, uniformities set out above, it shows the world depression of 1931-3 not as an inexplicable disaster whose repetition is unlikely, but as the lineal, if larger, descendant of all the earlier fluctuations which have brought insecurity to the industrial world through all its growing wealth for more than one hundred and fifty years. It shows that the same forces were at work and that history was repeating itself up to the outbreak of the second World War.

44. Table 28 and Chart III presenting its most important series are carried on to 1938. They show that while unemployment increased from 1937 to 1938 in every industrial group, the increase was startlingly greater in textiles and in metal manufactures than in any other group. In other words, metal manufacturing and textiles are seen leading into the new depression that would have come upon Britain and the world but for the second World War. The similarity of the movement from 1937 to 1938 and the movement from 1929 to 1930 is shown not only in this broad comparison of

groups of industries, but also if each of the hundred industries is examined separately; if the percentage contractions of employment in each of the 100 industries from 1929 to 1930 and from 1937 to 1938 respectively are correlated, there is a significant correlation co-efficient of + 0.58 between the two sets of percentages. What happened between 1937 and 1938 is essentially the same as what had happened from 1929 to 1930 in the beginning of a new cyclical fluc-tuation. It is the same as what had happened for a hundred and fifty years. 1937 was the top of a cyclical fluctuation true to type; 1938 repeats 1793 and each year of incipient depression between those dates. After the culmination of each cyclical fluctuation, as industrial activity turned downwards, the turn came first in the industries of Britain dependent on overseas demand.

OTHER TYPES OF FLUCTUATION

45. The term international trade cycle is used here to identify one particular type of fluctuation of industrial activity. It is not the only type of fluctuation to which different industries in different countries are subject. At least three other types of fluctuation are recognized by American authorities.

46. First, superposed on the larger movement identified here as the international trade cycle, there are found in the United States shorter and generally less violent fluctuations. This is well illustrated by the composite index of business conditions in the United States which is one of the curves on Chart V. This index, constructed by Miss Dorothy S. Thomas, represents, with equal weights, wholesale prices, commercial failures, bituminous coal production, pig iron production, railroad freight ton mileage, bank clearings outside New York, employment in Massachusetts, railroad mileage con-structed, and imports. The principal fluctuations of this index are clearly the same as those of the British index. In addition to the crests and troughs corresponding to those of the British index, the American index has a number of intermediate fluctuations, with crests at 1887, 1892, 1895, 1902, 1910, and troughs at 1887, 1891, 1896–7, 1901, 1911. But with one exception, the crest at 1910, all these are markedly less important than the crests and troughs agreeing with the British fluctuation. Some American authorities taking all those fluctuations together, speak of the business cycle in the United States as having an average duration of about three and a half years, less than half that assigned in this chapter to the British and international cycle. But it seems better, as Professor

Alvin Hansen suggests, to distinguish between major and minor cycles.

"The American experience indicates that the major business cycle has had an average duration of a little over eight years. Thus from 1795 to 1937 there were seventeen cycles of an average duration of 8·35 years. . . . In the eighty-year period from 1857 to 1937 there were ten major cycles of an average duration of 8·0 years.

"Since one or two minor peaks occur regularly between the major peaks, it is clear that the minor cycle is something less than half the duration of the major cycle. . . . In the eighty-year period from 1857 to 1937 there were twenty-three minor cycles with an average duration of 3·48 years."[1]

The "major cycles" of Professor Hansen are the movement described here as the international trade cycle, with an average duration of eight years. The minor cycles are peculiar to the United States, or at least are far more marked there than elsewhere. They are not traceable in Britain.

47. Second, the building industry in the United States, as in Britain, is subject to a special fluctuation of its own, of a length materially greater than the eight years of the international trade cycle. This phenomenon, for Britain, was described by me in a paper read to the Manchester Statistical Society in 1921, and is discussed in the 1930 edition of *Unemployment*[2] as the "hyper-cyclical fluctuation of the building trade." A chart at page 336 of that work shows that in building, underlying the five to nine-year waves of the trade cycle is a ground-swell, with a length in the period covered by the chart of about eleven years from crest to trough, that is to say, about twice that length or twenty-two years altogether from crest to crest. In the United States, there appears to be an equally well-marked special fluctuation of building construction in an average period somewhat shorter than that suggested by me for Britain, namely seventeen to eighteen years, or about twice the length of the major business cycle.[3] Professor Hansen discusses this phenomenon as one of great importance, though "one that, strangely enough, has been greatly neglected in the analysis of business cycles." He points out how large a part it played in deepening and

---

[1] *Fiscal Policy and Business Cycles*, pp. 18–19 (1941, New York).

[2] Pages 335–9. Reference is made there to the attention called by Mr. N. B. Dearle in 1908 to the special experience of the London Building Trade.

[3] See Hansen, *op. cit.*, pp. 19–27, citing various authorities from 1923 to 1930.

lengthening in the United States the cyclical depression of the nineteen-thirties.

48. This hyper-cyclical fluctuation of the building trade in both countries deserves far more attention than it has received hitherto. It has the effect, noted in my paper to the Manchester Statistical Society, of placing the building industry rather than the instrumental industries in the first rank of fluctuation: "for ten years together its unemployment is first far less and then far more than that of engineering."[1] It has an interesting reflection in the record of houses inhabited, uninhabited, and building at successive censuses. The process by which, in respect of houses, supply has been adjusted to demand hitherto, is very slow and imperfect in action. Under a market economy, the supply of houses does not follow the demand closely, and is alternatively excessive or deficient over considerable periods. In my study of 1930, after pointing out that many other industries might on enquiry show characteristic movements independent of the trade cycle, I emphasized the significance of this building trade fluctuation in the following terms: "The building trade is only one illustration of such movements independent of the trade cycle, though for several reasons specially worth choosing for illustration here. Its hyper-cyclical fluctuation is markedly violent and regular, is exceptionally productive of unemployment, and represents a factor of instability in modern life to which perhaps sufficient attention has not been paid—the instability due to many-headed control of industry. Other industries, like engineering and cotton, are disturbed by varying demand for their products. Building contrives to fluctuate exceptionally and violently though engaged largely in meeting demands which do not fluctuate." Both as a guide to policy, and for practical purposes, this special feature of hyper-cyclical fluctuation is of first importance. It cannot be dealt with by measures directed to evening out the general trade cycle.

49. Third, there is some evidence of alternation of good and bad times generally in the United States over still longer periods—thirty years or so—and some writers have developed this into a theory of "long waves," with varying explanations, running respectively in terms of technological improvement, of wars, and of gold and price movements. The facts and theories are discussed briefly by Professor Hansen[2] and are set out at length in the various works to which he refers. There is, as might be expected, considerable divergence between the experience of different countries.

[1] *Unemployment* (1930), p. 339.　　　　[2] *Op. cit.*, pp. 27–41.

CONCLUSION

50. In my first study of unemployment thirty-five years ago, I described cyclical fluctuation mainly by the use of the trade union statistics from the middle of the nineteenth century. Fourteen years ago, in a second study of unemployment, I explored the possibility of finding cyclical fluctuation in the early part of the nineteenth century and came, on the whole, to a negative conclusion; that it was not possible before 1858 "to find the cyclical fluctuation of trade in the sense in which such fluctuation is found later as an influence dominant alike over finance and trade in the narrow sense and over industry and the whole economic life of the nation."[1] Under the influence of those who described the trade cycle as a monetary phenomenon I was then inclined to date its development from the Bank Charter Act of 1844 and the banking policies developed thereafter. That negative conclusion of 1930 was based mainly on consideration of four indices; prices, bank rate, export values and marriages. In the light of the fuller information now available it calls for revision to-day. The conclusions suggested by a new study of additional facts may be summarized as follows:

1. Fluctuation of industrial activity in Britain in periods of an average length not very different from those of the modern trade cycle can be traced over the whole time for which data of construction industries are available, i.e. from 1785.

2. The two regular features of the trade cycle named by Professor Haberler, namely the parallel movement of prices and the greater violence of fluctuation in instrumental industries are certainly present throughout, except in respect of prices during the war period before 1815.

3. Two other regular features—the greater violence of fluctuation in British industries dependent on overseas demand, and the leadership in time of such industries—are also certainly present throughout.

With these four regular features and with other minor similarities, the substantial identity of the trade cycle in Britain is established over the whole one hundred and fifty years from 1785 to the outbreak of the second World War. This identity has persisted through all changes of banking and monetary policies and through a revolutionary change in the relative position of Britain economically in the world.

[1] *Unemployment* (1930), p. 342.

51. The identity of the trade cycle over all the whole period of one hundred and fifty years is established partly by a special study of British exports. But quite apart from the fact that the experience of the British exports is itself international, the trade cycle by other facts is shown to be not a British but an international phenomenon. It is the common scourge of all advanced industrial countries with an unplanned economy, and of the regions from which they draw the materials for their industry. It cannot be explained away by external accidents of war or domestic politics. It begins at least as soon as industry begins to take predominantly its modern form of work with machines in factories and must be regarded as deeply rooted in the economic structure. It is the common interest of all countries which desire to preserve free institutions to find a means, and they must largely find the means in common, for preventing the fluctuations which have brought recurrent insecurity to the world ever since industry began to take its modern and more productive form.

Table 22

NEW INDEX OF INDUSTRIAL ACTIVITY IN BRITAIN, 1785–1938

	Construction and Instruments	Textiles	Other Industries	All Industries	Official Export Values as % of trend
1785	75·0	95·7	99·1	92·1	98·8
1786	108·3	94·1	101·3	100·8	99·7
1787	102·0	96·9	103·5	100·9	96·4
1788	99·2	90·4	106·0	99·2	95·7
1789	98·0	98·2	109·6	102·8	98·5
1790	106·2	101·9	104·7	104·3	101·2
1791	111·1	106·4	106·8	108·1	108·7
1792	124·0	103·2	108·7	112·0	113·0
1793	115·3	86·9	99·6	100·5	82·1
1794	93·0	94·3	98·5	95·6	94·5
1795	91·3	94·6	97·9	94·8	88·5
1796	99·0	95·2	98·8	97·7	99·6
1797	80·5	79·8	93·4	85·1	84·9
1798	84·5	99·7	92·6	92·3	95·3
1799	86·5	113·9	94·4	98·3	112·5
1800	103·0	104·9	107·5	105·3	109·5
1801	102·5	99·9	100·8	101·0	112·0
1802	123·1	96·8	103·5	107·4	113·9
1803	125·7	98·1	101·3	107·8	91·1
1804	107·0	107·9	102·6	106·7	94·6
1805	109·5	108·3	104·3	107·2	96·0
1806	98·0	95·2	102·2	98·7	102·2
1807	95·1	100·1	98·2	97·8	91·3
1808	85·6	73·1	93·9	84·6	94·1

Table 22—Continued

NEW INDEX OF INDUSTRIAL ACTIVITY IN BRITAIN, 1785–1938

	Construction and Instruments	Textiles	Other Industries	All Industries	Official Export Values as % of trend
1809	90·6	109·0	100·8	100·4	120·2
1810	106·9	126·5	111·1	114·8	116·5
1811	112·9	91·7	99·1	101·1	78·3
1812	97·1	98·2	99·7	98·5	...
1813	99·2	103·6	96·7	100·2	100·0
1814	89·3	102·9	103·8	98·1	108·8
1815	97·3	100·3	99·2	99·0	111·0
1816	73·2	82·3	92·3	83·4	92·6
1817	81·1	99·6	93·1	91·6	103·7
1818	104·2	112·5	106·5	107·6	109·5
1819	109·4	93·8	97·7	100·0	84·8
1820	89·6	89·5	97·2	92·5	95·4
1821	85·6	96·2	93·3	91·9	99·0
1822	97·3	104·1	95·2	96·8	104·4
1823	108·3	101·1	102·9	103·9	100·2
1824	123·8	107·7	107·6	112·5	107·5
1825	162·8	132·0	111·1	133·4	100·3
1826	121·1	80·6	105·7	102·3	83·6
1827	100·0	107·4	108·0	105·4	101·8
1828	94·6	110·5	103·8	103·2	98·4
1829	91·1	94·3	104·4	96·8	99·9
1830	86·2	105·9	105·7	99·5	103·5
1831	87·8	103·7	106·4	99·6	97·7
1832	84·9	98·1	95·5	93·0	99·4
1833	84·5	100·3	97·3	94·1	101·7
1834	93·3	103·2	94·4	97·0	101·8
1835	105·4	98·3	98·2	100·6	102·7
1836	111·8	115·1	97·9	108·1	105·9
1837	106·9	102·0	95·6	101·4	85·5
1838	108·4	111·4	101·5	107·2	103·7
1839	111·8	101·4	102·7	105·2	103·7
1840	117·0	100·8	100·9	106·1	103·9
1841	101·0	98·2	98·5	99·2	98·3
1842	82·3	88·9	91·4	87·6	91·6
1843	70·4	97·1	91·6	86·6	102·6
1844	92·5	105·0	89·0	95·5	109·1
1845	125·2	103·9	105·1	111·4	106·4
1846	137·4	97·6	103·2	112·6	99·7
1847	121·1	77·1	109·8	102·3	90·7
1848	81·5	92·5	101·4	91·7	91·0
1849	78·6	98·8	97·7	91·6	107·9
1850	85·0	90·6	101·1	91·4	
1851	94·5	92·2	98·6	95·0	
1852	94·7	101·4	95·6	96·9	
1853	110·6	108·0	101·4	106·6	
1854	103·4	100·0	98·9	101·0	
1855	106·3	97·7	95·2	100·3	

Table 22—Continued

NEW INDEX OF INDUSTRIAL ACTIVITY IN BRITAIN, 1785–1938

	Construction and Instruments	Textiles	Other Industries	All Industries	Employment Rate (T.U.)
1856	106·1	105·0	101·8	104·4	96·75
1857	105·0	104·2	104·7	104·6	95·80
1858	90·4	98·8	97·8	95·2	92·65
1859	93·3	105·4	101·1	99·4	97·35
1860	95·5	117·0	105·0	104·2	98·15
1861	92·2	107·0	104·2	100·2	96·30
1862	93·4	65·1	98·9	88·6	93·95
1863	110·1	67·5	98·3	95·5	95·30
1864	115·6	70·0	100·6	99·1	98·05
1865	114·7	86·2	102·2	101·9	98·20
1866	100·2	92·7	103·1	98·9	97·35
1867	90·5	93·0	104·2	95·9	93·70
1868	91·7	98·8	102·9	97·2	93·25
1869	97·4	90·9	102·0	96·7	94·05
1870	101·6	101·8	102·3	101·9	96·25
1871	103·7	113·4	106·9	107·7	98·35
1872	109·7	107·1	106·6	107·8	99·05
1873	109·1	111·7	108·6	109·7	98·85
1874	117·4	110·7	106·0	111·5	98·40
1875	98·6	102·1	107·0	102·5	97·80
1876	101·7	104·0	108·3	104·6	96·60
1877	105·0	101·8	105·4	104·2	95·60
1878	95·4	94·8	101·4	97·3	93·75
1879	81·6	92·5	99·5	91·0	89·30
1880	100·0	104·8	106·3	103·6	94·75
1881	104·6	101·2	105·0	103·7	96·45
1882	119·1	104·9	105·5	110·2	97·65
1883	119·8	103·1	107·5	110·6	97·40
1884	96·3	103·6	103·1	100·8	92·85
1885	89·0	92·2	99·2	93·4	91·45
1886	77·4	96·2	95·4	89·2	90·45
1887	83·9	98·7	96·0	92·4	92·85
1888	98·8	104·1	97·8	100·0	95·85
1889	114·9	106·6	100·6	107·5	97·95
1890	105·8	105·8	100·4	104·0	97·90
1891	97·8	109·0	99·2	101·6	96·60
1892	97·4	96·3	95·6	96·5	93·80
1893	84·2	96·0	87·7	88·9	92·30
1894	91·8	99·1	95·0	95·1	92·80
1895	87·8	104·0	93·0	94·4	94·00
1896	100·2	102·6	94·8	99·0	96·65
1897	102·8	99·5	96·4	99·7	96·55
1898	103·4	106·7	95·2	101·6	97·05
1899	108·8	103·8	100·2	104·4	97·95
1900	108·3	94·2	99·4	101·1	97·55
1901	102·8	96·6	95·1	98·3	96·65
1902	103·7	94·6	96·7	98·6	95·80

Table 22—Continued

NEW INDEX OF INDUSTRIAL ACTIVITY IN BRITAIN, 1785–1938

	Construction and Instruments	Textiles	Other Industries	All Industries	Employment Rate (T.U.)
1903	98·8	89·0	97·0	95·2	95·00
1904	97·4	89·9	96·2	94·7	93·60
1905	103·3	99·9	96·2	99·9	94·75
1906	112·6	101·2	100·1	104·9	96·30
1907	105·9	107·7	105·0	106·1	96·05
1908	85·6	94·9	100·6	93·5	91·35
1909	86·7	98·6	99·7	94·7	91·30
1910	91·9	93·4	99·1	94·8	94·90
1911	100·5	102·5	100·1	101·0	96·95
1912	99·5	107·2	98·9	101·6	96·85
1913	111·2	107·5	106·4	108·5	97·90
					L.C.E.S. Index as % of trend
1920	141·9	117·5	85·9	117·9	122·7
1921	84·3	117·2	70·4	90·0	85·8
1922	92·8	102·3	101·2	88·6	98·8
1923	97·2	82·4	113·6	98·8	98·0
1924	126·6	97·9	113·1	114·7	104·8
1925	110·1	109·9	105·2	109·1	103·5
1926	76·1	99·5	72·5	82·4	90·0
1927	124·2	106·3	105·3	113·6	106·8
1928	120·4	99·2	105·5	109·9	102·9
1929	133·9	102·9	113·3	118·7	107·1
1930	119·8	87·0	109·3	107·4	96·2
1931	74·9	86·6	99·1	86·8	86·0
1932	61·1	91·5	95·0	81·1	85·2
1933	75·9	99·2	95·4	89·3	90·9
1934	100·2	93·0	100·3	98·6	99·4
1935	99·0	93·9	101·5	98·8	102·8
1936	86·8	111·5	104·6	100·1	108·8
1937	92·6	112·7	110·2	104·5	111·2
1938	81·9	89·2	98·3	89·7	100·0

Note: The Employment Rate in Trade Unions given above from 1856 to 1913 continues up to 1926 as follows:

1914	96·75	1919	97·50	1923	87·50
1915	99·00	1920	97·45	1924	90·90
1916	99·55	1921	84·45	1925	88·95
1917	99·40	1922	82·80	1926	87·30
1918	99·30				

These figures are represented in Chart I.

Table 23

DATA IN INDEX OF INDUSTRIAL ACTIVITY, 1785–1913

Industry	Nature of data and period covered	Weight Assigned		
		1785–1849	1850–1859	1860–1913
Construction and Instruments				
Bricks ..	Production (E.W.), 1785–1849	14 ⎫ 16	—	—
Tiles.. ..	Production (E.W.), 1785–1822	2 ⎭	—	—
Timber ..	Imports (U.K.), 1785–1913	4	14	14
Iron .. {	Net Imports (Bar, G.B.), 1790–1829, 1845–9 Consumption (Bar, G.B.), 1830–44 Canal Shipments (South Wales), 1804–40 Production (Pig, U.K.), 1852–1913	4	12	6*
Steel ..	Production (U.K.), 1875–1913	—	—	6
Railway Construction	Miles Authorized, 1829–49	1	—	—
Ships {	Production (Empire), 1789–1811 Production (U.K.), 1815–59 Production (U.K.), 1860–1913	6	10	10
Engineering	Production (Engines, James Watt), 1785–1849	1	—	—
Textiles				
Cotton ..	Consumption (Raw, U.K.), 1785–1913	3–16	16	16
Wool {	Production (Cloth, Yorkshire), 1785–1819 Imports (Raw, U.K.), 1815–59 Consumption (Raw, U.K.), 1865–1913	16–8	8	8
Silk	Imports (Raw and Thrown, U.K.), 1785–1913	4	2	2
Linen {	Production (Cloth, Scotland), 1785–1802 Imports (Flax, U.K.), 1788–1913	4	2	2
Hemp ..	Imports (Raw, U.K.), 1788–1913	1	1	1
Jute	Imports (Raw, U.K.), 1860–1913	—	—	1
Other Industries				
Coal {	Receipts (London), 1785–90 Shipments (Tyne and Wear), 1791–1849 Shipments (All districts), 1850–9 Production (U.K.), 1860–1913	12	15	15
Tin	Production (Cornwall), 1785–1834	1	—	—
Copper ..	Production (Cornwall), 1785–6, 1796–1848	2	—	—
Salt .. {	Shipments (Weaver), 1803–44 Production (U.K.), 1860–1913	1	—	1
Clay ..	Production (U.K.), 1860–1913	—	—	1
Leather ..	Production (E.W.), 1782–1828	9–4	—	—
Glass {	Consumption (Crown, G.B.), 1789–1844 Consumption (Common, G.B.), 1789–1844	1 1	— —	— —
Shipping {	Clearance Out (U.K.), 1785–1859 Clearance (U.K.), 1860–1913	15	10	10
Railways {	Goods Traffic (U.K.), 1860–1913 Passengers (U.K.), 1860–1913	— —	— —	5 2

* From 1860 to 1874 when no figures for steel are available a weight of 12 is assigned to iron.

The sources used from 1785 to 1859 are described in *Oxford Economic Papers*, No. 3 (February, 1940) and No. 4 (June, 1940).

STATISTICAL AND TECHNICAL NOTES

1. EMPLOYMENT AND UNEMPLOYMENT BY INDUSTRIES 1924–37 (Tables 33, 34 and 35).

2. UNEMPLOYMENT RATES IN COUNTIES AND CERTAIN DISTRICTS (Table 36).

3. UNEMPLOYMENT RATES BEFORE AND AFTER THE FIRST WORLD WAR (Tables 373–8).

4. A POLICY OF CHEAP MONEY.

5. THE INEVITABILITY OF CYCLICAL FLUCTUATION.

1. EMPLOYMENT AND UNEMPLOYMENT BY INDUSTRIES, 1924–37

1. This section contains three tables, 33, 34 and 35, illustrating the different experience of unemployment in different industries, which is discussed in paragraphs 63–74 of the Report.

2. In Table 33 the manufacturing industries are arranged in groups with reference to the change of employment from June, 1924, to June, 1937. The change of employment is shown by the figures in column 4, giving the numbers of insured persons in employment in June, 1937, as a percentage of the corresponding number in June, 1924. The service industries, supplying consumers' services, the transport industries and the extractive industries other than coal-mining, are also grouped; building and coal-mining are given separately. The table covers all the industries in the Labour Gazette classification except national government, local government, railway service, commerce and finance, public works contracting, musical instruments, fishing and "other industries." In the first four of these substantial proportions of those employed are excluded from general insurance. The table excludes also agriculture, insured under a separate scheme since 1936. All the figures relate to Great Britain and Northern Ireland.

Table 33

INSURED PERSONS: EMPLOYMENT AND UNEMPLOYMENT BY INDUSTRIES, 1924–37

Industry	(1) Class of Industry	(2) Insured Persons (000) July, 1924 (16 upwards)	(3) Insured Persons (000) July, 1937 (16–64)	(4) Employment June, 1937, as per cent of June, 1924	(5) 1924	(6) 1929	(7) 1932	(8) 1937	(9) Males only 1927–3
					Unemployment Rate				
I. EMPLOYMENT GROWING MORE THAN TWICE AVERAGE (MANUFACTURING)									
Heating and Ventilating Apparatus	C	5·8	18·7	343·3	5·3	4·8	20·1	5·3	10·8
Electrical Wiring and Contracting	C	12·9	41·2	327·4	9·3	6·8	18·3	9·8	12·7
Artificial Stone and Concrete	C	11·8	28·6	260·9	16·5	14·3	28·0	11·3	20·1
Electrical Cable Apparatus, Lamps, etc.	OP	74·9	177·7	247·3	7·4	4·8	12·7	5·2	9·5
Stationery and Typewriting requisites	OC	4·5	9·0	204·6	5·8	4·1	10·4	4·1	7·8
Scientific and Photographic Instruments and Apparatus	OC	19·7	37·1	196·9	4·7	3·0	11·2	2·8	6·4
Silk and Artificial Silk	T	41·7	80·7	194·5	6·3	10·5	18·9	8·3	15·2
Motor Vehicles, Cycles and Aircraft	I	203·3	351·6	179·5	8·5	7·1	20·0	4·8	12·0
Constructional Engineering	I	24·0	40·1	177·8	12·9	11·1	36·2	9·7	20·3
Toys, Games and Sports Requisites	OC	11·0	17·8	172·3	10·9	5·6	14·4	7·2	11·5
Electrical Engineering	I	71·5	114·6	167·2	5·5	4·4	16·3	3·1	9·4
Metal Industries, not separately specified	OP	175·6	266·0	162·7	11·4	8·0	19·3	6·0	13·6
Brick, Tile, Pipe, etc., Making	C	70·5	106·5	156·8	7·4	10·7	22·8	8·3	13·4
Furniture Making, Upholstering, etc.	OC	96·8	149·9	155·9	7·2	5·9	19·7	9·0	12·8
Paint, Varnish, Red and White Leads	OP	16·4	24·2	151·8	5·1	4·4	10·3	4·8	7·3
Stove, Grate, Pipe, etc., and General Iron-founding	OP	81·9	104·6	143·9	12·1	9·4	27·8	7·1	16·2
Brass, Copper, Zinc, Tin, Lead, etc.	M	40·0	50·2	140·8	11·7	8·9	25·9	5·6	15·7
Total with Weighted Means		962·8	1,618·5	178·5	8·9			8·9	

2. EMPLOYMENT GROWING MORE THAN AVERAGE (MANUFACTURING)

Textiles, not separately specified	T	43·9	58·0	139·1	11·8	8·7	16·1	9·1	11·7
Shirts, Collars, Underclothing, etc.	D	72·1	102·9	138·7	7·4	5·3	13·4	9·4	8·1
Cardboard Boxes, Paper Bags and Stationery	OC	54·9	72·2	135·6	6·9	4·1	8·9	4·3	6·6
Wall-paper Making	OP	5·5	7·5	134·2	4·6	4·2	12·2	6·7	7·2
Explosives	OP	19·3	22·3	129·3	9·4	4·6	11·4	3·5	7·8
Paper and Paper Board	OP	54·6	65·4	128·5	8·4	4·3	11·4	4·2	7·8
Hosiery	T	93·4	119·9	127·4	6·9	5·9	12·5	8·2	10·0
Iron and Steel Tubes	M	27·2	32·7	127·0	15·5	9·9	42·5	10·5	23·5
Food Industries, not separately specified	F	108·5	134·5	126·4	12·2	9·0	16·6	12·4	12·1
Bread, Biscuits, Cakes, etc.	F	144·5	176·5	125·5	9·4	7·1	11·8	8·6	11·2
Glass (excluding Bottles and Scientific Glass)	OP	27·0	31·3	123·7	12·6	9·1	19·9	8·7	15·2
Carpets	T	27·0	31·5	120·2	6·3	5·8	9·5	6·9	8·7
Total with Weighted Means		**677·9**	**854·7**	**128·5**	**9·4**			**8·4**	
Unweighted Means				**129·6**	**9·3**			**7·7**	

3. EMPLOYMENT GROWING LESS THAN AVERAGE (MANUFACTURING)

Printing, Publishing and Book-binding	OC	240·1	284·6	119·9	5·4	4·3	10·3	6·3	7·7
Brass and Allied Metal Wares	OP	29·8	30·3	119·0	16·2	8·3	19·9	4·5	13·6
Chemicals	OP	97·6	109·5	119·0	9·0	6·3	16·5	6·5	13·0
Hand Tools, Cutlery, Saws, Files	OP	31·7	34·1	118·9	14·9	14·6	34·3	8·6	22·8
Rubber	OP	58·2	64·8	117·7	11·0	8·0	19·2	7·8	13·7
Glass Bottles	OC	18·0	19·9	116·3	20·3	16·0	25·9	14·8	21·8
Brushes and Brooms	OC	9·8	11·3	115·8	10·9	11·3	20·1	10·1	18·5
Tanning, Currying and Dressing	OP	42·6	48·4	115·7	10·2	10·6	16·6	9·3	12·7
Saw-milling and Machined Woodwork	C	57·7	63·2	114·5	10·0	9·5	20·8	10·4	14·5
Wire, Wire-netting, Wire-ropes	M	24·5	25·7	114·5	11·0	10·7	26·2	8·2	19·6
General Engineering	I	627·4	613·9	114·1	15·2	9·6	29·1	5·4	17·3
Bolts, Nuts, Screws, Rivets, Nails, etc.	OP	27·5	28·2	112·9	13·7	9·6	25·9	5·9	17·4
Cement, Lime-kilns and Whiting	C	16·0	16·8	112·5	8·1	8·0	25·9	5·6	13·5

Table 33—Continued

INSURED PERSONS: EMPLOYMENT AND UNEMPLOYMENT BY INDUSTRIES, 1924-37

	(1)	(2)	(3)	(4)	(5)	(6)	(7)	(8)	(9)
Industry	Class of Industry	Insured Persons (000) July, 1924 (16 upwards)	Insured Persons (000) July, 1937 (16-64)	Employment June, 1937 as per cent of June, 1924	Unemployment Rate 1924	1929	1932	1937	Males only 1927-36
3. EMPLOYMENT GROWING LESS THAN AVERAGE (MANUFACTURING)—continued									
Grain Milling	F	31·5	33·5	111·8	5·5	7·1	10·2	6·7	9·0
Tailoring	D	189·5	215·1	109·7	9·5	7·8	15·6	10·8	14·7
Coke Ovens and By-product Works	OP	13·5	14·7	108·3	8·2	11·4	33·3	11·5	20·4
Drink Industries	F	108·9	114·0	107·1	7·6	6·6	14·1	7·5	9·2
Dress Industries, not separately specified	D	29·7	29·4	105·8	10·4	5·0	10·1	5·3	11·0
Cocoa, Chocolate and Sugar Confectionery	F	72·2	77·7	104·9	10·0	9·4	14·3	9·2	12·4
Saddlery, Harness and other Leather Goods	OC	27·8	26·9	104·2	10·2	7·4	16·0	5·7	13·2
Railway Carriages, Waggons and Tram Cars	I	52·2	50·6	102·3	6·1	9·7	27·4	3·6	13·8
Pottery, Earthenware, etc.	OC	73·3	74·9	102·2	12·7	14·3	32·2	14·6	21·8
Steel Melting and Iron Puddling, Iron and Steel Rolling and Forging	M	207·3	181·9	101·7	21·1	19·5	46·8	10·1	29·0
Tobacco, Cigars, Cigarettes and Snuff	OC	43·9	42·4	101·6	8·1	4·2	8·7	4·6	5·8
Hemp, Rope, Cord, Twine, etc.	T	20·6	19·8	101·0	15·2	11·1	23·1	13·2	16·6
Total with Weighted Means		2,151·8	2,281·6	111·6	12·1			7·6	
Unweighted Means				110·9	11·2			8·2	
4. EMPLOYMENT DECLINING (MANUFACTURING)									
Oil, Glue, Soap, Ink, Matches, etc.	OC	73·7	75·7	98·2	7·5	6·7	12·4	7·2	10·7
Wood Boxes and Packing Cases	OP	12·5	11·8	97·7	14·2	10·8	26·5	12·8	20·0

Watches, Clocks, Plate, Jewellery, etc. …	O	47·4	39·0	92·0	12·1	6·6		
Wood-working, not separately specified	OP	26·5	23·8	91·7	11·2	9·4	21·3	11·2	15·2
Tin Plates … … …	M	29·3	28·1	91·6	8·5	25·4	38·8	13·2	31·3
Marine Engineering, etc. … …	I	66·1	53·8	89·9	16·9	10·0	54·7	9·1	27·9
Hats and Caps (including Straw Plait)	D	33·6	32·5	89·3	9·9	7·5	15·0	14·2	11·8
Lace … … … …	T	20·3	15·0	87·7	18·0	9·1	14·7	8·9	14·6
Linen … … … …	T	83·1	76·3	87·6	10·6	13·8	25·4	18·5	22·9
Woollen and Worsted … …	T	260·9	223·3	86·2	7·0	13·7	20·7	10·2	16·9
Textile, Bleaching, Printing and Dyeing, etc..	T	117·5	102·5	85·9	12·7	17·0	27·4	17·0	23·4
Shipbuilding and Ship-repairing …	I	255·1	172·8	76·7	29·3	23·8	62·2	23·8	40·8
Cotton … … … …	T	562·4	408·6	76·6	13·7	13·1	28·5	11·5	22·1
Jute … … … …	T	41·2	30·0	65·9	9·9	12·9	42·2	26·8	26·8
Pig-iron (Blast Furnaces) … …	M	30·2	17·3	64·4	14·3	11·3	43·5	9·8	24·9
Carriages, Carts, etc. … …	I	24·6	13·1	56·1	11·5	8·7	21·1	9·7	14·6
Total with Weighted Means … …		**1,947·4**	**1,574·3**	**83·3**	**13·5**			**12·8**	
Unweighted Means … …				**85·5**	**12·1**			**12·3**	
5. CONSUMERS' SERVICE									
Entertainments and Sports … …	S	66·0	139·6	204·8	13·5	11·2	20·5	17·5	19·1
Tramway and Omnibus Service …	S	119·3	203·8	176·7	3·2	3·1	6·2	3·4	4·4
Hotel, Public House, Restaurant, Boarding House, Club, etc., Service …	S	289·9	444·1	157·5	12·3	8·9	17·3	14·6	15·8
Laundries, Dyeing and Dry Cleaning …	S	112·9	173·9	156·7	6·2	4·3	9·2	6·1	8·6
Professional Services … …	S	110·7	165·8	153·3	4·0	3·1	6·3	4·3	5·9
Distributive Trades … …	S	1,352·1	2,061·4	151·3	6·6	6·1	12·2	8·8	11·1
Gas, Water and Electricity Supply …	S	171·6	218·5	131·7	6·1	5·9	11·0	8·1	8·6
Total with Weighted Means … …		**2,222·5**	**3,407·1**	**153·7**	**7·2**			**9·2**	
Unweighted Means … …				**161·7**	**7·4**			**9·0**	

Table 33—Continued

INSURED PERSONS: EMPLOYMENT AND UNEMPLOYMENT BY INDUSTRIES, 1924-37

	(1)	(2)	(3)	(4)	(5)	(6)	(7)	(8)	(9)
Industry	Class of Industry	Insured Persons (000)		Employment June, 1937, as per cent of June, 1924	Unemployment Rate				
		July, 1924 (16 upwards)	July, 1937 (16-64)		1924	1929	1932	1937	Males only 1927-36
6. TRANSPORT									
Road Transport, not separately specified	Tr.	150·4	207·2	144·0	15·4	12·0	22·3	12·6	16·8
Shipping Service	Tr.	119·1	134·1	100·3	19·5	17·8	33·9	21·9	26·5
Dock, Harbour, River and Canal Service	Tr.	195·5	166·0	88·5	25·6	30·4	34·8	25·8	32·1
Transport, Communication and Storage, not separately specified	Tr.	23·3	22·6	106·9	16·8	11·9	17·5	13·4	16·5
Total with Weighted Means		**488·8**	**529·9**	**108·3**	**16·5**			**19·1**	
7. OTHER EXTRACTIVE									
Clay, Sand, Gravel and Chalk Pits	E	13·5	18·9	142·7	5·0	6·3	27·7	7·5	13·9
Stone Quarrying and Mining	E	36·1	49·0	133·5	5·3	10·2	27·9	13·5	17·6
Lead, Tin and Copper Mining	E	5·0	4·5	95·5	16·5	19·0	63·7	15·3	33·5
Slate Quarrying and Mining	E	10·1	9·7	94·7	1·6	10·2	22·6	6·3	12·3
Iron Ore and Iron-stone Mining	E	17·1	11·3	84·5	21·5	7·1	46·7	8·6	24·5
Other Mining and Quarrying	E	22·2	11·0	48·7	6·1	9·9	24·8	12·8	17·6
Total with Weighted Means		**104·0**	**102·9**	**115·7**	**8·3**			**11·2**	
BUILDING	C	721·6	1,035·3	146·0	10·6	12·2	29·0	13·8	17·5
COALMINING	E	1,260·4	868·4	60·0	5·7	15·5	33·9	14·7	24·6

3. Column 1 shows the classification of the industries according to type of product, as follows:—

C	Construction
E	Extractive
I	Instrumental
M	Metal Manufacture
T	Textiles
F	Food and Drink
D	Dress
OP	Other Producer Goods
OC	Other Consumer Goods
S	Service to Consumers
Tr	Transport

4. In Column 2 the numbers represent insured persons in employment aged 16 and over; those in column 3 relate to persons aged 16 to 64 inclusive, as persons of 65 and over ceased to be insured after 1927. The percentages in column 4 allow for this change. They are obtained by dividing the adjusted percentage change from 1923 to 1927, as given in the *Labour Gazette* for December, 1937 (p. 489), by the change from 1923 to 1924, as given in the 21*st Annual Abstract of Labour Statistics* (p. 43).

5. The unemployment rates in column 5 for 1924 and column 8 for 1937 represent the mean for twelve months—January to December—in each year. Those in columns 6, 7 and 9 represent the mean for four months—March, June, September and December—in each year. The figures in columns 5, 6, 7 and 8 relate to all insured persons. The figures in column 9 covering the years 1927–36 relate to males only. As is noted in paragraph B14 (*c*) below, the recorded rates of unemployment among females were violently affected in the years 1930 and 1931 by administrative changes. The weighted means for groups in columns 4 and 5 are weighted by the numbers in column 2; those in column 8 are weighted by the numbers in column 3.

6. In Table 34 the figures referred to in paragraph 65 of the Report are set out in detail, showing the different ways in which particular industries react to decline in the demand for their products. The table covers the twelve manufacturing industries having the greatest contraction of numbers in employment between 1924 and 1937. In the first six industries of this table, taken together, employment (that is to say the effective demand for labour) declined by 14·7 per cent from 1924 to 1937, but the numbers (in thousands) of

insured persons declined only from 549·2 to 492·7, or 10·3 per cent,
and the unemployment rate rose from 9·2 to 14·3; each of the
separate industries had a higher unemployment rate in 1937 than
in 1924. In the other six industries taken together, employment
declined 23·2 per cent, but the numbers (in thousands) of insured
persons declined even more from 946·9 to 680·6, or by 28·1 per
cent, and the unemployment rate fell from 18·0 to 14·3; each of
the separate industries had a lower unemployment rate in 1937 than
in 1924.

Table 34

UNEMPLOYMENT IN DECLINING INDUSTRIES, 1924–37

	Employ-ment June, 1937, as per cent of June, 1924	Insured Persons 16–64 (thousands)			Unemployment Rate	
		1924 (est.) *	1937	1937 as percentage of 1924	1924	1937
Tin Plates	91·6	27·9	28·1	100·7	8·5	13·2
Hats and Caps	89·3	33·7	32·5	96·4	9·9	14·2
Linen	87·6	80·9	76·3	94·3	10·6	18·5
Woollen and Worsted ..	86·2	251·8	223·3	92·6	7·0	10·2
Textile Bleaching	85·9	115·2	102·5	89·0	12·7	17·0
Jute	65·9	39·7	30·0	75·6	9·9	26·8
Six industries with unem-ployment rate rising ..	85·3	549·2	492·7	89·7	9·2	14·3
Marine Engineering ..	89·9	64·6	53·8	83·3	16·9	9·1
Lace..	87·7	19·4	15·0	77·3	18·0	8·9
Shipbuilding	76·7	245·5	172·8	70·4	29·3	23·8
Cotton	76·6	564·8	408·6	72·3	13·7	11·5
Pig Iron	64·4	28·3	17·3	61·1	14·3	9·8
Carriages, Carts, etc. ..	56·1	24·3	13·1	53·9	11·5	9·7
Six industries with unem-ployment rate falling ..	76·8	946·9	680·6	71·9	18·0	14·3

* The numbers of insured persons 16–64 in 1924 as given in this table are estimated
from the numbers in 1937, by using the percentages given in the *Labour Gazette*, November
1937, pp. 444–5, for the relation between 1937 and 1923, and those given in the 21st
Abstract of Labour Statistics, pp. 36–8 for the relation between 1924 and 1923. They are
directly comparable to the numbers recorded in 1937, as given in the next column, and
they differ from the numbers in column 2 of Table 33, which relate to insured persons
of all ages from 16 upwards.

7. Table 35 gives information supplementary to paragraphs 72–3,
showing in broad outline the movement in the numbers of insured
males from 1929 to 1932 and from 1932 to 1937. The figures repre-

ent thousands, and relate to Great Britain and Northern Ireland.
'he rapidly expanding industries are those shown in Table 4.
'he declining industries are coal-mining, cotton, wool, linen, jute
nd textile bleaching, shipbuilding and shipping. It will be seen
nat the insured males as a whole increased more slowly from 1932
ɔ 1937 than from 1929 to 1932, presumably owing to the declining
umbers of young men in the population. The difference of 53,000
year between 182,000 and 129,000 was the same as the difference
etween 106,000 and 53,000 in the entry to the rapidly expanding
ndustries.

Table 35

INSURED MALES IN GROUPS OF INDUSTRIES, 1929, 1932, 1937

(*thousands*)

	Insured Males			Change from—		Change per year	
	1929	1932	1937	1929 to 1932	1932 to 1937	1929 to 1932	1932 to 1937
apidly expanding Industries ..	1,858	2,176	2,440	+ 318	+ 264	+ 106	+ 53
eclining Industries	1,823	1,773	1,505	− 50	− 268	− 17	− 54
ther Industries	5,074	5,353	6,002	+ 279	+ 649	+ 93	+ 130
ll Industries ..	8,755	9,302	9,947	+ 547	+ 645	+ 182	+ 129

2. UNEMPLOYMENT RATES IN COUNTIES AND CERTAIN DISTRICTS

8. Table 36 shows separately all counties in England, and shows
lso the areas of lowest and highest average unemployment over the
ɔur years taken together, in each county with more than five em-
loyment exchange areas, and in a few others; for counties with
nore than twenty areas, the two areas of lowest unemployment and
he two of highest unemployment are shown. In Scotland and Wales
igures are given only for counties with five or more exchange areas.
'he figures for 1937 and those for 1934, 1935 and 1936 are not
trictly comparable. The figures for 1934, 1935, 1936 have been
btained by relating all persons insured and uninsured, aged 14
nd over, registered as unemployed, to the estimated number of
ersons aged 16–64 insured under the general scheme. The figures
or 1937 have been obtained by relating the numbers of insured
ersons aged 16–64 recorded as unemployed to the estimated
umbers of persons of these ages; persons insured under the agri-

Table 36

UNEMPLOYMENT RATES IN COUNTIES AND CERTAIN DISTRICTS, 193
1935, 1936 AND 1937

ENGLAND				1934	1935	1936	1937
Bedfordshire	..	..	..	**4·6**	**4·7**	**5·0**	**4·8**
Berkshire	..	..	..	**10·0**	**8·7**	**7·8**	**6·6**
Didcot	..	..	..	4·5	5·1	4·3	2·8
Wokingham	..	..	..	14·0	13·3	10·0	10·2
Buckinghamshire	..	..	..	**6·2**	**5·9**	**5·6**	**5·8**
Bletchley	..	..	..	3·1	1·9	2·3	2·1
Slough	..	..	..	8·5	10·1	9·3	8·5
Cambridgeshire	..	..	..	**8·1**	**8·6**	**7·5**	**6·5**
Cottenham	..	..	..	2·3	2·1	1·5	1·7
Wisbech	..	..	..	10·1	12·8	12·1	9·0
Cheshire	..	..	..	**19·8**	**18·4**	**15·4**	**13·6**
Froolsham	..	..	..	12·1	10·1	8·5	3·7
Wilmslow	..	..	..	11·1	10·5	9·8	6·1
Birkenhead	..	..	..	29·4	29·4	23·9	22·9
Wallasey	..	..	..	28·9	27·4	25·0	24·1
Cornwall	..	..	..	**19·4**	**17·8**	**16·2**	**12·9**
Newquay	..	..	..	7·4	7·6	6·5	5·4
Redruth	..	..	..	37·0	38·7	31·0	29·0
Cumberland	..	..	..	**28·7**	**28·5**	**28·5**	**21·7**
Penrith	..	..	..	16·4	14·8	12·4	7·6
Maryport	..	..	..	57·5	57·6	51·7	42·7
Derbyshire	..	..	..	**14·8**	**11·9**	**10·7**	**8·3**
Derby	..	..	..	6·9	5·2	4·6	3·9
Buxton	..	..	..	7·3	6·7	5·6	4·2
Glossop	..	..	..	26·7	22·6	21·2	15·7
Hadfield	..	..	..	45·4	48·4	43·3	34·7
Devon	..	..	..	**13·8**	**12·9**	**11·6**	**9·3**
Tiverton	..	..	..	8·9	9·4	6·7	4·9
Bideford	..	..	..	16·6	17·3	17·2	15·3
Dorset	..	..	..	**12·9**	**12·3**	**9·8**	**6·7**
Wareham	..	..	..	9·2	6·7	5·8	3·0
Poole	..	..	..	14·4	12·8	11·0	9·5
Durham	..	..	..	**34·2**	**33·9**	**27·6**	**19·5**
Consett	..	..	..	9·6	8·7	7·6	5·4
Horden	..	..	..	10·5	23·0	8·1	4·5
Shildon	..	..	..	49·4	46·5	42·6	34·8
Bishop Auckland		..	..	53·5	52·0	48·1	35·5
Essex	..	..	..	**11·4**	**10·3**	**8·5**	**7·3**
Chelmsford	..	..	..	4·3	2·9	1·6	1·6
Leyton	..	..	..	7·2	5·9	5·2	4·7
Rayleigh	..	..	..	21·4	24·0	20·7	20·5
Pitsea	..	..	..	32·9	32·4	32·3	36·4
Gloucestershire	..	..	..	**17·6**	**15·2**	**12·2**	**8·7**
Dursley	..	..	..	4·5	3·9	2·5	2·5
Cinderford	..	..	..	43·3	43·2	36·6	20·2

Table 36—Continued

NEMPLOYMENT RATES IN COUNTIES AND CERTAIN DISTRICTS, 1934, 1935, 1936 AND 1937

NGLAND—*continued*				1934	1935	1936	1937
Hampshire ..	..	..	..	**13·3**	**12·0**	**9·3**	**7·4**
Eastleigh ..	..	..	..	7·0	5·3	3·8	2·6
Ryde ..	..	..	..	15·8	16·0	12·0	10·1
Herefordshire	..	..	..	**16·6**	**16·4**	**14·3**	**10·2**
Hertfordshire	..	..	..	**6·1**	**5·8**	**5·6**	**4·9**
Hemel Hempstead	..	..	..	2·5	2·4	2·7	2·5
Letchworth	..	..	..	7·8	8·3	9·4	7·9
Huntingdonshire	..	..	..	**11·8**	**9·5**	**6·5**	**4·6**
Kent..	..	..	..	**9·9**	**9·3**	**7·9**	**6·3**
Beckenham	..	..	..	2·8	2·4	2·0	1·7
Cranbrook	..	..	..	3·5	2·7	3·2	1·4
Faversham	..	..	..	15·2	18·0	16·1	11·3
Ramsgate..	..	..	..	16·2	16·9	17·6	14·5
Lancashire ..	..	..	..	**21·1**	**20·5**	**17·8**	**14·3**
Leyland ..	..	..	..	4·6	5·1	4·1	2·9
Irlam ..	..	..	..	6·3	7·1	6·0	4·6
Westhoughton	..	..	..	31·2	33·9	32·5	27·4
Hindley ..	..	..	..	42·1	40·8	37·5	37·2
Leicestershire	..	..	..	**11·2**	**9·7**	**7·6**	**6·9**
Market Harborough	..	..	..	5·6	4·8	4·0	2·8
Ratby ..	..	..	..	33·5	28·4	20·5	20·7
Lincolnshire	..	..	..	**16·2**	**15·3**	**13·4**	**9·7**
Scunthorpe	..	..	..	7·9	7·7	5·4	3·2
Gainsborough	..	..	..	25·9	27·6	18·3	12·7
Grimsby ..	..	..	..	16·6	17·2	18·0	15·1
London ..	..	..	..	**9·6**	**9·0**	**7·7**	**7·1**
Greenwich	..	..	..	7·6	6·0	4·6	3·8
Woolwich	..	..	..	8·4	6·8	4·5	3·7
Southwark	..	..	..	13·0	12·6	11·1	10·2
Poplar ..	..	..	..	15·7	15·3	12·4	11·2
Middlesex ..	..	..	..	**6·1**	**5·9**	**5·0**	**4·8**
Wembley	..	..	..	3·8	3·7	3·8	2·9
Finchley ..	..	..	..	3·8	3·4	3·4	3·2
Staines ..	..	..	..	7·1	9·9	10·2	7·9
Hayes and Harlington	..	..	..	7·4	11·5	8·1	8·6
Norfolk ..	..	..	..	**14·5**	**14·8**	**13·7**	**11·5**
Cromer ..	..	..	..	11·0	11·2	16·2	9·1
Great Yarmouth	..	..	..	22·6	22·5	20·8	18·5
Northamptonshire ..	..	..	..	**12·1**	**8·5**	**7·2**	**6·2**
Peterborough	..	..	..	7·9	6·8	5·2	3·9
Daventry	..	..	..	23·3	21·1	16·0	9·3
Northumberland ..	..	..	..	**25·2**	**24·3**	**20·4**	**15·5**
Bedlington Station	..	..	..	8·1	8·9	8·0	6·9
Willington Quay	..	..	..	51·4	52·4	45·1	32·5

Table 36—Continued

UNEMPLOYMENT RATES IN COUNTIES AND CERTAIN DISTRICTS, 1934
1935, 1936 AND 1937

ENGLAND—*continued*				1934	1935	1936	1937
Nottinghamshire	..	..	..	**15·5**	**14·6**	**12·6**	**10·0**
Newark	..	..	..	11·2	8·6	6·3	3·7
Arnold	..	..	..	24·7	26·7	23·5	18·8
Oxfordshire..	..	..	..	**8·2**	**8·4**	**6·9**	**6·8**
Rutlandshire	..	..	..	**17·0**	**15·4**	**12·6**	**6·9**
Shropshire ..	..	..	..	**17·3**	**15·9**	**13·3**	**8·8**
Shrewsbury	..	..	..	12·5	12·2	10·8	7·7
Chobury Mortimer	..	..	..	17·5	19·0	16·3	14·7
Somersetshire	..	..	..	**12·8**	**11·4**	**8·8**	**7·0**
Keynsham	..	..	..	3·5	3·6	2·4	2·1
Bridgwater	..	..	..	19·2	17·7	14·1	13·0
Staffordshire	..	..	..	**16·8**	**15·2**	**12·2**	**9·7**
Stafford	..	..	..	8·0	5·9	4·2	3·4
Smethwick	..	..	..	9·5	7·6	5·0	3·7
Audley	..	..	..	32·8	33·1	27·8	24·8
Kidsgrove	..	..	..	53·1	56·2	50·1	44·5
Suffolk	..	..	..	**14·6**	**12·4**	**10·2**	**7·6**
Sudbury	..	..	..	9·5	9·3	6·4	3·8
Lowestoft	..	..	..	20·8	18·6	17·3	12·5
Surrey	..	..	..	**6·7**	**6·3**	**5·7**	**5·3**
Redhill	..	..	..	2·0	2·0	2·1	3·1
Sutton	..	..	..	8·9	8·5	8·8	7·9
Sussex	..	..	..	**6·8**	**6·6**	**6·3**	**6·3**
Hayward's Heath	..	..	..	2·2	2·2	2·6	2·2
Shoreham	..	..	..	10·3	10·9	10·4	10·2
Warwickshire	..	..	..	**8·0**	**6·9**	**5·3**	**4·4**
Rugby	..	..	..	6·6	3·7	2·3	1·6
Bedworth	..	..	..	13·4	11·7	9·3	9·3
Westmorland	..	..	..	**6·6**	**6·7**	**7·1**	**5·6**
Wiltshire	..	..	..	**9·6**	**7·2**	**5·6**	**3·8**
Chippenham	..	..	..	6·4	4·1	3·6	1·7
Salisbury..	..	..	..	11·7	8·8	7·1	6·7
Worcestershire	..	..	..	**12·7**	**11·5**	**8·9**	**7·4**
Halesowen	..	..	..	7·5	5·9	5·1	4·2
Dudley	..	..	..	21·2	18·2	13·8	10·1
Yorkshire	..	..	..	**19·5**	**17·9**	**14·7**	**11·4**
Tadcaster	..	..	..	6·0	5·2	4·4	2·9
Elland	..	..	..	8·2	7·0	4·7	4·3
Guisborough	..	..	..	44·7	49·9	31·3	20·9
Hoyland	..	..	..	47·2	52·5	42·9	32·9
SCOTLAND							
Aberdeenshire	..	..	..	**19·8**	**18·4**	**16·8**	**14·6**
Inverness	..	..	..	7·4	8·1	8·0	4·2
Peterhead	..	..	..	39·7	35·8	37·3	34·5

Table 36—Continued

UNEMPLOYMENT RATES IN COUNTIES AND CERTAIN DISTRICTS, 1934, 1935, 1936 AND 1937

SCOTLAND—continued				1934	1935	1936	1937
Angus	..	..	..	27·5	24·4	22·6	20·0
Forfar	..	..	..	10·1	10·2	18·4	11·5
Montrose		..	..	27·9	32·0	29·4	16·6
Ayr ..	..	..	..	22·6	21·1	17·9	13·8
Dalmellington	..	..		9·2	7·1	4·7	4·1
Kilwinnig		..	..	54·3	50·8	38·5	22·8
Fife ..	..	..	..	18·3	17·4	15·6	11·2
Leslie	..	..	..	7·0	6·9	5·2	4·2
Cowdenbeath	..	..		23·7	24·4	22·2	15·8
Lanark	..	..	..	29·4	27·4	24·2	18·2
Lanark	..	..	..	15·2	13·2	12·3	9·5
Airdrie	..	..	..	42·0	41·4	36·8	30·1
Midlothian ..	..	..		15·9	16·0	15·1	11·9
Dalkeith ..	..	..		9·6	10·2	9·4	7·6
Leith	..	..	..	24·2	23·8	21·7	17·3
Renfrew	..	..	..	27·2	25·5	20·5	15·5
Renfrew ..	..	..		14·9	10·0	6·3	4·1
Port Glasgow	..	..		46·0	42·3	31·2	23·1
Stirlingshire..	..	..		17·9	18·0	14·8	11·5
Bonnybridge	..	..		18·1	11·9	9·8	7·3
Kilsyth ..	..	..		17·1	19·8	18·9	14·8
WALES							
Caernarvonshire	..	..		18·3	19·4	17·6	15·2
Llanberis	..	..		6·2	5·2	5·4	5·6
Caernarvon	..	..		30·8	33·3	27·0	35·1
Carmarthenshire	..	..		21·2	24·4	22·8	21·3
Carmarthen	..	..		18·7	19·7	17·9	11·1
Garnant ..	..	..		18·6	26·4	29·8	36·2
Denbighshire	..	..		26·5	28·3	23·9	19·0
Colwyn Bay	..	..		14·9	16·7	15·0	16·3
Brymbo ..	..	..		44·4	43·9	36·0	30·0
Flintshire	..	..	..	19·8	19·3	15·8	14·5
Shotton	..	..	..	13·1	11·6	9·3	8·6
Mold	..	..	..	37·3	36·4	28·9	25·2
Glamorgan ..	..	..		36·9	36·4	34·9	23·7
Resolven ..	..	..		18·8	10·7	10·0	4·5
Clydach ..	..	..		21·7	24·5	16·4	10·3
Pontlottyn	..	..		64·9	55·3	56·8	39·8
Ferndale ..	..	..		62·2	67·6	67·1	48·1
Monmouthshire	..	..		36·0	33·5	32·7	21·1
Newbridge	..	..		28·9	20·2	27·4	12·0
Blaina	..	..	..	75·5	60·0	60·8	40·0

cultural scheme have been excluded. The figures for the earlie
years are thus a little higher than if they had been prepared on th
1937 basis; comparison of figures compiled on both bases fo
January, 1936, shows a difference of 0·6 in England (betwee
15·2 in the old and 14·6 in the new basis), of 1·9 in Scotlan
(between 24·6 and 22·7), of 2·3 in Wales (between 33·7 and 31·4
and of 1·1 in Britain as a whole (between 17·1 and 16·0).

3. UNEMPLOYMENT RATES BEFORE AND AFTER THE FIRST WORLD WA

9. One of the main technical problems in the evaluation o
statistics of unemployment in Britain is as to how far the unem
ployment rate derived from trade union returns before 1914 ca
be taken as a guide, not merely to the direction in which unemploy
ment was moving at any moment, that is to say its rise or fall
but also to the general level of unemployment over a period o
years. The mean unemployment rate recorded by the trade union
from 1856 to 1913 was 4·4; the mean rate from 1883 to 1913 wa
4·8. The mean rate recorded under unemployment insurance from
1921 to 1938 was 14·2. What would have been the rate recorded
under unemployment insurance if it had been in force from 188
to 1913? This question must be approached by examining the differ
ences in the basis of the trade union rate and the unemploymen
insurance rate.

10. First, the trade union returns cover only trade unionists
that is to say, they exclude the unorganized workpeople in the trade
to which they relate. The only direct evidence on the question
whether trade unionists as such were liable to more or to less un
employment than non-unionists, is that derived from the working
of the first unemployment insurance scheme in 1913–14. Under
this scheme members of associations providing out of work pay of
their own could under arrangements made by the association
obtain their State benefit through the association, in place of direct
from an employment exchange. The following table, derived from
the unpublished Board of Trade Report on Labour Exchanges
and Unemployment Insurance to July, 1914, shows for each of the
insured industries the benefit paid direct and through associations
(in practice these were always trade unions), and shows also, in the
last column, the association membership in each industry as a
proportion of the unemployment books current.

Table 37

UNEMPLOYMENT BENEFIT PAID THROUGH ASSOCIATIONS AND DIRECT,
1913–14

	Benefit paid 1913–14 (£000)			Association Benefit % of total	Association Members % of all unemployment books current
	Direct (1)	Association (2)	Total (3)	(4)	(5)
Building	242·7	78·9	321·6 ⎫	24·0	20·1
Construction of Works ..	10·7	1·1	11·8 ⎭		
Shipbuilding	22·3	23·6	45·9	51·4	36·6
Engineering and Ironfounding	69·5	50·3	119·8	42·0	32·1
Construction of Vehicles ..	20·0	6·9	26·9	25·6	14·4
Sawmilling	0·5	0·4	0·9 ⎫	33·3	29·1
Other Insured Workmen ..	4·1	1·9	6·0 ⎭		
	369·9	163·1	533·0	30·6	29·5

In this table it is necessary to look at each industry separately.
The closeness of the two percentages in columns 4 and 5 for all
industries taken together is misleading, being due to the fact that
building and construction of works combine a much higher rate of
unemployment with a lower proportion of association members,
thus lowering fallaciously the average for all industries in column
4. Shipbuilding, engineering and construction of vehicles all show
association members drawing markedly more benefit than in
proportion to their numbers; the difference is greatest in construction
of vehicles, probably due to the inclusion here of the railway workshops which would combine exceptional stability of employment
with relatively weak trade unionism. The difference is much smaller
in building and works of construction, but this is clearly due to the
fact that the association members here would be mainly skilled men
with a low rate of unemployment.[1] If it were possible to show the
skilled men and the labourers in building separately, it is clear

[1] In devising the financial basis of the first unemployment insurance scheme
of 1911 it was assumed on the basis of some highly speculative statistics that the
unemployment rate in building as a whole (including the building labourers)
would be about twice that of the skilled crafts of carpenters and plumbers to
which the trade union returns were confined. The statistics now available under
unemployment insurance show just this relation in 1936, 1937 and 1938. The
rates for building as a whole in these three years are 13·8, 15·1 and 14·9 respectively; those for carpenters and plumbers weighted by the numbers in each
craft are 7·0, 7·8 and 7·1.

that the trade unionists among the skilled men would be foun
drawing much more than in proportion to their numbers, probabl
at least as much more as in the other industries in the table.]
should be noted, on the other hand, that the figures in column
probably under-estimate the effective proportion of associatio
members which is put in sections 378–9 of the Board of Trade Repor
not at 29·5 per cent, but at somewhere between 29·5 per cent an
34·0 per cent. It is clear that raising the figures in column 5 t
allow for this would still leave the association benefit, industry b
industry, well above the proportion of association members; that
to say, the trade union rate should be reduced materially, to cove
unorganized as well as organized workers in the period before 1914
How great the reduction should be is hard to say exactly. But o
the figures a reduction by one-sixth, say from 4·8 to 4·0, is reasor
able.

11. Second, the unemployment insurance records after the wa
covered a greater variety of industries and occupations than thos
covered by the trade union returns, but this does not mean tha
they would necessarily or naturally show a higher percentage c
unemployment. The trade union returns, it is true, omitted occupa
tions so badly paid or so disorganized that they could not attemp
to pay out of work benefit, such as dock and wharf labour, buildin
labour and semi-skilled and unskilled occupations generally. Bu
the returns left out, on the other hand, occupations so regular tha
they had not felt the need to provide for unemployment; thes
included the service industries and others meeting the needs c
consumers directly. A test calculation covering the years 1927–3
suggests that, even if the building labourers are treated as a separat
industry of high unemployment not covered by the trade unio
returns, the industries substantially covered by the trade unio
returns had more rather than less unemployment than the averag
of all industries. This is not surprising, in view of the fact that the
were in the main men's industries and that the rate of unemploy
ment among insured men is normally higher than that amon
insured women. But the difference shown by this calculation is no
clear or decisive. It is safest to regard the occupations covered by
the trade union returns, as having had on an average much the
same general level of unemployment as all occupations taker
together, though less in good times and more in bad times. That i
to say, no correction either way should be made on account of the
narrower occupational basis of the trade union unemploymen
rate.

12. Third, the unemployment insurance recording was more complete within the trades covered. The trade union returns in some important industries, such as coal-mining and to a lesser extent textiles, included only those who were wholly unemployed and not those who were working short time, losing a few days each week. In the eight years 1906–13, in which the corrected general rate for all unions averaged 4·8, the percentages of unemployment recorded in coal-mining was 0·7 and that in textiles was 2·4; as these two industries provided about a third of the total membership represented in the returns, these low percentages lowered the general rate substantially. For coal-mining it is possible to make some estimate of the extent to which loss of work through short time escaped being recorded as unemployment; in this industry during the nineteen years 1895–1913 the average rate of unemployment returned by the trade unions was under 1 per cent. But the average number of days per week on which the mines were working was only 5·22, representing a loss of 0·78 of a day, or 13 per cent, on the theoretical maximum of six days a week and 0·36 of a day, or more than 6 per cent on the 5·58 days per week actually worked in the busiest year. For textiles no statistical estimate of short-time before the war can be made, but it must represent a substantial unrecorded loss of employment. In most industries it is probable that a good many short spells of unemployment went unrecorded; most unions had a waiting period for which benefit was not paid and most gave benefit only for a limited period, so that men just out of work who hoped shortly to return to work had more than one reason for omitting to record their unemployment. Finally, as a good deal of short period unemployment escaped record, so did some chronic unemployment. Some unions, indeed, provided out-of-work pay practically without limit of time; striking instances were given in my first study, of chronic unemployment recorded in the printing trade.[1] But trade union benefit generally did not last indefinitely; men who remained unemployed for long might lose their union membership and fail to be recorded. In contrast to these omissions of unemployment from the trade union record, both at the beginning of any period of unemployment and at the end of a long period, the recording of unemployment by the Ministry of Labour between the wars was singularly complete. In one way or another—to get benefit, to get unemployment assistance or public assistance, to get exemption from payment of health insurance contributions, to get the chance of work—it was made

[1] *Unemployment* (1909), pp. 140–1.

worth while for every person capable of work to get on to th
register of the unemployed as soon as he could, and to stay ther
whenever he was not working. Employers in the short-time industrie:
like textiles, soon learned to adjust their days of working so as t
enable their operatives to qualify for benefit. Undoubtedly, unde
this fourth head, the trade union record substantially under-state
the true volume of unemployment. Some measure of the unde;
statement, through omission of short intervals of unemploymen
is probably afforded by the proportion which persons "temporaril
stopped" bear to the numbers "wholly unemployed" in the insuranc
statistics. Table 11 shows that the former are about one-quarter (
the latter, so that on the assumption that, as a rule, the forme
would not and the latter would have been recorded as unemploye
by the trade unions, the trade union rate should be raised by
quarter on this account. It is suggested below that anothe
quarter should be added for the greater completeness of th
insurance record in respect of prolonged unemployment and i
other ways.

13. Fourth, the unemployment insurance record of unemploy
ment was swollen at times by people who were not really in th
labour market. There were some who were incapable of ordinar
work, but, as has been shown subsequently in the second Worl
War, the number of such people was very small; not more tha
about 25,000 of the unemployed have been judged to be unsuitab!
for ordinary industrial work when there was need for them. Moi
important was the occasional swelling of the register of the unem
ployed by people who were not fully in the labour market f(
employment because their main occupation was some independe!
work of their own, or was unpaid domestic work as married wome
or otherwise. Since 1932 the largest classes of such people ha\
been removed from the register of unemployment by the Anomali«
Act of 1931, which in the case of persons following seasonal occup;
tions and married women imposed special conditions for the recei[
of benefit. No doubt a certain number of people, particularly i
country districts, whose substantial occupation is that of the smal
independent worker on the land or in fishing, still contrive to con
within unemployment insurance by collecting insurance stamps i
one way or another.[1] But the addition to the record of genuir
unemployment in these ways is trifling in comparison to the whol
On the other hand, the record of unemployment in Britain, moi

[1] See *Report of Unemployment Insurance Statutory Committee on Share Fisherm*
(1936), particularly paras. 19, 20, 30.

ɔmplete as it almost certainly is than the corresponding record in
ther countries, still omits a certain amount of concealed unemploy-
ıent in lost time and lost work.

14. Fifth, the bases of the trade union and of the unemployment
ısurance were not only different from one another but each of
ıem changed from time to time. In the case of the trade unions
ıe change consisted in the gradual spread of the practice of giving
ut-of-work benefit and so widening the trade basis of the figures.
Ise of the corrected percentages, giving equal weight throughout to
ıe instrumental industries (engineering, shipbuilding and metals),
voids some but not all the results of this change of basis. The
ɔrrected percentages yield a substantially lower average rate of
ınemployment (3·9) from 1856 to 1882, than from 1883 to 1913
4·8), but from other evidence it is doubtful if unemployment was
:ally more severe in the later period. The higher rate was probably
ue to the more representative character of the returns. In the
resent comparison, accordingly, pre-war unemployment as recorded
y the trade unions is taken as 4·8 per cent, the mean for the last
ıirty-one years, in place of 4·4 per cent, the mean for 1856–1913.
ı the case of unemployment insurance the recording of unemploy-
ıent between 1921 and 1938 was affected repeatedly by adminis-
ative changes, of which the following are the most important:—

(a) Exclusion from unemployment insurance after 1927, of
persons aged 65 and upwards. The numbers insured till 1926
relate to persons aged 16 and upwards; those from 1928 relate
to persons aged 16 to 64. As figures of both kinds are available
for 1927, the Ministry of Labour is able to construct a continuous
table of index numbers from 1923, showing the numbers
insured and the insured persons in employment in July of each
year, as percentages of the corresponding adjusted numbers in
1923. For July, 1927, the number of insured persons of all ages
over 16 is given as 12,131,000 and that of insured persons
from 16 to 64 is given as 11,784,000; that is to say, the number
of insured persons of 65 and upwards was 347,000. The number
removed from the unemployment register by the change is
given in the *Labour Gazette* for February, 1930, as 25,000;
that is to say, little more than 7 per cent of the numbers of
insured persons of 65 and upwards. This is lower than the
average unemployment rate, so that the change presumably
had the effect of raising slightly the recorded rate of unemployment. Presumably persons of 65 and upwards only continued

to take out unemployment books if they had a relatively goo
prospect of work.

(*b*) Several minor administrative changes between 1924 an
1929, described in a note in the *Labour Gazette* for Februar'
1929, generally increased but sometimes decreased the numbe:
recorded as unemployed. Two of the most important of thes
changes were estimated to have added 65,000 persons to th
register between April and October, 1928.

(*c*) The dropping of the "genuinely seeking work condition
in 1930, followed by the Anomalies Act of 1931, made a majc
disturbance in the record of unemployment, particularly amon
women, and makes it desirable for any detailed study of ur
employment in particular industries covering those years to us
figures for males only. The first of these changes was estimate
to have added 60,000 to the unemployed register betwee
March and May, 1930, and many more later (*Labour Gazett*
November, 1930, and February, 1932). The latter was estimate
to have removed between 180,000 and 190,000 persons fror
the register between October, 1931, and May, 1932 (*Labo.*
Gazette, April, May and June, 1932). These changes and son
of their effects are discussed in the first part of my "Analys
of Unemployment" (published in *Economica*, November, 1936)

(*d*) A change in the conditions for unemployment assistanc
in April, 1937, increased the numbers recorded as unemploye
by about 20,000 and affected the comparability of statistics (
duration of unemployment, before and after the change (so
paragraph 80). The change is described in the *Labour Gazet*
for April, 1937.

(*e*) A change in the method of counting the unemployec
made in September, 1937, and described in the *Labour Gazet*
of the following month, lowered the general unemploymer
rate by $0 \cdot 3$ on an average. The extent of the change differe
in different industries as appears from a table at page 442 of th
Labour Gazette for November, 1937.

It has seemed worth while to set out these changes, knowledge (
which may be useful for those who make detailed study of th
British unemployment figures. But none of them are of first-rat
importance. Their general tendency is to make the offici:
figures an increasingly accurate and complete record of unemploy
ment.

15. It should be added that the table at pp. 68–9 of the 21*st Annual Abstract of Labour Statistics*, giving trade union unemployment percentages from 1881 to 1926, contains at the head the statement that "persons on strike or locked out, sick or superannuated are excluded." If this meant that such persons were excluded from the denominator as well as from the numerator represented by the percentages, this would make a further significant difference between the trade union rates and the unemployment insurance rates; the latter are based on all the unemployment books issued, i.e. include in the denominator persons sick or on strike or locked out. This would make a difference of about $3\frac{1}{2}$ per cent in the rates, i.e. the trade union rates would have to be reduced or the insurance rates increased by about $3\frac{1}{2}$ per cent to allow for this and be made strictly comparable. But from a note in the Second Series of Board of Trade Memoranda (Cmd. 2337, p. 97), it is clear that sick persons, though not counted as unemployed, were included in the membership on which the percentage was based, i.e. in the denominator of the fraction; they were included on the ground that they "were only temporarily disabled." The note at the head of the *Abstract of Labour Statistics* table presumably means only that they were excluded from the numerator.

16. Of the various heads of difference named above, the first suggests that, for comparison with the unemployment insurance record between the wars, the unemployment rate recorded by the trade unions before 1914 should be reduced materially; the second head suggests no change either way; the other heads (particularly the third) suggest that the trade union rate should be raised materially. If the rate of $4\cdot8$ recorded by the trade unions from 1883 to 1913 is first reduced under the first head to $4\cdot0$, then increased by a quarter to allow for the recording of "temporary stoppages" and by as much again to allow for the greater completeness of the insurance record in other ways, it yields an unemployment rate of $6\cdot0$. This, it is suggested, is the most probable rate of pre-war unemployment to use for comparison with the unemployment rate between the wars. It makes the latter at $14\cdot2$ per cent, nearly $2\frac{1}{2}$ times the true rate of unemployment before the first war.

17. From the working of the first unemployment insurance scheme in 1912–14 it is possible to make another direct comparison between trade union and insurance records, and between insurance records before and after the first World War. This is done in Table 38 below for 1913 and 1937. The main results are summarized at the end of the note to the table.

Table 38

TRADE UNION AND UNEMPLOYMENT INSURANCE RATES OF UNEM-
PLOYMENT IN 1913 AND 1937

	Building	Ship-building	Engineering and Iron-founding	Construction of Vehicles	Saw Milling	All above Insured Industrie
1. Trade Union Rate, 1913	3·8	3·1	1·9	2·1	2·9	2·7
2. Unemployment Insurance Rate, 1913	5·1	3·4	2·4	2·5	2·5	3·6
3. Unemployment Insurance Rate, 1937	13·8	23·8	5·5	5·0	10·4	10·4
4. Numbers covered by Trade Union Returns, 1908 (*thousands*)	60	57	164	9	5	305
5. Insured Persons, 1913–14 (*thousands*)	813	264	818	210	12	2,117
6. Insured Persons, 1937 (*thousands*)	1,035	173	822	402	63	2,495
7. Row 2 as per cent of 1..	134	109	126	119	86	125
8. Row 3 as per cent of 2..	271	700	229	200	416	279

The trade union rates and numbers covered in the returns in building relate only to carpenters and joiners and plumbers. The figures for construction of vehicles relate only to coach-builders; no doubt some of those who in the insurance statistics are assigned to construction of vehicles appear in the trade union returns under engineering. The numbers covered by the trade union returns are given as at 1908; the figures in 1913 would be higher but it is unlikely that the proportions would be materially different.

The unemployment insurance rate of 5·1 in the column "Building" covers both building and construction of works, as the two are not separated for this purpose in the Board of Trade Report. The other figures in this column relate to building, i.e. exclude "public works contracting."

In row 5 the numbers of insured persons, 1913–14, represent the numbers of unemployment books current in July, 1914. It seems better to take these later figures in preference to the lower figures given in Table LXI of the unpublished Board of Trade Report of unemployment books of 1912–13 currency exchanged during the period July, 1913–July, 1914. These figures no doubt omit a number of men who should have been insured but did not at once take out unemployment books.

In row 7 the figure of 125 for all insured industries is got by weighting the figures for separate industries by the numbers in row 5. In row 8 the figure of 279 for all industries is got by weighting the figures for separate industries by the numbers in row 6.

In rows 1, 2 and 3 the rates for all the industries taken together are got by weighting the rates in the separate industries by the numbers in rows 4, 5 and 6, respectively. The rate of 3·6 given in the Board of Trade Report for all insured industries, covers 144,000 persons in construction of works (at a rate of 5·1) and 65,000 in other insured industries (at a rate of 1·2), and works out at the same as that reached above.

The main results of the comparison made in Table 38 are:

(1) The unemployment insurance rate in 1913 taking all the insured industries together is 25 per cent above the recorded trade union rate. This accords with the suggestion made above of treating the 4·8 of recorded trade union unemployment from 1883 to 1913 as equivalent to 6·0 on an insurance basis.

(2) The unemployment insurance rate in 1937 is 279 per cent of that recorded in

Table 38—Continued

1913. If ship-building is omitted as being abnormally depressed, the percentage for the other industries becomes 248, i.e. corresponds almost exactly to the conclusion reached above treating unemployment between the wars as two and a half times as high as unemployment before the first World War.

18. These figures relate only to a single year in each case at the top of a cyclical fluctuation, but so far as they go they show good agreement with the inferences made on other grounds. They support the suggestion that the most probable figure to take for the mean rate of unemployment in Britain before the first World War for comparison with the rate recorded between the wars is about 6·0, but this is subject to large margins of error either way. The true rate may easily have been as low as 5·0 or as the recorded trade union rate of 4·8, or as high as, say, 7·0. At a rate of 14·2 between the wars unemployment was between two and three times as severe as before the first World War, most probably about $2\frac{1}{2}$ times.

4. A POLICY OF CHEAP MONEY

19. An integral part of a policy of full employment is a "cheap money" policy. The Government already possesses full *de facto* powers to control the long-term and short-term rate of interest. No new powers are required; but it is essential that the powers already in the hands of the Government by virtue of its control of the Bank of England should be consciously used and systematically applied.

20. The rate of interest used to be looked upon as a price which adjusted the demand for savings to the supply. It was thought that whenever business men desired to increase their outlay on new investment, the rate of interest would rise, and that such a rise would have the double effect, first, of inducing people to save more and, second, of discouraging the business man who was at the margin of doubt whether he should invest or not. In this way, the rate of interest was thought to adjust the supply of savings to the demand for savings. But this view has been exploded by modern economic research. The rate of interest cannot fulfil this function, because capital expenditure itself brings into existence the very savings necessary to finance it. There is no question of "equilibrating" the one to the other because they are kept in equality by changes in the level of income. Savings are the *result* of any expenditure (for whatever purpose) which is defrayed out of loans or reserves. The amount which any community is able to save is determined by the amount which the community spends out of loans or reserves.

A low rate of interest encourages such expenditure; it does not discourage savings, because savings are the inevitable concomitant of such expenditure.

21. It is extremely desirable that there should be a high level of investment—private or public—in post-war Britain. It is therefore desirable that the rate of interest should be as low as possible, so as to encourage every kind of outlay on capital goods. A housing programme, in particular, depends on finance being obtainable at a low rate of interest.

22. It is possible, and indeed likely, that the people of Britain after the war should desire and attempt to use for their current consumption a larger proportion of available manpower than would be in the public interest. Such an attempt would not exclude a parallel attempt by business men and the State to marshal manpower for purposes of investment. The result would not be that consumers' expenditure made it impossible to find money for capital expenditure or for budget deficits; the result would be that consumers' expenditure and capital expenditure (or budget deficits) together would add up to a total which exceeded the value of current output at the prices which it was desired to maintain. Inflation, in other words, would be the result. It might be theoretically possible to combat such an inflationary tendency by an enormous increase in the rate of interest, so that would-be borrowers would find it unattractive to raise funds for capital expenditure. To do so, however, would be a fatal mistake, since the re-equipment of British industry, a large expansion of investment in houses, and a considerable expansion of communal investment are surely the most immediately desirable objectives for post-war Britain. It follows that the rate of interest must be kept low—as low as possible. It follows, further, that a rise in the rate of interest must be ruled out as a weapon in the fight against inflationary tendencies. Recourse must be had to more direct methods. As long as inflationary tendencies exist as the aftermath of war, war-time controls must be maintained.

23. In war-time there is an unprecedented demand for loans—albeit a demand emanating almost exclusively from the State. But whether such demand is public or private, war-time experience shows that it can be satisfied at interest rates which are as low as ever before in peace-time. This alone is sufficient proof of the statement that the Government possesses full control over the rate of interest. How is this control exercised?

24. The volume of savings a community can make is determined, as stated above, by the volume of money it expends out of loans

or reserves. The rate of interest is controlled by controlling the form in which savings can be held. Savings may be held in the form of cash, or bank deposits, or bills, or long-term loans. The amount of savings held in the form of cash or bank deposits, once the rate of interest is kept stable, is determined by business turnover, that is to say, by the level of production and the level of prices. The amount of savings held in the form of short-term bills is determined partly by business turnover, but partly also by certain established ratios which financial and other institutions desire to preserve between their short-term and long-term assets. The amount of savings, finally, held in the form of long-term bonds is a residual item—all funds not held in another form. This applies when the rate of interest is kept stable. But how can it be kept stable? The answer is a simple one: The Government has to decide upon the rate it wishes to maintain and then to allow the savers to hold their savings in the form in which, with that rate of interest, they want to hold them. That is to say, the Government must offer long-term bonds and short-term paper "on tap" so that savings can flow into them according to the wishes of the savers.

25. It may be asked, what happens if the Government wishes to borrow and spend £100 millions and the public is not prepared to subscribe more than (say) £60 millions to the long-term or short-term issues "on tap"? The answer, again, is simple. A deficit expenditure of £100 millions having been decided upon in the light of the general economic situation, the Government raises the balance of £40 millions through "Ways and Means Advances" from the Bank of England. As it proceeds to spend the £100 millions, it increases the stock of the community's savings by £100 millions. These new savings will again have to be held in some form—in cash, deposits, bills, or bonds. Having spent £40 millions out of "Ways and Means Advances" from the Bank of England, the cash basis of the banking system has been increased by that amount. The banks will not want to hold more than their customary ratio of cash against deposits. Thus they will, during the next period, again subscribe to the "tap" issues. The public will not wish to hold all their new savings in the form of cash or bank deposits (these being determined by business turnover) and will also subscribe to "tap" issues. The banks can subscribe to these issues only to the extent that the public are prepared to hold more bank deposits. If the public refuse to hold any of their current new savings in additional bank deposits, because their demand for cash is satiated, all the subscription to the "tap" issues will come from the public and

none from the banks. Bank deposits and bank assets will cease to expand.

26. The essence of what has been said above is this: maintaining a stable rate of interest means, first, deciding what the rate of interest should be and, second, offering the citizens exactly what, in view of the thus determined rate, they are anxious to have. In practical terms, this means keeping long-term bonds and short-term paper on "tap," and "creating" additional cash or Central Bank money by borrowing from the Bank of England whenever "tap" subscriptions are insufficient to cover the budget deficit. This does not mean inflation, because the very size of the deficit is decided upon as an antidote to the "deflationary gap" which would exist in the absence of a deficit. If, as may well happen, "tap" subscriptions exceed the amount required by the government, this shows that the rate of interest offered is higher than is necessary, and should lead the government to lower the rate.

27. It might well be asked why the Government should not decide right away that the best rate of interest is a zero rate and proceed to finance all its deficits by the "creation" of new cash or bank money through "Ways and Means Advances." This question is a pertinent one. It does not raise, as many of the so-called monetary reformers seem to think it raises, an issue of principle. The difference between printing paper which is a claim to cash in ten years and carries an appreciable rate of interest and printing paper which is a claim to cash on demand and carries an insignificant rate of interest is merely a difference of degree, not one of substance. Equally, there is no difference of substance between "creating" cash and printing, say, short-term bills carrying 1 per cent interest. If it is demanded, therefore, that the Government should cease to borrow at interest and simply cover its deficit by creating cash, this, in effect, amounts to demanding that governmental monetary policy should reduce the basic rate of interest, that is, the rate on paper, which carries no private risk, not gradually, but suddenly and to zero. It would have to be shown that a sudden reduction is preferable to a gradual one. Can this be shown?

28. There are at least two objections against it. First, a sudden reduction in the rate of interest produces a sudden appreciation in the capital value of all outstanding long-term money claims and all durable capital assets, such as land, houses, industrial property and so forth. An appreciation of these values—particularly a sudden one—which means windfall profits to their owners, may induce them to increase their luxury expenditure on an appreciable scale. While

this, of course, would create additional employment, it would do so for purposes of small social value and might create social tensions that are wholly undesirable. Second, there are innumerable financial and other institutions, whose activities depend upon their being able to convert cash into interest-bearing paper that carries no appreciable private risk. If there is no further supply of gilt-edged Government paper, an important foundation of their activity crumbles away, and special arrangements are necessary to maintain them in being. This applies not only to insurance companies and banks, but also to pension funds, charitable organizations, research endowments, and so forth. These two objections lose their force when applied to a gradual and long-term policy of reducing the rate of interest; but they would appear to have considerable weight against a policy of sudden changes.

29. A policy of gradual reduction gives time for adjustment. The speed with which it proceeds can be adjusted to circumstances. If the long-term rate of interest is reduced by one-tenth of 1 per cent every two years, a total reduction from the present level of 3 per cent to a new level of 2 per cent is effected in twenty years. This rate of reduction may be considered too slow; it can hardly be considered too fast. If, through conversions of the existing national debt, it could be spread over the total of that debt, it would allow the annual amount of interest payable on the national debt to remain stationary in spite of an annual budget deficit of £400 millions. This calculation alone should dispose of the arguments of those who claim that annual budget deficits would impose an unmanageable "transfer burden" upon society.

30. The method that might be applied for the gradual reduction in the rate of interest on long-term bonds is the following: The length of the bonds offered "on tap" is increased every month, at a stable rate of interest. After a while, the length of the bond is reduced, and the rate of interest offered on the shorter bond is also reduced. This can be repeated over and over again, giving a perfectly smooth transition. As long as the method of issuing bills and bonds "on tap" is maintained, the rate of interest is controllable without any difficulty whatever.

5. THE THEORETICAL INEVITABILITY OF CYCLICAL FLUCTUATION

31. The inevitability of trade cycle fluctuations, in an unplanned market economy, can be deduced by two lines of argument: by showing the way in which a developing boom affects incomes and

savings, and by an analysis of the structure of industry, particularly the division of industry between trades producing primarily goods for current consumption and trades producing primarily goods for expanding the capital equipment of the country. Both roads lead to the same result, since the flow of money incomes and savings is merely the reflected image of what happens in the various departments of production. A full explanation of the trade cycle would require a book by itself. For the present purposes, it is sufficient to stress the following: the pattern of income distribution in our society is such that, whenever the national income expands, intended savings expand at a faster rate than the national income. Intended savings, however, become real savings only when they are offset by loan expenditure. As savings rise at an ever-accelerating rate, so somebody's loan expenditure must rise at an accelerating rate. This produces increasing internal tension, if only because of the growing volume of private indebtedness. A small curtailment of bank credit may stop this process and usher in depression. Even if no conscious policy of credit restriction is introduced, a small abatement in the optimism (i.e. profit expectations) of business men may do the same. But even without any special assumptions as to credit policy and business confidence it is at least plausible that a process cannot continue indefinitely when it depends upon some factor—current investment—growing at a steadily accelerating rate. Nor is this all. Current investment activity means making current additions to the existing stock of capital. The new capital, forthcoming in ever growing volume, competes with the old and reduces the profits obtainable on the old. Since new investment—in an unplanned market economy—depends upon favourable profit expectations on the part of entrepreneurs, it is not likely to grow at a rapid rate when the profits obtainable on older equipment show a continuously falling trend.

32. Additional equipment, moreover, in the majority of cases requires additional labour to work it. A boom derived from a rapid growth in the production of new industrial capacity finds its natural termination in an absolute shortage of labour. This inevitable end is foreshadowed by sectional shortages and rising labour costs, reducing the entrepreneur's eagerness to invest often long before all available labour has been absorbed. In short, it is inherent in the design of an unplanned market economy that every approach to full employment produces increasing inner tension, until this tension is relieved by the brutal cure of depression. Since consumption and private investment can only grow and fall together,

every movement of expansion or of contraction once inaugurated becomes cumulative. The instability of the unplanned market economy is not accidental: it is inherent. Modern analysis makes it possible to state categorically that, in the absence of planning there will be fluctuations. How severe they would be, in future, theory alone cannot tell us.

Appendix C

THE QUANTITATIVE ASPECTS OF THE FULL EMPLOYMENT PROBLEM IN BRITAIN

By NICHOLAS KALDOR

SECTION I: ALTERNATIVE METHODS OF SECURING FULL EMPLOYMENT BY FISCAL POLICIES

SECTION II: THE FULL EMPLOYMENT PROBLEM IN 1938

SECTION III: THE FULL EMPLOYMENT PROBLEM AFTER THE WAR

SECTION IV: THE LONG RUN CONSEQUENCES OF CONTINUOUS PUBLIC BORROWING

1. The purpose of this memorandum is to examine what a full employment policy would involve, in terms of the revenue and expenditure of public authorities, assuming that the principle is

accepted that the fiscal policies of the State are so regulated as to secure adequate total outlay for the community as a whole. Any such analysis of the quantitative aspects of the full employment problem requires a large number of hypotheses and assumptions resting on more or less firm statistical foundations. We shall set out these hypotheses and assumptions as fully as possible so as to enable the reader who has reason to differ from them to revise the estimate accordingly.[1]

2. We shall begin by giving a brief account of the nature of the alternative policies by which full employment may be secured, and showing their general implications. After this introduction, the actual statistical analysis will be tackled in two stages: first by examining the implications of the full employment policies in the circumstances of pre-war Britain; second, the nature of the problem in the conditions that will probably arise after the war.

I. ALTERNATIVE METHODS OF SECURING FULL EMPLOYMENT BY FISCAL POLICIES

3. There are many ways in which a Government desirous to ensure full employment can so regulate the fiscal policies of the State as to ensure adequate total outlay for the community as a whole; but they can all be reduced to four distinct types.[2] The first is by increased public expenditure covered by loans; the second is by increased public expenditure covered by taxation; the third is by increased private spending brought about through remission of taxation, and the fourth is by increased private spending brought about through changing the incidence of taxation or imposing a combined system of taxes and subsidies. The first two methods imply that idle resources are primarily absorbed for purposes that are determined by, or are under the control of, the State; the last two that they are absorbed in uses determined by private citizens. The first and the third (though not the second or the fourth) imply "deficit spending"—i.e. a state of affairs where aggregate State expenditure, for all purposes, exceeds total State revenue from

[1] The author is indebted to Dr. T. Barna both for working out the statistical correlations involved, and for allowing the use of yet unpublished estimates regarding the incidence of taxation.

[2] [The first three of these types are represented by Routes I, II and III, shown in Table 18 of the Report and discussed in relation to that table. The fourth type, though included in this memorandum for the sake of logical completeness, presents such extreme practical difficulties that it did not appear advantageous to discuss it in the Report itself.—W. H. B.]

taxation and public property, and where in consequence there is continuous public borrowing. We shall examine the implications of each of these policies.

4. An increase in the scale of public expenditure with given *rates* of taxation, will increase the total outlay of the community on home-produced goods and services by a greater amount than the rise in the public expenditure itself, since—on account of the increase in incomes and the increase in productive activity to which it gives rise—it will lead to increased private expenditures. The size of this secondary expansion will depend on three factors; first, on the way private citizens allocate the increase in their incomes (their "marginal" incomes) between taxation, savings, and consumption; second, on the extent to which increased spending by the Government, and increased spending by private citizens, leads to an increase in capital expenditures by industry (the increase in "private investment"); and third, on the proportion of the increased demand for goods and services of all kinds which goes to home-produced and to imported goods and services respectively. If by means of a policy of increasing public outlay, while keeping the existing rates of taxation constant, an expansion of demand is generated that is sufficient to absorb unemployed resources (i) the total increase in the demand for goods and services will be *greater* than the value of the potential output of unemployed resources, since part of the increase in demand will be directed abroad; (ii) the increase in public expenditure will be *less* than the total increase in demand, since there will be a consequential increase in private consumption and private investment; (iii) the increase in public borrowing (the size of the deficit) will be *less* than the increase in public expenditure, since the higher expenditure will increase the yield of existing taxation.

5. Full employment could be secured, however, by means of increased public outlay, even if the State expenditure is fully covered by taxation—dor the reason that an increase in taxation is not likely to reduce private outlay by the full amount of the taxes paid. It may be assumed that all taxes have some influence on the savings of the individuals on whom they fall; taxes which fall on the poor have a relatively large effect on consumption and a relatively small effect on savings; with taxes paid by the rich it is probably the other way round. Hence an increase in public expenditure will cause a net addition to the total outlay of the community, even if it is covered by taxation; and this net addition is likely to be all the greater, the more progressive is the incidence of the extra taxation

raised to cover it. But since the addition to total outlay brought about by a given expansion of public expenditure would in this case be necessarily much smaller than in the case where the rates of taxation are kept constant and there is an expansion in the rate of borrowing, the total expansion of public expenditure would have to be much greater.

6. The alternative approach to securing adequate total outlay, and hence an adequate total demand for labour, is to increase not the State expenditure, but the expenditure of private citizens. Here also there are two different methods of procedure, according as the policy chosen involves "unbalanced budgets" or not. The creation of a budgetary deficit by the simple device of reducing taxation relatively to a given rate of expenditure will increase employment, since it converts the ordinary expenditure of the Government into "loan expenditure" which is an offset to savings. Since some part of the additional incomes made available through tax remissions would be bound to be saved by the recipients, the necessary deficit would always have to be larger, in this case, than in the case of increased public outlay; there are, on the other hand, no technical obstacles to making the deficit sufficiently large.

7. The financially orthodox method of raising private outlay relies on the stimulus given by changing the incidence of taxation: reducing the taxes falling on the relatively poor (who can be expected to spend most of the additional incomes made available to them) and increasing the taxes falling on the relatively rich, and thereby reducing total savings at any given level of income. This can be done either by raising the degree of progressiveness of income tax and surtax at any given standard rate (increasing exemptions in the lower income brackets and graduation in the upper brackets) or by reducing indirect taxes and raising the standard rate of income tax. In order to secure an adequate expansion of outlay in this way, however, the required changes in relative taxation would have to be very large, while the scope for such changes—under the British system of taxation, which is fairly progressive in any case—is limited. To secure an adequate expansion under this method the State may have to supplement the reduction or abolition of particular taxes by the granting of subsidies (which are negative indirect taxes) either in the form of subsidies on the prices of necessities (such as are given in war-time) or subsidies on wages paid to employees.[1]

[1] A subsidy on wages paid to employers would—insofar as the benefit of lower wage costs is passed on to the consumers in the form of lower prices—have much the same kind of effect as subsidies on commodities or subsidies on earnings

In general, if considerable changes in the structure of income distribution were desired, it is better to tackle the problem directly— by forcing producers to sell at lower prices relatively to costs—than indirectly through changes in taxation or some combined scheme of taxation and subsidies. The main reason for this is that it is extremely difficult to devise a scheme where the consequential higher taxation on profits would not in itself have adverse effects on incentives and hence on employment.

8. It will be shown in Section II of this memorandum that in the kind of circumstances which existed in Great Britain in 1938, of the above policies those which did not involve loan expenditure would have been ineffective or impracticable. Full employment could have been secured (in principle) without deficit finance, either by enlarging sufficiently the range of public expenditure, or by changing (through taxation and subsidies) the distribution of available incomes, but in either case, the policy would have involved such major changes in the social framework as to have made it—from a political and administrative point of view—very difficult to carry out. The practical alternatives therefore were either the creation of budgetary deficits through higher public outlay, or the creation of deficits through tax remissions.

9. It will be argued in Section III of this memorandum that in the circumstances of the early post-war years this will probably not be so; the needs of private industry after the war, together with the higher ratio of exports to imports, are likely to set up, for a number of years, a demand for labour that will be much more closely related to the available supply than was the case before the war. This might enable a full employment policy, for a time, to be consistent with budgetary surpluses, rather than public borrowing. But taking a longer view, there appears to be no reason why the employment problem should not again present itself in much the same aspects as in the 1930's; and once this stage is reached, the practical methods of maintaining full employment will again be the creation of loan expenditure, either by increasing public outlay, or by lowering taxation.

10. In Section III, dealing with the post-war situation, it will be assumed that (i) a rigid separation will be made in the public

paid to employees. But insofar as owing to rigidity of prices in some sections of the economic system the cost-reduction cannot be relied on to result in corresponding price reductions in every case, a subsidy on wages paid to employers would be less effective as a means of raising employment than either subsidies on commodities or subsidies on wages paid to employees.

accounts between the ordinary running expenditures of the State and investment expenditures; (ii) that the Government will plan the rate of national investment as a whole, both privately and publicly financed; (iii) that the rates of taxation will be so adjusted as to secure continuous full employment with the planned rate of investment expenditure. It will thus be shown: first, what is the level of national investment consistent with full employment, assuming that the level of taxation is just sufficient to cover the ordinary expenditure of public authorities; and second, what are the adjustments in taxation necessary in order to secure higher levels of investments that may be more in accord with the objects of national policy. In Section IV, a brief examination will be made of the long run aspects of the problem, with particular reference to the long run effects of a rising National Debt.

II. THE FULL EMPLOYMENT PROBLEM IN 1938

11. In order to examine the implications of full employment policies, in the circumstances of 1938, in quantitative terms, it is necessary to make three kinds of estimate:—(i) how the value of the national output would have been changed as a result of the change in employment; (ii) how the various types of income would have been changed, as a result of the changes in the value of the national output; (iii) how the various elements of the national expenditure—consumption, taxation, the level of imports and the Balance of Payments,[1] private savings and private investment outlay—would have changed as a result of the changes both in the national output and in private incomes.

12. The estimates are based partly on the official estimate of the national income in 1938, as given in the White Paper on the National Income,[2] partly on a regression analysis of the relation between variations in the national income and its various components in the inter-war period, based on Professor Bowley's estimates of the National Income,[3] partly on other estimates relating to savings and the relation of undistributed profits to total profits.

[1] By the term Balance of Payments, here and throughout this paper, we mean the balance of payments on income account—i.e. the net sum of the balance of merchandise trade, the balance of invisible exports and imports (shipping, insurance, etc.), and the net income from foreign investments. It excludes gold and capital movements.

[2] Cmd. 6520, 1944.

[3] *Studies in the National Income*, 1924–38, Cambridge University Press, 1942. Professor Bowley's series have been adjusted for a number of factors, in particular for over-assessments and business losses in the figures for profits.

13. The calculations throughout are in real terms, i.e. they assume constant rates of wages and prices. In case a full employment policy had been associated with a rise in wages and prices, the resulting money totals (of the national income, consumption, Government expenditure, etc.) would have been higher but without necessarily changing, to any significant extent, the relative magnitudes of the various items.

The National Output in 1938

14. The estimate of the "net national income and expenditure at factor cost"—which is a measure of the value of the current national output of goods and services, plus the net income obtained on

Table 39

NET NATIONAL INCOME AND EXPENDITURE IN 1938

	£ millions		£ millions
Rents	380	Personal expenditure on consumption..	3,510
Profits and Interest..	1,385	Private net investment at home ..	420
Salaries	1,100	Balance of foreign payments ..	— 55
Wages	1,730	Expenditure of public authorities on goods and services out of revenue	725
Pay of H.M. Forces	80	Government expenditure on goods and services out of loans ..	75
Net National Income ..	4,675	Net National Expenditure ..	4,675

Note.—The estimates are from Cmd. 6520, Table I, except that the figures for profits, private net investment at home and the net national income (and expenditure) have each been raised by £70 millions, to adjust them for the amount of "inventory losses" in profits, as this adjustment gives a more correct picture of the value of the national output at constant prices. The figures on the expenditure side are measured at factor cost of production, i.e. all indirect taxes are deducted from, and subsidies added to, the relevant categories. The estimates in the latest White Paper show separately the expenditures incurred in the transfer of property and the investment of savings, which are here included in the item "private net investment at home." This item is therefore composed of the following: net investment in fixed capital, £335 millions; net increase in working capital and stocks, £25 millions; cost of transferring property, etc., £60 millions. The figures in this table are rounded off to the nearest £5 millions.

foreign investments—is given in Table 39. The national income, on this definition, is smaller than the sum of the separate incomes of all individuals and corporations, since it does not include "transfer incomes" (i.e. National Debt interest, pensions, payments in respect of unemployment relief, etc.) which, though regarded as income by the individuals concerned, are not earned in connection with the production of goods and services. These "transfer incomes" amounted to £478 millions in 1938. Similarly, the expenditure of public authorities shown on the right hand side of Table 39 is not the total expenditure of public authorities in that year, but falls short of this amount by the £478 millions transfer expenditures. The total amount of taxation paid by private individuals and corporations in 1938 was £1,176 millions, as shown in Table 42, p. 355, of which (after the deduction of £478 millions, which went to provide for transfer expenditures and £15 millions for subsidies) £683 millions was available to meet the expenditures on goods and services. This latter sum, together with £44 millions state revenue from public property, makes up the £727 millions "public expenditure on goods and services out of revenue." Since the total expenditure of public authorities on goods and services was £802 millions, there was a net deficit of £75 millions, covered by borrowing. (This was by no means typical of the pre-war period, since in most years there was a net surplus on the consolidated public accounts.[1] The deficit in 1938 was solely due to the fact that 1938 was a re-armament year.)

The National Output under Full Employment

14. In 1938 there were, roughly, 14·5 million wage-earners aged 16–64, of whom about 1·7 millions were unemployed.[2] On the assumption that under "full employment" 97 per cent of wage-earners are employed, the additional number of wage-earners to be brought into employment was 1·25 millions. On the assumption of constant returns (which seems well supported by the pre-war relation between variations of employment and output) the value of the additional net output of 1·25 million wage-earners in primary and secondary industries might be put at £375 millions.[3] We must also take into account, however, the consequential increase in the value of the output of "tertiary industry," i.e. in the distributive

---

[1] Cf. Clark, *National Income and Outlay*, Macmillan, 1937, p. 59.

[2] This figure was reached as follows. Of 13·7 million persons insured for unemployment under the general scheme, 1·8 millions were unemployed in 1938. Of the insured, about 2½ million persons were in non-manual occupations; and it was assumed that the general rate of unemployment was applicable to them. On the other hand, 3 million persons in manual occupations (1½ million men and 1½ million women) were in occupations outside the insurance scheme, such as agriculture, domestic service, etc. It was estimated that of these 3 millions, 200,000 were unemployed.

[3] On the basis of the 1935 Census of Production, but correcting for changes in wage rates, etc., net output per operative in 1938 can be put at £300.

trades and in services. The value added by distribution can b taken (on the average) as 50 per cent of the factory value, and sinc the increase in personal expenditure on consumption would hav been about half the increase in output (see below) the income earned in the distributive trades could be assumed to have increase by some £95 millions, while a further £30 millions can be added o account of the consequential increase in the income from pro fessional services,[1] etc. The net result is that full employment woul have increased the national output by £500 millions, or 11 pe cent, over the £4,675 millions actually reached, thus making i £5,175 millions.

The same result can also be reached by the following considera tions. As will be shown below, under pre-war circumstances, and i terms of constant wage-rates, 36 per cent of any increase in th national output went into wages, which means that the increase in the national output was 2·78 times the increase in the wages bi associated with a given rise in employment. Since the additiona employment of 1·25 million wage-earners would have added som £180 millions to the total wage payments,[2] it would have increased total income by £500 millions.

Incomes under Full Employment

15. We must next consider how the increase in the nationa output would have affected the different types of income. This i shown in Table 40. The average percentages of the different type of income relate to the actual income in 1938 and are taken from Table 39. The "marginal" percentages which show what woul have been the share of each type of income in the increase in the national income, were estimated on the basis of the pre-war relation between the variations in the national income, wages, salaries and rent, and of the pre-war proportion of marginal profits put to reserve. This estimate shows that while the share going into wage out of an increase in incomes is only slightly less than the share o wages in the whole income, the share going into salaries is little more than half the average, while the share going into rent is nil On the other hand, the share of profits and interest takes up 51

---

[1] Equivalent to a 5 per cent increase in services other than distributive services, and excluding the net output of dwellings and of services provided by the Government.

[2] Of the 1·25 millions, 1 million were adult men and 250,000 women or young men. The average weekly earnings of each category in 1938 have been obtained from the earnings inquiry of the Ministry of Labour. To obtain the annual wage bill, the weekly figures were multiplied by 48.

er cent of any increase in income (as compared with 29½ per cent
n average income) and since 45 per cent of this increase is put to
eserve the share of undistributed profits in marginal income becomes
3 per cent as against 7 per cent in average income. These differ-
nces between the average and marginal profits (and, in particular,
he high proportion of marginal profit going into undistributed
rofits) are chiefly responsible, as will be seen below, for the increase
n savings, following on an increase in incomes, being so much
arger than the proportion of savings in total income.

Table 40

SHARE OF DIFFERENT FACTORS IN THE NATIONAL INCOME

(*In Percentages of Total Income*)

	Average	Marginal
Rent	8	—
Distributed profits and interest ..	22½	28
Undistributed profits	7	23
Salaries	23½	13
Wages	39	36
Total..	100	100

Note.—Average percentages based on Table 39. *Marginal* percentages were obtained as
follows. Wages and home-produced national income, both deflated by an index of wage
rates, were correlated for the period 1924–38, on the basis of Bowley's estimates of the
National Income, corrected for various factors. Salaries, deflated by an index of salary
rates, were correlated with wages, deflated by an index of wage rates. Rents did not
fluctuate with employment. The share of undistributed profits in marginal profits is
based on Radice, *Savings in Great Britain*, page 71. There was no trend in the share of
wages during the period, but there was an upward trend in the share of rents and salaries.

The Level of Taxation

16. We must now consider the allocation of expenditures out of
the different types of income between taxation, savings and consumption. We shall first estimate the amounts taken in taxation from
the different incomes and then the allocation of income available
after taxation between savings and consumption.

The proportions of average and marginal incomes paid in direct
and indirect taxation in 1938 are shown in Table 41.

Applying these estimates to the distribution of incomes under full
employment (which is shown in Table 44, p. 359), it is possible to
estimate what the yield and the incidence of taxation would have

Table 41

TAXATION OF AVERAGE AND MARGINAL INCOMES IN 1938

(*In Percentages of Incomes*)

	Average Incomes			Marginal Incomes		
	Direct Taxes	Indirect Taxes	Total	Direct Taxes	Indirect Taxes	Total
Rent, interest and distributed profits	23	8	31	35	4	39
Undistributed profits	25	3	28	33	2	35
Salaries	4½	14½	19	10	10	20
Wages	—	18	18	2	14½	17
Average	11	12½	23½	19	8	27

Note.—The percentages are largely based on the estimates of the incidence of taxation in an unpublished thesis by T. Barna. Social insurance contributions have been included in indirect, and not direct, taxation, divided between salaries and wages. Taxes on undistributed profits include income tax at the standard rate, a proportionate share of stamp duties, N.D.C. and of indirect taxes on production in general (allocated to this item because they fall on investment goods bought out of undistributed profits). Taxes falling on the pay of H.M. Forces and on social incomes are not included in the figures. For the yield of different kinds of taxes, in the actual situation and under full employment, see Table 42 below.

been under full employment (assuming the 1938 rates of taxation in force) and how it would have compared with the yield and incidence of taxation in the actual situation. This is shown in Table 42.

Consumption and Savings

17. As regards the distribution of the expenditure between consumption and savings from *available* incomes (incomes remaining after taxation), the estimates shown in Table 43 were based on the following considerations. Total net savings (at factor cost) amounted to £440 millions in 1938.[1] This, however, excludes that part of the savings (amounting to £90 millions) which is offset by death duty, etc., payments. From the point of view of estimating the saving propensities of different classes, these have also to be taken into account and therefore the average percentages in Table 43 refer to the £530 millions *gross* savings, which were allocated between

[1] This is equal to the sum of the items private net investment at home, the balance of foreign payments, and Government expenditure out of loans, in Table 39, p. 350.

Table 42

ACTUAL AND FULL EMPLOYMENT TAXATION IN 1938

(At the rates of taxation in force in 1938)

	Actual Taxation						Taxation under full Employment					
	Direct Taxes		Indirect Taxes		Total		Direct Taxes		Indirect Taxes		Total	
	£Mn.	%	£Mn.	%	£Mn.	%	£Mn.	%	£Mn.	%	£Mn.	%
Rent, Distributed Profits and Interest	373	72	125	19½	498	43	418½	68	130½	19	549	42
Undistributed Profits	89	17	9	1½	98	8½	127	21½	11	1½	138	11
Salaries	50	10	160	25	210	18	56½	9	166½	24½	223	17
Wages	5	1	310	48	315	27	10	1½	336	50	346	27
Pay of H.M. Forces and Social Income	—	—	40	6	40	3½	—	—	40	5	40	3
Total	517	100	644	100	1,161	100	612	100	684	100	1,296	100

Note.—Social Insurance contributions included among indirect taxes.

Table 43

PROPORTION OF AVAILABLE INCOMES SAVED

(*In Percentages*)

	Average	Marginal
Rents, distributed profits and interest..	11	25
Undistributed profits	100	100
Salaries	9	15
Wages	6	10
Total Income	14	33

Note.—Average percentages were obtained by relating amounts saved to incomes received less taxation, but not deducting death duty payments, as the savings are gross of death duties. The large difference in the estimate of savings out of average and marginal total income is primarily due to the higher proportion of undistributed profits in marginal income, as shown in Table 40.

the different types of income as follows:—Savings out of undistributed profits (i.e. undistributed profits, less taxes)[1] amounted to £230 millions, leaving £300 millions savings out of personal incomes. The total savings of persons with incomes below £250 a year can be estimated at about £120–£140 millions,[2] thus leaving £160–£180 millions as the total savings of those with incomes over £250 a year. It was assumed that the savings of persons with incomes below £250 were divided between wage-earners, salary earners and the recipients of other incomes in proportion to the amount of wages and salaries and other incomes earned; while the savings of persons above £250 were divided between salary-earners and other incomes (i.e. the recipients of rents, distributed profits and interest) in proportion to the amount of salary income and other incomes in the latter category.[3] On these assumptions £300 millions personal gross savings were allocated as follows:—

[1] Undistributed profits were adjusted for stock valuation.

[2] Based on the method employed by Radice, *op. cit.* ch. vi, making certain adjustments.

[3] Total personal incomes below £250 a year amounted to £2,600 millions, of which £1,810 millions were wages, £520 millions salaries and £270 millions other incomes. Personal incomes above £250 a year amounted to £1,900 millions of which £580 millions were salaries and £1,320 other income. (These figures include interest on the National Debt, but not other transfers, i.e. unemployment benefits, etc., which are excluded on the supposition that no savings were made out of the latter.)

£ millions

Rents, interest and distributed profits ..	130
Salaries	80
Wages	90
	—
Total personal savings	300

These amounts were then applied to the incomes remaining after taxation in the respective categories and the results are as shown in Table 43. The estimate of the percentages of *marginal* income saved shown in the same table are based on the following considerations. The estimate of 33 per cent for savings out of total available income (which is the equivalent of 24 per cent of marginal income before deducting taxation) is based on the estimates of the "multiplier" before the war[1] which suggest that expenditure on consumption took up about one-half of an increase in income, while savings and taxation took up the other half. Since undistributed profits take up 23 per cent of marginal income, and therefore 63 per cent of marginal savings, only 37 per cent of marginal savings are made out of personal incomes. These were allocated among the three categories of wages, salaries and distributed profits as shown in Table 43. The percentage of savings out of marginal wages and salaries is supported by estimates based on the movements of working and middle-class savings.[2] The assumption that 25 per cent of the marginal income out of distributed profits is saved, is supported by the facts (i) that the typical profit income is larger than either the typical wage or salary income and it is reasonable to suppose that a higher proportion of any increase of income is saved, the higher the income; (ii) that individual incomes from profits are more unstable than individual wage or salary incomes and therefore a higher proportion of any increase of income tends to be saved.[3] While pre-war statistics tend to suggest that the total savings of the capitalists out of *personal* incomes are not much more than the payments of death duties, this is quite consistent with the marginal savings out of profits being relatively high.

[1] Clark, "The Determination of the Multiplier," *Economic Journal*, 1938, p. 435 *et seq.*; R. and W. M. Stone, "The Marginal Propensity to Consumer and the Multiplier," *Review of Economic Studies*, Vol. VI, p. 1.

[2] Radice, *op. cit.* p. 66.

[3] It should also be borne in mind that while the increase in the wage and salary bill is largely due to the increase in the number of persons earning wages and salaries, the increase in profit incomes implies an increase in income per income recipient.

Full Employment Income and Outlay

18. The assumption made in paragraphs 15–17 above makes it possible to estimate the distribution of private incomes and outlay under full employment and the effects of changes in the rates of taxation. It follows from these assumptions and from Tables 40–43 (*a*) that an increase (or decrease) in the national income by £100 millions, the rates of taxation remaining unchanged, will increase (or decrease) consumption by £49 millions, savings by £24 millions and tax payments by £27 millions; (*b*) that at full employment level of income, a proportionate change in all tax rates, increasing (or decreasing) revenue by £100 millions would decrease (or increase) consumption by £73 millions, and savings by £27 millions; (*c*) that a similar change in the rates of *direct* taxation (excluding social insurance contributions) would decrease (or increase) consumption by £60 millions, and savings by £40 millions; (*d*) that a similar change in the rates of *indirect* taxation and social insurance contributions would decrease (or increase) consumption by £84·5 millions, and savings by £15·5 millions.

The distribution of private income and outlay under full employment, under the assumption that the actual tax rates of 1938 are maintained unchanged, is shown in Table 44.[1] The distribution of the national expenditure under policies that would involve changes in the 1938 tax rates is shown in Table 46, p. 363.

Imports under Full Employment

19. A correlation analysis of the movements of imports and the national income in real terms shows that under the conditions of the 1930's the marginal propensity to import was 15 per cent— *i.e.* a £100 increase (or decrease) in the national income caused a £15 increase (or decrease) of imports. In 1938 visible and invisible imports exceeded visible and invisible exports plus the net income derived from foreign investments by £55 millions. This means that if the foreign demand for British exports is taken as given (irrespective of changes in the level of employment in Britain) the Balance of Payments under full employment would in the circumstances of 1938 have amounted to − £130 millions, since imports would have increased by £75 millions.

In the calculations in paragraphs 22–24 below, it is assumed that

[1] It will be noted that the figures in Table 44 refer to the national income looked at as the sum of private incomes, i.e., it is equal to the net national income shown in Table 39, plus £478 millions transfer incomes, less £44 millions government income from property.

Table 44

PRIVATE INCOMES AND OUTLAY IN 1938

(*£ millions*)

	Actual Incomes (a)	Hypothetical Incomes under Full Employment		Actual Outlay	Hypothetical Outlay under Full Employment
Rent, distributed profits and interest ..	1,595	1,735	Personal expenditure on consumption (d)	3,510	3,755
Undistributed profits(b)	330	445	Savings (d)	440	560
Salaries	1,100	1,165	Taxation (e)	1,160	1,295
Wages and social income (c)	2,085	2,265			
Total Income.. ..	5,110	5,610	Total Outlay ..	5,110	5,610

Notes.—(a) Based on Cmd. 6520, with an addition of £70 millions to undistributed profits and total income, on account of adjustment for inventory losses.

(b) Includes, in accordance with the White Paper definition, "the savings held in the business accounts of traders, farmers and other individuals," in addition to the undistributed profits of companies.

(c) Includes £278 millions cash payments on account of social insurance and allied services. It was assumed that this item is identical under full employment, which means since payments on account of unemployment benefit, at the ruling scales, would have been £70 millions less) that the scales of social benefit cash payments were raised by 83 per cent.

(d) At factor cost—i.e., after deduction of all indirect taxes.

(e) This is the total taxation falling on private incomes and differs from total tax receipts by the amount of taxation falling on public authorities.

British exports under a full employment policy would have been the same as in the actual case, while imports would have been allowed to increase freely with the increase in incomes. In paragraph 26, however, an estimate is made of the requirements of a full employment policy under the assumption that the adverse foreign balance is eliminated.

Private Investment Outlay

20. In 1938, net private investment at home[1] amounted to £420 millions which, together with £340 millions estimated depre-

---

[1] In accordance with the definition adopted in the White Paper, this item includes all investment which is financed privately or which forms part of the capital expenditure of the Post Office and the housing and trading services of local authorities.

ciation, made up the gross private investment of £760 millions
Gross and net private investment was made up of the various item
as shown in Table 45.

Table 45

GROSS AND NET PRIVATE INVESTMENT IN 1938

	Gross Investment	Net Investment
	£ millions	£ millions
A. Outlay on fixed capital:		
Public Utilities	140	60
Buildings	350	245
Plant and Machinery	120	20
Other fixed capital	65	10
B. Net Increase in Working Capital and Stocks	25	25
C. Costs incurred in the transfer of property and the investment of savings	60	60
Private investment at home	760	420

Note.—The estimates are those of Cmd. 6520, Table D, except that they are in term
of factor cost and not market prices (i.e. deducting the proportion of general indire
taxes falling on them); the investment in working capital, etc., is the value of th
change in stocks, and not the change in the value of stocks; and the item C has he
been included under private investment. *Public utilities* investment includes capit
expenditures of the railways and the L.P.T.B., dock and harbour, canal, water suppl
electricity and gas undertakings, and the Post Office. *Buildings* includes all house buildi
as well as other building, with the exception of those included in public expenditure
public utility investment. *Other fixed capital* includes merchant shipping and fishi
vessels, roads, goods vehicles and public service vehicles and passenger cars bought f
business purposes. The definition of "gross investment" here adopted differs from earli
estimates in that it excludes expenditure on repairs other than repairs to building
(This change of definition leaves, of course, the figure for net investment unaffected.)

In attempting to answer the question, "What would have bee
private investment under full employment?" we are confronted wit
the primary difficulty that the rate of investment varies not onl
with the level of output but to a large extent also with the change
in the level of output. Thus an *increase* in employment normall
involves a considerable increase both in investment in fixed capit
and investment in working capital. But the extra stimulus afforde
to both these types of investment is to a great extent temporary
as time goes on, and employment is kept at a constant level, priva
investment would gradually fall again to a level determined by th
rate of technical innovation and other long-run trends. It is impo
sible therefore to make any particular estimate for private inves
ment under full employment without specifying how long the fu
employment policy was supposed to have been in operation.

In the subsequent calculations, the pre-war private investment utlay on fixed capital and working capital under full employment as taken as £400 millions instead of the actual £360 millions in 938 (which means a total net investment—including the costs ncurred in the acquisition and transfer of property—of £460 nillions). This is not meant as an estimate of what private invest-nent would have been in 1938 if output had suddenly been raised o the full employment level, but rather as an indication—not un-easonable in view of the general pre-war experience—of what the .ormal annual private investment outlay could have been expected o be, under a continuous full employment policy.[1]

lternative Policies of Full Employment

21. We have now made all the assumptions necessary for exploring he quantitative implications of full employment policies.

As was shown in paragraphs 3–7, full employment could have •een secured in four different ways; these are specified by the)llowing "routes" :—

Route I: Assuming that the *rates of taxation* are maintained at the .ctual (1938) level and total Government expenditure is raised to he extent necessary to secure adequate total outlay;

Route II: Assuming that *revenue is kept equal to expenditure* (i.e. that here is no borrowing) while both are increased to whatever level is •ecessary to secure adequate total outlay;

Route III: Assuming that *total Government expenditure* is kept at the .ctual (1938) level and the total yield of taxation is reduced to the xtent necessary to secure an adequate expansion of private outlay;

Route IV: Assuming that the total Government expenditure on oods and services is kept at the actual (1938) level, and revenue ; kept equal to expenditure, but that the *structure of the tax system* i.e. the rates of the individual taxes and subsidies[2]) is so altered as o secure an adequate expansion of total outlay.

22. In the case of Route I and Route II, it will be assumed that he increased Government expenditure is similar in character to

[1] We shall also assume that the total outlay on private investment under full mployment will be the same, irrespective of whether full employment was •cured (primarily) by an increase in public outlay or an increase in private onsumption outlay. It may be that the actual rate of capital expenditure by rivate industry would have been different in the two cases; but it is quite im-ossible to say—without making detailed assumptions about the objects of Govern-•ent outlay—whether it would have been greater in the one case or in the other.

[2] Government expenditure on subsidies (either on wages or commodities) is •garded as negative indirect taxes.

investment expenditure, and hence does not react unfavourably on the proportion of income consumed by private individuals.[1] Route II and III admit several solutions, according to the nature of the taxes which are raised or lowered in the two cases respectively. The necessary expansion of taxation in the case of Route II will be all the less, the more the additional taxation is concentrated on those who save a high proportion of their marginal incomes; while the necessary deficit in the case of Route III will be all the smaller the more the reduction of taxes benefits those who consume a high proportion of their marginal incomes. This means that—since the bulk of the incidence of direct taxation is on the higher income groups, while the bulk of indirect taxes falls on the lower income classes—Route II would involve a smaller expansion of expenditure and Route III a smaller deficit, if in the former case only direct taxes were raised, and in the latter case only indirect taxes were lowered, than if all taxes were proportionately raised or lowered in each case. Accordingly two solutions are given for these two latter cases. "Route II" assumes a proportionate increase in all tax rates; "Route IIa" assumes that the increase is confined to direct taxation; "Route III" assumes that all taxes are reduced in the same proportion; "Route IIIa" that the tax reductions are confined to indirect taxation.

Similarly, in the case of Route IV, the actual solution depends on the precise nature of the changes of taxation. We shall assume that all direct taxes are proportionately raised and all indirect taxes are proportionately lowered, which makes Route IV a virtual combination of Routes IIa and IIIa.

23. It follows from the assumptions made above, particularly the estimates given in paragraph 18, that Route II would have implied an all-round increase in tax rates by 66 per cent; Route IIa an increase in the rates of direct taxation by 94 per cent; Route III an all-round reduction in the rates of taxation by 31 per cent; Route IIIa a reduction in the rates of indirect taxation by 50 per cent.

The full results for Routes I–III are set out in Table 46. It must be borne in mind, in interpreting the estimates given in this Table, that all the calculations assume that the marginal propensities shown

[1] This means that the objects of the increased Government expenditure are assumed to be either capital goods or goods and services for communal use, and not consumption goods destined for the individual use of private citizens. Subsidies on private consumption are treated as "transfer expenditures" and are covered by Route IV.

Table 46

ACTUAL AND FULL EMPLOYMENT OUTLAY IN 1938

(*£ millions*)

	Actual Outlay 1938	Hypothetical Full Employment Outlay, 1938				
		Route I	Route II	Route IIa	Route III	Route IIIa
Private Consumption Outlay ..	3,510	3,755	3,135	3,410	4,045	4,045
Private Home Investment Outlay	420	460	460	460	460	460
Balance of Payments Abroad ..	− 55	− 130	− 130	− 130	− 130	-- 130
Public Outlay out of Revenue ..	725	860	1,710	1,435	460	515
Public Outlay out of Loans ..	75	230	—	—	340	285
Total Outlay	4,675	5,175	5,175	5,175	5,175	5,175
Total Public Outlay	800	1,090	1,710	1,435	800	800
Increase in total public outlay as compared with actual amount	—	290	910	635	—	—

in Tables 40–43 above are constant over the relevant range; and that this assumption is all the more hazardous the more the hypothetical full employment situation diverges from the actual situation. There is greater uncertainty therefore concerning the estimates in Routes II and III—which involve more far-reaching changes in the amount of incomes available to the different classes—than is involved in the estimate for Route I. If, in particular, the marginal propensity to consume were found to be a diminishing function of available incomes and not a linear function, the estimates under Route II and IIa overstate the extent of the required increase in Government expenditure, while Routes III and IIIa understate the amount of deficits required.

24. In the case of Route IV, which is not included on Table 46, since its salient features could not be shown in terms of the categories here given,[1] full employment could not have been secured by redistributing the burden of taxation between direct and indirect taxes alone, since the total abolition of indirect taxes, and their replacement by additional direct taxes, would only have reduced full employment savings by £160 millions, and increased the total outlay on home-produced goods and services by £350 millions instead of the required

[1] In the case of Route IV, the various items shown on Table 46 are identical with those given for Route III, with the exception of the items of public outlay, which are identical with Route II.

£500 millions. Hence to have secured an adequate expansion o
outlay, the policy implied in Route IV would have required i
addition the granting of subsidies on consumption goods, to a
aggregate amount of some £250 millions. It would therefore hav
required an increase in the rates of direct taxation by 150 per cen
the total revenue from direct taxation (cf. Table 42), being raise
from £612 millions to £1,562 millions. In interpreting this resul
the limitation referred to in the previous paragraph should, of cours
be borne in mind; in case the proportions of marginal incomes save
are not constant, but diminishing, the scope of the necessary chang
in taxation would be smaller.

Full Employment and the Balance of Payments

25. The various solutions of the full employment policies give
above were all worked out on the assumption that the Governme
adopted a purely passive attitude as regards the reaction of th
higher outlay on the Balance of Payments. Hence, with the volun
of exports actually obtained in 1938, the full employment *adver*
balance would have amounted to £130 millions instead of the actu
figure of £55 millions.[1] As a long run policy, however, it woul
have been neither desirable nor even possible to maintain an adver
balance of that magnitude. To eliminate it, measures would hav
had to be taken either to increase exports, or if that proved impossibl
to cut imports by restricting purchases from abroad to those con
modities which are essential and for which it is not easy to fin
substitutes in home production. In the circumstances of 1938 (c
the assumption of constant terms of trade, i.e., a constant ratio o
export prices to import prices) and under full employment, th
would have meant either increasing exports by £120 million
i.e., by 25 per cent, or cutting imports by £140 millions or 15 p
cent[2] below their hypothetical full employment level or adoptir
some combination of both methods. Either of these two methods o
adjustment would have absorbed labour in Britain—though w
cannot, of course, be certain that they would have done so to th
same extent—and would thereby have made the required expansic

---

[1] It should, however, be borne in mind that the assumptions in para. 13 abo
tend to make the situation appear too unfavourable for (a) they make no allo
ance for the fact that 1938 was an exceptionally bad year for British export
(b) they do not allow for the effect of additional British imports on incom
abroad and hence on British exports.

[2] These estimates allow for the movements of the invisible exports (shippi
and insurance) consequent upon a change in the volume of visible exports a
imports.

ι Government expenditure (or alternatively, the required reduction
ι the rates of taxation) very much less.

Table 47

LTERNATIVE ROUTES TO FULL EMPLOYMENT IN 1938 WITH AN EVEN
BALANCE OF PAYMENTS

(*£ millions*)

	Route I*b*	Route II*b*	Route III*b*
·ivate Consumption Outlay	3,755	3,485	3,915
ivate Home Investment Outlay	460	460	460
·lance of Payments Abroad	—	—	—
·blic Outlay out of Revenue	860	1,230	640
·blic Outlay out of Loans..	100	—	160
·tal Outlay	5,175	5,175	5,175
·tal Public Outlay	960	1,230	800
crease in total public outlay as compared with actual amount	160	430	—

26. In Table 47 the three hypothetical solutions of the full employ-
·ent problem, given as Routes I, II and III, are worked out under
·e amended assumption that the adverse balance of payments is
·iminated by an expansion of £120 millions in the volume of
·xports. This gives three variations of the original routes which are
·escribed here as Routes I*b*, II*b*, and III*b* respectively.

It is seen that in Route I*b*—full employment secured by increased
·ublic spending, without changing the rates of taxation—the neces-
·ry expansion in public outlay is not £290 millions, but only
·160 millions, and the resulting deficit is only £100 millions, that is,
·nly slightly more than the actual deficit in 1938 with a *lower* level
·f public expenditure; while in II*b*—where full employment is
·cured without any deficit at all—the necessary expansion in public
·pending would amount to £430 millions, instead of £910 millions.
·Vhat these figures show is that if Britain had secured 25 per cent
·ore exports in 1938—which was the expansion necessary for
·curing the level of imports appropriate to full employment without
·n adverse balance—she would, in doing so, have absorbed about
·ne-half of her unused resources, and would thus have left less scope
·r other methods of utilising them.

27. Expanding exports would, of course, have been the more
·vourable method of eliminating the adverse balance; if Britain
·ad to be content with securing an even balance via a restriction

of imports, she could not have expected to enjoy the same real income from the use of her resources; nor would it have been certain that the expansion of home production consequent upon the restriction of imports would have given rise to the same increase in employment as an expansion of exports would have. To the extent that the commodities no longer imported would have been replaced by home-produced substitutes, the expansion in employment would have been greater; to the extent that the use of certain kinds of goods might have had to be foregone altogether, it might have been less. But in any case, the scope of the necessary Governmental measures under any of the alternative policies would have been much smaller than if the adverse balance of payments had not been eliminated.

III. THE FULL EMPLOYMENT PROBLEM AFTER THE WAR

28. The foregoing analysis referred to the full employment problem as it existed in Britain before the war. Its purpose, however, was not merely an historical one, but to provide the background for an analysis of the conditions of full employment in the post-war situation. It is, of course, quite impossible to make forecasts about the future except on the hypothetical postulate that in all matters where the nature of changes cannot be definitely foreseen and taken into account, the future is assumed to be a continuance of the past. The subsequent calculations should be interpreted in this light; they are not put forward as prophecies of future events but only as the joint outcome of the most reasonable hypotheses that can be made about post-war conditions in the light of present knowledge.

29. After the conclusion of hostilities there will be a period of transition and immediate reconstruction which, from the economic point of view, will have more affinities with the present war economy than with a peace economy. In order to examine the background of a post-war full employment policy it is best to ignore this transition period altogether, and to make forecasts of the relevant economic factors for a succeeding period, when the transition from a war-time to a peace-time economic structure will already have been largely accomplished—when the ordinary peace-time industries will have re-absorbed their labour, restored their pre-war output capacity and replenished their stocks. This does not mean, of course, that the period of reconstruction, as distinct from the period of transition, is assumed to have been completed. "Post-war reconstruction" is generally interpreted to mean the accomplishment of a large number

of things which go far beyond the restoration of the pre-war economic structure. If the present plans as regards post-war housing policy, agriculture, transport, etc., are even partially adopted, the reconstruction period will extend over a large number of years; and during this period the requirements of the reconstruction programme and the requirements of a stable full employment policy will have to be fitted in with each other.

30. It is impossible to foretell with any exactness how long the immediate transition period will last.[1] In the following calculations it is assumed that the war will come to an end somewhere in the middle of 1945, and that this transition period takes $2\frac{1}{2}$ years. The hypotheses therefore refer to "1948"—this being taken as the first normal post-war year. We shall attempt to make estimates—in an analogous manner to those given above for 1938—of the national income and its distribution under full employment conditions in 1948; of the level of Government expenditure, and of taxation, consumption and savings, under alternative hypotheses.

31. It will be assumed, for the purposes of this analysis, that the pre-war economic structure will, in broad outline, have been restored and that the pre-war economic relations will continue to operate, except in those particular cases where there are definite reasons for assuming a change. This means that as far as the distribution of income between profits, wages, etc., and the division of the outlay of the various income groups between consumption and savings are concerned, the estimates will be based on an extrapolation of pre-war trends, without taking into account the war-time shifts in those factors.[2] In the case of the ordinary expenditures of the Government, allowance will be made for the effects of the war and for other changes unconnected with the war (such as the expenditure on education) to which the Government is already committed. It will

---

[1] After the last war, 1924 was generally looked upon as the first "normal" peace year, i.e., five years after the conclusion of hostilities. But this was partly because the big post-war slump of 1921–22 was erroneously regarded as a phase of the transition period; and the position was further complicated by the period of large-scale currency disorders in Europe and the British policy of gradually returning to the gold standard at pre-war parities.

[2] The most important of these war-time shifts is, of course, in the proportions of income saved. The present enormous increase in the savings propensities of the public is due—apart from the patriotic appeal—to sheer inability to spend money owing to rationing and the complete disappearance of many objects of peace-time consumption. It is possible that the savings habits generated during the war will, to some extent, be retained afterwards (though this is not borne out by the experience of the last war). But it would be quite impossible to make an allowance for this factor.

be assumed that the Social Security Plan put forward in the Beveridge Report will have been adopted in full. In the case of foreign trade, it will be assumed that the terms of trade (the ratio of the prices of export goods to the prices of imported goods) will be the same as in 1938; but in the case of the income from foreign investment, allowance will be made for the war-time liquidation of assets owned abroad.

32. In one important respect the new setting of the problem calls for a change in procedure. Whatever justification there may have been for making a guess at the full employment level of private investment under the circumstances of 1938, it would clearly be idle to speculate on the corresponding magnitude of this item in the circumstances of 1948. For a considerable period after the war the demand for capital investment is likely to be considerably larger than that experienced in the 1930's. There will be the needs of the housing programme; the demand for new capital investment in industry, transport, agriculture, fed by a decade's accumulated backlog of technical invention and innovation; there will also be the need for capital expenditures arising out of Britain's participation in the reconstruction of Europe. In an unregulated economy—where the Government did not take positive steps to ensure that the total outlay of the community was adjusted to available man-power— the danger, for a number of years, might be more that of "inflationary gaps," with the consequent upward pressures on prices, than of "deflationary gaps," with large-scale unemployment.[1] If that proved to be the case, the Government might decide to limit private spending through the creation of budgetary surpluses (or the maintenance of rationing) and/or to limit the rate of private capital expenditures in accordance with a scale of national priorities. In a situation of this sort, the needs of public investment (whether that of the Central Government, of the local authorities or of public utilities) could not be treated as a "left-over," to be drawn on after the needs of private investment had been satisfied, but the Government would have to plan the allocation of the aggregate of resources available for investment purposes among investment of all kinds.

Hence in analysing the requirements of a full employment policy in 1948, we shall treat public and private investment together, and

---

[1] It may be objected that the big slump of 1921–22 points to a different conclusion. But after the last war, long-term capital investment (in housing and industry) did not get going until much later; the boom of 1919–20 was essentially a re-stocking boom, and the slump of 1921–22 signified that both the period of war expenditures and the period of post-war restocking had come to an end.

estimate the amount available for purposes of home investment of
all kinds, assuming either (*a*) that there is an even balance of payments (i.e. the amount of exports is sufficient to pay for all imports)
and that the level of taxation is just sufficient to cover the ordinary
expenditures of public authorities (i.e. that there is no surplus or
deficit on the current accounts of public authorities); or (*b*) that
the resources available for investment purposes are augmented by
heavier taxation (or other methods of restricting consumption), or
by an adverse balance of payments.

The National Income in 1948

33. We shall estimate the full employment level of the national
output in 1948 by assuming (*a*) that the working population will be
the same as in 1938; (*b*) that the average hours of work per week
will be the same as in 1938; (*c*) that the average unemployment
rate will be 3 per cent; (*d*) that the average real productivity per
man-hour will have risen, over the period 1938–48, by 13 per cent;
(*e*) that the Armed Forces of the Crown will be maintained at
double the strength of that of 1938, i.e. between 750,000–1,000,000
men; (*f*) that the real terms of international trade (the ratio of
export prices to import prices) will be the same as in 1938; (*g*) that
the income from foreign investment will have fallen to 40 per cent
of its 1938 amount; (*h*) that the average level of prices will be
stabilized at $33\frac{1}{3}$ per cent above the 1938 level.

The basic considerations behind the more critical of these assumptions are as follows:—

(*a*) The net change in working population will be the resultant
of the following factors: (i) the normal increase in the working
population, due to the change in numbers and age composition
which, in the absence of war, would have amounted to some 550,000;[1]
(ii) the war casualties (killed and permanently disabled) which are
put at 500,000;[2] (iii) the withdrawal of boys and girls from the
labour market, due to the raising of the school-leaving age to 16,
which implies a reduction of 850,000 juveniles (aged 14–15) at
work; (iv) the addition to the working population due to the increase
of the number of women in the labour market as a by-product of
the war. To obtain the net change in the working population, each
of these classes has to be weighed by its output per head, which

---

[1] Obtained by interpolation from the Registrar-General's forecast of population
(Actual increase 1928–38 was 1,700,000).

[2] War casualties (including civilians) killed and permanently disabled were
about 250,000 in the first four years of war.

may be assumed to be proportionate to the relative wages in 1938. Since the weekly wages of classes (i)–(iv) on the basis of Bowley's[1] and the Ministry of Labour's estimates were 50, 65, 13, and 32·5 shillings respectively, it would require an addition of 500,000 women under head (iv) to keep the aggregate working population unchanged. This last assumption is not unreasonable, in view of the fact that about 2½ million women were stated to have been drawn into industry and the Forces in the course of the present war; while after the last war, the number of women remaining in industry (up to the time of the slump of 1921, at any rate) was stated to have been about 30–40 per cent of those additionally employed in the course of that war.

(d) As regards the average productivity per man-hour, the estimate of a 13 per cent increase was arrived at as a result of averaging between (i) the actual rate of increase in productivity per man-hour over the period 1914–24; (ii) the rate of increase of productivity between 1924–38. The increase in hourly productivity, for the national output as a whole (including distribution and services) in the ten-year period covering the last war seems to have been around 10 per cent,[2] while in the inter-war period it was at the rate of 1·5 per cent per annum (which implies a rise of 16 per cent over a ten-year interval). It appears fairly certain (from various statements made by responsible authorities) that the increase in productive techniques in the course of the present war is much more substantial than that of the last war; and it is by no means improbable that when peace returns the rise in productivity will be found to be even greater than what would have resulted from the mere continuation of pre-war trends.[3] The estimate of a 13 per cent increase over the period should therefore be regarded as the minimum probable, rather than the most likely, figure of the rise in productivity.

(e) Our assumption is that by 1948 at any rate the war will have been concluded with Japan as well as Germany. At the same time it would be idle to expect that the immediate post-war situation would enable the strength of the Armed Forces to be reduced to

[1] *Studies in the National Income*, p. 67.

[2] Though the statistical estimates covering this period are not so extensive as for later dates, the estimate of a 10 per cent increase in hourly productivity is supported both by Rowe's production index, divided by an index of employment and of hours, and of Bowley and Stamp's estimate (*The National Income*, 1924, p. 58) that home produced real income per head in 1924 was about the same as in 1914, while the length of working hours was about 10 per cent less. Cf. also Clark, *National Income and Outlay*, p. 267.

[3] On the increase in productivity see also para. 56 below.

the pre-war level; the needs of military occupations, etc., will probably require the maintenance of a much larger number of effectives. In 1938, the complements of the Army, Navy and Air Force amounted to 400–450,000 men. For 1948, it will therefore be assumed to amount to (roughly) double that number, say between 750,000–1,000,000 men. This means, that (since the definition of the aggregate working population, which was assumed to be unchanged, included the Armed Forces) the number available in industry, etc., will be about 400,000–500,000 less. It means also that the real increase in home-produced output over the 1938 full employment level will amount to, not 13, but only 11 per cent (since the value of the output per head in the Armed Forces—represented by their pay and maintenance—is less than the output per head in industry).

(f) The assumption of an unchanged price of imports in terms of exports implies (roughly) that the world price level of foodstuffs and raw materials in terms of manufactured goods will be the same in 1948 as it was in the late 1930's. The experience of the aftermath of the last war was that of a considerable improvement in the terms of trade, so that Britain obtained the same amount of imports with about 20 per cent fewer exports than before. There is no reason to suppose that this favourable experience will be repeated, but neither is there any definite reason for assuming the contrary. The policies of control adopted in the course of the present war have prevented the spectacular rise in the prices of primary products which was such a prominent feature of the last World War, and it may be assumed that the same policies will continue in force during the period of immediate post-war scarcities. There is no sign at present of the world entering a more prolonged period of scarcities in foodstuffs and raw materials; the forces of technical improvement which made for the surpluses of the last two (pre-war) decades do not appear to be in any way exhausted.

It is possible, of course, that in the effort to obtain sufficient exports to pay for imports, Britain may deliberately set out to lower the prices of her exports of manufactures, not only in terms of the foodstuffs and raw materials which she imports, but also relatively to the prices of manufactured goods of other countries. It is not possible to take account of this contingency in calculating the national income, but the nature of the balance of payments problem will be examined in paragraph 43 below.

(g) In the five years 1939–43 the total amount of disinvestment abroad (through the loss of gold and foreign exchange, the sale of foreign assets and the accumulation of debt) amounted to £3,073 millions.[1] Since in the years 1942 and 1943 disinvestment proceeded at an approximately constant rate of £650 millions per annum, the aggregate of disinvestment, up to the middle of 1945, may be put at £4,100 millions, the loss of income from which may be estimated as follows :—[2]

	£ millions	
	Amount	Loss of Annual Income
Loss of gold and foreign exchange ..	700	—
Sale of securities	900	36·0
Sterling balances of foreign countries held in London and other loans ..	2,500	62·5
Total	4,100	98·5

On the other side, allowance must be made for the fact that the devaluation of sterling and the higher earnings of companies operating abroad (due to higher prices, etc.) would have raised the income from foreign investment, on the pre-war investments, considerably above the £200 millions obtained in 1938. If we allow for an increase of only some £10 millions on account of the last factor, the post-war income from foreign investments may be put at £110 millions at post-war prices or £80 millions at pre-war prices.

(*h*) The assumption made in the Beveridge Report on Social Services was that the average level of prices after the war will be 25 per cent above pre-war. The latest official estimates suggest, however,[3] that unless there is a reduction in the general level of money wages (which is not likely) the allowance of 25 per cent is likely to prove insufficient, and it is safer to reckon on post-war prices being 33⅓ per cent above 1938. This assumption was therefore preferred and in the subsequent calculations the estimates for

[1] Cf. Cmd. 6520 Table I, item 13.

[2] For sources of estimate cf. *Economic Journal*, June-September, 1943, pp. 261–62. It was assumed that since the securities sold consisted to a large extent of Indian, Canadian, and other Government bonds of a low yield, the average loss of income on securities can be put at 4 per cent. The loss of income due to the accumulation of sterling balances assumes that these balances are converted into long-term obligations with a yield of 2·5 per cent.

[3] Cf. Cmd. 6520, pp. 7–8.

Government expenditure, and in particular the scales of benefit of the Social Security Plan, were adjusted accordingly.

The net result of these assumptions is that the net national output (including foreign income) in 1948 is estimated to be £7,450 millions, in terms of post-war prices, or £5,600 millions in terms of 1938 prices. This allows for a substantial reduction in the national money income below its current war-time level (the official estimate for 1943 being £8,172 millions) a difference to be explained by a number of factors, among which the larger occupied population and the longer hours worked in war-time are the most important. The comparison between the pre-war and the post-war national income is shown in Table 48.

Table 48

CONSTITUENTS OF THE NATIONAL OUTPUT IN 1938 AND 1948

(£ *millions*)

	1938 (Actual)	1938 (Full Employment)	1948 (Full Employment) at 1938 Prices	1948 (Full Employment) at 1948 Prices
Home-produced output excluding the Forces	4,395	4,895	5,360	7,110
Pay and allowances of H.M. Forces	80	80	160	230
Net Income from Foreign Investments	200	200	80	110
Net National Income	4,675	5,175	5,600	7,450

Note.—The average prices of home-produced output are assumed to be 33 per cent higher in 1948. In calculating the pay and allowances of H.M. Forces at 1948 prices, cash pay was assumed to rise at the same rate as the average level of wages (see below) and payments in kind in proportion to output prices.

34. The division of the net national income between the different types of incomes, shown in Table 49 (p. 374), is based on the following additional considerations. It was assumed that the share of wages in wage-containing output will be the same in 1948 as it would have been under full employment in 1938. In other words, allowance was made for the change in the share of wages consequent upon full employment, but it was assumed—in accordance with the pre-war experience[1]—that the change in productivity leaves this factor unaffected. This implied that, taking into account the rise in output prices and the increase in productivity, the average level of wage

[1] Cf. note to Table 40 above.

rates was 54 per cent above that of 1938.[1] In calculating the total wage bill, allowance was made for the transfer of men (as compared with 1938) to the Forces. In the case of salaries, it was assumed that the average level of salaries increases by 33 per cent, i.e. in the same ratio as prices, while the number of salary earners will be the same as under full employment in 1938. In the case of rents, the assumption was that there will be one million additional houses by

Table 49

NET NATIONAL INCOME IN 1938 AND 1948

(£ millions, at current prices)

	1938 (Actual)	1938 (Full Employment)	1948 (Full Employment)
Rents	380	380	450
Profits and Interest	1,385	1,640	2,400
Salaries	1,100	1,165	1,550
Wages	1,730	1,910	2,820
Pay of H.M. Forces	80	80	230
Net National Income	4,675	5,175	7,450

1948 and that the average level of rents will be 10 per cent above 1938, on the presumption that the Rent Restriction Acts continue in force, while agricultural and other rents not subject to restriction rise with the increase in the price level. The amount of profits and interest was then obtained as a residue; it implies an increase (in money terms) of 57 per cent in home-produced profits and interest as compared with the 1938 full employment estimate.

Private Incomes in 1948

35. To obtain the amount and the distribution of private incomes (as shown for 1938 in Table 44, p. 359) the figures in Table 49 must be adjusted for "transfer incomes" (consisting of National Debt interest, social security cash payments and war pensions) and for Government income from property, and an estimate must be made of the amount of undistributed profits.

We shall assume Government income from property to be

[1] The average increase in wage rates, up to the end of 1943, was 39 per cent. Our assumption of a 54 per cent increase up to 1948 implies that the average level of wage rates rises at about 2 per cent per annum over the next five years.

£70 millions instead of the pre-war £44 millions.[1] For National Debt interest paid to private individuals and corporations (including accrued interest on National Savings Certificates, but excluding that part of the nominal interest burden which represents payments to public funds[2]) we allow £500 millions. This item was £200 millions in 1938 and £340 millions in 1943, having risen at a rate of about £50 millions per annum during 1942 and 1943. The assumption of £500 millions allows therefore for the continuation of borrowing on the present scale up to the end of 1945; it also allows for the conversion of £2,500 millions floating debt into long-term debt bearing 2·5 per cent interest after the war.[3] Social security cash payments—assuming that the Beveridge Plan is adopted in full, allowing for an upward adjustment of benefit rates owing to the assumption of a 33⅓ rise in the price level, and making a number of other adjustments, set out in note to Table 53, p. 378—will amount to £470 millions, while war pensions are put at £100 millions, which allows for some £70 millions for the pensions arising out of the casualties of the present war. The resulting comparison of transfer incomes in 1938 and 1948 is shown in Table 50.

Table 50

TRANSFER INCOMES IN 1938 AND 1948

(£ *millions*)

	1938	1948
National Debt Interest	200	500
Social Income:—		
Social Security cash payments ..	238	470
War Pensions	40	100
Transfer Incomes	478	1,070

[1] For 1943, this item was officially estimated at £97 millions, but some of the revenues under this head (such as the receipts under the Railway Agreement) are temporary in character.

[2] But without deducting National Debt interest paid to foreigners, because this has already been deducted in calculating the net national income.

[3] Account must also be taken of the repayments on account of post-war credits on income tax (say £600 millions), the repayment of 20 per cent of E.P.T. less income tax (say £250 millions) and the post-war payments under the War Damage Acts. There are, on the other hand, the accumulated tax accruals (which will amount to at least £1,500 millions by the end of the war) to cover these items.

36. In making the estimate for undistributed profits it was assumed—in an analogous manner to the assumptions about consumption and savings out of personal incomes, explained in paragraph 41 below—that over longer periods the share of undistributed profits in total profits varies not so much with the amount of profits, but with the level of unemployment. The high proportion of any increase in profits which is normally put to reserves is largely due to the policies of dividend stabilization followed by businesses; as time goes on, and profits increase, the standard around which businesses stabilize their dividends is also raised. Hence it seemed more reasonable to assume that the proportion of undistributed profits in home produced profits and interest will be no higher in 1948 than it would have been at the full employment income of 1938.

Table 51

PRIVATE INCOMES UNDER FULL EMPLOYMENT, 1938 AND 1948

(*£ millions*)

	1938	(1938)	1948
Rent, distributed profits and interest	1,735	(2,315)	2,640
Undistributed profits	445	(595)	640
Salaries	1,165	(1,550)	1,550
Wages and pay, etc., of H.M. Forces	1,990	(2,650)	3,050
Social Income	275	(365)	570
Total Private Income	5,610	(7,475)	8,450

Note.—For the sake of comparison, the middle column was inserted to show what the 1938 incomes would have been at the 1948 level of money values. Thus the difference between the third and the first columns shows the change in money income, and that between the third and the second columns the change in real income, between the hypothetical full employment earnings at the two dates.

Public Expenditure and Taxation

37. In estimating the post-war budgets of public authorities we shall assume the following principles: (i) that all ordinary expenditures will be financed out of taxation, but not capital expenditures which will be excluded from the ordinary budgets (It is estimated that in 1938 capital expenditures included in the ordinary budgets of the Central Government and local authorities amounted to £40 millions, of which £20 millions were spent on new road construction) ; (ii) that all services provided by public authorities before the war will be maintained (and in the case of defence expanded)

and, in addition, the services proposed in the Report on Social Insurance and Allied Services[1] and the Education Bill[2] will be provided in full, and a further allowance will be made for other similar contingencies; (iii) that all social security services will be consolidated in a Social Security Budget, which will be financed by insured persons, employers and public funds in the proportions recommended by the Social Insurance Report, but that the whole burden falling on public funds will be borne by the Central Government, thus relieving the local authorities from the finance of social security services altogether; (iv) that the poundage of local rates will be maintained at the 1938 level, and that the Central Government contribution will be the amount necessary to balance the local authorities' budgets, on this principle; (v) that the taxation

Table 52

CONSOLIDATED BUDGETS OF LOCAL AUTHORITIES IN 1938 AND 1948

(£ *millions*)

1938		1948	
Revenue	Expenditure	Revenue	Expenditure
Rates 211	Social Security Services .. 68	Rates .. 250	Ordinary Expenditure .. 415
Income from property .. 26	Other ordinary expenditures 311	Income from property .. 40	
Contribution of Central Government 169	Capital Expenditure .. 20	Contribution of Central Government 125	
	Total Expenditure .. 399 Surplus .. 7		
Total Revenue 406	Total Expenditure and Surplus .. 406	Total Revenue 415	Total Expenditure .. 415

Note.—For 1938, the figures are those of Cmd. 6520 (Table iv, items 83, 87, 115, 95) except for the division of local authorities' expenditure among the three categories of social security services (which consist of services included in the Social Security Budgets, i.e. health services and public assistance cash payments), other ordinary expenditures and capital expenditure which is derived from other sources. For 1948, it is assumed that only the second category (ordinary expenditures other than health and public assistance) is financed locally out of revenue, and that the cost of these is increased by 33 per cent as compared with 1938. The revenue from the 1938 poundage of rates in 1948 is based on the estimates of rent given in Table 49.

[1] Cmd. 6404, 1942. [2] Cmd. 6458, 1943.

of the Central Government will be such as to balance the Central Government budget.[1] The estimated budgets for 1948 (together with the actual budgets of 1938) are shown in Tables 52–54 and the basis of the estimates of individual items is explained in the notes attached to the tables. Table 55 brings the accounts of all public authorities together and shows the amount of Central Government tax revenue that will be necessary to balance the accounts of public authorities.

Table 53

SOCIAL SECURITY BUDGET IN 1938 AND 1948

(£ *millions*)

1938		1948	
Revenue	Expenditure	Revenue	Expenditure
Contributions:—	Civil Pensions (e) .. 91	Contributions:—	Social Insurance .. 315
Insured Persons (a) 55	Unemployment Payments (f) 90	Insured Persons (l) .. 176	National Assistance .. 47
Employers (b) 67	Public Assistance (g) .. 23	Employers (l) 124	Children's Allowances .. 107
Local Authorities (c) .. 68	Health Payments (h) .. 34	Central Government (m) .. 355	Cost of Administration of above .. 26
Central Government (d) .. 152	Workmen's Compensation 13		Health Services.. .. 160
	Cost of Administration (i) 20		
	Health Services (j) .. 49		
	Total Expenditure 320		
	Surplus (k) .. 22		
Total Revenue 342	Total Expenditure and Surplus .. 342	Total Revenue 655	Total Expenditure .. 655

Note.—The Budget for 1948 is on the basis of the estimated budget for 1945, given in Cmd. 6404, p. 209, adjusted for the following factors: (i) the cost of social insurance was raised by £20 millions, owing to the higher cost of old age pensions in 1948 (as compared with 1945) in accordance with the scheme; (ii) the estimates for the cost of the health services revised in accordance with the estimate given in Cmd. 6502; (iii) owing to the assumption of 3 per cent unemployment, the cost of social insurance was reduced by £73 millions (i.e. two-thirds of the cost of unemployment benefits), and the cost of children's allowances (on first children) by £10 millions; (iv) all items were increased

---

[1] On the question of sinking funds, see para. 48 below.

Table 53 (continued)

by 6⅝ per cent owing to the assumption of a 33 per cent (instead of 25 per cent) rise in the price level. The contributions proposed in Cmd. 6404 were reduced to balance the budget, allocating to the Exchequer one-third of the saving in the cost of unemployment and the whole saving on children's allowances. The corresponding Budget for 1938 was brought together for purposes of comparison from published sources, itemized below.

(*a*) Cmd. 6520, Table IV, item 78.

(*b*) Ibid., item 82, plus £13 millions estimated expenditure on workmen's compensation.

(*c*) Includes payments of local authorities on public assistance cash payments and part of health services. See also note (*i*) below. Identical with similar item in Table 52.

(*d*) Residue. Includes £63 millions Exchequer contribution to social insurance. (Identical with item (*c*) in Table 54).

(*e*) Pensions to widows and orphans, contributory and non-contributory old age pensions. Cmd. 6520, Table II, item 22, *less* war pensions.

(*f*) Unemployment insurance benefits and allowances. Cmd. 6520, Table II, item 23 *less* public assistance.

(*g*) Cmd. 6520, Table IV, item 107.

(*h*) Ibid., Table II, item 24.

(*i*) Cmd. 6404, p. 204.

(*j*) Cmd. 6502, Appendix E. Of this £4 millions was expenditure by the Central Government, and £45 millions by local authorities.

(*k*) The surplus of unemployment, health and pensions insurance funds. Cmd. 6520, Table IV, item 90.

(*l*) The contributions were reduced, as compared with the proposals in Cmd. 6404, in order to balance the budget under the assumptions stated above. After estimating the Exchequer contribution as stated in note (*m*) below, this implied a reduction in the *total* revenue from contributions of 10 per cent and a reduction in the *per capita* rates of contributions by 16 per cent (owing to the increase in the numbers of insured, as a result of full employment). Hence, in spite of the higher rates of cash benefits assumed, the required rates of contributions per adult man are 3s. 7d. for insured persons and 2s. 9d. for employers (as compared with 4s. 3d. and 3s. 3d. respectively, proposed in Cmd. 6404).

(*m*) The Exchequer contribution under the Beveridge Plan (including interest on insurance funds) was estimated at £366 millions in 1945. (Cmd. 6404, p. 209.) Since, of the adjustments stated above, (i) and (ii) offset each other, (iii) implies a reduction of £34 millions, and (iv) an addition of £23 millions, the net result is £355 millions.

38. Tables 52–55 show that after making full allowance for the additional commitments of the Government and for the higher expenditure due to the rise in prices, and making an allowance for unforeseen contingencies, the Central Government will have to raise £1,655 millions in taxation to balance the budgets of public authorities as a whole. To find out the rates of taxation that will be necessary to obtain this revenue we shall first of all estimate what the yield of the 1938 rates of taxation would be at the full employment national income of 1948. We shall assume the same taxes in force as in 1938[1] and the same *ad valorem* tax rates—which means

[1] I.e., war-time taxes other than N.D.C.—which was already in force in 1938—are not taken into account.

Table 54

CENTRAL GOVERNMENT EXPENDITURE IN 1938 AND 1948

(£ millions)

	1938	1948
Interest on the National Debt (a)	200	500
Other Consolidated Fund expenditure ..	16	20
Defence Services (b)	379	480
Civil Votes:—		
Social Security (c) 152		355
War Pensions (d) 40		100
Grants to local authorities (e) 169		125
Other Civil Votes (f) 23		50
Other post-war contingencies (g).. .. —		40
	384	670
Cost of tax collection	14	15
Capital expenditures, included in Civil Votes in 1938 (h)	20	—
Total Expenditure	1,013	1,685

Notes.—(a) For bases of estimate, see paragraph 33 (g) above. Interest paid to public funds is excluded from this item, but included in social security payments.

(b) For 1938, this item includes issues under the Defence Loans on rearmament as well as expenditures on the preparation for war (such as A.R.P.) usually included under the Civil Votes. The 1938 figure is not representative of the pre-war rate of expenditure on defence, which amounted to only £100–£120 millions before rearmament began.

For 1948, the defence expenditure was based on the assumptions stated in paragraph 33 (c) above. The estimate of £480 millions was reached as follows. Pay and maintenance of the Forces, £230 millions (see Table 49). Expenditure on armaments and auxiliary materials, £250 millions. The latter item is more than twice the corresponding normal pre-war rate of expenditure, after allowing for a 33 per cent rise in prices.

(c) See notes (d) and (m) to Table 53.

(d) See paragraph 35 above.

(e) See corresponding items in Table 52.

(f) Includes cost of civil administration, justice, etc. For 1948, it includes an additional £20 millions on account of the new Education Bill, in addition to the rise in the cost of education due to the 33 per cent rise in prices. See Cmd. 6458, Appendix.

(g) This item represents an allowance for unforeseen commitments, other than expenditure on capital account.

(h) See paragraph 37 above.

that *specific* tax rates are deemed to have been adjusted for the rise in the general price level, and all allowances in direct taxation (i.e. the various income tax allowances, the surtax limits, etc.) to have been raised in the same proportion, so that the proportion paid in taxation out of any given real income is the same.

Table 55

THE CONSOLIDATED ACCOUNT OF PUBLIC AUTHORITIES IN 1938 AND 1948

(£ millions)

Revenue	1938	1948
Taxation:—		
Central Government	888	(1,655)
Social Security	122	300
Local Authorities	211	250
Total Taxation	1,221	2,205
Income from property	44	70
Total Revenue	1,265	2,275
Deficit	78	—
Total Revenue and Deficit	**1,343**	**2,275**

Expenditure	1938	1948
Central Government	1,013	1,685
Social Security	320	655
Local Authorities	399	415
Gross Total Expenditure	1,732	2,755
Less Transfers from—		
Central Government to Social Security	− 152	− 355
Central Government to Local Authorities	− 169	− 125
Local Authorities to Social Security	− 68	—
Total Transfers	− 389	− 480
Net Total Expenditure	**1,343**	**2,275**

Note.—For the individual items except Central Government taxation in 1938, see Cmd. 6520, items 33, 40, 77, 81. For Central Government taxation see Tables 52–54. Central Government taxation in 1948 is derived as a residue being the amount necessary to balance the total budget of public authorities. The difference between the £78 millions deficit in 1938 shown in this table and the £75 millions shown in Table 39 is due to the fact that in Table 39 items are shown at factor cost, while in the present table they are at market prices. The difference between the total taxation of £1,161 millions in 1938 shown in Table 42 and the £1,221 millions shown in the present table is due to (i) general indirect taxes falling on the Government, £32 millions; (ii) subsidies, £15 millions; (iii) workmen's compensation—which was added to public expenditure in Table 53 for purposes of comparability of social security expenditure—£13 millions.

Table 56

YIELD OF CENTRAL GOVERNMENT TAXATION, 1938 AND 1948

(*At the Rates of Taxation in Force in* 1938)

(*£ millions*)

	1938 (Actual)	1938 (Full Employment)	1938 (Full Employment, 1948 prices)	1948
	(1)	(2)	(3)	(4)
Income Tax	333	398	529	620
Surtax	69	83	110	140
N.D.C.	25	36	48	50
Death duties, and stamp duties on the transfer of property	90	95	126	140
Total Direct Taxes	517	612	813	950
Taxes on alcohol, tobacco, matches and entertainment	204	219	291	340
Other specific indirect taxes	94	100	133	150
General indirect taxes	73	81	108	120
Total Indirect Taxes	371	400	532	610
Total Taxation	888	1,012	1,345	1,560
Central Government Income from property ..	18	18	24	30
Total Revenue	906	1,030	1,369	1,590
Total Expenditure (see Table 54)	1,013	—	—	1,685
Deficit	107	—	—	95
Deficit as percentage of expenditure	**10**	—	—	**6**

Note.—The figures in column (1) based on Cmd. 6520 and other official sources. As regards column (2) the general principle was explained above; the most important individual estimates were that the marginal rate of income tax on *distributed* profits was 20 per cent and of surtax 10 per cent, and that the average rate of N.D.C. was 4½ per cent of assessed profits. It was assumed further, that there is no increase (consequent on full employment) in death duty receipts, but stamp duty receipts increase owing to the higher turnover of shares and other capital assets; the yield of specific indirect taxes was related to the estimated change in their consumption; the yield of general indirect taxes to the change in consumption and investment. As regards the adjustment from column (3) to column (4), the increase in incomes shown in Table 51, between the second and the third columns of that Table, was assumed to bear income and surtax at the marginal rates given above. Death duties, etc., allow for the expansion of the National Debt. The volume of alcohol and tobacco consumption and entertainments were assumed to be 25 per cent above the *actual* 1938 level. For other indirect taxes, the assumptions were the same as those stated for column (2) above.

This estimate is given in Table 56. The first column in Table 56 shows the actual yield of the different taxes in 1938. The second column shows what the same taxes would have yielded under full employment in 1938; this estimate is based on the same assumptions as were employed in making the estimate in Table 42, p. 355. The change in the yield of taxes due to the difference in incomes between the full employment income of 1938 and that of 1948 is shown in the third and fourth columns. The third column shows the change in tax yields due to the change in money values; in accordance with our assumption, this implied an increase of 33 per cent in the yield of each kind of tax. The fourth column adjusts these figures for that part of the change in tax yields which is due to the change in the real income of each income category, between 1938 and 1948; here the additional taxes payable by each income group were calculated separately, on the assumption that the proportion of marginal income paid in taxation is the same as that assumed for the purposes of the second column, but making certain allowances for the trend in consumption habits.

39. The result of this analysis is that the combined effect of the change in money values, of higher productivity and of full employment is that the tax system of 1938 would yield £1,560 millions in 1948 (instead of the actual £888 millions in 1938) and thus would fall short of the required amount by only £95 millions or 6 per cent. Thus, in spite of the considerably higher post-war expenditure, the 1938 tax system would be consistent with a *smaller* deficit in 1948 than it was in the actual situation in 1938. In order to eliminate the deficit, the average rates of taxes would have to be raised by 6 per cent—which means an income tax of 5s. 10d. (instead of 5s. 6d.) in the £, if all taxes were raised proportionately.[1]

40. We are now in a position to estimate the total tax burden falling on private incomes by adding together the taxes raised by all public authorities and by deducting subsidies and the general indirect taxes falling on goods and services purchased by public authorities. This is given in Table 57 and shows that the proportion of private incomes paid in taxation (including the higher social insurance contributions under the Social Security Plan) will be 25 per cent, instead of the pre-war 23 per cent. The distribution of this tax burden between the different categories of

[1] It should be borne in mind that in this estimate of a standard rate of 5s. 10d. income tax, it was also assumed that the pre-war income tax allowances were fully restored not merely in money but in real terms, i.e., the tax exemption limit was raised to £165, the allowance for married persons to £240, etc.

Table 57

TAXATION OF PRIVATE INCOMES, 1938 AND 1948

(*£ millions*)

	1938 (Actual)	1938 (Full Employment)	1948
I. Direct Taxes:—			
Central Government	517	612	950
Social Security Funds	55	60	176
Total	572	672	1,126
II. Indirect Taxes:—			
A. Specific Indirect Taxes:—			
Central Government	298	319	490
Local Authorities	141	141	170
Less Subsidies	− 15	− 15	− 20
Net Total	424	445	640
B. General Indirect Taxes:—			
Central Government	73	81	120
Local Authorities	70	70	80
Social Security Funds	54	60	124
Less Taxes falling on Public Authorities	− 32	− 32	− 50
Net Total	165	179	274
III. Increase in Central Government Taxation to cover prospective deficit	..	..	95
Total Taxes on Private Incomes	1,161	1,296	2,135
Private Incomes	5,110	5,610	8,450
Taxes as percentage of private incomes	**23**	**23**	**25**

Note.—The derivation of individual items is explained in previous tables, except the yield of social security taxes between the first and the second columns which is in proportion to the rise in employment; the revenue from local rates in the first and the second column is assumed to be the same, in accordance with the assumed behaviour of rents given in Table 40 (while their expansion between the second and the third column is as explained in Table 52). Taxes falling on public authorities for 1938 is derived from Cmd. 6520 (being the difference between item 16 in Table II and item (4) in Table F). For 1948 this item was adjusted to the rise in prices and the expansion of public outlay on goods and services.

income is shown in Table 58 on the assumption that *all* Central Government tax rates were raised by 6 per cent (as compared with 1938).

Table 58

INCIDENCE OF THE BURDEN OF TAXATION, 1948

	Direct Taxes		Indirect Taxes		All Taxes	
	£Mn.	%	£Mn.	%	£Mn.	%
Rent, distributed profits and interest	700	69	200	18	900	42
Undistributed profits	195	19½	15	1	210	10
Salaries	85	8½	250	22	335	16
Wages and Social Income ..	30	3	660	59	690	32
Total	1,010	100	1,125	100	2,135	100

Note.—For the corresponding estimate for 1938, and 1938 full employment, see Table 42, and for the methods used see notes to Tables 41, 42, 56 and 57. Social insurance contributions are here included in indirect taxation, as in Table 42. It is assumed that the 1938 level of Central Government taxes would be raised by 6 per cent, local rates remain at their 1938 level and social insurance contributions will be as given in note (*l*) to Table 53.

Consumption and Savings

41. We next have to estimate the distribution of available incomes between consumption and savings. The available evidence points to the conclusion that with the long run rise in incomes, consumption rises more or less proportionately;[1] the disproportionate rise in savings following upon an increase in incomes—which was shown in Table 43, p. 356—is a typically short-run phenomenon. In estimating post-war savings it would be erroneous therefore to apply the same assumptions for the change in incomes over the ten-year interval 1938–48, as were applied for the change from the actual to full employment income in 1938.

The most reasonable hypothesis for estimating savings out of available incomes in 1948 appeared to be to assume that for that part of the rise in real income which is due to long-run factors (i.e. the rise in productivity) savings rise in the same proportion as real income (i.e. in the proportions shown in the "average" column in Table 43); while for that part which is due to the elimination of unemployment, savings increase in a higher proportion (i.e. in the proportions shown in the "marginal" column in Table 43). This assumption implies that in the long run the proportion of

[1] Cf. Clark, *National Income and Outlay*, ch. viii.

income saved varies, not with the amount of real income, but with the level of employment.[1]

42. On this assumption, and by taking the distribution of private incomes and taxation as shown in Table 51 and Table 58 above, gross savings come to £905 millions, and net savings (i.e. after deducting death duty, etc., payments) to £765 millions, both calculated at post-war factor cost of production. From the same assumption it follows that consumption in 1948 would amount to £5,550 millions at post-war factor cost, or £4,170 millions at pre-war factor cost, which implies an increase in real consumption of 19 per cent over the actual 1938 level or 11 per cent over the hypothetical full employment level in 1938. An increase in real consumption of this order (which implies moreover a rise of 46½ per cent over the current war-time level) presupposes, of course, that there are no restraints on consumption *other than taxation*; that war-time rationing and scarcities have disappeared and that the consumer has much the same range of choice in spending money as he had before the war. To the extent that these suppositions will not be completely fulfilled by 1948, private savings will be larger and the expenditure on consumption less, than in this estimate.

The Post-War Balance of Payments

43. In order to estimate the requirements of a post-war full employment policy, we must finally make an assumption about the post-war balance of payments. Our provisional assumption will be that exports (visible and invisible) and foreign income will balance imports, i.e. a zero balance of payments on current account. It may be worth while to set out, however, what this implies.

On the assumption that the importance of imported goods in the British national economy will be the same as before the war—i.e. that there are no measures taken to reduce the proportion either of imports of raw materials, etc., in total production or of imported consumers' goods in total consumption—the total volume of imports can be assumed to expand by 15 per cent of the increase in real income, that is, by £140 millions (at 1938 prices) or 16 per cent as compared with the actual level of imports at 1938. At the same time the income from foreign investments, at pre-war prices, will be some £120 millions less.[2] In addition, as we have seen, there was already an adverse balance of £55 millions in 1938. Finally, there is the

[1] A similar assumption was made in calculating undistributed profits in para. 36 above.
[2] Cf. para. 33 (*g*) above.

income from "invisible exports" (mainly shipping and insurance) the amount of which cannot be assumed as given—independently of the policies followed about exports and imports—since it varies more or less in proportion with the volume of international trade. Before the war, our invisible exports represented about 10 per cent of the value of our trade (the sum of exports and imports). After the war, owing to the fall in the proportion of British shipping in world tonnage they might be less.

44. We shall estimate the requirements of an even balance of payments after the war on two suppositions:—

(i) On the assumption that the terms of trade will be the same as before the war, but that invisible exports will amount to only 7 per cent (and not 10 per cent) of the value of trade, it would require an increase in exports by £325 millions (at pre-war prices), or by 68 per cent over the 1938 volume, to compensate fully for the various factors specified above. Alternatively, a zero balance of payments might be achieved by a cut of £375 millions[1] or 37 per cent in imports below the level it would have reached without restriction.[2] Finally, if imports are to be restricted, but only to the 1938 volume, the increase in exports required would be £205 millions, or 43 per cent over 1938.

(ii) On the more favourable supposition that the terms of trade remain the same and that shipping and insurance will regain their pre-war position (i.e. that they will represent 10 per cent of the value of trade) the required expansion in exports is 57 per cent; alternatively, with the volume of exports at the pre-war level, the required restriction of imports (below the hypothetical post-war volume) 34 per cent;[3] while the maintenance of the 1938 level of imports would in this case require an expansion of exports by 33 per cent.

44. It may be that none of these policies will be practicable in the early post-war years and that the position of equilibrium in the balance of payments will only be achieved gradually. Though the traditional position of Britain was that of a lending country with a favourable balance of payments, there need be no great harm in allowing an adverse balance of say, £200-£300 millions per annum for a number of years—either by borrowing from abroad, or by liquidating foreign investments still further—provided that the addi-

---

[1] The difference between this sum and the required increase in exports (£325 millions) is due to the change in the amount of invisible exports in the two cases.

[2] This implies a cut in imports by 27 per cent below its actual 1938 amount.

[3] I.e. 23 per cent below its actual volume in 1938.

tional resources made available in this way are used to improve the balance of payments position in the future—i.e. either in developing new industries suitable for exports, or industries (such as agriculture) whose product is a substitute for imports. In other words, provided that the Government adopts a long-term plan for the development of industries, the maintenance of an adverse balance over the reconstruction period might be a means of improving (instead of aggravating) the position of the balance of payments in the long run.

Full Employment Policies in 1948

45. We are now in a position to answer the question posed in paragraph 32, what is the rate of investment outlay (public and private) which would assure full employment in 1948? Our hypothesis is that the Government, through a National Investment Board, will so regulate the rate of capital expenditure (by fitting together the investments undertaken by public authorities and by private industry into a common national plan) as to ensure stability and adequacy in the national outlay as a whole. The question which then arises is whether the "required" rate of investment expenditure which emerges from our assumptions is an adequate one, from the general social point of view; and what Governmental policies should be followed if it is not.

46. On the assumptions that Government taxation is just sufficient to cover ordinary expenditure, that the level of exports is sufficient to pay for imports, and that the division of private incomes between consumption and savings is as explained in paragraph 41 above, the rate of net investment consistent with full employment in 1948, as shown in Table 59, is £765 millions—the equivalent of £575 millions in terms of 1938 prices. This is just 25 per cent greater (in volume) than the actual rate of investment in 1938, which was £460 millions;[1] but it is 13 per cent lower than the implied rate of investment expenditure under full employment, and a zero balance of payments, in 1938 which would have been £660 millions.[2]

[1] £420 millions net private investment (see Table 45) plus £40 millions public capital expenditure, financed in 1938 out of Central and local Government revenue, but excluded from the post-war budgets.

[2] See Table 47, Route I b. Out of the total public expenditure of £960 millions, £200 millions should be regarded as investment expenditure, i.e. the additional public outlay of £160 millions, plus the £40 millions referred to in the previous footnote. This, together with the "private investment outlay" of £460 millions, amounts to £660 millions. The reasons why despite the higher national income, the corresponding item for 1948 is smaller are: (i) the higher level of public consumption outlay in 1948 (£855 millions at 1938 prices, instead of £760

Table 59

FULL EMPLOYMENT INCOME AND OUTLAY IN 1948

(£ *millions*)

	1948 Prices	1938 Prices		1948 Prices	1938 Prices
Private Consumption ..	5,550	4,170	Private Consumption Outlay	5,550	4,170
Private Saving	765	575	Public Consumption Outlay	1,135	855
Taxation of Private Incomes	2,135	1,605	Balance of Payments	—	—
Private Incomes.. ..	8,450	6,350	Net Investment Outlay		
Government Income ..	70	55	(Public and Private)	765	575
Less Transfer Incomes ..	−1,070	−805			
Net National Income ..	7,450	5,600	Net National Outlay	7,450	5,600

Note.—The derivation of all the items in this Table was explained above, with the exception of "public consumption outlay" (i.e. the expenditure of public authorities on goods and services on current account) which was derived as follows:—

	£ *millions*
Total Expenditure of Public Authorities (see Table 55) ..	2,275
Less Transfer Expenditure (see Table 51)	− 1,070
Subsidies (Table 57)	− 20
Total Expenditure on goods and services at market prices ..	1,185
Less General indirect taxes falling on public authorities (Table 57)	− 50
Total Expenditure on goods and services at factor cost ..	1,135

47. An examination of the requirements of post-war reconstruction in the field of capital expenditure is now being undertaken by various Government Departments, and until their results are published the material for a more detailed analysis will not be available. But without any such examination, it is fairly certain from the considerations mentioned earlier, that if Britain after the war goes in for a vigorous policy of renewing her capital stock—of scrapping

millions), (ii) in the calculation of "Route I*b*" in Table 47 there is implied a budgetary surplus over public consumption outlay of £100 millions, which augmented the resources available for investment purposes (as compared with the situation postulated for 1948, where the surplus is zero) by £73 millions. (The reason for the difference is that in the calculation of Route I*b* for 1938, the existing rates of taxation were assumed to be given; in the calculations for the full employment outlay for 1948 in Table 59 the taxes were determined by the condition that the ordinary budgets should balance.)

obsolete houses and obsolete industrial equipment, and providing for the development of new industries—she would have to spend on capital projects at a far higher rate than in 1938.

In Table 60 an attempt is made to relate the available information about pre-war capital expenditure (given in Table 45) to the requirements of post-war investment under three alternative hypotheses: (i) that the rate of net investment will be as given in Table 59 above (Plan I); (ii) that net investment will be planned at the rate of £750 millions (Plan II); (iii) that net investment will be planned at the rate of £1,000 millions (Plan III); all at 1938 prices. The allocation of the totals among the various categories shown in this Table is largely in the nature of guesswork based on the broad facts about post-war needs, not on the result of a separate examination of the individual categories.

Plan I—apart from allowing for the minimum increase in stocks that can be expected in a normal year—only permits a modest increase in the rate of capital expenditure in industry and in housing. Plan II allows for a rate of expenditure on buildings that would probably be sufficient for the building of 500,000 dwelling houses annually;[1] it also allows a much higher rate of new investment in industrial plant and machinery, public utilities and other fixed capital. Plan III would allow doubling the pre-war volume of *gross* investment in plant and machinery; it also includes an allowance for the British contribution towards the reconstruction of Europe.

48. It is not possible to decide at this stage which of these possibilities comes nearest to fulfilling the requirements of an adequate post-war reconstruction programme; we may, however, discuss their implications for a full employment policy. Plans II and III require that the Government restrict real consumption below the level it would reach with a balanced budget and thereby release resources for investment purposes. This could be done in various ways; the simplest, perhaps, is by creating a surplus in the ordinary budget in the form of a sinking fund, to be covered out of taxation. In making the estimate for post-war Government expenditure in Table 54, we have made no provision for a sinking fund—for the simple reason that the desirable sum to be set aside for this purpose could only be determined after all the relevant factors in the total economic situation were known.

49. It follows from the estimates of taxation, consumption and savings, in paragraphs 40–42 above, that at the full employment

---

[1] This is regarded as the necessary rate of building if an adequate number of houses are to be provided, and all slums abolished, in a period of 15 years.

Table 60

ALTERNATIVE FRAMEWORKS FOR THE NATIONAL INVESTMENT PLAN

(£ *millions, at* 1938 *Prices*)

	Actual Net Investment, 1938	Hypothetical Net Investment, 1948		
		Plan I	Plan II	Plan III
Public works (new roads, etc.)	40	40	40	60
Public utilities	60	60	90	100
Buildings	245	300	400	400
Plant and Machinery	20	45	80	140
Other fixed capital	10	30	40	50
Net increase in stocks and goods in process	25	40	40	40
Costs incurred in the transfer of property and investment of savings	60	60	60	60
Contribution to the reconstruction of Europe	—	—	—	150
Total Net Investment	460	575	750	1,000

Note.—For the definitions of the various categories in this Table, see note to Table 45, p. 360. (In case Recommendation 23 of the Beveridge Report were adopted—i.e. industrial assurance made a public service—the item "costs incurred in the transfer of property" should be reduced by £15 millions.)

level of income in 1948 (i) a proportionate increase in *direct* taxes, increasing revenue by £100 millions, would reduce consumption by £62 millions, and savings by £38 millions; (ii) a proportionate increase in the rates of *indirect* taxes, augmenting revenue by £100 millions would reduce consumption by £85 millions, and savings by £15 millions; (iii) a similar proportionate increase in *all* Central Government tax rates would reduce consumption by £71 millions, and savings by £29 millions.

This means that if, in connection with the policy of restricting consumption (in order to maintain a higher rate of investment), all Central Government taxes were increased proportionately, Plan II would involve a sinking fund of £331 millions, and Plan III a sinking fund of £800 millions. As is shown in Table 61, each of these plans is consistent with a higher level of private real consumption than obtained in 1938, and would thus leave the community better off, in terms of current standard of living, than they were before the war. But in the case of Plan III at any rate, the required increase in taxation is so stiff—it implies an income tax of 8s. 8d., instead of 5s. 10d. in the £, if all Central Government taxes were raised proportionately—that it might be preferable, in this case, to secure the required reduction in consumption (at least in part) by other means of control, such as rationing.

50. Table 61 also shows the implications of these plans in case the level of exports is not sufficient to secure an even balance of payments, and an adverse balance of £200 millions is maintained. These are given as Plans I*b*, II*b* and III*b*. The second plan in this case is consistent with a practically unchanged level of taxation, while the first plan would require a *negative* sinking fund of £282 millions—i.e. a 17 per cent deficit in the current Central Government budget.

Table 61

ALTERNATIVE PLANS FOR FULL EMPLOYMENT OUTLAY IN 1948

(£ *millions at* 1948 *prices*)

	Plan I	Plan II	Plan III	Plan I*b*	Plan II*b*	Plan III*b*
Private Consumption Outlay ..	5,550	5,315	4,982	5,750	5,515	5,182
Public Consumption Outlay ..	1,135	1,135	1,135	1,135	1,135	1,135
Balance of Payments	—	—	—	− 200	− 200	− 200
Net investment outlay (public and private)	765	1,000	1,333	765	1,000	1,333
Total Outlay	7,450	7,450	7,450	7,450	7,450	7,450
Sinking Fund	—	331	800	− 282	49	518
Percentage increase in rates of taxation as compared with Plan I ..	—	20	49	− 17	3	31
Percentage increase in private real consumption as compared with 1938	19	14	7	23	18	11

Note.—It is assumed that the tax revenue for the payment of sinking funds is obtained by a proportionate increase in all taxes raised by the Central Government, and the percentage changes in tax rates relate not to all taxation, but only to taxation raised by the Central Government.

IV. THE LONG RUN CONSEQUENCES OF CONTINUOUS PUBLIC BORROWING

51. The above calculations were worked out for a particular post-war year, 1948. A plan for a continuous full employment policy would also have to take into account that under conditions of capital accumulation and technical progress, the national income would not remain stationary, but would be steadily rising, with the conse-

quence that the necessary Governmental policies to ensure full employment would also have to be steadily adjusted. Since any addition to incomes could be expected to be only partly devoted to increased consumption and partly to increased savings, a *given* rate of investment outlay would not be adequate to maintain full employment in successive years unless measures were taken to enable the rising production to be fully absorbed in rising consumption. This means that the Government, in order to maintain full employment in conditions of rising productivity, would either have to plan for an expanding rate of investment expenditure over time, or for a gradually diminishing rate of the "sinking fund"—i.e. for a gradual reduction in tax revenue, relatively to any given level of public expenditures.[1] Ultimately, the Government may have to raise the propensity to consume by more radical methods of income redistribution—when it will no longer be possible to afford the degree of inequality of incomes that can be sustained during the period of relatively high investment.

52. It would be beyond the scope of this memorandum to examine the implications of this problem on a full employment policy over a longer period in any detail. The remainder of the paper will be restricted to an examination of one particular aspect of the long run problem: the effects of a policy of continuous public borrowing under peace-time conditions.

53. If a plan providing for a high rate of investment expenditure were adopted over the reconstruction period, and if the analysis of the various elements of the post-war situation given in the previous section is correct, the Government during the early post-war years would have to provide for surpluses rather than deficits in its "ordinary" budget, i.e. taxation would have to be higher than the level of running expenditures. On the other hand, the Government would have to undertake loan expenditures as part of the national investment budget; the latter might well exceed the "sinking fund" in the ordinary budget so that the net national indebtedness might

[1] This is, of course, merely a different way of stating the proposition that if as a result of the accumulation of capital there is a steady increase in productive capacity, steps must be taken to ensure that the increase in potential output is matched by a corresponding increase in "purchasing power"—otherwise the increased output will not materialize and unemployment will result. The maintenance of full employment would automatically ensure, of course, that adequate purchasing power is created to absorb the potential output (indeed, the latter is merely a different aspect of the former); but in order to maintain full employment in these circumstances it is not enough to maintain the level of expenditures—these must be steadily increased.

be growing rather than diminishing, right from the start. Moreover, as time went on and the national real income increased, either the rate of loan expenditure on capital account would have to be raised, or taxation would have to be lowered, relatively to expenditure; in both cases the annual net increase in the public debt would tend to get larger. Further, in the more distant future, when the reconstruction programme will be nearing completion and it will be desirable to reduce the proportion of output devoted to investment, and to raise the proportion of output consumed, remission of taxation might prove the most convenient method of maintaining full employment. Hence, as part of the full employment policy we may have to reckon with a steadily rising public debt in peace time.

54. Ever since the inception of the British National Debt in 1688, money was borrowed in time of war and gradually repaid during periods of peace; the war borrowings always exceeding the peace repayments (see Table 62). As a result, a strong prejudice grew up against a policy of borrowing in peace time. But there is, in fact, *less* justification for incurring debt in war than there is in peace time. Borrowing in time of war does not increase the productive powers of the community and does not sustain employment; also, a great deal of borrowing is concentrated over a relatively brief span of time, so that war-borrowing increases rentier incomes not only absolutely, but as a proportion of the national income.

55. What is the "real burden" of a growing National Debt? Against the popular notions which regard borrowing as a means of "throwing the burden on future generations" and the Debt as a net loss of real wealth, economists rightly emphasized that internally held debt does not diminish the total real income of the community; all that the service of the Debt implies is a transfer of income between different members of society; and even this "transfer-burden" can be minimized by an appropriately chosen tax system.

This interpersonal transfer is not, however, the sole relevant aspect of the problem; the existence of the debt would have some economic consequences even if the interpersonal transfer were nil. Let us suppose, e.g. that everyone saves during war time (when the borrowing takes place) a constant proportion of his income; so that, when the period of borrowing is over, everyone's interest-income on past savings bears a constant proportion to his other sources of income. If we then assumed that the annual interest charge is paid out of the proceeds of an income tax which is proportionate to income, there is no transfer at all in consequence of the Debt. Yet economic incentives have altered; for in the new situation, everyone

eceives a higher proportion of the same *net* income in the form of
rent (which is independent of current effort) and a lesser propor-
ion as a reward for current effort. Hence the incentive to current
effort is diminished.

55. It is difficult to say how much importance should be attached
to this factor, but whatever its importance is, it clearly depends not
on the size of the Debt or the annual interest charge, but on the
proportion of the latter to the national income; and it could only
become significant when this proportion is large. In Britain, the
annual debt burden as a proportion of the national income reached
a maximum on two occasions, 1815 and 1924, and in each case
amounted to some 7 per cent of the national income. After the
present war, on the assumptions stated above, it will be just under
5 per cent, i.e. £500 millions on £8,450 millions private income.[1]

56. In estimating the effects of a rising National Debt in peace
time, we must first of all consider the probable growth of the national
income. This will be the resultant of the following four factors:
(i) the change in productivity per man hour; (ii) the change in the
working population; (iii) the change in the length of the working
week; (iv) the change in the price level.[2] Let us examine them in
turn.

(i) Since the beginning of this century at any rate (and probably
over a much longer period, though this cannot, in this country, be
established statistically) output per man hour in primary and secondary industry has increased (as the result of technical progress and
the accumulation of capital) at the compound rate of 3 per cent per
annum. The national real income per man hour (i.e. including the
output of distribution and services) has increased at the rate of
1·5 per cent per annum.[3] There is every reason to expect that this
movement will continue in the post-war era; under a full employ-

[1] Between 1924 and 1948 the National Debt on our assumptions will have
increased by 300 per cent, the annual interest charge by only 66 per cent, while
the national (private) income in money terms by 108 per cent. Thus, despite a
second world war, which—in terms of borrowing—was twice as costly as the first,
the burden of the Debt is likely to be smaller after the present war than it was
after the last war—a striking consequence of the cheap money policy inaugurated
by the Treasury in the 1930's.

[2] A fifth factor, namely the level of employment relatively to the working
population, is here ignored, on the supposition of a full employment policy.

[3] The difference is due to the fact that the other sections of the economy have
not participated in the increase in industrial productivity, and tended to absorb
a rising proportion of the total labour force. Output per man hour in distribution
has tended to diminish in the sense that the number of people engaged in distributive services has increased faster than the volume of goods to be distributed.

Table 62

HISTORY OF THE BRITISH NATIONAL DEBT, 1688 TO 1944

(£ millions)

		Borrowed	Repaid	Debt (at end of period)
War	1688–97	21	—	21
Peace	1697–1701	—	5	16
War	1702–14	39	—	55
Peace	1714–39	—	8	47
War	1739–48	31	—	78
Peace	1748–55	—	3	75
War	1755–63	72	—	147
Peace	1763–75	—	11	136
War	1775–86	121	—	257
Peace	1786–93	—	13	244
War	1793–1815	604	—	848
Peace	1815–53	—	79	769
War	1853–55	39	—	807
Peace	1855–99	—	172	635
War	1899–1902	159	—	794
Peace	1902–14	—	144	650
War	1914–18	7,180	—	7,830
Peace	1919–39	—ᐟ	33*	7,797*
War	1939–	11,796†	—	19,593†

* Excluding the National Defence Loans, 1937–39, which should more properly b[e] allocated to war borrowing. There was a substantial amount of net debt repayment ove[r] the period which is concealed in the above figures, since they include the borrowing o[f] the Exchange Equalization Fund (offset by holdings of gold and foreign exchange[)] and do not deduct the public debt held by public departments.

† Up to 31st March, 1944.

ment policy, it is bound to be even greatly accelerated for thre[e] reasons: (i) owing to the higher rate of capital accumulation unde[r] full employment; (ii) owing to the extra stimulus given to the intro-duction of more labour-saving methods of production under a system where the scarcity of labour (and not the scarcity of markets) is the factor limiting the scale of production, and under conditions of approximate stability of population where a much higher pro-portion of investment expenditure than in the past will be available for purposes of "deepening," i.e. of increasing capital per head; (iii) owing to the fact that with a high demand for labour in industry, the past tendency towards an exorbitant number of people entering the field of distribution might be arrested, in which case the annua[l]

ncrease in productivity, for the system as a whole, would automatically be greater. It seems, therefore, that at a minimum, the
rate of increase in productivity under full employment conditions
n peace time could be put at 2 per cent per annum.

(ii) The future movement of the working population is partly the
result of the changes in the age composition of the existing popu-
ation (due to the past fluctuations in the annual number of births),
partly of the movements of fertility and mortality rates in the future.
We shall estimate the change in the working population in the period
1945–70 on two assumptions: (a) a minimum estimate, on the
assumption that fertility rates will resume their declining trend after
the war; (b) a maximum estimate, on the assumption that fertility
rates will rise sufficiently to maintain the actual number of births
at the average level of the years 1936–40.[1] The first assumption
implies a gradual decline in the gross reproduction rate, over the
period 1945–70, from 0·8 to under 0·6, the second a gradual rise
n the rate from 0·8 to about 1·0.[2]

On the first assumption the population of the United Kingdom
aged 15–64 will decline by 2·2 millions, or 6·6 per cent, between
1945 and 1970; on the second assumption, by only 700,000, or
2 per cent. These figures conceal, however, the unfavourable change
n the age composition within the group; the numbers in the most
productive age group, 20–49, will decline, over the same period, by
14 per cent in the case of assumption (a) and 10 per cent in the
case of assumption (b). Hence the fall in the *effective* working population (i.e. in terms of units of constant labour power) during the
quarter of the century following the war, and assuming that the
balance of migration will be zero, might be put at a minimum of
6 per cent and a maximum of 10 per cent. For the purposes of
estimating the movement of the national income up to 1970, we
shall assume the maximum figure and put the fall in the *effective*
working population at 10 per cent.

Beyond 1970, the different assumptions about fertility will yield,
of course, much more divergent results. On the assumption that the

[1] The estimates were largely derived from the recent League of Nations Report
on "The Future Population of Europe and the Soviet Union," by Frank W.
Notestein and others of the Office of Population Research of Princeton University. The hypotheses about the trend of mortality rates and of fertility rates
n case of assumption (a), are those given in pages 22–36 of the Report.

[2] The base of a 0·8 gross reproduction rate for 1945 is founded on the fertility
rates of the last three pre-war years, ignoring the war-time jump in fertility.
The *net* reproduction rate was estimated by the Registrar General at 0·9 for
1943).

gross reproduction rate will fall, in the manner specified above, u
to 1970, and thereafter be maintained at that very low level, th
working population will fall by about a third every twenty-five year
On the assumption on the other hand that over the next twenty-fiv
years there will be a sufficient increase in fertility to push the n
reproduction rate to around unity by 1970—a very modest aim to s
to social policy; it implies only a 10–15 per cent rise in fertility ove
the current war-time level—the population will be eventuall
stabilized at a level only slightly below that of 1970, with an effectiv
working population of some 12·5 per cent below that of 1945.

(iii) In the above estimates for the year 1948 it was assumed tha
working hours in 1948 will be the same as in 1938. It is reasonab
to suppose, however, that the trend towards shorter hours will b
resumed, in the post-war period, though at a slower rate; and w
shall assume that the average hours of work will fall by 10 per cen
every twenty-five years.[1]

(iv) It will be assumed that post-war Governments will pursu
a monetary and wage policy which maintains the prices of fin
commodities constant. This implies that given the share of wages i
the total value of output (which in the past showed remarkably littl
change over long periods), the average rate of money wages will ris
in the same proportion as productivity per man hour. A policy of
falling price level, implying constant money wages, quite apart fror
its other disadvantage of enhancing rentier incomes, would mak
the task of monetary stabilization under full employment needless
difficult; while a policy of a rising price level might be incompatibl
with the maintenance of stability in the long run.

There is one particular case in which a policy of rising price
would be preferable to that of constant prices. If the supply of good
and services freely provided by the State were to form an increasin
proportion of the national real income (i.e. the supply of thing
which just because they are not provided through the market, do n
enter into the calculation of the price level) the maintenance of
stable relation between the movements of money income and tha
of real income—which is necessary in order to keep money wage
constant in terms of productivity—would require that the price leve
of marketable goods and services should be allowed to rise.

57. The net result of these assumptions is that, setting off th
effects of rising productivity against the fall in the working popu

[1] This would bring average hours of work to 42 per week by about 197
(In the period 1914–24 average working hours fell by about 10 per cent; but ther
was little change in the period 1924–38).

lation, and the reduction of hours, and assuming a monetary policy which maintains a stable relation between money income and real income, the national money income rises over the period 1948–1970 at the rate of 1 per cent per annum, i.e., that it rises on the average by some £90 millions per annum, over the period. This implies that the Government could go on borrowing an amount which adds some £5 millions to the interest charge annually without thereby increasing the interest burden as a proportion of the national income. Assuming that the Government borrows on the average at 2 per cent, it could borrow an average annual amount of £250 millions without increasing the ratio of the annual interest burden to the national income above the level it will have reached at the end of the war. After 1970, assuming that the fertility will have risen sufficiently in the meantime for an approach to a stable population, it could, of course, borrow at a higher rate still—at the rate of some £325 millions per annum. It could moreover borrow at an increasing rate through time, since with an even rate of increase in the national income, the annual increment in income will get steadily larger.[1]

58. The above calculation shows the amounts that could be borrowed annually while maintaining the ratio of the interest on the National Debt to the national income constant. They are not, of course, the true limits of the amounts that could be borrowed while maintaining budgetary equilibrium at a constant level of taxation. With the tax structure postulated in paragraph 40 above, and with the rates of taxation at the level necessary to balance the post-war Central Government budget, 25 per cent of any increase in the national income could be expected to be paid in Central Government taxation.[2] This means that with an average annual. increment of £90 millions in the national income, Central Government tax revenue would expand annually by £22·5 millions, while the annual increase in Central Government expenditure could only be put at £7 millions.[3] Hence after meeting other commitments,

[1] Over the period 1948–70, the national income could not be expected to increase at an even rate through time, because the fall in the effective working population will not proceed at an even rate. Up to about 1960, the working population is likely to remain fairly stable, most of the reduction occurring in the decade 1960–70.

[2] See Tables 51 and 54 above; tax rates were raised by 6 per cent, in accordance with paragraph 40. In case post-war taxation is higher than that (i.e., it allows for the payment of a "sinking fund") the marginal yield of taxation will be more than 25 per cent.

[3] The total annual increase in expenditure over the period 1948–70 being put at £152 millions. This is the net result of the increased cost of retirement pensions under the Beveridge Plan, £196 millions (Cmd. 6404, p. 199; allowing for a

a sum of £15·5 millions will be available each year to cover additional interest on the National Debt. This means that—assuming the average rate of interest to be 2 per cent—the National Debt could be allowed to expand at the average rate of no less than £775 millions per annum over the period 1948-70, without having to raise any new taxes for the maintenance of "budgetary equilibrium."

Thus the contention that a policy of increasing the National Debt in peace time involves a steadily increasing potential burden on the taxpayer is very far from the truth. This could only be the case with a rate of borrowing that is far in excess of anything that might be necessary under peace time conditions in order to sustain a full employment policy.

59. These estimates are based on the annual growth of the national income that can be expected under any full employment policy. They do not take into account the direct effect which the Government loan expenditure—if wisely invested—would have on the increase in the national income in the future; they hold even if the loan money is spent on objects of current consumption, or on completely useless purposes, such as digging holes and filling them up again. Insofar as the loan is spent in ways which directly raise the productive efficiency of the community, we must also allow for the further increase in income and tax revenue resulting from it. On the above assumption of 25 per cent of any increase in income being paid automatically in taxation, any public investment which increases the future national income by more than 6 per cent of the loan expenditure will actually make the prospective tax burden relatively *smaller* than it would have been without the loan expenditure; since it will augment the yield of taxation in the future by more than it increases the interest charge.

60. It follows therefore that even if the State policy were guided by purely fiscal considerations—that of reducing the rates of taxation to a minimum—the best course to pursue would still not be to refrain from borrowing, but to undertake public investments which lighten the future tax burden through increasing the national income and

10 per cent increase in the number of old age pensioners between 1965 and 1970); the net saving in war pensions, £70 millions; the further increase in the cost of education, £60 millions; an allowance for the automatic rise in the yield of death duties, due to the change in age composition (not included in the above estimate of the marginal yield of taxes), £34 millions. This makes no allowance for any saving on other items, such as defence, which in the case of a prolonged period of peace, might be considerable.

thus the yield of given rates of taxation. In the past State investments were only regarded as "self-liquidating" when the prospective money return of the asset created by the investment was by itself sufficient to cover the interest charge. It is now fairly generally recognized however that the price mechanism, even under the most favourable conditions, can register only some of the gains and losses which result from any particular piece of economic activity; there is a cluster of effects (what the economists call the external economies and dis-economies) which escape the net of price-cost measurement. Thus an investment may be highly remunerative from the social point of view even if its direct return is nil; if, in consequence of the invest-ment, the real income of the community is increased. To the extent to which the State, through the tax system, automatically partici-pates in any increase in the incomes of its citizens, such investments may be "remunerative" from the point of view of the State, even though they would not be remunerative when undertaken by private enterprise.

Hence the test of profitability which is decisive in the case of private investments, is not adequate when applied to public investment. This would be true even if the policy of the State were guided by purely fiscal considerations—that is to say, by the object of reducing the burden of taxation to a minimum. It is totally inadequate when the economic policy is governed, as of course it should be, by social considerations—not merely of minimizing the tax burden, but of maximizing the national income as a whole.

Appendix D

EXPLANATION OF TERMS

1. ECONOMIC TERMS

Balance of Payments

Bilateral Trade

Business Investment

Cyclical Fluctuation

Discrimination

Downward Phase

Effective Demand

Exports Visible and Invisible

Frictional Unemployment

Instrumental Industries

Investment

Liquidity

Marginal Efficiency of Capital

Multilateral Trade

Multiplier

Outlay

Propensity to Consume

Real Wages

Saving

Seasonal Unemployment

Structural Unemployment

Transfer Payments

Unemployment, Frictional, Seasonal
    Structural

Upward Phase

2. STATISTICAL TERMS

Correlation Coefficient

Employment Rate

Employment Volume

Index Numbers

Means Weighted and Unweighted

Relative and Index Number

Standard Deviation

Trend and Deviation from Trend

Unemployment Rate

The terms explained in this Appendix are divided into two sections, economic and statistical. The accounts given of them are not so much definitions as explanations of the way in which the terms are used in this Report. Some of them, e.g. investment, are used in popular language in a different sense from that adopted here, and others are used differently by other writers.

On the first use in the text of any of the terms appearing to need explanation, a footnote is added, calling attention to Appendix D. This footnote is not repeated on subsequent uses of the term. The bracketed paragraph reference after each term dealt with in the Appendix gives the paragraph in which the term first appears in the text. Paragraph numbers without letters refer to the Report. Paragraphs in the Appendices referred to have the letters A, B, C prefixed to their numbers in references.

1. ECONOMIC TERMS

Balance of Payments (paragraph 183).

The term "Balance of Payments" is used in this Report for "International Balance of Payments" indicating the relation between two nations or countries which use different currencies. The citizens of each country use their own currencies in dealing with one another. In dealing with citizens of another country, they make and receive payments across a currency frontier. Incomings and outgoings, including both immediate payments and promises to pay later, must always balance, as the two sides of a balance sheet or an income and expenditure account always balance. The important question is how this balance is brought about.

If the goods and services supplied by the people of one country to the rest of the world are less in value than the goods and services received by that nation from the rest of the world, then either (a) some of the goods and services received must have been supplied on credit or in cancellation of an old debt previously owed to that country from abroad, or (b) the country must have parted with some of its stock of gold or other international currency to pay for them. In the first case (a), there is a movement of capital, in its financial sense, which balances the deficit on goods and services. In the second case (b), the account is balanced by a movement of gold or other international currency. The second of these ways of balancing the international account of a country which buys more than it sells obviously depends on its having a stock of gold or international currency and depletes that stock. It cannot go on indefinitely, and ends by making the country illiquid. (See "Liquidity" below.) The assumption of all proposals for the establishment of an international currency or freely inter-changeable national currencies is that such movements of currency can be made purely temporary.

The International Balance of Payments of a country is normally presented in two sections, the "current account" and the "capital account." The current account shows all payments made or received in respect of goods and services including payments of interest on past lendings or borrowings, that is to say in respect of exports and imports, visible and invisible. (See "Exports Visible and Invisible" below.) The capital account shows all payments made or received by way of settling old debts or creating new debts. The current account and the capital account may each of them be unbalanced and normally are so, but, in the absence of any movement of international currency, the current and capital accounts taken together must balance. The positive unbalance of one is offset by negative unbalance of the other and vice versa.

A country which has an excess of imports over exports, visible and invisible, is said to have an "unfavourable balance of trade" or a "deficit in the balance of trade," while a country which has an excess of exports over imports, visible and invisible, is said to have a "favourable balance of trade" or a "surplus in the balance of trade." "Deficit" and "surplus" in this connection always refer to the current account; payments can be balanced by movements in the capital account, i.e. by lending to adjust a surplus, or borrowing or dis-investing to adjust a deficit in the balance of trade. If the payments are not balanced in this way there is a "deficit (or a surplus) in the balance of *payments*," and this involves either a loss of liquid resources (such as an outflow of gold), or an acquisition of liquid resources (such as an inflow of gold).

The "Balance of Payments" of any country may refer either to its relations to a single other country or to its relation to all other countries taken together.

Bilateral Trade (paragraph 40).

This term is described and illustrated, together with "Multilateral Trade," in paragraphs 311–13.

Business Investment (paragraph 33).

See "Investment."

Cyclical Fluctuation (paragraph 21).

The economic activity of nearly all industrial countries shows alternations of prosperity and depression, in periods of length normally ranging between five and eleven years and averaging (in Britain) about eight years. This phenomenon is illustrated in Chart I (in paragraph 55), showing the course of the employment rate (see below) in British trade unions from 1856 to 1926, and is described at length under the name of the International Trade Cycle in Appendix A. The term "cyclical fluctuation" is used both to describe the movement generally and, as in paragraph 21, to denote as "a cyclical fluctuation" one wave of the movement, from one crest (or boom) of activity and prosperity to the next, or from one trough (or depression) to the next. The "upward phase" of a cyclical fluctuation is the movement from trough to crest, and the "downward phase" is the movement from crest to trough.

Discrimination (paragraph 313).

This term refers to international trade practices. A country is said to "discriminate" if it allows considerations other than those of price to determine its international buying and selling. "Non-discrimination" implies that goods are always bought in the cheapest and sold in the dearest market. Relative cheapness or dearness is measured exclusively in terms of market prices. That is to say, an article offered at (say) 5 pesos is to be considered cheaper in sterling than an identical article offered somewhere else at 5 escudos, if at the current rate of exchange with sterling pesos are cheaper than escudos. "Discrimination" is said to take place if other considerations but those of the market price are allowed to enter: if, for instance, the article offered at 5 escudos is given preference, because the Central Bank of the purchaser happens to possess an ampler supply of escudos than of pesos.

It is obvious that the motive of discrimination may be a different one in different circumstances. It may arise out of social, political, or economic considerations; preferences, such as those granted by various parts of the British Commonwealth to one another under the Ottawa Agreement, are a leading instance of such discrimination. It may arise out of relative scarcity or abundance in the supply of different currencies. "Non-discrimination" implies that the distribution of trade between a number of potential suppliers is decided solely by the price calculations of private traders.

Downward Phase (paragraph 72).

See "Cyclical Fluctuation."

Effective Demand (paragraph 20).

Effective demand means desire for goods or services backed by willingness to pay the price of those goods and services. Mere need not clothed with purchasing power is not effective demand. Need backed by willingness and ability to pay less than the producer of the goods and services is prepared to accept is not effective demand, though it is sometimes described as demand, without the adjective "effective." The adjective is also commonly omitted in writing when there is no need to emphasize the "effectiveness" of demand, as in paragraphs 21 and 22.

Exports Visible and Invisible (paragraphs 307).

All exports which are tangible and visible, that is to say, all exports of goods are called visible exports. They alone enter into the statistics of trade. But they do not represent the only things which the people of one country can sell to the people of another country and so become entitled to payments abroad. In addition to visible exports there are invisible exports of various kinds, of which, for Britain, the most important are:

(a) *Services Abroad.* A British ship carrying goods for a foreign merchant earns income in his currency. So may an insurance company or a bank or a commercial house render services to be paid for in a foreign currency, as much as if they were goods shipped from Britain.

(b) *Sales and Services to Foreign Travellers in Britain.* Foreigners travelling in Britain consume goods and services produced here, and in order to pay for them have to exchange their currency into British currency.

(c) *Payments by Foreigners on former Borrowings from Britain.* When money is lent from country A to country B, B is able to buy goods from A without sending goods in return. Subsequent payment by B of interest and dividends is called an "invisible export" from A to B, because it enables A to obtain imports in virtue of having had an export surplus in the past. Invisible exports of this nature bulk largely in Britain's account with other nations.

It should be added that gold, though tangible and visible, is not usually included among the visible exports of the country which sends it abroad. It is treated as international currency.

Frictional Unemployment (paragraph 3).

See "Unemployment: Frictional, Seasonal, Structural."

Instrumental Industries (paragraph 98).

The industries described in this Report as "instrumental" are those engaged in making or repairing instruments of production, in particular machinery of all kinds, ships and vehicles. The actual industries of the Ministry of Labour list treated here as instrumental are identified by the letter I in Table 33; they include engineering in all its forms, shipbuilding, the making of motor vehicles, cycles and aircraft, and railway carriages. They do not include building, which is grouped with a number of ancillary industries as constructional, or metal manufactures.

Investment (paragraph 15).

Investment in this Report means a form of outlay directed not to goods or services desired for their own sake (for immediate enjoyment), but to goods and services desired as the means to producing other goods and services. It means spending on means of production such as factories, machinery, ships, railways, or on materials to be used in producing other things.

The term "business investment" (paragraph 33) is used for spending directed to the production of goods or services which are marketable, i.e. will be sold at a price to the person who proposes to use them. As is explained in paragraph 178, "business investment" may be either private, such as that of a private business or limited liability company, or public, such as investment in a municipal tramway or a State railway. Spending money on the means of producing goods and services which are not marketable, i.e. which will be provided without charge to those who use them, is "communal investment." Typical subjects of communal investment are battleships, roads and elementary schools.

In common speech "investment" is often used also in a sense quite different to the foregoing. People speak of "investing" their money when they use their cash resources to buy stocks or shares or War Loan, or lend their money on mortgage or in some other way, or buy an existing house; they describe their holdings of stocks or shares or War Loan or their houses as "investments." This popular use of the term "investment," though quite correct in itself, is avoided in the present Report.

Liquidity (paragraph 327).

Liquidity means ability to meet current financial obligations in cash or its immediate equivalent, such as a bank deposit on which one can draw. It relates to the form in which wealth is held, not to its amount. It does not mean wealth, just as being illiquid does not mean that one is poor. A poor man who owes much more than he possesses is liquid, if his debts are not due for immediate settlement and he has cash in hand or a deposit in the bank on which he can draw for daily needs. A rich man whose wealth consists wholly or mainly of land and houses may be illiquid if he has to meet a sudden demand, say for death duties, and cannot sell any of his property or can sell it only at what seems to him an inadequate price.

Internal liquidity, that is to say the liquidity of individuals within a country and the varying importance which they attach to liquidity at various times, enter largely into the General Theory of Employment set forth by J. M. Keynes. In this Report, liquidity is considered only in its international aspects, as the liquidity or the reverse of one country in its dealings with other countries. International liquidity means ability to meet current financial obligations in another country. Since those obligations have ultimately to be discharged in the currency of that other country, liquidity means having supplies of that currency or of something that will be accepted as its equivalent. So long as all countries are willing to accept gold in settlement of obligations from other countries, any country with a stock of gold is liquid. So long as, and to the extent that, countries are willing to place supplies of their currency at the disposal of other countries for settling obligations to them, all countries are liquid. The object of the joint proposals by experts for an International Monetary Fund[1] is to ensure initial international liquidity in this way. But if the stock of gold held by a country or its right to supplies of other currencies is limited, as it normally is, a country which continually incurs deficits in its current account of international trade and cannot secure long term loans is bound in time to become illiquid.

Marginal Efficiency of Capital (paragraph 129).

This term refers to the ability of capital equipment to earn an income for its owner. It is an economic not a technical concept, and in popular language is fairly well represented by "earning power." Even a technically inefficient piece of capital equipment may possess a high economic efficiency when it is in scarce supply and may enable its owner to make large profits. The word "marginal" means that it is not the earning power of all capital that is under consideration,

---

[1] Cmd. 6519.

but only the earning power of additional capital, that is to say, the expected return on money laid out on new capital.

J. M. Keynes, from whose work the passage in paragraph 129 referring to marginal efficiency of capital is taken, defines the term as follows: "More precisely, I define the marginal efficiency of capital as being equal to that rate of discount which would make the present value of the series of annuities given by the returns expected from the capital-asset during its life just equal to its supply price" (*General Theory*, p. 135). When, in the passage quoted in paragraph 129, J. M. Keynes speaks of aiming at "a progressive decline in the marginal efficiency of capital," he presumably has in mind the possibility of reducing its rate of earning by making it abundant.

At the same time it should be noted that, in a passage quoted in paragraph 135, J. M. Keynes attributed the acuteness of the contemporary problem in 1936 in part to the fact that the marginal efficiency of capital is already much lower than it was in the nineteenth century.

Multilateral Trade (paragraph 40).

This term is described and illustrated, together with "Bilateral Trade," in paragraphs 311–13.

Multiplier (paragraph 187).

Every act has an infinite chain of consequences. Therefore, the act of employing an unemployed man and paying him wages does not stop there. The man who is taken on and gets wages which are more than he was getting as unemployment benefit or assistance, will spend most or all his additional income on goods and services supplied by others, and bring others into employment. They in turn will have more income; will spend some of it giving fresh employment and so on. So long as there are any unemployed men in a community, employing one of the unemployed for wages will increase the number employed by more than one and will add to the national output more than what he himself produces. The primary effect will be multiplied owing to secondary and tertiary effects. How much it will be multiplied depends on the circumstances of the time and country, and different values are assigned to the multiplier by different authorities. As a first approximation, the multiplier in Britain in 1938 can be taken as two; that is to say, it can be assumed that setting to work one of those who were then unemployed would have led on an average to employment and wages for another man.

The multiplier applies to contraction of employment as much as to expansion. Putting one man out of employment and wage-earning leads to more than one man's loss of employment and earning.

Outlay (paragraph 15).

This term is described fully in paragraphs 175–9.

Propensity to Consume (paragraph 129).

The term "propensity to consume" of a person or a class of persons is used in the Report to indicate the proportion of his or their total income which that person or class may be expected to spend on consumption. What people do not spend on consumption they "save" and the savings become available for "investment" by themselves or others, i.e. for spending on means or materials of production. As a broad generalization, the smaller the income, whether of an individual or a community, the larger is the propensity to consume; people individually and collectively spend on consumption a larger proportion of a small income than they do of a larger income. Therefore, out of a given total income of a community more is likely to be spent on consumption and less is likely to be saved if the income is divided evenly between the individual members than if it is divided unevenly.

The sense in which the term "propensity to consume" is used in this Report appears also to be that in which it is used in the passage cited from J. M. Keynes in paragraph 129, as something which could be changed by altering the distribution of income. J. M. Keynes's own definition of the term is given at page 90 of the *General Theory*.

Real Wages (paragraph 127).

Money wages are wages reckoned in money. "Real Wages" are wages in terms of how much they will buy of the things on which they are spent by most people, that is to say they take account of the cost of living. Real wages may rise though money wages are falling, if the money cost of what the wage-earner buys is falling still more rapidly. Real wages may fall, even though money wages are rising, if the cost of living is rising even more rapidly. Obviously the calculation of real wages is affected by what articles one takes into account.

Saving (paragraph 15).

Saving in this Report, like "investment," is used to indicate a course of action, though a negative course. Saving means not spending part of one's income. Saving is discussed in paragraphs 120–4.

Seasonal Unemployment (paragraph 169).

See "Unemployment: Frictional, Seasonal and Structural."

Structural Unemployment (paragraph 6).

See "Unemployment: Frictional, Seasonal and Structural."

Transfer Payments (paragraph 183).

This term covers all payments made by public authorities which are not made in consideration of goods and services currently produced. Thus they are not a part of public outlay, since outlay has been defined as "the laying out of money as demand for the products of current industry" (paragraph 175). Unemployment benefit and assistance payments, for instance, are transfer payments, while wages paid to a State employee are outlay. The former are made without the State obtaining any goods or services in return; the latter are made in consideration of services rendered. When the State purchases land, or any other existing asset, the payment made is a transfer payment, because the mere change in the ownership of such an asset does not in itself make any demand on the available manpower of the nation. Transfer payments, therefore, are payments made by public authorities on account of pensions, relief, grants-in-aid, insurances, interest on public debt, or the acquisition of property already in existence.

Unemployment: Frictional, Seasonal, Structural

"Frictional Unemployment" is unemployment caused by the individuals who make up the labour supply not being completely interchangeable and mobile units, so that, though there is an unsatisfied demand for labour, the unemployed workers are not of the right sort or in the right place to meet that demand.

"Seasonal Unemployment" means the unemployment arising in particular industries through seasonal variation in their activity, brought about by climatic conditions or by fashion.

"Structural unemployment" means the unemployment arising in particular industries or localities through a change of demand so great that it may be regarded as affecting the main economic structure of a country. The decline of international trade after the first World War, involving drastic contraction of the demand for labour in British export industries, is a leading instance of structural change of this character. The northward movement of industry in Britain before the first World War is a less striking instance, though perhaps sufficiently great to be called a structural change. Structural unemployment may or may not be a form of frictional unemployment.

On the definition given above there cannot be actual frictional unemployment, unless there is an unsatisfied demand for labour somewhere. If the total demand for labour is less than the total supply, those who are unemployed are so because of deficiency of demand not because of friction.

This does not mean that the problem of industrial friction, that is to say friction in adjusting the supply of labour to the demand, is unimportant. Assuming an unsatisfied demand for labour there may still be frictional unemployment, arising in several ways:

(a) Through technical change, that is the development of new industries, machines and methods, superseding old industries, machines and methods. Innumerable small technical changes take place constantly. Assuming that they do not diminish the total demand, but only change its character or location, the extent to which they result in unemployment depends on the ability of the labour supply to adjust itself to the changes in the character of the demand, that is to say on the adaptability and mobility of labour. The amount of unemployment will vary with the strength of industrial friction.

(b) Through local variations of demand. So long as production is conducted by a number of independent businesses, the demands of different employing units may vary, one rising and the other falling, even though demand remains adequate and steady in total. How much frictional unemployment will result from this depends on the degree of mobility of labour and the way in which the engagement of men is organized. The chronic over-stocking with labour of the casual labour industries (paragraphs 57–9) represents an acute form of frictional unemployment.

(c) Through seasonal variations of demand. Nearly all industries are seasonal to some extent, though to very different extents, but the slack and busy seasons respectively of different industries do not coincide. The amount of unemployment involved in the seasonal variations of separate industries depends therefore on the extent to which they are separate for the purpose of labour supply, i.e. the ease or difficulty with which men can change from one industry when seasonally slack to another which is seasonally busy. Assuming adequate total demand, seasonal unemployment is a form of frictional unemployment.

Whether structural unemployment should be regarded as a form of frictional unemployment or not depends on the effect of the structural change on total demand for labour. Where, as between the wars, the structural change destroys demand for labour of one kind without adequate compensating increase of demand for labour of another kind, it brings about unemployment due to deficiency of demand, rather than to friction. If the structural change involves both a great decrease of demand for one kind of labour and a compensating increase of demand for another, the unemployment which results through men not being qualified or willing to meet the new demand is frictional unemployment.

The degree of industrial friction, relatively unimportant when total demand is deficient or weak, becomes of decisive importance when demand is strong, as in war, and would be of great importance under a full employment policy in peace.

Upward Phase (paragraph 72).

See "Cyclical Fluctuation."

2. STATISTICAL TERMS

Correlation Coefficient (paragraph A.6).

The correlation coefficient is a measure of relationship between two sets of quantities. It is a fraction always lying between $+ 1.0$ and $- 1.0$. At $+ 1.0$ it represents perfect positive correlation; deviation from the mean of one of the elements compared is accompanied by an exactly corresponding (equal or proportionate) deviation of the other element in the same direction. At $- 1.0$ the correlation coefficient represents perfect negative correlation; the correspondence of movements is as great, but the movements are exactly contrary to one another. In either case one of the elements contains the sole cause of all the movements in the other element or both sets of movement have a common single cause. At 0.0 the correlation coefficient indicates that there is no connection at all between movements of the two elements. At any point between 0.0 and $+ 1.0$ there may be a positive connection, and at any point between 0.0 and $- 1.0$ there may be a negative connection.

Whether or not in any particular case there is an actual connection depends on a calculation of probability; and this depends largely on the number of pairs of quantities compared. Thus the odds against getting by pure coincidence, i.e. without any real connection, a correlation coefficient as high as $.40$ whether positive or negative are more than 100 to 1 if 40 pairs are being compared and are less than 20 to 1 for 20 pairs.[1] The former is all but certainly significant of a real connection; the latter is merely suggestive.

All the actual coefficients mentioned in this Report are high enough to leave no reasonable doubt of a real connection between the two sets of data compared. The two weakest of them ($- .35$ in paragraph A.35 for relation between British industrial activity and textile exports of a year later in the forty-five years from 1815 to 1859, and $+ .42$ for the relation between British industrial activity and

---

[1] These probabilities are derived from a table given by Professor R. A. Fisher, *Statistical Methods for Research Workers*, which is reproduced by Professor F. C. Mills, *Statistical Methods* (Pitman, 1932), p. 701.

French pig iron production in the thirty-six years from 1824 to 1849) have odds of about 50 to 1 and about 100 to 1 respectively in favour of their representing a real connection.

The correlation coefficient is used most commonly to discover whether the quantities in two times series, e.g. wheat prices and marriages recorded over a period of years, have a definite tendency to rise and fall together. But it is equally important for discovery of relations of other kinds, such as that between the increases of unemployment in each of one hundred different industries from 1929 to 1930 and from 1937 to 1938 respectively which is referred to in paragraph A.44; this example illustrates the fact that the correlation coefficient, however high, establishes only correspondence of variation and not a causal connection between the two elements. High correspondence may point simply to a common cause outside both elements. In the case mentioned in paragraph A.44, the co-efficient of + .58 on comparison of one hundred pairs of quantities is high enough to be decisive evidence of a real connection between the two sets of quantities. It does not mean that unemployment had a tendency to rise in a certain way from 1937 to 1938 *because* it had risen so in that way from 1939 to 1940. It means simply that some common cause was at work on both occasions, i.e. that the trade cycle was repeating itself.

A special use of correlation, illustrated in paragraph A.34 and Table 31, is in examining the time relation between different economic elements by comparing two time series simultaneously and with one of the two series advanced or lagged a year or some other period upon the other. Another example of this is mentioned in the footnote to paragraph A.12, and many other examples are given in my two articles on "The Trade Cycle in Britain before 1850," in *Oxford Economic Papers*, Nos. 3 and 4.

The correlation coefficients used in this study are all cases linear, and are obtained by the product-moment method described by Professor F. C. Mills in *Statistical Methods*, pp. 345–53.

Employment Rate (paragraph 55).

The employment rate of any body of persons available for employment at any time is the percentage of those persons who are actually in employment at that time. The employment rate, as is explained in paragraph 55, is usually got by deducting the unemployment rate from 100.

Employment Volume (paragraph 68).

The employment volume of any industry or region at any time is the number of persons actually in employment at that time in that industry or region.

Index Number.

See "Relative and Index Number."

Means, Weighted and Unweighted (paragraph 64, footnote).

In an unweighted mean each of the quantities whose mean is being sought is treated as of equal importance. In a weighted mean the quantities are given weight according to the assumed differences in their importance.

Thus in Table 26, the unweighted mean of 26.0 in the right hand column is the average of the 11 figures above it, got by adding them and dividing by 11. The small industries like lace and hemp, rope, etc., contribute as much to this

mean as the large industries like cotton and wool. The weighted mean of 28.6
is got by multiplying each of the industry figures in the column above by the
number of insured males in that industry, adding the products and dividing
the sum by the total number of males in all the 11 industries. The largest industry
—cotton—with a high percentage contraction, contributes more than any other
industry to the weighted mean, which is by consequence higher than the unweighted mean.

Relative and Index Number (paragraph 64).

A relative is the quantity recorded for any economic element at any given
time; e.g. the price of an article in a particular month or year, expressed as a
percentage of the corresponding quantity at some other time, described as the
"base," e.g. the price of the same article in another month or year, which may be
called the "base month" or "base year." The "base" quantity need not refer to
a time of the same length as is covered by each of the quantities related to it,
and commonly does not do so. In setting out a table of relatives the base period
is usually indicated as = 100. The figures for separate industries in column 4 of
Table 33, and the figures in Tables 3 and 6 are relatives. An index number is
a combination of relatives for a number of economic elements which are regarded
as sufficiently homogeneous to justify the treating of them as a group: thus in
Table 28 the relatives expressing the male unemployment rate in each separate
industry (on the basis 1927–36 = 100) are expressed as index numbers for groups
of industries of the same general type, e.g. instrumental, textile, etc. An index
number being a mean of relatives may be weighted or unweighted. The heading
to Table 28 indicates that the relatives for the separate industries have been
weighted by reference to the numbers of insured persons (men and women).

A relative is a percentage expressing the relation between corresponding
quantities in a time series. The term is not used when a quantity of one kind is
being expressed as a percentage of a quantity of another kind, e.g. when the
number of trade unionists unemployed at any time is expressed as a percentage
of the total trade union membership as in paragraph 54. This is an "unemployment percentage" or, in the language of this Report, an "unemployment rate."
It is not a relative.

It should be added that in using the term "relative" when the quantities of a
single term series are being expressed as percentages of the corresponding quantity
in a base period and restricting the term "index number" to averages of relatives
for groups, I am following the American rather than the British practice. Among
British writers a common practice has been to use the term "index number" to
cover both single series (i.e. simple percentages) and groups (means of percentages).
Figures such as those given in column 4 of Table 33 and in Table 6, which are
described here as "relatives," are described as "index numbers" in the Ministry
of Labour tables from which they are taken. As "relative" is both the shorter
and less pretentious term than "index number," and as the making of an average
involves the question of weighting and thus introduces a new set of problems
whose presence it is convenient to indicate by a new word, the American practice
is in several ways more economical of language than the British practice.

Standard Deviation (paragraph A.24, Table 27).

The standard deviation of a number of quantities is the square root of the
mean of the squares of the deviations of those quantities from their arithmetic

mean. To obtain it, therefore, all that is needed is to calculate the arithmetic mean of the quantities, express each quantity as an arithmetic deviation, + or — from the mean, square the deviations, obtain their arithmetic mean and extract its square root. The standard deviation is the most convenient single measure of the degree of dispersal of those quantities from their mean and so from one another. Applied to a time series, such as the rate of unemployment of an industry over a period of years, or the new index of industrial activity in Table 22, it reflects the range of fluctuation and thus makes easy the comparison of a range of fluctuation for different industries. In Table 27 the standard deviation is used to compare the range of fluctuation in different groups of industries in different periods from 1785 to 1938.

Trend and Deviation from Trend (paragraph A.3).

Owing to growth of population and other progressive changes, most economic and social time series (e.g. the number of tons of pig iron produced each year or the number of marriages each year) have a general movement over a period of years and may or may not be subject to fluctuations. It is necessary and important to be able, so far as possible, to distinguish between general movements and fluctuations. The general movement is described as the "secular trend" or, more shortly, "trend." For the purpose of this study the trends have been calculated by the method of least squares described by Professor F. C. Mills, *Statistical Methods*, pp. 244–64. This method gives a line (straight or curved) which is assumed to represent what would have been the quantity in each year, if the economic element recorded had grown (or declined) steadily according to its general movement and apart from the short fluctuations. Deviation from trend means the difference between the actual quantity in any year and the corresponding point on the trend line described as the trend ordinate. This difference may be expressed either arithmetically (as + or — from the trend) or geometrically (as a percentage of the trend ordinate). In this study the deviations are all geometrical.

Unemployment Rate (paragraph 54).

The unemployment rate of any body of persons available for employment at any time is the percentage of those persons who were unemployed, i.e. capable of work and willing to work but unable to find employment, at that time. The unemployment rate is often called the unemployment percentage, but, as it is often necessary to express the "unemployment rate" of one group or at one time as a relative, i.e. as a percentage of some other unemployment rate, it is less confusing to speak of unemployment rates than of unemployment percentages.

INDEX

GEORGE ALLEN & UNWIN LTD

London: 40 Museum Street, WC1

Auckland: P.O. Box 36013, Northcote Central, N.4
Barbados: P.O. Box 222, Bridgetown
Bombay: 15 Graham Road, Ballard Estate, Bombay 1
Buenos Aires: Escritorio 454-459, Florida 165
Calcutta: 17 Chittaranjan Avenue, Calcutta 13
Cape Town: 68 Shortmarket Street
Hong Kong: 105 Wing On Mansion, 26 Hankow Road, Kowloon
Ibadan: P.O. Box 62
Karachi: Karachi Chambers, McLeod Road
Madras: Mohan Mansions, 38c Mount Road, Madras 6
Mexico: Villalongin 32-10, Piso, Mexico 5, D.F.
Nairobi: P.O. Box 4536
New Delhi: 13-14 Asaf Ali Road, New Delhi 1
Ontario: 81 Curlew Drive, Don Mills
Rio de Janeiro: Caixa Postal, 2537-Zc-00
São Paulo: Caixa Postal 8675
Singapore: 36c Prinsep Street, Singapore 7
Sydney, N.S.W.: Bradbury House, 55 York Street
Tokyo: P.O. Box 26, Kamata